HARRISON GRAY OTIS

1765–1848

Harrison Gray Otis, by Gilbert Stuart.

HARRISON GRAY
OTIS

1765–1848

The Urbane Federalist

SAMUEL ELIOT MORISON

With portraits and other
illustrations

BOSTON

HOUGHTON MIFFLIN COMPANY

1969

TO THE MEMORY OF MY MOTHER

EMILY MARSHALL MORISON

1857–1925

WHOSE ENCOURAGEMENT OF A YOUNG HISTORIAN

MADE MY EARLIER BOOKS POSSIBLE

AND TO MY BELOVED WIFE

PRISCILLA BARTON MORISON

WHOSE ENCOURAGEMENT OF AN ELDERLY HISTORIAN

MADE THIS BOOK POSSIBLE

Preface

In 1913 there appeared, in two formidable volumes, *The Life and Letters of Harrison Gray Otis, Federalist,* by a young and unknown historian, Samuel Eliot Morison. It became a *succès d'estime,* opening the doors to more than one history department, but a financial failure. It was even remaindered by the publishers at two dollars. Time and change have made it a relatively rare book — I had to pay twenty-five dollars for a secondhand copy — and the requests for facsimile publication became so frequent that the publishers and I decided to bring out a new edition ourselves. But, after reading my expensive copy, I decided that the public needed a new book rather than a new edition. So it has been almost completely rewritten, condensing or omitting much of the political material and all the bibliographical footnotes, adding a few important facts which have come to light since 1913, and increasing the space devoted to the social life of Boston, Philadelphia and Washington. It is amusing to recall that scholarly reviewers attacked my 1913 book as containing too much trivial and frivolous detail; one even called it "a chronicle of small beer"; and Professor Caudel, my *cher maître* at l'École Libre des Sciences Politiques, scolded me for including *anecdotes un peu grises.* When I gave a paper on the Republican Court before my mother's chapter of the D.A.R., she would not let me read about Maria Bingham, and (at the request of a South Carolina friend) burned the letter in which John Rutledge told about his wife's adultery.

What a change of taste and of *moeurs* since 1913! A new school of social history has arisen to which no detail of how people lived is inconsequential. Fashionable table talk has become infinitely more earthy than as Otis describes it at dinner tables in Philadelphia during John Adams's administration. Historians may deplore my omission of political data, letters and footnotes; but there are plenty of copies of my 1913 publication in public and college libraries which they may consult.

Surprisingly little of historical importance has been published during the last fifty years about New England Federalism; and (to my knowledge) no novelist or playwright has used the theme. Historians and other writers probably regarded this subject as a blind alley leading nowhere, which in a sense it was. But, when the study of human behavior is so much to the fore, what can be more entrancing than a story so fraught with emotion and passion as that of the New England Federalists? What could be more pathetic than to watch intelligent and conservative Americans, brought up to worship the principle of union, forced (as they thought) to fall back on the state rights theories of their alleged persecutors, whipping up factious opposition to a nationalist war? Otis's role as appeaser of these passions was unheroic but highly valuable. No racial issue was involved, but Federalist emotions in the New England of 1808–14 were no less genuine than those later aroused in the South by the prospect of a Republican president; and it is owing largely to the work of moderates like Otis that the New England sectional movement had no such catastrophic results.

After all, plenty of other political blind alleys in American history, from the Anti-Masons to the America Firsters, have been explored by historians; properly so, since all indicate subterranean streams of emotion in the American Republic. As Marcel Proust has written, *"Les faits ne pénètrent pas dans le monde où vivent nos croyances."* Federalist *croyances* were deeply rooted, and although subject to scorn and contumely, they frequently reappear under other names. No series of Democratic victories in state and nation have suppressed the fundamental Federalist creed that liberty is inseparable from union, that men are essentially unequal, that *vox populi* is seldom if ever *vox Dei,* and that sinister outside influences are busy undermining American integrity.

When my first biography of Otis came out, a more witty than kind local critic passed the word, "Sam Morison has tried to build up a second-rate politician into a great statesman." I never considered Otis a great statesman; but he was not second rate in politics or anything else. He conceived and promoted one of the most significant urban developments of the early nineteenth century, the building-up of Beacon Hill. In so doing, and in many other ways, he enriched the social life of his community. Dr. Johnson's epitaph for Oliver Goldsmith, *nihil tetegit quod non ornavit* — "He touched nothing that he did not adorn," is peculiarly appropriate to Harrison Gray Otis.

From the preface to my 1913 book I repeat with enhanced gratitude, "This undertaking would have been impossible without the assistance and advice rendered by many individuals and institutions. I am indebted most of all to Professor Albert Bushnell Hart, at whose suggestion this work was begun, and under whose direction and encouragement it has been carried out; to Professors Edward Channing and Frederick J. Turner for their helpful criticism . . . and to the historical training that I received at Harvard University." To this I should add, for the present volume, the careful research of my secretary, Miss Antha E. Card, and the suggestions and encouragement of my beloved wife, Priscilla Barton Morison.

S. E. MORISON

44 Brimmer Street, Boston
1 March 1968

Contents

PREFACE, ix

I. CHILDHOOD, 1765–1775, AET. 1–9
End of the Colonial Period, 1; Boston Latin School, 11; Patriot Otises
and Loyalists Grays, 17

II. A YOUTH OF PROMISE, 1775–1783, AET. 9–17
The Tragic Separation, 23; Parental Activities, 30; Harvard College, 33

III. LAW, FUN, AND REBELLION, 1783–1789, AET. 18–23
John Lowell's Law Student, 39; The Fast Young Set, 42; Shays's Rebellion, 49; Legal Business, 51

IV. MARRIAGE, BUSINESS, AND FAMILY LETTERS, 1790–1797,
AET. 24–31
Marriage to Sally Foster, 57; Theater and Loyalist Property, 59; Business
Tours and Prosperity, 64; The Copley Purchase, 75

V. HAMILTONIAN FEDERALIST, 1794–1796, AET. 29–31
Harry Embraces Federalism, 83; The French Revolution, 90; Jay's Treaty
and Election to Congress, 93

VI. FIRST TERM IN CONGRESS, 1797–1798, AET. 31–33
Maiden Speech, 97; Fears of France, 102; "Wild Irish" Speech and a Fight
in Congress, 107; Quasi-War with France, 112; Alien and Sedition Acts,
116

VII. THE REPUBLICAN COURT, 1797–1801, AET. 31–35
Federalist Society in Philadelphia, 122; The Bingham Family, 131; Miscellaneous Occurrences, 138; Primitive Washington, 145

VIII. FRANCE BACKS DOWN, 1798–1801, AET. 33–35
Visits to Adams and Gerry, 153; Reëlection and the French Problem,
155; Adams Asserts Himself, 158; Sixth Congress, 165

IX. THE ELECTION OF 1800–1801, AET. 35
Political Maneuvers, 170; Sixth Congress Concluded, 175; Congress
Elects Jefferson, 178

X. HARRY OTIS, FRIEND AND HOST, 1801–1817, AET. 36–52
Harry and Sally, 186; The Adams Relationship, 190; Houses, Hospitality, and Harvard, 193; Politics and Social Life, 204; Eating, Drinking,
and Scandals, 208; The Otis Wit, 215

XI. BUSINESS, ORATORY, AND FAMILY AFFAIRS, 1800–1828
AET. 34–63
Boston Real Estate, 218; Maine Lands, 226; Literature and Art, 232;
Otis Oratory, 238; Boston Society and Poor Relations, 242

XII. FEDERALIST REORGANIZATION, 1801–1814, AET. 35–48
Caucus System and Central Committee, 246; Methods of Nomination,
249; Educating the Voters, 253; The Secret National Conventions, 257

XIII. CONSPIRACY AND THE Chesapeake AFFAIR, 1801–1807,
AET. 35–41
Otis in the State House, 264; State Rights and Secession Plot, 268; Feast
of Shells and Selfridge-Austin Affray, 275; Boston and the Chesapeake
Affair, 279

XIV. TRIP TO MONTREAL, 1806, AET. 40
Boston to Montreal by Chaise and Boat, 284; To Quebec and Back, 290

XV. EMBARGO TO WAR, 1807–1812, AET. 41–46
Jefferson's Embargo, 298; New England Wrecks the Embargo, 300;
Madison and Gerry, 313; The Approach of War, 319

XVI. MR. MADISON'S WAR, 1812–1814, AET. 46–48
Our Most Unpopular War, 325; Boston During the War, 332; Intensified Opposition, 342; The Crisis of 1814, 348

XVII. THE HARTFORD CONVENTION, 1814–1815, AET. 48–49
Why a Convention?, 353; The "Wise and Good," 358; Extremist Demands, 362; Sessions and Report, 372

XVIII. The Mission to Washington, February 1815, aet. 49
"Three Black Crows," 383; Thoughts on the Convention, 395

XIX. Good Feelings and the United States Senate,
1815–1821, aet. 49–55
Post-War Life at Number 45, 400; Era of Good Feelings, 402; Harvard
Happenings, 406; Social Life at the Capital, 411; National Politics,
420; Missouri Compromise, 424

XX. State Politics and Manufacturing, 1822–1837,
aet. 56–72
Indian Summer of Federalism, 433; Running for Governor, 437; Finis
Federalism, 442; Manufacturing and the Tariff, 448

XXI. Mayoralty and Slavery, 1829–1835, aet. 64–70
Third Mayor of Boston, 455; Boston and the Abolitionists, 464; Otis
Attempts to Solve the Slavery Question, 470

XXII. A Brisk Old Age, 1834–1848, aet. 69–83
The Irish Catholics, 478; Social Life and Family Gossip, 484; The Last
Years, 499

Appendix, Descendants of Harrison Gray Otis, 517

Bibliography and Notes, 527

Index, 551

Illustrations

HARRISON GRAY OTIS, by Gilbert Stuart, 1809.   frontispiece
Owned by Society for the Preservation of New England Antiquities.
Courtesy Vose Galleries. Photograph by Herbert P. Vose.

COLONEL JAMES OTIS, by John Singleton Copley, 1758.   3
MRS. MARY ALLYN OTIS, by John Singleton Copley, 1758.   5
Photographs taken c. 1900, courtesy James Otis Esq. Originals are in
Wichita, Kansas, Art Museum.

BOSTON IN OTIS'S BOYHOOD, THE BONNER MAP OF 1769.   12–13
Courtesy New York Public Library.

THE BOSTON LATIN SCHOOL IN HARRY'S DAY.   15
From H. F. Jenks Catalogue of the Boston Public Latin School (1886), p. 89.

JAMES OTIS THE PATRIOT, by Thomas Crawford.   19
Courtesy Fogg Art Museum, Harvard University.

HARRISON GRAY, by John Singleton Copley, 1767.   20
Courtesy Hon. Robert H. Thayer of Lorton, Virginia. Photograph by
Corcoran Art Gallery, Washington.

SAMUEL ALLYNE OTIS, by Gilbert Stuart, 1809.   25
ELIZABETH GRAY OTIS, by John Singleton Copley, 1764.   26
Courtesy Hon. Robert H. Thayer. Photographs by Corcoran Art Gallery,
Washington.

HARVARD COLLEGE IN HARRY'S DAY.   35
From the model by Pitman in the Harvard College Library.

MRS. MERCY OTIS WARREN, by John Singleton Copley, c. 1762. 45
Courtesy Boston Museum of Fine Arts.

HARRISON GRAY OTIS, 1785. 46
From a miniature owned by Mrs. Elizabeth Gray Spingarn.

SALLY FOSTER OTIS, by Edward G. Malbone, 1798. 56
Courtesy Society for Preservation of New England Antiquities.

JOHN HANCOCK, by John Singleton Copley, 1765. 62
Presented by Otis to the city in 1830, now in Boston Museum of Fine Arts.

THE NEW STATE HOUSE, BOSTON. 77
From cover of a March dedicated to Otis, Harvard College Library.

JONATHAN MASON, by Gilbert Stuart, 1805. 78
Courtesy of the owner, Henry Sears Esq. of New York. Photograph by
Peter A. Juley & Son.

THE BRICK HOUSE, 141 CAMBRIDGE STREET. 80
From a sketch by Bulfinch in the Otis Mss.

THE BRICK HOUSE IN 1966, WITH THE WEST CHURCH. 81
Photograph by author.

DRAWING ROOM AT THE BRICK HOUSE. 81
From Charles A. Place Charles Bulfinch (1925).

"A NEW DISPLAY OF THE UNITED STATES," engraving by
Amos Doolittle, 1799 99
Adams Mss., Massachusetts Historical Society. Photograph by
George M. Cushing.

MRS. JOHN ADAMS, by Mather Brown, 1785. 129
Courtesy of New York State Historical Association, Cooperstown, New York.

MRS. WILLIAM BINGHAM, by Gilbert Stuart. 133
Courtesy Frick Art Reference Library and the owner, Francis F. Hart Esq.

MARQUISE DE BLAIZEL (MARIA BINGHAM),
by Thomas Lawrence. 135
Courtesy Miss Helen Frick.

MARQUESA DEL CASA YRUJO (SALLY MCKEAN),
by Gilbert Stuart. 143
Courtesy Duque de Sotomayor y Marques del Casa Irujo, Madrid.

HARRY'S LETTER OF 23 FEBRUARY 1801 TO SALLY. 151
Facsimile from the Otis Mss.

AARON BURR, by Gilbert Stuart, c. 1794. 179
From Lawrence Park Gilbert Stuart

SALLY FOSTER OTIS, by Gilbert Stuart, 1809. 183
Courtesy Reynolda House, Inc. Photograph by Herbert P. Vose.

NO. 85 MOUNT VERNON STREET. 194
NO. 45 BEACON STREET. 195
Photographs by Samuel Chamberlain, 1960.

NO. 45 BEACON STREET, MAIN FLOOR AND GARDEN. 198
From plan in Otis's hand in his Mss.

NO. 45 BEACON STREET, YARD AND STABLES. 199
Photograph by author, 1968.

OTIS'S SKETCH OF HIS DINNER TABLE. [In Text] 210
From the Otis Mss.

THE OTIS AND SEARS MANSIONS, c. 1817. 222
Watercolor by Ogden Codman, c. 1900. Courtesy Somerset Club.

THE GRANITE BLOCK ON BEACON STREET, BELOW RIVER. 222
Photograph by author, 1968.

THE EXCHANGE COFFEE-HOUSE. 224
From State Street Events (1916). Courtesy State St. Bank and Trust Co.

INDIA WHARF. 224–225
*Photograph c. 1855 in Herbert F. Otis Story of India Wharf (1916).
Courtesy Miss Mary Otis.*

TWO GROUPS OF OTIS TOWNSHIPS IN MAINE. 228
From the Wallis and Chase map of 1862 in Northeast Harbor Library.

MAP OF "NO. 2" (LEXINGTON), 1808.   229
From the Otis Mss. Photograph by George M. Cushing.

OTIS'S "REMBRANDT" — DE POORTER'S "MUSIC LESSON."   237
Photograph by Herbert P. Vose.

SAMUEL DEXTER, by Gilbert Stuart, 1806.   241
Courtesy Franklin Dexter Esq. Photograph Frick Reference Library.

TIMOTHY PICKERING, by Charles Willson Peale.   273
Courtesy National Park Service, Independence Hall, Philadelphia.

A CANADIAN CALÈCHE.   296
From a drawing by Cornelius Krieghoff in E. C. Woodley's Province
of Quebec *(1944), p. 135. Courtesy Public Archives of Canada.*

CHRISTOPHER GORE, by John Trumbull.   302
Courtesy Fogg Art Museum, Harvard.

GOVERNOR CALEB STRONG.   304
From Burdick's Massachusetts Manual for *1814.*

THE ORIGINAL GERRYMANDER.   317
*From broadside in the Massachusetts Historical Society. Photograph by
George M. Cushing.*

ROULSTONE'S RIDING SCHOOL.   318
Bill in the Otis Mss. Photograph by George M. Cushing.

"SHIPS OF THE LINE," Federalist ballot in 1814.   337
From S. E. Morison Maritime History of Massachusetts.

JOHN LOWELL, by Gilbert Stuart, 1824.   365
From Lawrence Park Gilbert Stuart, *courtesy Ralph Lowell Esq.*

THE HARTFORD STATE HOUSE, EAST ENTRANCE.   369
From Crofut Guide to the History of Connecticut, *courtesy
Frederick S. Bliss.*

THE HARTFORD STATE HOUSE, COUNCIL CHAMBER.   371
Newton C. Brainard The Hartford State House of *1796, courtesy
Connecticut Historical Society.*

"A TRIP TO WASHINGTON CITY." 384
Satire of the three ambassadors. Courtesy Massachusetts Historical Society.

THOMAS HANDASYD PERKINS, by Thomas Sully. 387
Courtesy Boston Athenaeum.

WILLIAM SULLIVAN, by Gilbert Stuart Newton. 388
Courtesy Mrs. Francis Oakey, Southampton, New York.

SOME OTIS RELICS 409
Arranged by Priscilla B. Morison. Photograph by Herbert P. Vose.

WILLIAM EUSTIS, by Gilbert Stuart, 1806. 438
From Lawrence Park Gilbert Stuart.

TREMONT STREET, c. 1840. 462–463
From Gleason's Pictorial of 1853, reproduced in Bulletin *Boston Public Library, 1894.*

BISHOP JOHN CHEVERUS, by Gilbert Stuart, 1823. 481
Courtesy Boston Museum of Fine Arts.

MAP OF BOSTON IN OTIS'S LATER YEARS. 482–483
From T. G. Bradford Illustrated Atlas of the United States, *1838.*

NUMBERS 43, 44, 45 BEACON STREET IN 1968. 485
Photograph by author.

FANNY ELSSLER. 489
From a poster in the Harvard Theater Collection.

EMILY MARSHALL, by Chester Harding, 1827. 493
Courtesy of Mrs. Emily Morison Beck.

WILLIAM FOSTER OTIS. 494
From a daguerreotype, owned by author.

HARRISON GRAY OTIS IN 1844. 503
From a miniature signed "D.P." Courtesy Society for Preservation of New England Antiquities.

WILLIAM CHURCH OTIS AND MARY ELLEN (LYMAN) APPLETON. 521
From photographs owned by author.

MARTHA CHURCH OTIS. 522
From engraving of painting by Charles C. Ingham. Courtesy Miss Mary Otis.

ELIZABETH OTIS (BOOTT) DUVENECK, by Frank Duveneck. 522
Courtesy Cincinnati Art Museum.

HARRISON GRAY OTIS

1765–1848

CHAPTER I

Childhood

1765–1775, AET. 1–9

END OF THE COLONIAL PERIOD

"GET UP, Harry! Come to the window and see the Redcoats march out of Boston!"

It was shortly before midnight of 18–19 April 1775, and a very hot night for that season. A sense of uneasiness, of doom, hung over the town; rumors flew back and forth; Harry's parents, Mr. and Mrs. Samuel Allyne Otis, never went to bed. The nine-year-old boy rushed to a window of their house on Bowdoin Square and saw the British regulars, almost concealed by the mist rising from Colonel Chardon's pasture, marching along jaunty and confident, on their way to Lexington and Concord. At seven the next morning, Harrison Gray Otis, to give the child his full name, started for school. Earl Percy's brigade, about to march to the relief of the column that had been so roughly handled by the minutemen, had been drawn up from Scollay Square along Tremont Street to the Common, blocking off School Street where Boston Latin was then located. A corporal directed Harry to go down Court Street. He rounded the corner where the old bookstore still stands and entered the school door opposite the present "old" City Hall, just in time to hear Master Lovell say, "War's begun, and school's done. *Deponite Libros.*" Harry did just that, and ran all the way home for fear of the regulars.

This boy, born in Boston on 8 October 1765, came into a good inheritance. Harrison, Gray and Otis were names of respectable English families who had been in New England for three generations or more. John Adams, who detested the egalitarian notions of Thomas Jefferson, once said to General James Warren, who married Harry Otis's Aunt Mercy, "There has been a natural aristocracy here ever since the country was settled — your family at Plymouth, Mrs. Warren's at Barnstable, and many others in very many places, that have kept up a distinction similar to nobility."

At the time that Harry bawled his entry into this natural aristocracy, it was being shaken by the writings and speeches of his Uncle James. Owing to him, the name of Otis was already famous throughout the North American continent, and infamous in Great Britain.

The Otises were landowning farmers of Glastonbury, Somersetshire, who came to New England in the Puritan migration of the 1630's. They first settled in Hingham, where they named a hill "Wearyall" after the one at Glastonbury where Joseph of Arimathea is said to have rested. Two John Otises, father and son, emigrated; the younger moved to Barnstable in Plymouth Colony and built a homestead beside the Great Salt Marshes that served the family for several generations. We know nothing else about him except that he was once fined £2 for selling cider without a license; but his son, the third John, rose to provincial eminence. Judge Otis, as he was generally called, held various military and judicial appointments in Barnstable County and represented his town for twenty successive years in the general court of Massachusetts Bay, to which Plymouth had been annexed. In 1708 he was chosen a member of Her Majesty's Council, the highest position that the province could offer a native son, and until his death in 1727 he was annually reëlected to that honorable board. His character was easygoing and genial, with the same humor and charm of manner for which his great-grandson Harrison Gray Otis became famous.

James, his sixth child, born at Barnstable in 1702, followed a career similar to his father's but possessed a very different temperament. Copley's portrait shows a man of strength, conscious of his

Colonel James Otis, by John Singleton Copley.

dignity, lacking in humor. Colonel James (as he was called because of his militia commission to distinguish him from his famous son James Jr.), became the undisputed head of the bar in the Old Colony, and in 1748 received the appointment of Attorney General of the Province. In 1762, three years before his grandson Harrison Gray Otis was born, the colonel was elected to the Council.

Although entitled to by his rank, the colonel never joined the court circles in Boston. Whenever business did not require his attendance at the capital, he lived in the ancestral homestead at Barnstable. There thirteen children were born to him and his wife Mary Allyn of Plymouth.[1] No fewer than six of the babies died in infancy. But the record of those who survived shows that quality was not sacrificed to quantity in the family of James and Mary Otis. Of those who reached maturity, James, Mercy, Joseph and Samuel contributed to the American Revolution, and to American culture.

Samuel Allyne Otis, father of Harrison Gray Otis, tenth child of this large family and the youngest to reach maturity, was born in 1740. He graduated from Harvard College in 1759 and returned to Barnstable to study law. At that time his eldest brother and senior by fifteen years, James Otis "the Patriot," had become one of the leading lawyers of the province. Jim, who took a great interest in the education of Sam, wrote their father in 1760 a letter of sound advice about legal education. It was wasted. Sam dropped the law like a hot potato and begged his father to set him up as a merchant in Boston. The Colonel humored him, and before long we find advertisements in the Boston *Evening Post* to the effect that "Samuel Allyne Otis will sell very cheap, at his store No. 5 South Side of the Town Dock, New Flour, cordage & boltrope, Lead & Shott, New England Rum made under his own inspection

[1] Phonetic spelling proves that this name was pronounced "Allen." The Otises added first one and then two e's to the name, eventually both spelling and pronouncing it "Alleyne"; but H. G. Otis refers to his son of that name as "Allen" in letters as late as 1815.

Mary Allyn Otis, by John Singleton Copley.

etc." He owned the 100-ton ship *Industry,* built at Barnstable in 1773, and traded in her with London. Samuel A. Otis never developed the high ability of his father and grandfather; but he inherited from the latter, and transmitted to his son, a gift of personal charm that stood him in good stead.

On the last day of 1764 Sam married Elizabeth, only daughter of Harrison and Elizabeth (Lewis) Gray. Both sides of her family were well-to-do Boston merchants. Elizabeth's grandfather, Edward Gray, owned long ropewalks, the profit from which allowed him to bring up a family of nine children in considerable luxury. At the time of his death in 1757, his son Harrison, Elizabeth's father, was serving a fourth term as treasurer and receiver-general of the province, a well-remunerated position of great dignity. Harrison Gray married Elizabeth Lewis, daughter of Ezekiel Lewis and descendant of Ezekiel Cheever, the famous seventeenth-century schoolmaster. Elizabeth, their only daughter and youngest child, is said to have been a beautiful woman; and her character, as we shall have occasion to observe, was one of singular beauty.

After their marriage, Mr. and Mrs. Samuel Allyne Otis purchased a house on Bowdoin Square, Boston. There on 8 October 1765 their first child was born, and named Harrison Gray Otis after his maternal grandfather, whom his mother adored. But nobody ever thought of calling him Harrison. "Harry" he was nicknamed from the first, and Harry Otis he always remained to his family and friends.

Boston, surrounded by water and including many open spaces and hilly pastures, was then an ideal place in which to bring up a boy. Harry made full use of his opportunities for play and mischief, and developed a rugged constitution that carried him past his eighty-third birthday. He was a sturdy, healthy little fellow with a broad, humorous face, ruddy cheeks, brown hair and inquisitive dark blue eyes.[1] Thomas Handasyd Perkins, one of his

---

[1] The eyes in the miniature of 1785 and the Stuart portrait of 1814, which we have reproduced, are dark blue, as are the eyes in a later miniature portrait of Otis

lifelong friends, said, "Harry Otis was always the handsomest, brightest, and most charming boy of all our companions. Everything he did was better done than any of the rest of us could do it."

Do not imagine that life for a Boston boy was strict or dull in the 1770's. In a town of predominantly wooden houses and wharves, against which sailing vessels moored, there were frequent fires at which every small boy assisted, in the French sense. At one waterfront fire, Captain Jordan of the Royal Navy lost his temper and damned the volunteers as a pack of rogues and thieves, for which he made up by causing the following bluff apology to be printed in the Boston *Gazette:*

> Captain Jordan, of the Royal Navy, Presents his Compliments to the good People of this Place, who attended at the fire on Thursday morning last and begs leave to return them his sincere Thanks for their ready and faithful Assistance he experienced from them on that occasion, which will ever make him think very highly of their Honor. But from his not being acquainted with the well regulated and conducted Police of Boston, and having in similar cases (in other Parts of the World) known great Thefts committed at Fires, occasioned his making Use of improper Expressions in his Warmth, which he is very sorry for, and hopes they will excuse.

In addition to street rows and unscheduled brawls between Redcoats and Bostonians, there were three important holidays — Guy Fawkes Day, Election Day, and Harvard Commencement, which everyone observed.

> Please to remember
> The Fifth of November,
> The Gunpowder treason and plot.

All boys looked forward to this; Harry especially, as that day was

---

owned by the Society for Preservation of New England Antiquities. But the eyes in the Chester Harding portrait are hazel. All portraits agree that he kept his ruddy complexion well into old age.

chosen by his parents to give him a new pair of leather breeches which would be preserved for best until the next Fifth of November. A few days before the anniversary, boys ran around to every front door in town ringing handbells and singing:

> Don't you hear my little bell
> Go chink, chink, chink?
> Please to give me a little money
> To buy my Pope some drink.

North End and South End each had its "pope." Dawn of the Fifth was announced by a screech of conch shells which woke everyone up, and by midmorning each End of the town had a pageant prepared and rolling. A wheeled stage drawn by four horses carried the Pope's "court." At the forward end stood a big lantern of oiled paper covered with satirical inscriptions alluding to recent events, and lampooning the royal governor. A puppet suspended from a gibbet represented the Stuart Pretender. Following him came a man-sized wax or straw-stuffed, corpulent figure, wearing a preposterous miter, representing the Pope; and behind him a very live devil which occasionally jabbed his holiness in the rear with a pitchfork. Other figures representing unpopular characters, such as a tomcod for Governor Bernard who used to handline for that despised fish to save money, were added to the float. Boys under the float's floor held sticks which could turn and elevate the heads of the figures and cause them to bow and leer into second-story windows; the effect was irresistibly droll. Each float paraded about the town during the day, stopping frequently for refreshments, and when the shades of evening fell both met on their agreed boundary, Union Street near the Old Oyster House. There then ensued a terrific struggle on each side to capture the other's "pope." If North End won, it bore the trophies to Copps Hill; if South End won, to Boston Common; and the festivities concluded with a jovial supper and as much drink as the public's contributions would buy.

Thanksgiving Day was a family festival and Christmas was not observed in colonial Boston except by the Anglicans. For another big time Harry and his friends had to wait for the annual celebration of the Boston Massacre on 5 March. That was a rather lugubrious affair. Ghastly relics were exhibited in Paul Revere's shop-window, and an orator declaimed on the "Bloody Massacre." After March they had to wait for Election Day, the last Wednesday in May. This was really inauguration day for the newly elected house of representatives and council; but custom had turned it into an uproarious holiday, and it owed the nickname "Nigger 'Lection" to the fact that all blacks whether slave or free, and all apprentices whether white or black, were given a holiday and took over Boston Common. As a popular ballad on Election Day states,

> Long before Phoebus looks upon
> The outskirts of the horison,
> The blacks their forces summon,
> Tables & benches, chairs, & stools
> Rum-bottles, Gingerbread & bowls
> Are lug'd into the common.
> Thither resorts a motley crew,
> Of Whites & Blacks & Indians too
> And Trulls of every sort.
> Swear, sing, play paupaw,[1] dance and stink
> There Bacchus holds his court.

A pretty pageant began when the scarlet-coated First Corps of Cadets conducted the royal governor from Province House to the meeting house of the First Church, near the head of King (now State) Street, to hear the annual Election Sermon. That was a great honor for a divine and usually a great bore to the audience, since it lasted at least an hour. His Excellency then attended an official banquet in Faneuil Hall for deputies, councillors, preachers and prominent citizens. By 4 P.M., dinner over and drink exhausted, they

---

[1] The game of pawpaw or props, precursor to craps, was played with four cowrie shells filled with sealing wax, the convex side ground flat.

proceeded to the Town House (now the Old State House), where
the new deputies and councillors were sworn in and His Excellency
delivered a speech telling how King George loved New England
and expected the people to prove their loyalty by behaving better
the ensuing year than in the past — which they seldom did.

Everyone, rich or poor, white or colored, attended the next celebration, Harvard Commencement; but as Harry was only seven
years old at the time of the last one before the war, he probably
never saw one until after he entered college. He undoubtedly attended the celebration in mid-August of the repeal of the Stamp
Act around the Liberty Tree at the foot of Boylston Street. His
father and uncles belonged to the Sons of Liberty, and Harry hung
around the outskirts with other town boys watching what went on,
and trying to snitch food from the well-laden tables. All Boston
lads considered him "one of the boys," and it was said that his first
election to Congress was carried by the local Irish and Negroes.

In addition to participating in annual celebrations and unscheduled occasional brawls and parades, there was plenty of fun for the
little boys of colonial Boston: swimming, fishing and sailing in
river and harbor in the summer; coasting on the Common and
Beacon Hill, skating on Mill Pond and Frog Pond in the winter.
It was fun even to ramble through the narrow, crooked streets
where signs such as King's Head, Red Lion, Orange Tree, Unicorn,
Thistle and Crown and Indian Queen proclaimed the owners'
patriotism — for not until the 1770's was it safe to say a word
against good King George. The waterfront, too, was an endless
source of amusement; vessels arrived and departed daily from
Down East, Out South, and even Europe. Boston streets themselves were an entertainment; instead of the standardized garb of today's businessmen, you encountered the sartorial variety of a fancy-
dress ball: foreign sailors "with bearded lips" and gold earrings,
red-coated British soldiers, cocked-hatted gentlemen in red-lined
cloaks and nankeen breeches, ladies in muslin and dimity with
towering hairdos, girls of the town with come-hither eyes, husband-

men and mechanics in smocks, and an occasional Indian from Natick, Gay Head or 'Quoddy. The small-paned shopwindows were enticing: apothecaries showed great earthenware jars of drugs and herbs and bowls of squirming leeches; haberdashers displayed the latest London and Paris fashions; vintners stimulated thirst with puncheons of West Indies rum and pipes of Madeira wine; and for the learned, Samuel Eliot's bookstore featured the latest London books and controversial pamphlets. In addition there were country wagons with barrels of cider whose drivers allowed small boys to suck as much as they could through a straw for a penny, and itinerant venders crying their wares — "Scissors to grind, knives to sharpen!" "Here's berries, plump strawberries!" and "Oy, here's Oy!" by the oystermen. There then reigned a gaiety, freedom and color in colonial Boston's streets which one now has to seek in the Mediterranean or the Orient.

BOSTON LATIN SCHOOL

Harry received the best education that time and place afforded. Luckily for him, old Puritan ideas of education had been greatly mitigated among broad-minded people like his parents. They belonged to the West Church where Simeon Howard now preached; and he, like most Boston Congregational ministers of the day, was a religious liberal tending to Unitarianism, although he would have repudiated the label. Accordingly, Harry's childhood was not clouded by severe repression of his natural boyish impulses or by a constant reminder that the old Adam resided in him. He never showed much interest in speculative religion, but remained all his life a faithful Bible reader, and, after he changed his residence, joined the liberal Brattle Square Church and became a communicant.

At an early age Harry attended schools where female teachers were unheard of, and liberal use was made of the rod. The first,

in AMERICA

Bartons Point.

Charles River

Ferry to Charles-Town
is about half Mile over.

EbN Mill Damm

N. Water Mill.

Mill Pond.

No 7

No 7

No 7ᵃ

No 9

7

No 9

No 6ᵃ

4

No 8

No 9

M Cornhill

No 9

G

No 8

No 10

FortHill
No 10ᵃ

S. Battery.

Old Wharfe.

Long Wharfe.

Old Wharfe.

HARBOUR

Meeting built 1742.
Town, large brick building Worthy of the Gov.
the year 1742. Gave it to the Town for the use of a
Saturdays

on Hanover Street, was kept by one Master Griffiths, a queer old fellow who used to reward the good scholars every Saturday by letting them scramble for hickory nuts which he threw from his window into the courtyard. At the age of seven, Harry was promoted to the Boston Latin School where Master John Lovell and his son James were the reigning tyrants. We shall let Harry recall his school life in his own words, written over sixty years later:

I perfectly remember the day I entered the School, July, 1773, being then seven years and nine months old. Immediately after the end of Commencement week, I repaired, according to the rule prescribed for candidates for admission to the lowest form, to old Master Lovell's house, situate in School Street, nearly opposite the site of the old School house. . . . The probationary exercise was reading a few verses in the Bible. Having passed muster in this, I was admitted as second boy on the lowest form. . . .

The School was divided into seven classes. . . . The books studied the first year were Cheever's Accidence, a small Nomenclature, and Corderius' Colloquies. The second year, Aesop's Fables, and towards the close of it, Eutropius and Ward's Lilly's Grammar. The third year Eutropius and Grammar continued, and a book commenced called Clarke's Introduction. In the fourth year, the fourth form, as well as the fifth and sixth, being furnished with desks, commenced "making Latin," as the phrase was, and to the books used by the third form Caesar's Commentaries were added. After this were read in succession by the three upper classes, Tully's Orations, the first books of the Aeneid, and the highest classes dipped into Xenophon and Homer. School opened at 7 in summer and 8 in winter, and at 1 P.M. throughout the year. It ended at 11 A.M. and 5 P.M., at which hours the greater part went to writing school for an hour at a time — but a portion remained and took lessons in writing of "Master James," son of the Preceptor, and some young girls then came into school.

The discipline of the School was strict but not severe. The Master's — Old Gaffer, as we called him — desk was near the south-west corner of the room; Master James's desk was in the

First School House, 1748–1810

north-east corner. I remember to have seen no other instrument
of punishment but the ferule in Master Lovell's day. Gaffer's
ferule was a short, stubbed, greasy-looking article, which, when
not in use, served him as a stick of sugar candy. The lightest
punishment was one clap, the severest four — the most usual,
two, one on each hand. The inflictions of the old gentleman
were not much dreaded; his ferule seemed to be a mere continuation of his arm, of which the center of motion was the shoulder.
It descended altogether with a whack, and there was the end of
it after blowing the fingers. But Master James's fashion of wield-
ing his weapon was another affair. He had a gymnastic style of
flourishing altogether unique — a mode of administering our
experimentum ferules that was absolutely terrific. He never
punished in Gaffer's presence, but whenever the old gentleman
withdrew, all began to contemplate the "day's disaster," and
to tremble, not when he "frown'd," for he did not frown, nor
was he an ill-tempered person, but rather smiled sardonically,
as if preparing for a pugilistic effort, and the execution as nearly
resembled the motion of a flail in the hands of an expert thrasher
as could be acquired by long practice.

Otis's granddaughter Emily remembered hearing her grandfather recite an old Latin School ditty about the flogging:

> *Hic haec hoc,* strap him to the block;
> Noun and pronoun, pull his breeches down,
> Verb and participle, the rod begins to whistle.

Returning to Harry's own account:

School opened with *attendamus* to a short prayer. It ended
with *deponite libros.* The boys had a recess of a few minutes to
go out in the yard — eight at a time. No leave was asked in
words; but there was a short club of a yard in length which was
caught up by some boy, round whom those who wished to go
out clustered, and were drilled down to eight. The club was
then held up near Master's nose, who nodded assent, when the
eight vanished, club in hand. Upon their return there was a
rush to seize the club which was placed by the door, and a new
conscription of eight formed, and so *toties quoties.*

PATRIOT OTISES AND LOYALIST GRAYS

During Harry's first ten years, the struggle between Parliament and the Colonies passed through the stages of resistance, compromise, unorganized rebellion, attempted punishment, and civil war. In this struggle Harry's family played an important part from the first. At the time of his birth, both sides of his family belonged to the Whig or Patriot party: Grandfather Otis a prominent opposition member of the Council, and Uncle Jim at the height of his reputation. His two most famous pamphlets, *Rights of the British Colonies Asserted and Proved,* and *Vindication of the British Colonies,* came out in 1764–65; he represented Massachusetts in the Stamp Act Congress which met at New York on 7 October 1765, the day before Harry was born. The following years were the most active, if not the most fruitful, in the career of James the Patriot. Politics gradually absorbed his entire time, to the exclusion of his law. His genius seemed to burn itself out under the stress of agitating; and his nature, formerly easygoing and genial, became resentful and irascible. John Adams's diary as early as 1763 records extravagant behavior and violent temper on James Otis's part which can only be accounted for by mental unsoundness. In 1769 occurred an altercation with a crown official, in which he received a severe cut on the head. This blow permanently unbalanced his reason. With the exception of a few lucid intervals, the brilliant orator, lawyer and patriot was never again himself. He became madly violent, and in December 1771, on representation to the probate court that James Otis, Jr., was *non compos mentis,* Harry's father was appointed his guardian.

Another cause of uneasiness in Harry's family was the growing toryism of his maternal grandfather. Treasurer Gray, a somewhat shaky member of the popular party, began shortly after Harry's birth to gravitate toward the other side. John Adams subsequently ascribed his apostasy to the death in 1766 of his political and reli-

gious mentor, the Reverend Jonathan Mayhew, who is now regarded as one of the clerical precursors of the Revolution. "Had
Mayhew lived, it is believed that Gray would never have been a
refugee; but the seducers prevailed, though he had connected his
blood with an Otis." The worthy treasurer was, indeed, fond of
religious exercise and devoted to his pastor, but no particular circumstance is necessary to explain his march toward the right. Men
of means and established position, although liberal in their ideas,
generally take the conservative side when the issue is fairly joined
between rebellion and loyalty. Self-interest would have led Harrison Gray to remain a Whig, for his tenure of office was dependent
on the popularly elected general court. But he believed that Parliament had conceded enough in repealing the Stamp Act; and,
abhorring boycotts, riots and other illegal methods employed by
the patriots, he refused to make an issue out of the tax on tea.

Until the time came when everyone had to choose sides, Harrison Gray remained a moderate Tory, even managing to retain his
official position by advancing salaries to impecunious representatives out of his own pocket when the treasury was empty. But in
1774 came an event that forced him to take a stand. Among the
Acts of Parliament intended to punish rebellious Boston for mobs
and tea parties was one suspending the Province Charter and providing that the Council henceforth be appointed by the royal governor on a legal writ of *mandamus*. Harrison Gray's name appeared high on that list. Against the advice of most of his friends,
he accepted the call, thus recognizing the right of King and Parliament to suspend at will the rights and liberties of Massachusetts
Bay. The immediate consequences were loss of his position and
unwelcome attentions from the mob; the final consequences were
confiscation of his property and permanent separation from friends
and country.

Harry never had any doubt about which side he was on. His
uncle, Harrison Gray, Jr., only a few years older than Harry, who
later followed the treasurer into exile, recalled over forty years

James Otis, by Thomas Crawford.

Harrison Gray, by John Singleton Copley.

later their playing together at his father's house. "I was very fond
of you," he wrote, "tho' not nine years old and a most Violent *little
democrat, so* much so that I had a difficult task to keep you within
bounds."

Nevertheless, the fact that Grandfather Gray became a loyalist
had an important effect on the mind of young Harry. In after
years he could testify that it was possible to be at the same time a
Tory and an honest man, and that persecution of the loyalists,
though inevitable, went too far.

The Otis family, who had as much at stake as Treasurer Gray,
never wavered from the Patriot cause. Colonel Otis in 1770 renewed his active opposition in the Council, his election to which
had been vetoed by Governor Bernard since 1766. In 1774, at the
age of seventy-two, he was chosen to the revolutionary provincial
congress at Watertown, one of the first of whose acts was to order
the people to cease paying taxes to Treasurer Gray.

Harry's father, in close business and personal relations with the
Adamses, Warrens, and Gerrys, did not take an active part in
politics until after the war broke out. In the meantime his sister
Mercy, Harry's "Aunt Warren," rose to fame as a poet. Married
in 1754 to James Warren, a well-to-do country gentleman of Plymouth, Mercy Otis led the humdrum life of a New England house-
wife down to the Boston Tea Party, when her husband became a
prominent member of the general court and Mercy blossomed as a
femme politique. With heart and soul in the Patriot cause, she
applied her pen to its aid — a proceeding that other and less gifted
wives believed highly unbecoming to her sex. In 1774 she published a serious poem, "A Political Reverie," in which she looks

> . . . with rapture at the distant dawn
> When Patriot States in laurel crowns may rise,
> And ancient kingdoms greet them as allies.

Although not derelict in her duties as wife and mother, Mercy
loved public life. Throughout the war she advised her husband on

political matters, corresponded with statesmen, and shot barbed shafts of satire into the enemy's flank. Harry she regarded as the young hopeful of the rising Otis generation, but deplored, as we shall see, his favorite amusements and Federalist politics.

The year 1775 was Harry's tenth, when he could observe great events that were taking place in his native town. His vivid recollections of 18–19 April 1775 we have already described. News of the Concord fight brought thousands of armed country people swarming around Boston, until it became apparent that the town would be besieged in order to force the British garrison out. Harry's father decided to follow the example of many Patriot families and remove his before it became too late. The Otis homestead at Barnstable offered a convenient refuge. In the second week of May 1775, Harry and his mother, bidding good-bye to Grandfather Gray and the Gray uncles and aunts, set out in the family chaise for the Great Salt Marshes. Samuel A. Otis followed by sea with part of the household goods. It was the final parting of the ways for the Otis and Gray families. Luckily for Harry, his father remained true to the cause which his Uncle James had done so much to promote. That cause must have seemed desperate enough in May 1775 to an intelligent man who compared the resources of Great Britain with those of the Thirteen Colonies. But his father's choice meant for Harry an opportunity for distinguished public service in a republican state, whilst his Gray uncles and cousins were doomed to a monotonous life of pensioned exile near the court in which they had placed their trust.

CHAPTER II

A Youth of Promise

1775–1783, AET. 9–17

THE TRAGIC SEPARATION

SHORTLY AFTER the Otis family arrived at Barnstable, Harry's
mother wrote to her Tory father as follows:

Barnstable, May 1775.

Hond Sir

I have only time to inform you, I arrived here this day at
twelve, and have been treated with the greatest kindness upon
the Road, every one rejoicing that we have left *Boston.* The
Sloop did not arrive here till yesterday; I have not seen Mr.
Otis yet, he thinks it best not to come on shore, until he can
get his goods all out of the Vessel, which will be to morrow, the
children are all well with me, except the Baby, who I have left
for the present, with her Nurse. I wish you with the rest of my
dear Friends were out of Town, not that I am apprehensive of
any danger, except that of *starving.* I have many things to say,
but I forbear as I know not whose hands this may fall into, so
with wishing you all the support of Heaven which is necessary
at this day of Trial and distress, I conclude

Your dutiful Daughter   E OTIS[1]

---

[1] Her letters are copies made by the recipient, and sent by his granddaughter
Sophia to her cousin, Harrison Gray Otis, in 1833. He writes in reply, 17 January
1833: "You did me a greater favor than you were aware of in sending me the little
rubrics of my Grandfather. They have reference to scenes impressed on my bosom
in childhood, with indelible interest. I was with my mother when she wrote those
letters which showed that her heart was beginning to break as break it did at her
separation from her father tho' united to a worthy and affectionate husband, whom
she loved."

Harry looked on the removal to Barnstable as a huge lark. He was not allowed to waste time, being sent to school with the nearest clergyman, at whose house he passed every week from Monday to Saturday. His progress satisfied his mother, who wrote to his grandfather on 8 January 1776, "I shall inclose you a letter from Harry of his own handwriting as well as of inditing, which will enable you to form a Judgment of his Genius which his Tutor tells me is very uncommon to say the least." Tom Perkins, Harry's young friend who studied at the same school, told in after years of the famous times he and Harry used to have in the Old Colony:

> In vacation and on Saturday during fishing season we used, with my brother James, to go trout fishing in Mashapee and Santuit Rivers with great success. We never kept trout much under a pound, putting the smaller ones back into the stream. Although we were so young, we were allowed to use guns; my mother saying that she did not know but that we might be called upon some day or other to fight for our country and she wished us to understand the use of a gun. Sometimes we joined the deer-hunts on the hills, or during the autumn shot flight-birds on Barnstable Great Marshes.

For the boys' elders, however, it was a time of deep anxiety. They had not been long in Barnstable before news came of the battle of Bunker Hill and the burning of Charlestown. "This came to us," Harry remembered, "not in the shape which it has since assumed, as a real victory, though nominal defeat; but with the unmitigated horrors of conflagration and massacre, and as a specimen of the mode in which our peaceful villages were intended to be swept with fire and sword." Barnstable lived in a state of almost perpetual alarm, the coast being frequently threatened by British tenders and privateers. Harry's mother, full of grief at the parting from her father and brothers, and of apprehension for their welfare in the beleaguered town, wrote pathetic letters. "I must entreat you dear Papa," she writes on 24 July, "to write me, and

Samuel Allyne Otis, by Gilbert Stuart.

Elizabeth Gray Otis, by John Singleton Copley.

inclose it to General Thomas, I shall then be sure of having it. Do not write any thing for the sake of keeping up my Spirits, but let me know exactly how you all do. Every Wish and Prayer that a heart can pour out await you and my Brothers Letters."

So difficult were communications between Boston and the outside world that for three months in the autumn of 1775 there came no word from Grandfather Gray. Later in the year communication became fairly easy, to judge from a letter of Christmas Day 1775 from Elizabeth Gray Otis to her father:

> If it would not be giving my Papa and Brother too much trouble, I should be exceeding glad [if] they would send me out a trunk of Apparel I left in the little Chamber, with my beding counterpin Curtains and Carpets which may be put in a Trunk. I should not have asked this had I not been credibly informed Mr. Bowdoin has lately got out several large Trunks over the Neck and the things I mention are absolutely necessary. I need not add I most ardently long to see you, but whether ever I shall is known only to him, who orders all things with unerring Wisdom.
>
> We have already felt heavy trials — and are daily expecting greater. May Heaven take pity on us, and remove those heavy Judgments that are now hanging over us — prays your obedient Daughr.   E O

The family at the Otis farm consisted of Harry's father and mother, his younger brother Sam, two babies, Grandfather Otis, and Harry's Uncle Joseph. The last two were absent a large part of the time — the old gentleman being president of the council at Watertown, and Joseph a member of the lower house of the provincial congress. Early in 1776 they received an unexpected acquisition in the person of Mrs. Otis's youngest brother John Gray. Jack was a spirited young loyalist of twenty, with a faculty for getting into trouble. At the beginning of the siege he sailed for England; but not long after, thinking that the rebellion would soon be over, he reëmbarked for Boston. His vessel was captured

by an American privateer and brought to Newburyport, where the
boy was thought sufficiently dangerous to be put under close confinement. By the intercession of his Otis relatives the provincial
congress passed an order releasing him into their custody, on giving a bond for £1000 not to leave Barnstable or to have any dealings
with the enemy. Under these conditions Jack was allowed to join
the family at the Great Salt Marshes. Since his sister writes "He
is in very good spirits, and treated like a gentleman," the young
loyalist, highly pleased with himself and his adventure, was doubtless a great source of entertainment to his relatives.

After the evacuation of Boston, 17 March 1776, the Otis family
returned and reopened the house that Grandfather Gray had abandoned. It was a different town from the Boston they had left ten
months before. The change was not so much in the outward aspect of the place, although cannon balls were still scattered about
and many houses had been pillaged by the British soldiery during the confusion of evacuation. The real change that the war
had brought about lay in the social structure. When Lord Howe
came to his sudden decision to retire from the town, the Boston
Tories saw that they too must leave. In the words of one loyalist,
"Neither Hell, Hull nor Halifax" would be as bad as facing the
enraged and victorious patriots. For three days confusion reigned
while panic-stricken British sympathizers rushed to and fro, trying
to find corners for themselves and their household goods on one
of the transports. When they were all finally embarked, Abigail
Adams could look down from Penn's Hill upon the largest fleet
ever seen in America, upward of a hundred and seventy sail ready
to set forth for Halifax.

This emigration was comparable to that of the royalists from
France sixteen years later. It drained Boston of some of her most
prosperous and valuable citizens, leaving great gaps in the social
structure. Among the exiles were Harrison Gray and his sons,
Lewis and Harrison. Their absence alone made it a sad homecom-
ing for Harry's mother, as her letters indicate:

My dear, dear Pappa [she writes on 29 June 1776] — Although I see no great probability this will ever reach you, yet I cannot let the opportunity pass without a few lines. It's not in the power of words to express how much I have suffered for you and the rest of my dear friends since you left Boston, having never received any Intelligence from Halifax, till yesterday. A few lines from Mrs Hughes informs me you with my Brother and Sister embarked for London May 12th. Hard is my fate to be thus separated from the tenderest, the best of Parents. . . . You may well suppose the Town wears a gloomy appearance to me who has lost so many dear connections. . . . I had no other Inducement to return to it, but on account of the little folks, who were destitute of Schools when in the Country.

And again, on 15 August:

My dear papa I must entreat, if there is any possible way of conveying a line, you would improve it, and tell me whether you think there is the least probability of our ever meeting again on Earth. I own I sometimes indulge the pleasing hope, however slender the foundation. As I ever make it a rule not to say any-thing upon political matters, you will not expect anything in that way now. I have many things to say in the domestic way, but as I know not whose hands this may fall into I forbear. . . .
                                                Your dutiful Daughtr   E. O.

My good partner with the little folks joins me in duty and Love. I wish you would not mention anything in the political way, as it may be a means of my not seeing it.

Harrison Gray had placed himself beyond the pale by a pam-phlet that he published in 1775, attacking both the continental and the provincial congresses. Tories called it "The Two Congresses Cut Up"; patriots called it "The Gray Maggot." He dwells on the "gross, immoral, . . . malignant, atrocious nature" of the Boston Tea Party, and on "treasonable" resolves which could only be ex-plained by the congressmen having voted "immediately after drinking thirty-two bumpers of the *best Madeira*." With his sons he left Boston in the British evacuation and settled in London.

There he lived on a pension of £200 per annum from the crown,
and whatever grandson Otis managed to salvage from his New England property. Harrison Gray never regretted his loyalty. On
1 March 1777 he wrote to his brother John, who had adhered to
the American cause, that he was sorry for his low spirits; but, cheer
up! The glorious period is hastening when "You will be emancipated from the tyrannical, arbitrary, congressional government
under which you have for some time groaned. A government for
cruelty and ferocity not to be equalled by any but that in the lower
regions, where the prince of darkness is president, and has in his
safe custody a number of ancient rebels, who are reserved in chains
of darkness to the judgment of the great day!"

For his apostasy (as patriots regarded his loyalty) Harrison Gray
had the compliment of being placed fourth, after Governors Bernard and Hutchinson and Lieutenant Governor Oliver, on a list of
"notorious conspirators" whose estates were confiscated by a Massachusetts law, and who were permanently banished from the
United States.

PARENTAL ACTIVITIES

Samuel Allyne Otis and his children adjusted themselves well
enough to wartime Boston. Harry returned to the Latin School in
the fall of 1776 to prepare for college. He and his friend Tom
Perkins used to shoot snipe on the site of the present playground
at the foot of Boston Common, and went gunning for teal in a salt
creek near the site of Dover Street. On one memorable occasion,
in a vacation at Barnstable, "Otis and I" (wrote Perkins) "went
out to the marshes to shoot against one another, he going to the
north toward Sandwich and I keeping to the south. At the end of
the day I brought in some seventy large birds, half of them killed
by single shots with a gun having but one barrel and a flint lock,
and was delighted to find I had beaten Harry, who had, however,
killed but a very few birds less than I had."

Harry's father now resumed his mercantile business, in partnership with a Mr. Andrews, and also entered politics. In May 1776 he was chosen one of the Boston representatives to the general court. Shortly after, the legislature appointed him to the state Board of War, together with his brother-in-law James Warren. This was a responsible and important position. The Board of War acted not only as a state executive for military affairs but as intermediary between the state and Congress. In the meantime the Otis business prospered. It is a mistake to suppose that the majority of Americans suffered hardship and privation during the War of Independence. In that contest, as in all wars, fortunes were made out of speculative enterprise, supplying government, and contraband. The early enthusiasm for homespun and raspberry tea soon passed away; and from 1778 on, the demand for luxuries and British goods was so great as to make advocates of Roman virtue like Sam Adams and Mercy Warren feel that corruption and decay had already entered the body politic. There is no reason to suppose that Samuel Allyne Otis shut his eyes to any legitimate modes of making money.

In November 1777, Messrs. Otis & Andrews received the appointment of collectors of clothing for the Continental Army. Although, as Otis acknowledged, "the emoluments were considerable," it was an exacting and difficult position. Continentals were in constant need of clothing. A sudden order would come for ten thousand uniforms to equip Pulaski's Legion, and Messrs. Otis & Andrews would first have to procure the materials as best they could, then see that the garments were made up, and finally forward them to the clothier-general. They wrote to Colonel Timothy Pickering, the quartermaster-general, on 2 July 1778: "we have sent on from the beginning of Dec. from 16 to 18000 suits of cloathes, besides shirts, shoes, Hatts, blankets, &c.; . . . for about six months we were near £200,000 lawful money in debt on account of the United States, during which time, we were perpetually embarrassed by people calling for their money, & much of our time was taken up, in apologizing." General Washington on one occasion complained of the "Scantiness of the Cloaths" provided by Otis & Andrews, and desired the sergeants' uniforms in future be made of better quality than those of the private soldiers.

Otis owned a privateer, the *Phoenix,* which did not do well. But he had many other lines, as revealed in his letters to brother Joseph, brigadier general of the militia of Barnstable County, country merchant, and member of the local committee on clothing. On 8 June 1778, he wrote:

> Dear Brother
> Will procure the 160 hard dollars if I can and write you. Am sorry for Weeks's Misfortune. am indifferent about the Cloth but wont refuse it at 10/.
> Have no thots of reducing the price of anything past, future reductions is all I have an Idea of. — The melasses cost Andrews 26/ he refused 40/ declined letting you have it at less 24/ and as is riseing you must not think hard of it. You may as well keep yourself calm because if you sware as you threaten at this distance nobody will mind it. Salt Works Freeman insists on managing and we cant honorably decline it tho his political fagaries hurt all he is connected with. Have so many Irons in the fire dont incline to Speculate at Sea but will sell you the Salt. Yours Affectionately, SAM A OTIS.

And on 10 September of the same year:

> Am afraid you will be in too much in a hurry about your winter goods, but you may as well make 100 prc as 5 they grow exceedingly scarce and will be at 20 for one in a short time yours were put at 12 . . .
> As you are a farmer Mr. Andrews & myself will help you to a sale of forty bushell good potatoes, 200 head of Cabbages, few bushells onions 20 bushell of turnips Carrots & parsnips & few onions, or what you can spare of these articles.
> Mrs. Otis desires you would take her in a pail or two of Eggs if they come handy.
> We have no News here, but find ourselves alarmed by the burning of Dartmouth. Cruel Men! Are these their olive branches?

Mrs. Otis is miserably sick & weak & am very much distressed with the apprehension that she w[ill] not recover.

Give my Duty & Love to all friends, & send namesake home first opportunity, and if he is scandalously ragged as I fear he is let the shoe maker & Taylor put him in decent kilter.

The forebodings that Samuel Otis expressed for his wife were well founded. Separation from her beloved father inflicted on Elizabeth Gray a wound from which she never recovered. With gentle submission she accepted the course that her husband had taken; but, as her letters show, she remained a loyalist at heart, inwardly protesting against the course of events that had placed an insuperable barrier between her husband's family and her own. There was nothing in the new order of things to make up for the friends she had lost. "You can have no Idea of the situation of this wretched place," she wrote to her father from Boston on 10 July 1777. "Those who never knew what it was to live in a gentle way are now the first people here, while others, who were brought up in the most delicate manner, are by these unhappy times reduced to great distresses."

Anxiously her husband and children saw depression turn into poor health and continual illness. A painful confinement after long months of sickness hastened her decline, and on 22 January 1779 she passed away, clasping her father's miniature to her breast. She was only thirty-two years old, and had borne five children. "As she lived a saint, she died an Angel," wrote her husband to Harrison Gray, who answered, "The tenderness and affection you had for my dear child, make you stand high in my Estimation, notwithstanding we widely differ in our political principles."

HARVARD COLLEGE

When the shadow of this calamity fell across his life, Harry was thirteen years old, and in his last year at Latin School. The following summer he entered Harvard College with the class of 1783.

Here his active intellect and charming personality made him a leader in work and play.

Harvard College had changed little since the war. The "Antient Customs" were still read to incoming freshmen: they must not wear a hat in the Yard ("unless it rains, hails or snows"); they must run errands for any student senior to them, and not linger; a freshman must open his door immediately whenever anyone knocks. No student may halloo out of a window or play "Foot Ball or any other game in the College Yard." A playground on the site of Holworthy had been set aside, but the poor freshmen had to provide the "Batts, Balls and Foot Balls" for all four classes. In addition to said Ancient Customs there was a fat pamphlet of College Laws which entering freshmen had to learn by heart.

Any undergraduate who wanted a "cellar" — a locker in the basement of Hollis Hall — could hire one from the college. This practice tempted students to appropriate one another's supplies. George Fairservice's cellar, when searched, yielded a bottle of olives, fifteen bottles of Madeira and four of rum that belonged to Harry Otis. The thief was "degraded" ten places in the class order but recovered his status before graduation.

Young Otis could be counted upon for fun and mischief. In a letter of his riper years he alluded to "our old College practice, of putting a bullet at the end of a whip and when we passed near a flock of geese full speed, of throwing it over the neck of one and jerking it into the chaise. When the goose was caught he must be roasted and eaten or the sport was spoiled. No matter whether fat or lean, goose or gander, down he went before Billy Darling's fire." Billy, besides his regular job of cleaning the College Yard, extended unauthorized hospitality to the "young bloods" who indulged in illegal sports.

In Harry's class of 1783 of thirty members and the slightly larger classes of 1782 and 1784, his principal friends were future congressmen, senators or judges such as New Englanders Benjamin Pickman and Prentiss Mellen, Ambrose Spencer and Stephen Van

Harvard College in Harry's undergraduate days.
Front to rear: Holden Chapel, Hollis Hall, Harvard Hall, Old Stoughton
(roof showing), Meeting House of First Church, Wadsworth House.

Rensselaer of New York, and John Dawson of Virginia. The last-named (nicknamed "Beau" Dawson owing to his courtly manners) and Van Rensselaer graduated a year ahead of Harry. The New Yorker left many debts in Cambridge, but next fall he sent Otis a purse of gold to pay them off; and Harry, in accounting for them, did his best to woo the future patroon back to Boston:

Boston October 20, 1782

My dear Stephen, . . .

The Expectation of your passing the Winter in Town is universal and I am continually questioned concerning the Period of your arrival. The Subscription is open for the Assembly: may no unpropitious Occurrence prevent your coming here and enjoying with your usual Polish, the Pleasures of this Metropolis. D[awso]n is in Philadelphia: Quiri: if his Eclat is as Brilliant as it was among us *Yankees*. It is now Vacation and I have a temporary Respite from Pedantry and Logic. May Father Time ameliorate his tardy Pace and hasten the desired Period when I shall bid adieu to the Sophisticated Jargon of a superstitious Synod of pension'd Bigots and ramble in the Fields of liberal Science.

I inform'd you that I paid Webber, and the Remainder waits for Mr. P. As I apprehended the Gold was weighed, I did not hesitate to pay Webber in Part, deducting Mr. Parkers Amount. I find however it is deficient to the Value of nine Shillings; if it is necessary that I should make up the Sum I can do it with Facility. P. knew I had the Money six Weeks ago, and will positively call for it tomorrow. do write Me and oblige Me by putting it in my Power to do you Service, which at all times will be chearfully undertaken by your affectionate Friend

HARRISON GRAY OTIS

It has been somewhat irritating to historians of Harvard College that these smart remarks of one young blade have been quoted as an accurate description of Harvard College during the 1780's. President Joseph Willard was no intellectual giant, but an amateur scientist second to none; he not only broadened the curriculum but got the Harvard Medical School founded during Harry's junior year. There were three professors — of divinity, natural philosophy and Hebrew — and at least one young tutor, the Reverend William Bentley, who became famous. The study of modern languages began when the corporation appointed Albert Gallatin, a twenty-one-year-old graduate of the University of Geneva, instructor of French in Otis's senior year. And since he mentioned "Oatis" as one of his pupils, and Harry used French readily during the rest of his life, we may assume that Albert Gallatin was as capable a tutor as he afterward proved to be a statesman.

There is abundant evidence in the faculty records that Harry was "one of the boys," or, in the phrase of that day, a "young blood" or "rake-hell." He prided himself on being well dressed and having courtly manners. One heady Saturday eve in May of sophomore year he, Van Rensselaer and five others "supped at a Tavern in Cambridge . . . in direct violation of the Laws respecting the Lord's Day and against frequenting Taverns," and said supper was followed by "disorderly conduct in the Yard" and window-breaking. They were fined £15 each, with double for the window smashers. At the same faculty meeting it appeared that "Haskins, Sohier and Otis" left Cambridge without leave on a fast-day afternoon and "were guilty of such disorderly behaviour as gave great disturbance to the inhabitants of Medford, and has brought great dishonour upon this society." Each was fined £30. Old Sibley, the chronicler, recorded that Harry at times was too noisy for the comfort of his next-door neighbor in Hollis Hall, Librarian James Winthrop, who once fined him eightpence "for ill manners." Harry, it is said, considered this fine insulting — the noise he made was well worth at least five shillings!

Otis and his friends "Beau" Dawson and Sam Quincy committed a "heinous violation of the Lord's Day" — playing ball in the Yard during divine service, but the faculty could not ignore their talents. At a public exhibition sophomore year, in the presence of the Reverend the Board of Overseers, Harry was honored with a "part." He declaimed Lord Lyttelton's *Second Dialogue of the Dead* with his classmate Joseph Bond; and when Bond, by a macabre coincidence, died within a month, Otis delivered the

funeral oration in the college chapel. Junior year, Harry delivered
a Greek oration at an exhibition; and at the beginning of senior
year, a Latin salutatory. Shortly after, he and ten other students
were fined 10s. each for "disorderly behavior and noise" in Hollis
Hall; and in March, when winter was breaking up, the same group
violated the Sabbath by obtaining horses and gaily galloping off in
the direction of Boston, "to the dishonour and injury" of Mother
Harvard's reputation. Massachusetts having resumed specie pay-
ments, they were fined only 3s. each.

Although Commencement was still the great college festival in
which the entire community took part, the seniors in June held a
celebration of their own, which developed into Class Day. Harry
and the usual gang were fined £2 each "for making a riotous and
disorderly entertainment" on that day. Nevertheless, as the top
scholar of his class, Harrison Gray Otis delivered "An English Oration upon the American Revolution, and the Happy Prospects
Arising from the Peace now Restored to these United States," on
Commencement Day, 16 July 1783. It had to be good, coming at
the end of an eleven-part program of disputations in English and
Latin, Greek dialogues, and orations in English, Latin and Hebrew. Harry, as he later recalled, painted "in somewhat gorgeous
colors the prospects unfolded to our country by this achievement
of its liberties, and its probable effect on the destinies of other
nations."

A pleasant picture it is to look back on — the dark-haired, keen-
eyed boy of seventeen pouring forth glowing prophecies of the
future before the grave and reverend dignitaries of college, church,
and state. It was a triumphant end to his boyhood and beginning
of his manhood. He had every advantage a youth of his age could
ask. Gentle birth, an alert and active mind, a winning personality,
and the heritage of a great name; all were his. Surely no boy was
ever launched into the battle of life with more brilliant prospects
than Harrison Gray Otis, "the first scholar of the first class of a
new nation."

CHAPTER III

Law, Fun, and Rebellion

1783–1789, AET. 18–23

JOHN LOWELL'S LAW STUDENT

HARRY OTIS in college determined to study law. Grandfather and Uncle Jim had excelled in that profession, and the latter, having entered one of the lucid intervals that lightened the darkness of his later life, proposed to initiate Harry into the legal mysteries. Uncle and nephew had a long and delightful conversation on the subject in the course of a drive from Andover to Boston. But James Otis soon lapsed into his previous state, and shortly before Harry graduated he was slain by a stroke of lightning when watching a summer thunderstorm. Samuel A. Otis then proposed to give his son the best legal education that could be procured, at the Temple in London. This plan also fell through, since his father, affected by the general depression following the war, became bankrupt; doubly unfortunate because he had just married again.[1] A contributing cause of Samuel A. Otis's bankruptcy was the failure of his elder brother Joseph, owing him £6000 and losing by mismanagement the estate left by his father, the Colonel.

As Channing somewhere observes, the American Whigs inherited from their English brethren the firm conviction that patriots and their relatives should be "taken care of" by government, especially by "feeding at the public crib." Popular Samuel A. Otis,

---

[1] Mary (Smith), widow of Edward Gray and a first cousin of Mrs. John Adams. She bore Otis two daughters, Harriet Allyne and Mary, who adored their half-brother Harry, and he became very fond of them and his stepmother.

elected annually to the general court, was sent in 1787 as delegate to the almost expiring Congress of the Confederation. There he hung on almost until the Confederation's last day, then really landed on his feet in the new Federal Government. The exertions of Vice President Adams and Senator Langdon of New Hampshire procured for him the important post of secretary to the United States Senate. Owing to his uniform courtesy and moderate political views, Otis retained that office to the day of his death in 1814, without missing a single day's session.

Uncle Joseph Otis, to whom the colonel left the Barnstable farm as compensation for not putting him through college like his brothers Jim and Sam, stayed put. He kept a country store in the old house, farmed the property with notable lack of success, but kept so busy during the War of Independence harrying Tories and slackers as to be promoted to the rank of brigadier general in the county militia. He, too, was taken care of by the Federal Government, as collector of the port of Falmouth, Cape Cod.

For Harry Otis, his father's bankruptcy was a blessing in disguise. He needed to be thrown on his own resources at the age of eighteen, to toughen his character and develop self-reliance. And he had the best legal education then obtainable locally, through the generosity of the senior John Lowell, who took him without charge into his law offices as a pupil, out of friendship for the Otis family. Harry earnestly applied himself to the study of law, as an anecdote later told by Benjamin Bussey proves. Every morning on his way to his shop, Bussey saw one of Squire Lowell's office windows decorated by a pair of boots that evidently belonged to some early riser who preferred to read with his heels higher than his head. Curious to know how early they occupied that position, he arose before daybreak one morning and, passing before the Lowell office, found the boots posted at their usual place. Upon entering the office he discovered, deep in Blackstone, young Harry Otis who said he was simply keeping his usual hours for study.

In the autumn of 1783 this diligent student was invited by John

Lowell to accompany him on a journey to Philadelphia. Recalling this tour in his old age, Otis wrote:

> This afforded me a better opportunity of seeing Mr. Lowell in hours of unguarded relaxation from the cares of business, than afterwards occurred. The whole journey was a continued scene of pleasant and instructive conversation, and on his part of kind and condescending manners, sparkling anecdotes, and poetical quotations. . . . We came to New York before the evacuation by the British army was consummated. There Mr. Lowell found Col. Upham, aid of Sir Guy Carleton, and Mr. Ward Chipman, judge-advocate, as I recollect, of the British army, — both old acquaintances and early companions. Their interview, after eight years' separation and various fortune, was most cordial. They introduced Mr. Lowell to Sir Guy, with whom he and my other fellow-travellers dined with a large and splendid party of military and civilians, into which they had me worked in as an attaché to the Boston legation, and it seemed to me as brilliant as Alexander's feast. While in New York, Mr. Lowell received the hospitality and attentions of the distinguished citizens who had begun to return from exile. In Philadelphia, among others, he was waited upon by Mr. Robert Morris, who was still in his glory, and regarded in public estimation next to Washington, as the man on whose financial exertions had depended the success of the Revolution. He entertained *us* — I still hanging on as a bob to the kite — at a dinner of thirty persons, in a style of sumptuous magnificence which I have never seen equalled. I left him at Philadelphia, and went on an excursion to Baltimore for a few days. Upon my return to Boston, I resumed my desk and books in his office.

After three years' study with Lowell, Harry Otis, reommended by the Suffolk Bar Association, took his oath as attorney and counselor-at-law, rented chambers in Scollay's Buildings (on the site of the now-demolished Scollay Square), and hung out his shingle. His first client, a member of the Newport Jewish family of Touro, found him at work early in the morning before any other lawyer had arrived; and this satisfied client lent Harry fifty guineas to purchase a law library. John Lowell in 1786 turned over to Harry his practice in the lower courts, and by the end of the year he had paid his debts.

THE FAST YOUNG SET

Every revolution, including those pulled off by communists in the present century, has an austere, puritanical side. The promoters of revolt want everyone to concentrate on organization and propaganda; fun and games are frowned upon as decadent and counter-revolutionary. Even the Greeks, after their coup d'état in 1967, banned mini-skirts and censored Aristophanes. So it happened in the American Revolution. The Continental Congress and Massachusetts general court passed sumptuary legislation, and the British blockade kept out many luxuries. After the war was over, leaders such as Samuel Adams were eager to hold the line. They regarded the Revolution as a golden opportunity to revive the moral strictness of the early Puritans. The austere Roman Republic, as described by Sallust, was the model they wished their country to follow. But young people like Harry Otis and his friends did not see why they should not have a little fun now that independence had been achieved.

The fortnightly dancing assemblies in Concert Hall, to which Otis had alluded in his letter to Van Rensselaer, were too stiff and formal for the younger set. So, in January 1785, Harry and several young friends, such as Edward Sohier and Isaac Winslow, Jr., encouraged by two gay young matrons, Mrs. Perez Morton and Mrs. James Swan, organized an association called the "Sans Souci Club." It met fortnightly at Concert Hall for card playing, dancing and general jollity. There were twenty card tables at which no bet above twenty-five cents was permitted; tea, coffee and chocolate were served free; and wine, negus (sweetened wine and hot water), punch and lemonade could be obtained at reasonable rates. A couple of fiddlers and a flautist provided music for square dances, and festivities ended promptly at midnight.

This seems very innocuous, but some of the Boston "Old Romans" attacked it as savagely as if it were a gambling hell. The "Tea Assembly" (as they nicknamed the club) received violent abuse in the newspapers, and vigorous defense by the young smart set. The town was torn apart on the question whether this "innocent amusement" (as Harry called it) should be suppressed as immoral or allowed to continue as a much needed enhancement to the amenities of puritan Boston. Sam Adams himself, under the pseudonym "Observer," fired the first shot. His public letter rings the changes on luxury, extravagance, effeminacy, prodigality, profligacy and pernicious dissipation. "Say, my country, why do you suffer all the intemperances of Great Britain to be fostered in our bosom, in all their vile luxuriance?" He closed with an ill-disguised exhortation to his old mobsters to break up so unvirtuous an organization as Sans Souci.

Two days later Harry Otis, using the club's name as a pseudonym, opened a counterattack, characterizing "Observer" as "a baleful comet"; and, for urging the mob to rough up a gentle social club, "a son of sedition." As for Rome and Athens, whose example Adams had invoked, intrigues and seditious speeches of ambitious or disappointed demagogues had done more to undermine republican institutions than "pernicious luxury." Harry's Aunt Mercy Warren, torn between admiration of her nephew for his biting satire (an act she had practiced on the Tories), and regret that he should be on the wrong side, wrote to her son that Harry "is a youth of genius and fire, and I hope he will always have self command to temper discretion with wit."

"Nestor Ironside," "Crito," "Cato," "Slam Bang" and "a Bostonian" now galloped into the newspaper field. "Crito" denounced "Observer" as one of those "who consider all improvements as innovations on the principles of their grandfathers, and that all those who wish to be either wiser or happier than their ancestors are heretical upstarts and degenerate citizens." He scored one on Sam Adams by recalling that the previous summer, when the mall on Boston Common was improved with gravel and trees, the great patriot had opposed it as "a luxurious outline of their country's ruin." "Observer" retorted that the Tea Assembly, admitting gentlemen of nineteen and girls of fifteen without their parents, was "leading the way to vice," especially gambling; and "Mediator" predicted that Sans Souci, though but a foetus, would "quickly grow to a monster of an hideous form." Harry produced a satirical epitaph for "Observer," picturing him as brooding over the virtues of ancient republics and "pining upon the contemplation of pleasures which he is not qualified to enjoy."

"Candidus," the pen name of Benjamin Austin, a consistent advocate of republican virtue, now entered the lists with a solemn warning against "a publick institution where is practised card playing, . . . introducing YOUTH and others to the practice of gaming." One who called himself "Sans Six Sous" defended Adams as an "Illustrious Watchman over Public Morals," observing that "among the first symptoms of a depravity of manners is *youth* treating *old men* with disrespect." He exhorted Harry Otis thus: "Hold thy peace, forward youth, nor profane his name!" Harry retorted with references to his critic's "puerile genius." "Candidus," he asserted, had "reduced buffoonery to a system" and acquired proficiency in "the dialect of the stable." That brought "Thoughtful" and "Considerative" into the fray, attacking Otis as an "arrogant stripling" and "vain youth of matchless impudence."

The tempest in a teapot now boiled over. Editor Benjamin Russell of the *Massachusetts Centinel* advertised a pamphlet entitled *Sans Souci, alias, Free and Easy: Or, an Evening's Peep into a polite Circle.* Sam Jarvis, one of the young blades, threatened to horsewhip him, but Russell went ahead and printed the squib. It appears to have been successful, as a second edition came out the same year. Otis, in this mildly amusing literary performance, appears as "Young Forward" and opens the play as follows:

Mrs. Mercy Otis Warren, by John Singleton Copley.

Harrison Gray Otis in 1785, by an unknown miniaturist.

Sans Souci — free and easy! This is high bon ton — Ante-revolution days — routs — drums, &c. This would do for my Lord *Paxton,* that essence of Chesterfield:[1] We want some of that *Sans Souci* air and address, which were so conspicuous in that great character; but however we practice very well in the school of politeness, and a few years will produce many a BEAU NASH in our modern circles.

To which "Little Pert" (Isaac Winslow, Jr.) replies:

D——n the old musty rules of decency and decorum — national character — Spartan virtues — republican principles — they are all calculated for rigid manners, and Cromwelian days; — they are as disgusting as old orthodoxy: — Fashion and etiquette are more agreeable to my ideas of life — this is the independence I aim at — the free and easy air which so distinguishes the man of fashion, from the self formal republican — the court stile — the *je ne scai quoi* — give me but this and away with all your buckram of Presbeterianism. . . . Thank Heaven we can now hold up our heads amidst the most polite circle at Raneleigh, or join with full eclat the brilliant assembly at Vauxhall.

A dialogue follows, in almost unintelligible Negro dialect, between two black servants, Cuffee and Jack, sitting up for master and mistress who are spending an evening at the club. Cuffee wishes they would stay at home and be in bed by ten, as formerly. Jack, who has visited England, is all for late hours. He predicts that "Cornshort-Hall" will no longer be enough for Boston's "masserades," and that servants in livery are coming in.

At Concert Hall itself, "Dr. Gallant" deplores the "levelling spirit of republicanism" and declares that this club will enable distinguished Bostonians to stand out from the common herd. A rubber of whist is played between Mesdames "Importance" and "Brilliant" (Mrs. Morton and Mrs. Swan), and the Doctor and

---

[1] Charles Paxton, one of the unpopular royal customs commissioners before the Revolution, noted for "the finished politeness and courtesy of his manners," used to be lampooned every Pope Day.

"Mr. Bon Ton" (William Cutler). The session concludes, when the clock strikes twelve, by Cutler's gallant remark, "The hours pass most rapidly; — but however, Madam, we must not find fault with time, for in your company *eternity* can be the only measure of our *happiness.*"

Mrs. Catharine (Macaulay) Graham, the celebrated lady historian who had recently visited the United States and stayed with the James Warrens at Milton Hill, is brought in as a "Republican Heroine" in Act II. She reports to "Mrs. W——n" (Harry's aunt) her dismay that Americans "should so early plunge into the utmost excesses of dissipation." Mrs. W. thanks the learned lady for her just observations but calms her fears by predicting that the club will soon fold up, as apparently it did. Sans Souci gradually faded from view, and soon the people of Boston had something more serious to think about.

Harry Otis, in his middle age, remembered lovingly another social diversion, the sleighing party. On a winter night around full moon, with snow on the ground, the boys and girls and young married couples borrowed their papas' horses and open sleighs, recruited a fiddler or two, and after moonrise drove to a well-known tavern in a nearby town, such as Ames's in Dedham, the Punch Bowl in Brookline, or Porter's in Cambridge. There they drank mulled wine, square-danced to their own music, and, after lots of giggling about who would pair off with whom, bundled into the sleighs and raced home through the crisp air, singing ballads of long-forgotten wars. The "Old Romans" had no objection to this form of fun; they regarded sleigh-riding as "virtuous," having done the same in their youth, although Jonathan Edwards had fulminated against it at Northampton early in the century.

At Harvard Commencement 1786 Harry "incepted" — took his master's degree — according to the ancient ritual. In the afternoon exercises he responded with a Latin oration to a self-imposed *quaestio.* Harry's question was, *An jura jurisconsulti quodam communi et indissolubili vinculo enter se conjungantur?* — "Whether the laws expounded by a jurist are united by a certain common and indissoluble bond?" We know nothing about this oration except that Harry answered in the affirmative, and that John Quincy Adams, a junior in college, thought it very good.

SHAYS'S REBELLION

The year 1786, in which Otis was admitted both to the bar and to his second degree, brought a crisis in Massachusetts. The smoldering discontent of the huge debtor class created by recent hard times flared up in the western part of the state. Shays's Rebellion as it was called, broke out; county courts were forcibly prevented from sitting and county conventions demanded radical alterations in the state government. It seemed to many patriots that the "goodly fabric, that eight years were spent in raising," was about to be pulled down over their heads. When the insurrection approached Boston, young gentlemen formed a new militia company, the Independent Light Infantry, and chose Harrison Gray Otis their captain. Cambridge being threatened by an armed body of insurgents in November, the Light Infantry, stationed at the Charles River Bridge, prepared for action but did not get it. Then Governor Bowdoin appointed General Benjamin Lincoln commander of the state militia and ordered him to raise enough men to break the rebellion. He called at once for volunteers, and Otis offered the services of his company in a letter of 27 January 1787 to the Governor:

> May it please your Excellency,
> The Independent Lt. Infantry, ready to serve their Country & share the Dangers of their fellow Citizens beg leave to tender their Services to your Excellency upon ye present occasion, and are ready to march at the Shortest notice — & to continue in service untill regularly discharg'd.
> Yr Excellency's most obedt Servt
> HARRISON G. OTIS — Capt. Indt Lt Infantry.

This letter is endorsed: "Capt. Otis will proceed with his Company to join General Lincoln and until the junction will be under the command of General Brooks." The company was dismissed after advancing no further toward enemy territory than Cambridge. Otis promptly volunteered his services as aide to General Brooks, whom he accompanied through the remainder of that bloodless but successful campaign. He continued to head the same organization for a number of years. In 1789 "The Independent Light Infantry, under Major Otis," headed the cortège that escorted President Washington into Boston. This was Harry's first and only military service, but he always retained an honorary command in the Light Infantry Company and gave it a "splendid reception" at his residence shortly before his death.

Harry made a reputation for oratory at the beginning of his career. In 1788 he was chosen by the town authorities to deliver the annual Fourth of July oration — a singular honor for a young man of twenty-two. The oration seems labored and bombastic according to our modern ideas of eloquence. We feel the "scorching rays of supreme majesty" and the "pestilential breath of a despot"; the Americans are "elevated, patriotic, godlike," etc. Otis was evidently a little ashamed of the effusion himself, for on sending a copy to his grandfather Gray, he remarked that these expressions "are as necessary for an oration in this Country, as the Lemon juice for punch." He seems, however, to have pleased his hearers; for one of them, John Quincy Adams, by no means an easy critic of other persons' performances, wrote: "The composition and the delivery were much superior even to my expectations, which were somewhat sanguine. It was greatly superior, in my opinion, to that which he delivered when he took his second degree; the only public performance that I had heard before from him."

LEGAL BUSINESS

The bulk of Otis's law practice, at the beginning of his professional career, was derived from admiralty and maritime litigations which were always coming up in Boston. One of the most amusing, if not the most important of his cases, was that of Lemon *v.* Ramsden. Captain Clement Lemon, it appears, had so unsavory a reputation for drinking at sea, that he secured a ship only after signing the following agreement:

Boston December 31st, 1790

Be it Known; I Clement Lemon do hereby Agree to, and with, Thomas Ramsden of Boston Mercht. that if I am seen or known to be disguised with drinking Liquors, or in any wise drunk or disorder'd with drinking during the Voyage now bound on from Boston to Liverpool in the Brigantine Mary Ann and back to Boston — I will forfeit and give up all my Wages or demands I may have against the said Thomas Ramsden or Brigantine Mary Ann. In Witness whereof I have hereunto set my hand and seal this thirty first day of december One thousand seven hundred and Ninety.

CLEMT. LEMON

Alas, Captain Lemon became very much "disguised with drinking Liquors" during the voyage, and the brigantine meandered all over the North Atlantic before returning to Boston. The captain, nevertheless, sued the owner for the full amount of his wages when the owner, according to the agreement, refused to pay. Otis, retained as attorney for the defendant, during the trial produced in evidence of the Captain's condition the following gem of English composition from the mate of the *Mary Ann*. It is addressed to "Mr. Thomas Ramsdel Marchant Boston head of the Long Whorf."

March 2d 1791   Liverpool

Sir

With the utmost Satisfaction I take this opportunity To In
from you that I have Left your Brig and The Reason there off
is upon the aCount of the Capting Who has treated me with
very onsivel [la]ngeage — Nothing but quorling and fighting
has ben on board Sence we have ben out we got here in 37 Days
but more by good Luck then good Conduckd and Now had I a
Long bote I wold not trust him as fare as Castle William in hir.
I Dont say he gets Drunk but I say that he can grink groge as
well as my Self nor due I say he Neckglecks his Duty but he
Loves to Slipe.

I wish your vesel safe home and I am very glad that you have
hir Inshured I have no more Sir But am you humble Sarvent

DANIEL LEWIS.

P S Sir

I wold in from you that the 2 small pigs Died and Capt
Lemon Lost the Dipsy Line and both Leades out of his hand
overboard and then took all the Lead of the hase hole when
there was plenty of bolts and Speaks that wold answer the same
purpose I say Dam such a fellow that Stoes away Cags of Rum
on be none to the oner.

By aid of more direct and grammatical evidence, Otis won the
case for Mr. Ramsden.

A scattered practice added more to Otis's reputation than to his
income, as the following extract from one of his letters to Harrison
Gray, dated 14 January 1790, indicates:

My business calls me and keeps me so frequently from home
that I am really able with truth to say that I have hardly had
time to sit down and write you deliberately since my last. If
these avocations into the Country were as profitable as they are
troublesome, you would perhaps be reconciled to my apparent
negligence, but this is far from true. Our profession in this
Country is not lucrative and I feel already that I am doomd to
a hard life and scanty fortune.

One of these journeys, however, took Otis to New York in season to witness the first inauguration of a President of the United States, on 30 April 1789. The ceremony was especially interesting to the young man on account of the important part taken in it by his father, secretary to the United States Senate. As he stood in the crowd outside Federal Hall, Harry could see his father among the impressive group on the balcony, bearing on a crimson cushion the open Bible on which the President took his oath of office. As the solemn words of the inaugural oath concluded, Samuel Otis made a motion as if to raise the Bible to the President's lips, but Washington gently restrained him and bowed to kiss the book. The scene impressed itself indelibly on Otis's memory; sixty years later he wrote: "No one can describe the silent tearful ecstacy, which pervaded the myriads who witnessed the scene; succeeded only by shouts which seemed to shake the canopy above them."

Otis served as counsel in several famous cases, as we shall see in due course; none more so than the most celebrated local murder case of a century.

Jason Fairbanks, aged twenty-one, and Betsy Fales, eighteen, were lovers. They belonged to respectable farmers' families of Dedham, but the Fales parents, regarding Fairbanks as unreliable, unhealthy and unemployed, refused consent to the marriage. Jason and Betsy frequently made secret rendezvous in a thicket not a mile from her home. On 18 May 1801 Jason staggered into the Fales house, bleeding and lacerated, declaring that Betsy had killed herself with a knife, after which he had tried to do the same but lost courage. He was indicted for murder and tried before the full bench of the Supreme Judicial Court in Dedham meeting house, on 6 August. In contrast to modern murder cases, all the evidence was presented in one day.

Harrison Gray Otis and John Lowell, Jr., were Fairbanks's counsel; the attorney general, James Sullivan, prosecuted for the Commonwealth. Otis and Lowell defended Jason, according to the

Boston *Gazette,* "in a torrent of eloquence with all that ingenuity, sagacity and learning . . . could invent." Otis summed up the defense with emotion, and analyzed the evidence in a way to leave a very definite reasonable doubt in the mind of a reader today. He concluded with a strong statement of the doctrine of Lord Chief Justice Hale, that it is better five guilty persons should escape than that one innocent man should suffer. The attorney general "closed with a masterly and pathetic plea," in which he pointed out the evils of young people's disobeying their parents. The jury retired at 10 P.M., and at 8 A.M. 8 August brought in a verdict of guilty of first-degree murder. Chief Justice Samuel Dana promptly pronounced sentence of death by hanging. One infers from the printed evidence that the jury were convinced that the multiple wounds inflicted on the poor girl with "a certain knife, of the value of ten cents," could not have been self-inflicted; that she was murdered by Fairbanks for refusing to elope with him; and that he then stabbed himself for effect.

That was not the end of it. Ten days after the sentence, Fairbanks broke jail with the aid of friends and fled toward Canada. After a reward of a thousand dollars had been offered, he was apprehended at Lake Champlain, incarcerated in Boston jail for safekeeping, and there dictated to his counsel a statement reaffirming his innocence. A military escort conducted him to Dedham Common where he was hanged on 10 September 1801 in the presence of some ten thousand people who had come from Boston and other neighboring towns to witness the grisly spectacle.

John Lowell was so upset by this outcome, as he firmly believed Fairbanks to be innocent, that he had a nervous breakdown, gave up his law practice and made a trip to Europe. And there is no doubt that Otis, too, believed that great injustice had been done.

The trial created an immense sensation, being reported in the press throughout the United States, and it became the subject of pamphlets and broadside poems such as this:

> Now parents all where ere you be,
> Who hear this sad catastrophe,
> Now let you this one caution take,
> Where love is fix'd — don't matches break.

James Sullivan, on the contrary, ascribed the murder to what is now called "permissiveness." "The most prevailing error," he said in his summing-up for the prosecution, "is a false fondness and misapplied tenderness towards children."

Sally Foster Otis, by Edward G. Malbone.

CHAPTER IV

Marriage, Business, and Family Letters

1790–1797, AET. 24–31

MARRIAGE TO SALLY FOSTER

EARLY IN 1790, Otis offered himself to a young lady whom he had been courting for some time. In a letter that passed between two of his former college mates, Timothy Williams and Timothy Bigelow, we get an unofficial view of this important event in Otis's life:

> H. G. Otis is to be married in three months to Miss Sally Foster — poor girl who has been kept in the twitter of expectation these two years by his attention to her, but never received an explicit declaration till within a month. In this situation a girl must possess uncommon fortitude and virtue not to express or degrade herself in a thousand ways to which she is liable — court instead of being courted.

Whatever may have been her feelings, the diffidence of young Otis was probably due more to the lack of wherewithal than to lack of courage. Long engagements were looked upon askance in those days, and a young man was not expected to declare himself until he was capable of supporting a family. Sally Foster, a beautiful and vivacious girl of twenty, was the daughter of a well-to-do Boston merchant, William Foster, and Grace, daughter of Nathan Spear.

Family correspondence regarding the engagement of Sally and Harry throws light on eighteenth-century formalities. Mrs. Samuel A. Otis, Harry's stepmother, sent Miss Foster this somewhat qualified approbation of the match:

Mrs. Otis's love to Miss Foster, & cannot refrain from expressing the pleasure she feels in the connection which is like
to take place, & wishes Miss Foster all possible felicity and happiness. — Mrs O. intends to do herself the pleasure of Personally
testifying her approbation of Mr Otis's choice the moment she
has receiv'd the form of his Father's consent [of] which She's
persuaded there can be no doubt.

Mrs O. compliments to Mr & Mrs Foster.

Were she led to expect a chilly reception into the Otis family by
the tone of this letter, Miss Foster was soon relieved by a gallant
epistle from her future father-in-law:

New York Jan 24 '90
Dear Madam

When an old Gentleman writes to a fine young Lady his first
care should be to provide an apology. A declaration of Love
would be worse than none. But dont be alarmed my dear Miss
Forster, for altho' it must be a cold heart indeed that is not
half in love with you at least, I shall not make a declaration,
for many obvious reasons. Love to a very worthy & dutiful
son I may however declare; Nor will it I hope offend your delicacy if I add, I am almost jealous too; For I am convinced you
have engrossed so much of his regard that I must submit to a
transfer. Give me credit for a little candour if I confess it could
not in my opinion have been made to a more worthy object; And
to whom I should with greater pleasure resign the first place in
his affections than to, — I had like to have said — *my* Sally.
And will Miss Forster permit me at some future time to call her
so? I have lost an amiable daughter. In my Harry's wife I can
only hope to recover her. You may rely upon the most cordial
reception into our family, if you will consent to become one of
us, & because we all love Harry, tis impossible to withhold our
affections from the Lady of his choice, even if it was not one,
whose "bland accents" & whose "female attractions steal the
hearts of the wise." I can only promise you a continuance of
that solicitude for the dear youth, & all that are dear to him,
which has invariably attended him from his cradle, & will I have
no doubt, go down with me to my grave; On the verge of which,

I shall retrospect the pleasing reflection, that he is happy in loving & being beloved, by such an one as yourself. I should say more on this agreable subject but I fear my affectionate heart has already made me too expressive. Permit me to present my kind regards to your good Mamma, and to entreat her entire approbation of a plan of happiness, on which I felicitate at least one family, & to believe me with great sincerity and respect, her &

Your most Humble Sert.

SAM: A: OTIS.

The young couple — he twenty-four years old and she twenty — were married on 31 May 1790 by the Reverend Samuel Parker of Trinity Church. A daughter was born to them a year and a day later and christened Elizabeth Gray, after her sainted grandmother. The first son, Harrison Gray Otis, Jr., arrived in 1792; a second daughter, Sally, near the end of 1793. Mary, the fourth child, died in infancy; and a fifth, Allyne, was born in 1796. There were six more to come.

The correspondence of Harry and Sally Otis indicates that for the forty-six years of their married life their union was almost perfect. Perhaps the secret lay in the fact that Sally's temperament resembled her husband's, and that Harry never ceased to be her ardent lover as well as her faithful husband.

THEATER AND LOYALIST PROPERTY

Shortly after his marriage, Harry's name began to appear prominently in accounts of Boston town meetings. An interesting controversy revolved about the theater. "Stage plays" were forbidden by an act of 1750, the repeal of which a more enlightened public opinion now demanded. Otis, strangely enough in view of the Sans Souci business, at first took the contrary side and opposed, at a town meeting of October 1791, a petition to the general court to repeal the act. "So strong was his rhetorical power," says James S.

Loring, author of *The Hundred Boston Orators,* that Governor
Samuel Adams, who had attacked him as a frivolous gamester in
1785, now "lifted up his hands in ecstacy and thanked God that
there was one young man willing to step forth in defence of the
good old cause of morality and religion." Loring is so inaccurate
that one suspects this story; but that Harry did oppose the theater
is rendered certain by the quaint letter that he received from his
grandfather Harrison Gray in London:

> It affords me great pleasure my child to hear of the Christian
> as well as the political opposition you made to the motion in
> your Town meeting to petition the General Court for the re-
> peal of the Act against *plays.* If your Legislators have any re-
> gard for the morality of the people, they will not give the least
> countenance to the Stage, which by the late Doc. Tillotson is
> called the *Devil's Chappel;* and which is condemned by the
> primitive church. The Fathers have given their Testimony
> against it; I could quote many extracts from the holy Fathers
> condemning plays, but shall content myself with one from
> *Chrysostom,* who in his preface to his commentary upon St.
> John's Gospel, speaking of Plays and other public Shews says
> "But what need I branch out, the Lewdness of these spectacles
> and be particular in description, for what's there to be met with
> but Lewd laughing, but Smut, railing and buffoon'ry? In a
> word it is all Scandal and confusion. Observe I speak to you all.
> Let none who partake of the holy Table unqualify themselves
> with such mortal Diversions."

Although the general court refused to repeal the prohibitory
act, a company of comedians visited Boston the following year,
fitted up an old stable with a stage, and advertised their performances as "moral lectures" to get around the law. Thus matters
continued for some time; but on 2 December 1792, while the audience was enjoying a moral lecture entitled *The School for Scandal,*
a sheriff erupted onto the stage and arrested one of the actors. The
audience became greatly excited, and a party of enraged young
men tore down and trampled underfoot a portrait of Governor

Hancock that hung on one of the boxes. To satisfy public interest, the examination of Harper, the arrested actor, took place in Faneuil Hall. Otis, who had changed his opinion about the nefariousness of stage plays, appeared as Harper's counsel, made a clever defense on technical grounds, and won his case. The actor was discharged amid loud applause, and thereafter Boston was permitted to enjoy the theater.

What Harrison Gray thought of this backsliding on the part of his grandson in favor of the "Devil's Chappel" he was careful to keep to himself, for Harry was at that time engaged in the delicate business of attempting to recover some of the Gray property, which had met the same fate as that of most loyalists. By the end of the Revolution all his real estate, to the value of about £2000 lawful,[1] was long past recovery. In addition to this loss, however, there were outstanding debts owed to him in Massachusetts to the amount of £8036. Here young Otis was able to effect something, although with endless trouble. There were no legal impediments in the way of collecting loyalists' debts, but public opinion was so hostile to the old Tories that few juries would give a verdict in their favor; and even the fact of Otis's being retained by Tory clients, if generally known, might have killed his political aspirations. It was a very ticklish business, but Harry persisted, out of a sense of justice and family duty, and (as later he boasted) saved more from his grandfather's fortune than did any other agent of a Boston loyalist. His usual method, when forced to resort to a lawsuit, was to procure an assignment of the debt from his grandfather to himself, so that the jury could not be appealed to on the ground that the creditor was an outlawed Tory.

Among the debts were amounts totaling £3468 10s.9d. advanced from time to time to Gray's son-in-law, Harry's father. That went down the drain with Samuel A. Otis's and Joseph Otis's bankruptcies after the war, and Gray never pressed his grandson for

---

[1] This and previous sums mentioned in this book are in "lawful money of New England," six shillings to the silver dollar.

John Hancock, by John Singleton Copley.
Otis purchased this from the heirs of Mrs. Scott (formerly
Mrs. Hancock) in 1829 and presented it to the City.

any of it. But the John Hancock debt of over £1000 lawful, equiv-alent to £956 16s.5d. sterling, was another matter. This sum had been lent to the great patriot by Treasurer Gray prior to the Revo-lution as an advance on his salary. Otis was obliged to proceed with more than ordinary caution. Hancock wielded so great an influence that even the Harvard Corporation dared not press him hard for the settlement of his long-outstanding debts to the college; and had Otis gone to law, the governor could easily have procured an act from the general court permitting him to erase his debt to a Tory by a nominal payment thereof to the Commonwealth. Be-tween 1789 and Hancock's death in 1793, Otis wrote letter after letter, danced attendance in his waiting room, received appoint-ments only to have them broken on the plea of illness, but never succeeded in obtaining a direct reply, oral or written. "I have taken such unwearied pains with regard to this debt for years past," Otis wrote to his grandfather; "I have experienced such dis-appointment deceit & falsehood, that I have almost despaired of receiving a farthing." Finally, in 1795, after both John Hancock and Harrison Gray were dead, Otis thought up a clever move on the governor's widow. She became engaged that year to Captain James Scott, commander of a packet ship between Boston and Eng-land. "As all former arguments had failed," Otis wrote to his Uncle Harrison Gray, Jr., "it occurred to me that some advantage might arise from the intended connection of Mrs. H. and Capt. Scott, especially as an idea prevailed of her intention to accompany him to England. I therefore gave intimation, which I knew would reach her ears, of a determination to prosecute for the debt in Eng-land, if Mr. Scott should ever be found there after marriage, and this suggestion though it could never have been executed, very unexpectedly produced its effect, and induced the parties con-cerned to hearken to terms of accommodation." Harry actually recovered two thirds of the original debt, without interest, retain-ing twenty-five percent for his commission; but this meant a wind-fall of some £500 for Uncle Harrison.

Another piece of Gray property which Harry failed to recover
has been the occasion of much merriment in this writer's family.
It was a tract of 500 acres, including rich meadowland, in the town
of Peterborough, New Hampshire. As that state had passed no
general confiscation act, the town authorities, led by the constable,
Deacon Robert Morison, arranged to put it up for auction in
1779, and by intimidating all other would-be bidders, or getting
them drunk, secured it for a few pence an acre, plus £92 12s. costs
in continental currency. The costs were mostly for "rum drank,"
costing £2 16s. a gallon, at the auction. The town then proceeded
to sell lots from the tract, giving two to the town minister, a circumstance which aroused the late treasurer's and his grandson's
utmost indignation. Harrison Gray hoped that the minister thus
endowed would remember that "Righteousness exalteth a nation";
and young Harry wrote of the Morisons and other local worthies,
"Those fellows are so versed in iniquity that I shall be cheated."
He was; Peterborough refused to disgorge one cent.

BUSINESS TOURS AND PROSPERITY

In the meantime, Boston was recovering her ancient prosperity.
The population, having declined from 15,500 in 1770 to 10,000 in
1780 owing to the loyalist exodus and the war, rose to 18,000 in
1790 and to 24,000 in 1800. With commerce and business rapidly
expanding, Harry was not one to be left behind. Samuel Breck,
in his *Recollections,* gives a pleasant picture of Otis in 1792 toiling
away at his profession. He borrowed a thousand dollars from
Breck, and on repaying it, told him that "the utmost extent of his
desires as to riches was to be worth ten thousand dollars" — certainly a very moderate ambition. "It has pleased God to allow us a
very full measure of domestic felicity hitherto," wrote Harry in
December 1792, "We have two fine children, one of each sex; my

affairs have been prosperous beyond my most sanguine expectations, and I have a full share of business."

Part of his business lay in New York and Philadelphia. Harry hated travel by sea, but he never seemed to mind long journeys by coach or chaise over the execrable roads of the period. Until the railroad era, at least three days were required to travel from Boston to New York, spending nights at Providence and New Haven; and a day and a half or two days were required to get from New York to Philadelphia. The winter journeys which Harry had to make on business were attended by amusing accidents and hardships which today would be inconceivable short of the polar regions. As Randolph Churchill has written, "The separation of lovers delights the heart of the biographer"; and the letters that Harry wrote to Sally are noteworthy for wit and tenderness.

Hartford Decr. 11 [1791] Sunday

I sit down to write my dearest friend from the house in which I penn'd my letter when on a former Journey. . . . My Journey hither though barren of incident has been by far less tedious than I could have expected. We made our Stages by early hours in the evening; My Companions were indeed Strangers incapable of contributing to my instruction or amusement, but being civil and decent did not disgust me with insolence or impertinence. So that on the whole the days have worn away without tediousness, and my slumbers have been strengthened by fatigue, though not Sweetened by the sympathy of love. At Watertown I met your Uncle Josiah, who had purposely waylaid me to consult me on the subject of old Mr. Jackson's will. . . . I was sorry to remark in him a want of decision and firmness, and some wavering remains of fondness for his infamous wife. He is weak enough to doubt her having ever been unfaithful to his bed, and if he indulges himself in frequent access to her, you may be assur'd he will cohabit with her again. How Strange that a man of spirit can be thus willingly blind to the shame of his wife and to his own consequent disgrace! . . .

I hope you will endeavor to enjoy yourself by seeing your

friends at home and by going abroad, and even to the Assembly or Concert if you are at all inclin'd.

Let me hear from you, and write from time to time every little circumstance that occurs, without minding its importance. Tell me the visits you make and receive, the births deaths marriages and news both liberal and Scandalous. No matter what you write so that it is *written by you*. Embrace our little Cherub, with tenfold fondness if possible as you have double duty, and kiss it so as to make it cry a little that it may think of *my fader dere*. . . . Continue to love me as you will ever be loved by your

H G OTIS

New York Decr. 14, 1791
Wednesday Evg.

My dear Girl,

I have just this moment arrived after an extremely fatiguing jaunt; Yesterday morning we broke down and were obliged to walk nine in number, four miles thro' a violent Snow Storm, and made heavy & late progress, notwithstanding which, we were all cheerful and I have escap'd without even a slight cold. I am now at Mrs. Lorings[1] and have just received the sad and un-expected Tidings that one half of our army in the western Country is cut off[2] and that our Cousin Winslow Warren, Sam Newman, Capt Phelon, Nat Balch and others are missing and have probably fallen a prey to the merciless Savages. Good God, what a dismal Stroke for poor Aunt Warren, it will kill her I fear. I proceed on friday for Philadelphia & shall make but a short stay; As I am surrounded by all Mrs. Lorings family & several Boston Friends who ask me a thousand questions, I can only repeat to you that my Heart pants for the sight of you, and I am inconceivably anxious for my return. . . . The Theatre is opened and the play is begun, but the pleasure I take in penning a line to my dearest Girl exceeds any that I could there experience, more especially under the weight of the bad news. How happy I am — nay happy ought I to feel if destitute of a thousand Comforts, to possess in quiet so inestimable a treasure

[1] A well-known boardinghouse in New York.
[2] St. Clair's defeat on the upper Wabash, 4 Nov. 1791.

as yourself, while others of my age are called out and exposed to such hazards. Yes my dear Girl, forever will I cherish you as my own soul, and should fortune ever change and frown upon me, I can never despond while you continue to love your sincere

H. G. OTIS

New York, Friday Dec. 16, 1791.

My dear Girl,

By Capt. Bernard who sails on Sunday I shall send you a very elegant muff which I could not resist buying for you. Mr. Craigie has also bo't one for his Sister and another for Betsey Foster. Mrs. Foster's is a sable yours a white delicate kind of hair and Betsy Fosters a stained hair, all elegant. So that about Wednesday or Thursday, you must send to Mr. Blagge to know if the Vessell has arriv'd. God bless my dear Angel and her Babe. The Stage waits for me.

yr affectionate Husband

H. G. OTIS

Mr. Craigie has bo't a silver rattle for your Daughter which he purchased at 5 Dollars.

Philada. Decr. 18, 1791

My dear Girl,

Owing to the extreme badness of the roads I did not arrive untill this day about noon, and found all well and happy to see me. It being sunday I cannot judge of the probability of finishing my business soon, but unless I find this can be accomplished, I shall return immediately, and in no event do I intend to remain here more than four days. As I have now got to dress, and afterwards to see two or three Members of Congress I shall disappoint you of a long Letter, but I think it more likely I may have leisure to talk with them this day, than any other time on the subject of my excursion. My journey hither was not very pleasant, My Companions were a crazy man, a blind man and a lame man, with several others too *tedious* to be enumerated. I came however on business. My pleasures are at home, and all the gaiety and brilliance of great Cities are lost in the comparison with my domestic comforts. I din'd with Babcock the day I spent in N York & received numerous invitations for a week which I neither could nor wished to accept. I mean to call on Sophia this Evening and tomorrow I go to the Vice Presidents, and next Day to the *great man's* himself. Of all my visits given and receivd I will yield a faithful account and shall soon hold you to the heart of your affectionate

H. G. Otis

Phila. Thursday Evg. Decr 22d 1791

My dear Girl,

You can hardly conceive my mortification in not receiving from you a line since I left Boston. Why did not you write me by the next post? What more agreeable friend or engagement occupied your time! But I will not chide, especially at this distance, Tomorrow I hope will bring me news. My time here has been principally occupied in business, and though I have re-received many civilities I have been in no parties of Ladies, yet have din'd constantly abroad. This Evening I was persuaded by my Father, Sophia &c to go to the Assembly, but one hour sufficed me & I ran home. My spirits were dejected and my thoughts continually dwelling on my dear friend, in whose absence, brilliance and gaiety lose their charms. There was an immense collection of Ladies and Gentlemen, their dresses for the most part splendid and tawdry, and the greater part of the She's immers'd in the full persuasion of their respective fancied charms. But I shall reserve particulars for our approaching interview. . . . Tell your Papa I have not the most distant prospect of bringing his business to a close, as Griffin is determined to delay and finally cheat him if possible.

Harrison of late visits at Mr. Francis's, so I suppose things will soon come about.[1] I have left some Gentlemen below stairs, and can only say I grudge each moment that detains me from your arms. God bless you. Yrs, H. G. Otis

The following summer he made another business trip to New York and wrote home a revealing letter about his feelings for fame, and for Sally.

[1] They did. George Harrison and Sophia Francis, a girlhood friend of Sally's, were shortly afterward married. They became the Otises' lifelong friends.

New York July 5, 1792.

My dear Sally,

I arriv'd safe and sound on tuesday night and have taken my abode with Mrs. Loring. Circumstances render my going to Philadelphia very precarious, but I rather think I shall *not* go. . . . Yesterday was by no means celebrated with the pomp and splendor worthy this great City. A noisy peal of most infamous bells, and the firing a few cannon, alone distinguished it from other days. This City is as usual full of Strangers and full of bustle. I sleep in Mrs. Lorings parlour, with two other Gentlemen. The room is large, and an immense screen stretch'd across forms a partition, behind which are our three beds. So that you see I have no chance of introducing any *pretty lasses,* without observation whatever may be my wish.

Last Evg I called at Platts, to see my old friend & acquaintance Sally Aspinwall; I was admitted, although he is a Bank——t, and shut up. Your friend Peggy Aspinwall was there, & made many kind enquiries after your welfare. What a subject for philosophy and moral reflection does this family afford among others. Raised in appearance to the zenith of affluence, her house a palace, her Equipage an elegant Coach and four, in the heyday of youth & spirits, poor Sally is in a moment roused from the gilded dream, and presented with splendid ruin. Her husband cannot pay six pence in the £. Such also is the situation of Mr. Comb and many others. Are we not then happier my dearest friend in mediocrity? Is not our situation safer, and more agreeable than to be placed on these giddy heights? Why then am I so anxious for riches & honors? Why do mankind eternally sigh to explore the latent charms of affluence, regardless of the dangers and the stings? Indeed, I already tremble in my own situation. Rich in the best of women, in a dear offspring, possessed of competency, with flattering and expanding prospects of success in business, what have I to gain? How much to lose? I am happy, already, and we will so conduct our little bark as to secure if possible the continuance of our Enjoyments. And now, what would I not give to run into my Entry and call my Sally to her breakfast table, to spread her biscuit, to solicit her appetite, and sooth her gentle languid feelings by imprinting fifty kisses on her dear cheek; to romp with my little Pet, and teaze her into a repetition of her three or four monosyllables! But a little patience, and I will repeat these dear delights; I can never prize them enough, and never more highly than I now do.

Remember me to Saml., to all your Papa's family, kiss my Baby, and keep up good spirits. I cannot yet talk of returning but do not expect to transgress the time fixed at my departure. I do not wish that Sam or my father should have the key of my little Desk unless all the papers are taken out. What shall I buy for you?

Yr affect. H G OTIS

The "little Pet" was year-old Elizabeth Gray; "Saml." was his brother, back from Haiti and glad to be alive. Two days later Harry gave his views on married love:

New York July 7, 1792

"Absence is a cure for Love," is a proverb which my dear Sally has heard and to which she alludes, but like all maxims it admits of exceptions. It is happily a cure for those transient attachments, of which in the ardency of youth the sexes are susceptible, and which they cannot gratify, but it is no remedy for the loss of the pleasures and sympathies of the full & consummated raptures of *wedded* love. Nature in this as in other cases is kind & provident. It would be unfortunate if unsuccessful Lovers could not forget each other, it would be not less unfortunate if man & wife could easily forget. . . .

How happy then to make use of a solecism ought we to be, in the reflection that we are unhappy apart! How thankful should we be that we are so necessary to each other, that time has only encreased our mutual affection; that we never felt the *resentment of a moment,* & never the *coldness of an hour!* Are there *many* who can say so much, are there *any* who can say more!

Be under no apprehensions on the score of my health. If possible I am more firm than ever. Three hearty meals a day, and an *Ice Cream* (dont long, you little Hussey)[1] at eleven o'clock, hardly excuse me.

---

[1] The letters of Abigail Adams indicate that ice cream was a rare treat in Boston.

But be careful of yourself, and dont expose your health, let me know if your cough & appetite are better or worse. Get a little Iron Coat of mail made for Dove, so that I may not kill her with the first squeeze. Take care of my *boys!*[1]

God bless you my dear Sally. Yr affect. H. G. Otis

Harry's next recorded journeys were on the business of one or more of the many speculative western land schemes which flourished in the last decade of the century. A letter of late 1792 relates the details of a Boston-New York journey that was worse than usual:

N. York, Sunday Novr 11, 1792

My dear Girl,

After a very tedious passage and journey I arrivd here this morning. My journey has been the most unpleasant I ever experienced. We got into New Haven on thursday Evg and went immediately into a Pacquet, about sunset, but the wind blew a hurrican, so that we lay tossing out in the harbour all night; About Day break it moderated and we saild with a fine wind & in less than six hours we ran half the distance to this place, when it suddenly became calm, and after continuing so untill dark, the wind came round in our teeth and blew so violently that we tho't proper to make a harbour in Long Island where we anchord all night. On Saturday morning the weather was still unpromising and the wind continued ahead, so that finding no chance of beating up, we went ashore in quest of land carriage, and after walking three miles we hired *two waggons,* and in these we went jaunting, bag and baggage, forty miles by land and rode till 12 at night. You will have an idea of our carriage by supposing a large open sleigh fixed on four wheels instead of runners, and drawn by two horses. Our trunks served for seats and away we drove five in a waggon like pigs to market. However in spite of our misfortunes we were all except one or two in good spirits, and I in excellent health. We were not however in any danger, as the whole coast and Island are lined with excellent Harbours. I find the winds so precarious at this season that I am resolved not to attempt the water again but shall jog

[1] Sally was expecting twins, but only Harry Jr. was born a month later.

by Land. I hope to be with you next Saturday Sen'night. I should have felt more happy to have left you and our dear Infant in better health and spirits, but I flatter myself you are well 'ere this. Give the precious Babes a thousand for their Father and don't suffer Elisa to forget my name. Distance as usual is irksome to me, and nothing deserves the name of Enjoyment in your absence. I shall hasten with my wonted affection to partake with you the amusements of the Season, and the delights of our dear Domestic Scenes. . . . God bless and preserve my dear Angel and her Baby. Yrs, H. G. Otis

I find I have got the key of my office, it must be broken open & a new lock put on.

Fairfield [Conn.] Monday July 1 [1793]

Here I have this moment arrived, & have not before had an opportunity of writing a line to my dearest friend. My ride has been extremely agreeable. This morning We dismissed our Coach, and two of us have taken the stage & shall reach New York tomorrow night. If [a]ny pleasures could reconcile me to absence from you, the beauty of the Country the pictoresque landscape, waving fields and loaded orchards would be likely to produce that Effect, but without my Sally to partake, Nature in her loveliest Garb loses half her charms. . . .

Take care of your health, & keep up your spirits. Consider that my exertions are for you & yours, and that we have reason to be thankful, that such occasion[s] offer to promote the advantage of our family. Kiss my little angel for her father, & present me kindly to your Fathers family & to Saml.

God bless & preserve my dear Girl, for the arms of her H G O

Letters of the 1795 journey start from Connecticut:

Hartford Tuesday Evg Augt 3ᵈ

My dear Sally,

In Spite of the heavy and excessive rains and Still more heavy roads which I have constantly encountered since my departure I am just safely moor'd in Bull's tavern; my thoughts & ideas which (thank) God have no dependence upon rains or roads fly back to my dear mansion and the objects which it contains. . . . We found our vehicle almost too much for the poor horses. My journey tho' not diversified by incident, nor enlivened by the Society of anny intimate associate has been however quite tolerable. It is yet impossible to form an opinion of the probable event of our Enterprise. Competitors arrive from all quarters every moment, & it is an equal chance that we return without doing any thing of consequence.

Will you believe that the theatrical rage has reached this once puritanical City, and I have actually taken a ticket for *Venice preservd* by Hodgkinson's Company, *to which will be* added *a Cure for the Spleen;* a medicine which never comes amiss to me when absent from all I love.

The violent rains here have done great damages, the Cornfields are in many places Swept down & the grain which is in the ears, and not dried will be destroyed. What a variable Climate! & what needy mortals! Should the Season continue wet, I shall fear the prevalence of autumnal disorders, but the fine air of W. Boston is a great Security, & good spirits which will enable you to attend to your little flock is a still greater Security. I hope and desire you will take, & give them frequent airings without regarding the expence of coach hire, & omit no possible enjoyment or amusement that does not expose you to the Evg air, during the few days of my absence.

Remember me to our fathers & mothers & all friends, & remember me yourself as you are always remembered by your invariably affectionate H G Otis

Suffield (16 miles from Hartford)
Sunday August 9 1795

I did not expect to address my dearest friend again until I received her to my bosom and impressed upon her lips the ardent pledge of the affection which increasingly animates my exertions, and supports my spirits, but altho I am now 16 miles nearer to my happy home than when I last wrote to you; I must return again to Hartford, where however I hope to remain but a few hours & set my face homeward on tuesday morning. My business has been prolonged beyond my expectation, and whatever may be the event, I am so far *committed* that I cannot look back.

After witnessing a scene of intrigue, negotiation, management,
& Connecticut cunning such as I never anticipated, I have nearly
accomplished my objects, and presume that its completion will
not be delayd beyond the morrow. Perhaps I shall be disappointed, and "the heavy hours may not be almost past." To
judge from the violent competition of persons engaged in the
same pursuit with myself & from their number and respectability, one would think that success must be followed by fortune.
Agents from the most opulent associations in various parts of
the Continent are anxiously embarked in the same enterprize,
and consider the road to the Wilderness of Lake Erie, as the
highway to Riches. You know I am not so sanguine; but it is
my duty to improve every *probable* occasion of encreasing the
means of happiness for the dear dear objects that depend upon
my industry. I am now at the house of Mr. Phelps who has invited Blake and myself to pass Sunday with him. Tomorrow we
return to Hartford and the next day I expect to depart homeward and to be with you on thursday. But should I not return
untill Saturday be not disappointed. I hope my dear Girl you
are tranquil and not perplexed or afflicted by any domestic concerns. Should our little Cherub continue to droop (which God
forbid) arm yourself with resolution by reflecting upon your
duty to the rest of the flock, and by considering that your health
may depend upon your serenity & composure but *she will not*
droop; and *you will not* lose your health. I am surrounded by
company and cannot enlarge. I write this upon the corner of
a table occupied by several persons engaged in this same employment, and I am my dear Sally, your tender & affect. H. G. OTIS

When a political career opened in 1796, Otis had already risen
to a leading position in the bar of Suffolk County which, though
small in numbers, was rich in talent. Theophilus Parsons, Christopher Gore, Jonathan Mason, James and William Sullivan, Samuel Dexter, Benjamin Austin, Jr., William Prescott, Josiah Quincy
and John Lowell were among Otis's brother lawyers and competitors. Parsons, Dexter and Otis were the acknowledged leaders in
the period between 1795 and 1815. Each excelled in some one
quality: Parsons in learning and intellect, Dexter in reasoning

power, and Otis in eloquence, tact and personality. It would be difficult to say whether his power of graceful oratory or his capacity for pleasing almost everyone was his greater asset as a lawyer. The rich and varied vocabulary at his command was the despair of his rivals. When Chief Justice Lemuel Shaw heard that Noah Webster was about to issue a dictionary containing three thousand new words, he exclaimed, "For Heaven's sake, don't let Otis get hold of it!"

Since all leaders of the Boston bar except the elder Sullivan and Austin, and all judges of the superior court without exception, were Federalists and close personal friends, there was an informality about court procedure that later became impossible. Otis was allowed free rein for his oratory until Theophilus Parsons was elevated to the supreme bench in 1806. The new chief justice wished to shorten the length of trials, which had become a crying abuse. Many were the flowers of eloquence about to blossom from Otis or Lowell or Prescott that his ruthless authority nipped in the bud. A story is told of one case in which Judge Parsons broke in on Otis's argument with, "Brother Otis, don't waste your time on that point, there is nothing in it." Otis stopped, bowed to the bench in a somewhat surprised manner, and went on to another point. After a moment: "Nor in this either, Brother Otis; don't waste your time." Otis bowed once more and took up a third point, only again to be interrupted. "I regret to find myself, your Honor, unable to please the Court this morning," he remarked with some asperity. "Brother Otis," replied the judge, with his most winning smile, "you *always* please the Court when you are *right*."

THE COPLEY PURCHASE

Before the age of thirty, Otis not only had achieved an enviable reputation as a lawyer, but also had laid the foundation of a fortune by investments in Boston real estate. His largest and most profitable venture was the purchase of the Copley pasture in 1795. Early in that year he was appointed one of a committee to procure a site for a new State House in Boston. The committee found by far the best situation to be the so-called governor's pasture near the middle summit of Beacon Hill. This land they purchased for the Commonwealth from Governor Hancock's heirs, and there the new (and still existing) State House was built from designs by Charles Bulfinch. Otis foresaw that this would give Beacon Hill prestige and make its sunny southwestern slope, facing the Common and the Back Bay, an ideal residential district. The entire area at that time was upland pasture, broken only by three wooden houses, and owned by John Singleton Copley, the celebrated painter, who had resided in England for twenty years. Wishing to sell, he placed this property in the hands of an agent who, on being approached by a syndicate formed by Otis and Jonathan Mason called the Mount Vernon Proprietors, signed on 22 February 1796 a bond for the sale of eighteen and a half acres of Beacon Hill for $14,000.

Copley, having paid around $3000 for this property, stood to make a profit of several hundred percent. Nevertheless he felt that he had been swindled; and he had complicated matters by independently deeding the tract to William Hull, the general later famous for the surrender of Detroit. Copley disavowed his agent's act, refused to execute the deed, and sent his son (afterward Lord Lyndhurst) to Boston in order to break the bond. But the future Lord Chancellor of England found that young Mr. Otis had taken care of all the technicalities. The contract was binding; but the Proprietors, fearing that English courts would decide against them, bought off Hull for $9777.77. And Copley also kept Hull's down payment of $1000.

The matter did not end there. Since no deeds to Copley could be found, one claimant after another came forward during the next forty years to contest the title of the Mount Vernon Proprietors; several had to be bought off, and Copley received from the Proprietors about a thousand guineas for furnishing evidence in regard to his title.

Grand Centennial March.

As performed by the

BOSTON BANDS.

Composed & respectfully dedicated to the

HON. HARRISON GRAY OTIS,

Mayor of Boston

BY

CH: ZEUNER.

BOSTON

Published by C. Bradlee 164 Washington Street.

1830.

Jonathan Mason, by Gilbert Stuart.

It was some time before the Mount Vernon Proprietors paid dividends, but eventually the old pasture proved a gold mine for its purchasers. It covered the territory starting at the Back Bay, running up Beacon Street to Walnut, and, from the other end of Walnut, along a diagonal line to the farther end of Louisbourg Square and down Pinckney Street to the Charles River. Originally more than eighteen acres, this tract was extended by the purchase of three adjoining pastures and by filling in the mudflats at the foot of Beacon Hill. Before Otis died, the entire territory exclusive of the flats was covered with first-class houses by such architects as Bulfinch, Asher Benjamin and Parris; the Copley pasture, as he foresaw, had become the most desirable residential district of Boston. Despite a few ups and downs, owing to the Back Bay being filled in and built up, this south slope of Beacon Hill has retained its character to the present day. As Otis shrewdly predicted, the hill was too steep to be given over to business as later happened to the older residential districts in the South End; and owing to the distinguished architecture of the buildings, it has been designated a historic district.

Otis also invested in Boston wharf property but never, to my knowledge, sank any money in ships or mercantile transactions, the most reputable Boston investments of his era. Probably his father's and Uncle Joseph's losses as merchant-shipowners dictated this prudence; but Harry disliked the sea and avoided it as much as possible after his already described attempt to sail from New Haven to New York. The longest "voyages" he ever took were on ferryboats crossing rivers en route to Washington, and on the Boston-Nahant boat. Even after the Cunard Line had made ocean crossings shorter and less uncomfortable than those of the sailing packets, Otis refused to visit England.

For several years the Harry Otises hired houses in Boston. They joined Dr. Peter Thacher's Brattle Street Church, another liberal Congregational society which would soon be Unitarian. And in 1795 Harry employed Charles Bulfinch, the local architectural

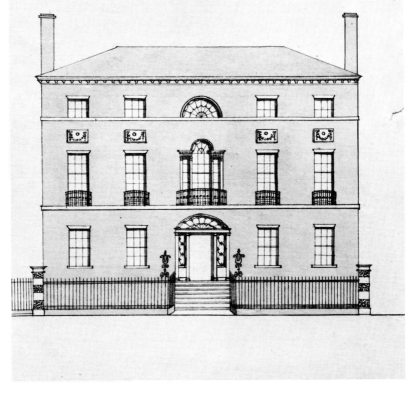

"The Brick House," 141 Cambridge Street. Designed by Bulfinch.

"The Brick House" and
West Church in 1966.

The drawing room
in 1925.

genius, to design for him a three-story brick mansion on Cambridge Street, across Lynde Street from the West Church. The land, with several more acres, Harry bought from his father-in-law for £450 in 1793. "The Brick House," as Otis called it, was an ambitious project for a man of thirty; Senator Bingham of Pennsylvania had used a very similar design for his Philadelphia mansion which became the center of social life in the Washington and Adams administrations.

Harry, Sally and their four little children — Elizabeth, Harry Jr., Sally Jr., and Allyne — moved into the new house in the spring of 1797. By the fall of that year Harry was doing so well as to contemplate buying a country estate on Fresh Pond, Cambridge; but he concluded (in a letter to Sally), "It will be time enough to procure a box in the country for a summer residence when my lands in town are sold and I am sure of being able to give up business; till then the fewer objects, the better."

Shortly after settling in the new house, Harry made himself a reputation as a member of Congress.

CHAPTER V

Hamiltonian Federalist

1794–1796, AET. 29–31

HARRY EMBRACES FEDERALISM

IT WAS inevitable that Harrison Gray Otis should enter politics. By heredity, education and character he was especially fitted for a political career. In New England during the eighteenth century, as in Old England, social position helped one in politics — it was almost a prerequisite. His forebears had been in public life since 1688, and few families in the United States had played a more important part in the Revolution than the Otises. Harry, moreover, not only inherited the name, but the ancestral traits that win success in politics. He possessed the gift of eloquence, and the essential tact and popularity. He liked people; not merely those of his class but all people — even some Democrats! In his day, as now, a public career was unremunerative to honest men; hence it was necessary for Harry to provide for the support of his family before he could enter politics. With the accomplishment of that task, in 1796, came the opportunity.

Tories having been eliminated from the American scene by the Revolution, the victorious Whigs split into Federalists and Anti-Federalists on the question of adopting the Constitution of 1787. The Anti-Federalists, somewhat halfheartedly reconciled to the new government, remained watchfully suspicious lest it justify their worst fears. Opposition to the triumphant Federalist party, developing as Alexander Hamilton unfolded his financial system, found a leader in Thomas Jefferson, farmer, scientist, diplomat and philosopher fresh from revolutionary Paris. The date of his return — March 1790 — marks the birth of the two national parties that occupied the stage for the next quarter of a century: the Federal or Federalist party under the lead of Hamilton; and the Republican or Democratic party[1] under the guidance of Jefferson. He appealed to the southern planters who looked with suspicion on financial schemes they did not understand, and saw in the Hamiltonian system only an attempt to corrupt the government and pave the way for monarchy. Hamilton rallied the merchant-shipowners, who required sound finance and a sane but vigorous foreign policy. The principles of Federalism appealed also to men who felt that consolidation and strength were necessary to preserve the Union. Conversely, the underdogs in the northeastern states, who envied the rich, went for Jefferson; and western Virginians, underdogs to tidewater and piedmont planters, went Federalist.

Despite these generalizations, an individual's political choice depended more on local friendships, personal contacts and basic ideas than on class or section. The frontier or sectional test does not work in Massachusetts, where the two frontier counties of Berkshire and Washington went and stayed Federalist; whilst the rich farming county of Middlesex, extending from Cambridge to the Merrimac River, could always be counted on to vote Republican. Class certainly was no determinant; the Republican leaders in Massachusetts, as throughout the country, were as well born as the Federalists. The only politically active members of the ancient Winthrop family, James, the Harvard librarian who fined young Harry 8*d.*, and Thomas Lindall Winthrop of Boston, were Jeffersonians. Of two leading shipowning families of Salem, the

---

1 According to the custom of the time, I have used Federal and Federalist interchangeably, and Republican and Democratic interchangeably for the party of Jefferson. He preferred "Republican," as it implied that the Federalists were monarchists; "Democratic," at first a term of opprobrium, was accepted by the Jeffersonians as early as 1795 (*Independent Chronicle* 14 May 1795). Since I first wrote the above, much ink, paper and print have been wasted to prove that the two-party system began at a later date than 1790. The answer really depends on how you define "party."

Derbys were Federalist and the Crowninshields, Republican. Even families split: Fisher Ames, the Edmund Burke of the Federal party, had a physician brother living across Dedham village square who was a "howling Jacobin" in the phrase of that day, and who cheered events which Fisher deplored and moaned when Fisher rejoiced — which he did not often do. Harry Otis's father-in-law, William Foster, and both brothers-in-law were Republican. The proud colonial family of Amory, one member of which used to say, "If there were a nobility in this country the Amorys would be dukes," split between Federalists and Republicans. Governor James Bowdoin, a Federalist of Federalists, had a son who contested Harry Otis's seat; Governor James Sullivan, Republican, inveighed against his son William's party associates as monarchists and secessionists. Edmund Burke had written on the colonial lawyers, "They augur misgovernment at a distance, and snuff the approach of tyranny in every tainted breeze." The habit lasted, and not only among lawyers; innkeepers like William Manning continued to smell tyranny in tainted breezes from Boston or Philadelphia as well as from London. (Curiously enough, the odors from the political sewers of Paris seemed sweet in comparison.) Thus Harry's aunt and uncle, the James Warrens, morbidly suspicious of tyranny, saw evidence of a monarchical plot in Washington's dignified aloofness and John Adams's love for titles and trappings. But their brother Dr. John Warren and his son Dr. John Collins Warren were staunch Federalists.

One difference between Massachusetts and Virginia was this: the great majority of F.F.V.'s followed Jefferson; whilst in the Bay State, gentlemen Democrats were in short supply and village demagogues, ambitious for office which they could never get under Federalist rule, thrust themselves forward. For instance, there were George Partridge of Duxbury who got into the Otises' hair, and Barnabas Bidwell, a Berkshire congressman whose subservience to Jefferson caused John Randolph of Roanoke to call him the President's "clerk of the watercloset." Most fellows of that kidney, however, had to await the advent of Andrew Jackson to make politics pay.

Joseph Varnum of Dracut, a self-educated farmer and veteran of the War of Independence, was the only successful Massachusetts politician of the Jacksonian type during Otis's heyday. He represented the Middlesex district in Congress from 1795 to 1811 when, by virtue of the famous gerrymander, he became United States senator. Varnum controlled the federal patronage in Massachusetts when Jefferson and Madison were presidents, and had his own district well "sewed up," carrying the Republican word to "every Middlesex village and farm" before each election day. Despite his long service in House and Senate, Varnum never made his mark on the national scene; he silently and faithfully followed the party line, as did the few other local Democrats who got to Congress. On the whole they were a pretty sad lot.

For a Massachusetts gentleman — which few of these men were — it became politically profitable to support the Republicans; or, if originally a Federalist, to defect. John Quincy Adams, in so doing in 1807, stepped aboard a Republican escalator which led, through several diplomatic appointments and the secretaryship of state, to the presidency. William ("Billy") Gray, a wealthy shipowner of Salem, supported the embargo and became lieutenant governor; Elbridge Gerry became governor of Massachusetts and vice president of the United States. James Bowdoin, Jr., defeated by Otis for Congress in 1796, received the Madrid legation; and James Jarvis, son of Dr. Jarvis whom Otis (as we shall see) defeated in the town meeting on Jay's Treaty, received the Lisbon Consulate, both by favor of President Jefferson. Dr. William Eustis became Madison's war secretary and minister to the Netherlands. Two Salem Crowninshields in succession were offered the secretaryship of the navy, and one accepted. In comparison with these gentlemen, Harrison Gray Otis and others who remained true to the Federalist faith never got very far politically.

Otis never had any doubt about becoming a Federalist, or any thought of abandoning the party. His merchant-shipowner clients wanted sound federal finance, and after experiencing Shays's Rebellion, he learned the value of good order. By birth he belonged to a class most of which went Tory; but families like the Otises who joined the Patriot cause abandoned none of their conservative principles. They had fought for independence from Great Britain, not for independence from government and social restraint. They expected the wheels of democratic evolution to stand still in 1783. Otis wrote in a Boston newspaper fifty years later, "Those mistake altogether the nature of the political controversy between the American Colonies and the British Ministry, who suggest that our fathers were actuated by a *radical* spirit. They acted on the defensive, and contended only for *constitutional* rights and privileges." And a few years later, to his old friend George Harrison, "You and I did not imagine when the first war with Britain was over that revolution was just begun, & that the spokes in the wheel had only moved a little from the former position. Are not the changes in manners, principles, & *the spirit of the government,* greater since the peace than those which happened between 1775 & 1783 — I think so."

In the early 1790's Fisher Ames, Theodore Sedgwick, Jonathan Mason and Samuel Dexter were the most popular leaders of Massachusetts Federalism. But from the first there stood out from the party ranks a dominant group, not interested in office but in sound political principles. This was the Essex Junto, composed chiefly of hardheaded merchant-shipowners and lawyers of Essex County who had moved to Boston. Stephen Higginson, George Cabot, Timothy Pickering, Theophilus Parsons and Jonathan Jackson were the Junto's earliest members; and Higginson's grandson thought it significant that they had originally been sea captains or admiralty lawyers and proposed to run the ship of state like a ship at sea; for them, Thomas Jefferson was a mutinous first mate who deserved to be hanged at the yardarm. Both John Lowells, the judge with whom Otis read law and his son "Jack" the "Boston

Rebel," were from Essex County and naturally belonged to the Junto. Fisher Ames and Chief Justice Parsons were their oracles. This ultra-conservative and ultra-sectional wing of the party refused to compromise with Democrats or democracy, failed to recognize that the South and West had legitimate sectional interests; in short they were as blind as the theoretical democrats and "Old Romans" to the fact that the world had moved forward since 1775. They undertook, as Elbridge Gerry once remarked, "to establish a nobility of opinion," of right thinking, and this they did so effectively that Boston became known to Federalists everywhere as the Headquarters of Good Principles.[1] They believed thoroughly in government by the wise, good and virtuous (like themselves!), for but not by the people. Ames, quoting numerous examples in antiquity, warned that democracy would lead to mob rule, anarchy and then despotism. Parsons, more knowledgeable of the peculiar conditions in America, predicted that democratic institutions, offering great elective prizes to unscrupulous adventurers and demagogues, would drive men of character and ability out of politics, that "mediocrity would gain possession of nearly all power, by the free use of all the means of management," and professional politicians would seek to augment their income "by any means within their reach." The end, for our Republic, will be "an oligarchy as absolute as was that of the old republic of Venice," resting on intrigue and composed of men "with little pretence to any higher talent, than that of craft, and still lower in moral character." This oligarchy finally becomes so disgusting that the people rally around some "strong man" who will tear up what is left of the "fabric of constitutional liberty."

A popular young man such as Otis the Junto instinctively dis-

---

[1] Of course the same thing has been done many, many times by political leaders and groups in the United States, Canada and Great Britain. If you do not conform, people turn their backs on you at parties or in the street, and blackball you for clubs. The Essex Junto worked largely through personal contacts; they appeared almost daily on 'Change or in the insurance offices on State Street; and for those who asked, "What does this news mean?" they always had an answer.

trusted; they feared he would turn out to be another John Hancock, with less cunning perhaps but more brains, and so more dangerous. Harry, in return, happily characterized the Essex group in a letter to Josiah Quincy: "There is not one of these sworn brothers who is, or ever was, a politician, or who ever had what old John Adams calls the tact of the feelings and passions of mankind; but they are men of probity, of talent, of influence, and the Federal party may say of them, *Non possum vivere sine te nec cum te!"*

Provincialism marked this Junto; not even Pickering, after many years in the cabinet and in Congress, made friends outside New England; and although some had sailed the seas in their youth and Jack Lowell made the grand tour of Europe, they proved to be perfect examples of Horace's apothegm *caelum non animum mutant qui trans mare currunt.* They changed their sky, not their dispositions, by travel, returning to Boston as bigoted as when they departed. Another characteristic of the Junto was inflexibility — they believed with Fisher Ames that the question was not *whether* they should fall, but *how* — "that we may fall, like Antaeus, the stronger for our fall." Otis, in contrast, was a compromiser; like Franklin before him and Clay and Lincoln after, he regarded politics as the art of the possible, not the ideal best.

In justice to the Essex Junto one must admit that every member we have mentioned, save the dour Pickering, was a charming and cultivated gentleman who indulged a taste for improved husbandry and horticulture; that all were religious liberals; and that every one founded a family whose members have been conspicuous in the financial, professional, artistic and scientific life of Massachusetts to this day. No difference may be discerned between them and moderate Federalists like Otis in taste or manner of living, and at times their political ideas coincided as well. But Otis, Mason, Dexter, Quincy, Strong, Sullivan, Perkins and others whom we shall frequently meet as Federalist leaders, were never let into the inner councils of the Junto, and most of them were suspected by the Junto as being unreliable compromisers and popularity seekers.

The French Revolution

The two groups, Federalist and Republican, crystallized as parties on the question of the nation's attitude toward the struggle between Revolutionary France and the rest of Europe. Otis well expressed the evolution of American opinion on the French Revolution in his *Eulogy on Alexander Hamilton* (1804):

The principles professed by the first leaders of that revolution were so congenial to those of the American people; their pretences of aiming merely at the reformation of abuses were so plausible; the spectacle of a great people struggling to recover their "long-lost liberties" was so imposing and august; while that of a combination of tyrants to conquer and subjugate, was so revolting; the services received from one of the belligerent powers, and the injuries inflicted by the other, were so recent in our minds, that the sensibility of the nation was excited to the most exquisite pitch. To this disposition, so favorable to the wishes of France, every appeal was made, which intrigue, corruption, flattery and threats could dictate. At this dangerous and dazzling crisis, there were but few men entirely exempt from the general delirium. Among that few was HAMILTON. His penetrating eye discerned, and his prophetic voice foretold, the tendency and consequence of the first revolutionary movements. He was assured that every people which should espouse the cause of France would pass under her yoke, and that the people of France, like every nation which surrenders its reason to the mercy of demagogues, would be driven by the storms of anarchy upon the shores of despotism. All this he knew was conformable to the invariable law of nature and experience of mankind. From the reach of this desolation he was anxious to save his country, and in the pursuit of his purpose, he breasted the assaults of calumny and prejudice. "The torrent roared, and he did buffet it." Appreciating the advantages of a neutral position, he cooperated with WASHINGTON, ADAMS, and the other patriots of that day, in the means best adapted to maintain it. . . .

We beheld the republics of Europe march in procession to the funeral of their own liberties, by the lurid light of the revolutionary torch.

The Federalists, following Hamilton's lead, became as strong partisans of Great Britain as the Republicans were of France. With Lafayette in exile and Louis XVI executed, and a Reign of Terror, when property and religion were no longer respected, conservatives felt that the very bases of society were threatened from a center of infection in Paris. They agreed with Edmund Burke that the French Revolution had become "irrational, unprincipled, proscribing, confiscatory, plundering, ferocious, bloody and tyrannical." Otis well expressed the Federalist view in a speech of 1797. In Europe, he said, "a revolution of manners of the most formidable nature threatens the subversion of all moral principles, of all social order, and a system of profligacy has swept off every vestige of whatever was most amiable and respectable in the eye of humanity." And conservatives were seriously alarmed by the attitude of Republican orators and the press, which followed the fluctuating party line of Republican France as faithfully as, of late, the *Daily Worker* followed the party line of Moscow. Thus it was not strange that conservatives feared lest the "Jacobin conspiracy" overwhelm and set up guillotines in the United States. After James Swan, a Boston speculator in Paris, had sent to Otis a letter from an American consul giving the French republican point of view, he replied that it was mere "sansculottic impudence." "These fellows," he continued, "have a chime of words, such as despotism, tyranny, liberty & the like which issue from their lips mechanically. They are *hand organs* on which are played certain tunes to please the mob." Substitute the now familiar chime of "colonialism, imperialism, fascism, gangsterism and revanchism," and one perceives a certain affinity between Otis's time and ours.

In like manner foreign events and foreign issues continued to dominate American politics until the Peace of Ghent brought an end to this political and intellectual thralldom.

Otis took part in several contests with the local democracy. Boston, a mob town in the 1760's and 70's, went Federalist after the war. In 1788 it elected to the First Congress Fisher Ames, one

of Hamilton's closest friends and allies. The local democracy, however, made up in noise and activity what it lacked in strength. And
its leaders, as we have seen, were every bit as respectable as those
of the Federalists.

Harry helped to prevent the town from falling into the "wrong"
hands on a memorable occasion in 1794. The Federal party that
year suffered great embarrassment from the British, who continued
to occupy western posts in American territory, and whose privateers
and prize courts were sweeping American commerce from the seas.
James Madison, now Republican leader in Congress, introduced
resolutions on 3 January 1794 providing for retaliation on British
commerce. That did not suit the seaboard merchants. The bulk
of their trade being with Great Britain, they preferred to enjoy it
on her terms rather than risk the whole by retaliation — an attitude that they steadily maintained for the next twenty years. Madison's resolutions caused intense excitement in Boston. Jarvis and
Austin, reviving a custom of Revolutionary days, called a town
meeting "to take the sense of the inhabitants." They hoped, by
playing on the old hatred of England, to overrule mercantile interests and procure resolutions ordering congressmen to support
Madison; and they very nearly succeeded. The town meeting,
begun at ten in the morning of 24 February, adjourned (owing to
the crowd) from Faneuil Hall to the Old South at three, lasted
there until after dark and adjourned until the next day. Only at
one in the afternoon of the 25th did the Federalists succeed in
wearing out their opponents, and in having the whole matter indefinitely postponed. After the end of this long oratorical contest
the *Columbian Centinel* remarked, "We cannot omit mentioning
in a particular manner Mr. Otis, who took a conspicuous part in
the course of the debate, in opposition to the Report. His fellow
citizens did justice to his abilities, and eloquence." And Christopher Gore wrote, "Otis also took a decided part and greatly aided
the cause of good government & order."

In recognition of his part in this victory for good sense, Otis in

1794 and 1795 received a place on the Federalist ticket for the "Boston Seat"; i.e., the town's quota of representatives in the general court. On both occasions the ticket was defeated, owing mainly to the influence of foreign affairs. Between the town meeting in February and the state elections in May, news arrived of a fresh British decree against neutral commerce, and of Lord Dorchester's inflammatory speech to the Indians of the Northwest. The Federalists, for refusing to recommend retaliation earlier in the year, were temporarily discredited.

JAY'S TREATY AND ELECTION TO CONGRESS

In the meantime, President Washington had averted war by sending John Jay to London. All hung fire until the result of his negotiation should be heard. Otis described the situation in a letter of 15 November 1794 to his Uncle Harrison Gray, Jr., in London:

> We have just passed through the turbulent period of the election of members for Congress. Strenuous exertions have been made by the anti-federal faction throughout the Union, but generally without success. Mr. Ames is reelected here, and the Friends to peace and good order are greatly encouraged by the appearance of our public affairs. Much however you are sensible depends on Great Britain. The moderate and respectable part of the Community wait with patience and anxiety the result of Mr. Jay's mission; but should justice be denied to our claims, I think a very general sentiment of indignation & spirit of resentment will prevail here among all classes of people & produce a rupture between the countries.

In July 1795 the text of Jay's treaty was made public and, as Henry Adams said, "threw a sword into the body politic." Howls of rage greeted the news throughout the country, and effigies of John Jay went up in smoke all the way from Maine to Georgia. The treaty seemed humiliating, and all parties at first united in condemning it. At a crowded town meeting in Faneuil Hall on 10 July not a single vote was registered in its favor. George Cabot was willing to swallow the treaty whole, but he had to attend Harvard Commencement to find sympathizers. Gradually, however, the conservative elements came to see that Jay's treaty was better than none, and that the only honorable alternative was war. When Washington finally signed the agreement, without one very objectionable article, the Federal party to a man approved.

But the last chance to defeat the Jay Treaty had not expired. The House of Representatives, through its power to defeat the necessary appropriations to carry it into effect, held a veto over the treaty; and under the lead of Edward Livingston and Albert Gallatin a determined effort was made by the Republicans to kill it. The Boston Federalists called a town meeting for 25 April 1796 to meet this crisis. Dr. Jarvis opened the debate. At this meeting, wrote James S. Loring, historian of Boston oratory, "The rolling thunder of Jarvis was again heard; but a new and bright planet blazed through the darkness, and dispelled the clouds — Harrison Gray Otis." At the conclusion of his speech Bishop Cheverus "threw his arms around Otis, and while tears were streaming down his cheeks, exclaimed, 'Future generations, young man, will rise up and call thee blessed!'"

Unfortunately for the dramatic side of history, this touching scene cannot be true. The Abbé Cheverus — three years younger than Otis — had not yet arrived in Boston and did not become a bishop until 1810. And the only contemporary report of this town meeting is in the *Independent Chronicle* which, as a leading opposition journal, took a dim view of the "new and bright planet." Otis, it says, "concluded the debate by a very pathetic eulogy on the President, and a very illiberal reflection on Mr. Gallatin, who Mr. Otis said was the *leader* of the majority in Congress. Shall we (said Mr. O.) join a vagrant foreigner in opposition to a Washington; a foreigner who to his knowledge ten years ago came to this Country without a *second shirt to his back?* A man who in comparison to Washington is like a Satyre to a Hyperian?"

This version is undoubtedly correct, for Otis's "second shirt speech" became notorious and although he apologized to Gallatin when they met in Congress, he had it thrown at him again and again. His former French tutor at Harvard belonged to the Geneva aristocracy, proud as that of Boston and far more ancient; and the time came when the Otis family were delighted to have a grand-daughter of the "second shirt" orator marry a grandson of the allegedly shirtless Genevan.

Returning to the town meeting, a vote of confidence in Washington's administration, proposed immediately after Otis's speech, carried by an overwhelming majority; a personal triumph for Otis indeed. He had met democracy in its citadel and conquered by logic and eloquence. Immediate recognition came from the party. On 26 May 1796 the President commissioned him United States District Attorney for Massachusetts. Having higher objects in view, Otis only consented to act temporarily under the commission until a successor could be procured. At the same time he became a director of the Boston branch of the United States Bank, and to that office he clung.

In the spring elections of 1796 to the general court, the Federalists regained their hold on Boston. Otis and the entire Federalist ticket were elected to the lower house by a strong majority.

In the autumn came Otis's great opportunity. Fisher Ames, having represented the Suffolk-Norfolk district in the first four Congresses, decided to withdraw from politics, and regarded Otis as his most promising successor. Jonathan Mason, a power in the state party who had been impressed with Otis's character and ability as his close partner in the development of Beacon Hill, worked hard to get him the nomination. The *Columbian Centinel* announced on 2 November: "The Federalists are determined to be united on . . . Harrison G. Otis for a Representative." As a striking evidence of the changed balance between country and city between 1796 and 1968, Boston belonged to one congressional district with fourteen country towns, some as far away as Medway and Weston.

Candidates were not expected to make speeches in those days;

newspapers and pamphlets performed all the electioneering. On behalf of James Bowdoin, Jr., the Republican candidate, the *Independent Chronicle* attacked Otis for his second shirt speech, and accused him of being "a mere *Automaton* of funds, banks, and land-jobbing speculators." But on 7 November 1796, when Massachusetts as a whole voted for John Adams for President, Harrison Gray Otis was elected to Congress by a substantial majority, carrying Boston and seven of the country towns.[1]

---

[1] His district comprised *Boston, Roxbury, Dorchester, Dedham, *Weston, *Brookline, *Newton, *Needham, *Natick, *Sherborn, Hopkinton, Holliston, Sharon, *East Sudbury, Medway. Those marked * gave Otis a majority.

CHAPTER VI

First Term in Congress

1797–1798, AET. 31–33

MAIDEN SPEECH

OTIS'S CONGRESSIONAL career, from 1797 to 1801, covered a period when foreign relations were paramount. What would the United States do about France? Nineteen twentieths of the congressional business during this period concerned the French Republic, directly or indirectly.

From the ratification of Jay's treaty with Great Britain, relations between the United States and France went from bad to worse. That agreement was a blow to French influence in the United States, since it settled controversies between the United States and Great Britain which the French Republic had counted upon to produce hostilities. So France attempted to coerce the United States through commerce-destroying. Beginning in July 1796, the Directory (as the French government was styled) promulgated a series of decrees against neutral commerce. Under their authority French privateers began to capture, and French prize courts to condemn, every American vessel bound to or from ports in the British Empire. By the month of June 1797, over three hundred captures had been made. French picaroons impudently pushed their operations into American territorial waters. One from Guadeloupe fired on an American ship departing from Philadelphia harbor. Another corsair pillaged and then burned a British ship in the inner harbor of Charleston. Numerous American prizes were made by these corsairs on the coasts of the United States, in their waters, in their bays, in their rivers — as Victor DuPont, a French consul, admitted.

President Washington, when he obtained news of these aggressions, recalled the minister to France, James Monroe, who had proved himself incapable of caring for American interests, and appointed in his place Charles Cotesworth Pinckney, a South Carolina Federalist. The French Directory took leave of Monroe with threats and insults toward his country, refused to receive his successor until the "grievances" of France were redressed, and on 3 February 1797 threatened Pinckney with arrest if he remained in Paris.

As a result of this attitude and of the commerce-destroying, President Adams summoned the Fifth Congress to a special session in the spring of 1797. Otis was present at the first quorum, on 15 May.

Congress Hall, the brick building north of Independence Hall, Philadelphia, was the scene of Otis's political activities during the next three years. That portion occupied by the House of Representatives is unpleasantly described by a contemporary as "a room without ventilators, more than sufficiently heated by fire, to which is superadded the oppressive atmosphere contaminated by the breathing and perspiration of a crowded audience." The House at full strength numbered 106 members. Among those prominent in his own party, Otis found Jonathan Dayton of New Jersey, the speaker; James A. Bayard of Delaware, and Roger Griswold of Connecticut. South Carolina sent a small but notable Federalist delegation — William Smith, Robert Goodloe Harper and John Rutledge. Harper had become the ablest debater and pamphleteer on the Federalist side of the House, and Rutledge turned Federalist after the insulting rejection of his fellow citizen Pinckney by the French Directory. Both men were of Otis's age and tastes; they became his lifelong friends and, like him, never deserted the Federal party. Prominent among the "Jacobins"[1] in the Fifth Congress

---

[1] A term applied to the Republican party by the Federalists as early as 1793, on account of their opponents' attachment to the cause of the French Revolution. It remained in current use until 1815. Jefferson, in retaliation, coined several nicknames for the Federalists, such as "Anglomen" and "Monocrats," which never became popular.

MILLIONS FOR OUR DEFENCE NOT A CENT FOR TRIBUTE.

NEW HAMPSHIRE	VERMONT	MASSACHUSETTS	CONNECTICUT	RHODE ISLAND
2 Senators 4 Representatives 183.858 Inhabitants	2 Senators 2 Representatives 106.943 Inhabitants	2 Senators 15 Representatives 422.845 Inhabitants	2 Senators 7 Representatives 251.002 Inhabitants	2 Senators 2 Representatives 69.122 Inhabitants

NEW YORK
2 Senators 11 Representatives 581.170 Inhabitants

NEW JERSEY
2 Senators 5 Representatives 11.114 Inhabitants

DELAWARE
2 Senators 1 Representative 64.273 Inhabitants

JOHN ADAMS President of the United States

PENSYLVANIA
2 Senators 14 Representatives 602.365 Inhabitants

MARYLAND
2 Senators 9 Representatives 300.035 Inhabitants

VIRGINIA
2 Senators 23 Representatives 878.959 Inhabitants

NORTH CAROLINA	SOUTH CAROLINA	GEORGIA	TENNESSEE	KENTUCKY
2 Senators 11 Representatives 78.003 Inhabitants	2 Senators 9 Representatives 34.591 Inhabitants	2 Senators 3 Representatives 162.686 Inhabitants	2 Senators 1 Representative 976.80 Inhabitants	2 Senators 4 Representatives 219.943 Inhabitants

A New DISPLAY of the UNITED STATES

New Haven. Printed & Sold Wholesale by Amos Doolittle. August 15. 1799

were John Nicholas and William B. Giles of Virginia; Nathaniel
Macon of North Carolina, serving the fourth of his fifteen terms
in Congress; Edward Livingston, future lawgiver of Louisiana,
representing his family interests in New York; and the ablest man
in the House, Otis's former tutor of the alleged single shirt, Albert
Gallatin.

Harry served in Congress during one of the most intense periods
of party feeling that the country has ever passed through. The
principles of the two parties were opposite and irreconcilable; the
one believed in a government by the "wise and good and rich," as
Fisher Ames put it; the other in a popular government led (of
course) by themselves. The one feared French influence and
democracy; the other, British influence and monarchy. A rigid
social cleavage deepened the rift. Although the Republican leaders, by and large, were as well born as the Federalists, members of
the two parties studiously avoided each other on the street and in
society; there were Republican taverns and Federalist taverns, Republican salons and Federalist salons. Party warfare raged in the
partisan press with a violence and bitterness of language which
became the norm until after the War of 1812.

The first business before the House was to draft an answer to
the President's speech. At that time the President delivered his
opening message in person, and each house went in a body to his
residence to present its reply. This practice was happily done away
with by President Jefferson, for the framing of a suitable reply
in times of high party feeling took weeks; in this instance, until
3 June. When the committee on the answer presented the House
with a draft that responded to the President's sentiments, John
Nicholas of Virginia proposed an amendment to the effect that
"We flatter ourselves that the Government of France," by dismis-
sal of Pinckney, "only intended to suspend the ordinary diplomatic
intercourse" in favor of "extraordinary agencies," and that a disposition to remove the inequalities of treaties would produce the
desired accommodation. In other words, that Jay's treaty be
scrapped.

Words like these made the Federalists' blood boil and precipi-
tated a vigorous debate. Otis, as a new member, was not expected
to sound off. "His talents will distinguish him," wrote his predecessor Fisher Ames, "and I hope he will be careful to wait patiently
in Congress until they do, but he is ardent and ambitious." Stephen Higginson of the Essex Junto wrote to their member in
Adams's cabinet, Timothy Pickering:

> Mr. Otis who succeeds Ames will not be his equal in any view,
> and it may be very uncertain in some cases how he will act. he
> is a seeker of office, his ambition has no bounds and whoever can
> offer him the best station for honor and profit will have him. at
> present he thinks, I believe, that his best chance is from the
> Government, and whilst he conceives his interest connected with
> and dependent upon Them, he will be on your side, saving such
> variations as he may think essential to his standing so fair with
> opposition, as to keep a way open to join them whenever he shall
> think it for his interest.

This was completely unjust to Otis, who never wavered in his
essential Federalism or had the slightest idea of going over to the
opposition. But Ames was right in calling him "ardent and ambitious." Burning with anti-Jacobin fire, Harry refused to keep
silent, and on 23 May 1797, a week after the session began, delivered his maiden speech on the Nicholas Resolution:[1]

> The injuries sustained by us are of a high and atrocious na-
> ture . . . If any man doubts of the pernicious effects of the mea-
> sures of the French nation, . . . let him inquire of the ruined
> and unfortunate merchant, of the farmer whose produce is fall-
> ing, and will be exposed to perish in his barns. Where are your
> sailors? Listen to the passing gale of the ocean, and you will hear
> their groans issuing from French prison-ships!
> There was a time when I was animated with enthusiasm in
> favor of the French Revolution, and I cherished it, while civil
> liberty appeared to be the object; but I now consider that Revo-
> lution as completely achieved, and the war is continued — not

---

[1] In quoting speeches made in Congress, I have transposed them, for the sake of
clearness, to the first person and the present tense.

for liberty, but for conquest and aggrandisement, to which I do not believe it is the interest of this country to contribute.

Otis stigmatized the Nicholas Resolution as "an absurd and humiliating apology." He then argued for national defense: "If negotiation fail, will the French give us time to equip our vessels, fortify our ports, and burnish our arms, in order to show us fair play?" And he concluded with a grand burst of rhetoric:

> The tide of conquest has deluged Europe; it may swell the great Atlantic and roll towards our shores, bringing upon its troubled surface the spirit of revolution, which may spread like a pestilence, possibly in the Southern States, and excite a war of the most dreadful kind — of slaves against their masters, and thereby endanger the existence of that Union so dear to my constituents, and the separation of which would be as painful as the agonies of death.

This speech gave Otis a national reputation for oratory. Judge Iredell wrote to Oliver Wolcott, "Mr. Otis' speech has excited nearly as warm emotions as Mr. Ames' celebrated one, on the treaty. It does indeed the highest honor to his patriotism abilities and eloquence, and I confess, much as I expected from him, far exceeds my expectations." Abigail Adams, too, warmly approved.

Otis's maiden speech was not simply a display of rhetoric; it was his confession of faith as a Federalist and an indication of his party's considered opinion of French policy.

FEARS OF FRANCE

By the time the Fifth Congress assembled, the Federalist leaders had a fairly correct idea of the different lines of French policy; their only mistake was in overestimating the final goal toward which it tended. Current events of Europe seemed full of ominous lessons for the United States. The French Directory, after suppressing the Jacobins at home, cynically used Jacobinism as an "article of export" to subvert neighboring countries. Almost every

European mail brought news of some fresh aggression on a neighboring country. One after another, the ancient governments of the old world fell victim to a "fifth column" of local Jacobins, supported by an invading French army. By the spring of 1797 France had annexed Belgium and secured control of Holland and Genoa. The news of Napoleon's partition of Venice, arriving during the first session of the Fifth Congress, and the sad tale of Switzerland's subjection, reaching America in the summer of 1798, demonstrated the fate of republics that could not or would not defend themselves against French force and intrigue. The spoliations of American commerce, the machinations of French ministers with the Democrats, and the presence of French spies, all pointed to similar intentions on the part of France toward the United States; and by the middle of 1798 most Federalists, from Washington down, believed that the French Directory intended to invade the United States via Hispaniola, raise a slave insurrection in the South, and seek to set up a vassal republic west of the Alleghenies or south of the Potomac.

Highly influential in spreading this creed was a powerful pamphlet by Otis's fellow congressman Robert Goodloe Harper: *Observations on the Dispute between the United States and France* (1797). It ran through at least seven American and fourteen British editions, as well as one in French and one in Portuguese. Otis, too, helped to spread the word through his first political pamphlet, a published letter to General William Heath of Roxbury, dated 30 March 1798. General Heath, a Revolutionary War Veteran, had acted as chairman of a Roxbury town meeting which drew up a petition against permitting merchant vessels to arm in their defense, a measure that was then under discussion in the House. Otis predicted that the French Republic would proceed

> to last extremities against this country, whenever she shall be at leisure for this purpose, and shall be confirmed in the belief that our internal divisions, and blind infatuation in her favor, will enable her, if not to conquer, at least to divide the Union. . . . War is not the most effectual instrument, nor the first which

France employs in the manufacture of the rights of man: Spies, emissaries, exclusive patriots, and the honest but deluded mass of the people, are the tools with which, in other countries, she carves revolutions out of the rough material. The Generals and soldiers are reserved to give the finishing stroke. . . . Can you, Sir, seriously doubt of their hopes and expectations that Georgia, the Carolinas and Virginia will pass under their yoke? That they have an eye upon a *Cis Apalachian* as well as upon a *Trans Apalachian* Republic?

What reason can be assigned to make it probable that we may rely upon an exemption from this general deluge? . . . Already their Geographers, with the scale and dividers, mark out, on the Map of America, her future circles, departments and municipalities. Already their Buonapartes and Bernadottes, are planning future triumphs; *here* with the army of the Mississippi and Ohio; *there* with the army of the Chesapeake and Delaware. — Remember, Sir, things much less probable have come to pass.

Extravagant as it may seem at this distance, Otis's prophecy of a French invasion was then within the bounds of possibility. France, by the Treaty of Campo Formio of October 1797, was at peace with all the world but England. Her boundaries had been extended to the Rhine, the Alps, and the Pyrenees, and several satellite republics beyond acknowledged her control. By March an *Armée d'Angleterre* was being mobilized at Boulogne; it made two unsuccessful landings, one in Ireland and another, led by an American renegade named William Tate, in South Wales. A regiment of Quislings was ready to welcome French invaders of England. Should England fall, whose turn would come next? That Otis's apprehensions on this subject were genuine and not merely published for political effect is shown by a letter to his wife of 14 March 1798:

The state of the country is alarming and if the Southern States do not change their representation, or that Representation change their measures, that part of the country will be lost, and the Eastern States will be compelled to take care of themselves. My principal hope is that the affairs of Europe cannot long remain in their present posture; but who can calculate the event. Should Great Britain be compelled to yield, it is my opinion that our liberties and independence would fall a sacrifice. She is the only barrier to the dreadful deluge, and when that is broken down, it will be time for us to prepare to be good and dutiful subjects to the French.

Whilst the French Directory never had any plan to invade the United States, they did flood Quebec with secret agents to stir up the Canadians to revolt. A half-breed Creek leader in French pay, named Milfort, tried to detach Florida from Spain; and the Spanish monarchy, beaten to its knees in 1795, was being pressured to return Louisiana to France. It seemed ominous that the opposition Republican press followed every twist in the French party line, openly condoning the spoliations on American commerce as a proper *riposte* to Jay's treaty, and denying the territorial ambitions of their favorite country. Naturally the Federalists suspected the existence of a good understanding between the French and the American Jacobins. Otis remarked in debate on 2 March 1798:

> If my private sentiments are required, I am ready to profess my sincere persuasion that our difficulties with France are not to be imputed to any one man, but to a desperate and misguided party, existing in the bosom of our own country, who are in league with other bad citizens resident in France, and with the French nation; and I have no doubt that regular information and instructions are conveyed from this country to influence the measures of the Directory, and impede our attempts to negotiate with success.

Jefferson excepted, a number of Democratic leaders were not unwilling to attain power through the good offices of France. French ministers in Philadelphia maintained a lobby in Congress, receiving inside information from Republican congressmen, and ordering the defeat of legislation unfriendly to French interests. Minister Adet took an active part in the election of 1796 in behalf of Jefferson. During the previous summer he made a tour of New England, in the course of which he "raised the courage" of the local Democrats and assured them that "France would never abandon them," while they in turn urged France to continue her policy of commerce-destroying in order to frighten the merchants.

As Otis probably knew, the mighty personages in his party had already decided on a program for the special session, in the execution of which he was expected to aid. Alexander Hamilton, who usually settled these matters in New York through correspondence with President Adams's cabinet, decided against any effort to rush the country into war. He recommended and the President decided to make a second attempt to settle the dispute by sending three envoys extraordinary to Paris, and that Congress in the meantime should put the country into a state of defense. If the Directory were willing to negotiate decently, peace would be preserved and the Federalist party would receive the credit; if the new mission were treated as Pinckney had been, the country would be prepared for war, and the French party would be discredited. Adams acted accordingly, and sent John Marshall, the young Virginia Federalist, and his friend, the politically neutral Elbridge Gerry, to act with C. C. Pinckney as a mission of three.

Congress was expected to act with a vigor noticeably lacking in its predecessor. The President sounded the keynote in his opening message, recommending increase of army and navy, reorganization of state militia, and permission for merchant vessels to arm in their defense. But it was found impossible, without further French provocation, to carry out the President's recommendations. In the Senate a sufficient majority existed; but in the House, party Federalists and party Republicans were almost equal in numbers. The balance of power rested with a group of moderate Federalists led by Speaker Dayton, who were unwilling to take even simple measures for defense.

That this situation occurred was no fault of Otis. Tireless in debate, he proved to be a tower of strength to his party. He made it his particular duty to answer Gallatin's able speeches — "to ferret him in his retreats, and to strip his designs of the metaphysical garb which conceals their turpitude," as the *Columbian Centinel* put it. He stood out with his young Carolina friends Harper and Rutledge in favor of war preparations, most of which were defeated by the combined votes of Jeffersonians and Federalist moderates. So the net result of the session was a loan of $800,000, a slight increase in taxes, and an act for the completion of three frigates, *Constitution, President* and *United States,* whose keels had been laid down in 1794.

"Wild Irish" Speech and a Fight in Congress

One thing that troubled the Federalists was the fact that their opponents were absorbing the foreign vote. From 1792 on, a stream of Irish, British and German malcontents began to flow into the United States. These people naturally joined the party that stood for Gallomania and democracy. By 1798 the alliance between native democracy and the Irish vote, which has endured to this day, was already cemented. The apprehension of his party is reflected in a remark of Otis in a letter to his wife: "If some means are not adopted to prevent the indiscriminate admission of wild Irishmen & others to the right of suffrage, there will soon be an end to liberty & property." Otis decided to do something about it. On 1 July 1797 he proposed a tax of twenty dollars on certificates of naturalization. The opposition immediately charged that the object of this resolve was not to raise revenue but to restrict immigration. Otis acknowledged the charge and defended the purpose. After an attack on the French Revolution he remarked:

> The Amendment will not affect those men who already have lands in this country, nor the deserving part of those who may seek an asylum in it. Persons of that description can easily pay the tax; but it will tend to foreclose the mass of vicious and dis-

organizing characters who can not live peaceably at home, and who, after unfurling the standard of rebellion in their own countries, may come hither to revolutionize ours. I feel every disposition to respect those honest and industrious people. . . . who have become citizens . . . but I do not wish to invite hordes of wild Irishmen, nor the turbulent and disorderly of all parts of the world, to come here with a view to disturb our tranquillity, after having succeeded in the overthrow of their own Governments.

The twenty-dollar proposition failed to pass, but Otis's "Wild Irish" Speech as it was called, caused him considerable embarrassment; for "wild Irish" was an offensive English cliché, like the southern "damn Yankee." Although it is commonly supposed that the Boston Irish all came over with the Kennedys around 1848, that is not so. The Charitable Irish Society of Boston was founded in 1737; and a noticeable Irish immigration took place before the Revolution. During 1796–1798, the period of "the troubles," a lot more came in; and the fact that most of them were Protestants did not make them less Irish, prone to resent the epithet "wild." The Philadelphia *Daily Advertiser,* edited by an Irishman, attacked Otis in a long screed which included the irrelevant argument that Ireland was a "nursery of arts and sciences" when England and Europe were "steeped in savagery," and that the War of Independence was won by the Irish. This was gleefully reprinted in the Boston *Independent Chronicle* of 27 July 1797, together with the following "Irish Epistle to H. G. Otis" by "A Tame Wild Irishman":

> I was born, Sir, a true *Paddy Whack*
> Tho' I live on American land.
> I came here with *"two shirts to my back"*
> And I paid for them down, cash in hand.
>
> I was lucky so soon to get here
> Before you *"plac'd bars in the way,"*
> By my shoul, "twenty dollars" is dear
> For the "wild Irish horde" all to pay. . . .

For tho' you "don't want population"
By Jasus your credit is poor,
'Twas the *Irish* and *African* nation
That made your *Election* so sure.

Young man, we would have you remember
While we in this country can tarry,
The *"Wild Irish"* will choose a new member
And will ne'er vote again for *young Harry.*

All Frenchmen are bone of our bone,
We embrace them as being good brothers.
We wish *slavish chains,* Sir, on *none*
But such as would make *slaves* of others.

Otis of course claimed that he had been quoted out of context; he loved Ireland and was only trying to keep out "vicious and disorganizing characters who could not live peaceably at home." The Federalist press defended Otis on the ground that he did not mean all Irish but only "the restless malcontents, the *wild* beasts of all nations, natives of America as well as Europe — scribblers of *Chronicles* and of O'Carey's *Gazette."* This only made matters worse. "Paddy Whack replied in the *Independent Chronicle:*

But faith, lawyer Otis, we like not your jests,
For instead of "wild Irish" you make us "WILD BEASTS."
This character surely don't suit *Paddy Whacks*
For *Tigers* and *Wolves* have no "shirts to their backs."

After several more insulting exchanges, the controversy concluded with a letter from "Citizen" John D. Burk: "Mr. Otis, if you can succeed in overthrowing the wild English government in Ireland, I will engage that sufficient charms will be found in Ireland to keep its wild men at home." A good prophecy, fulfilled after a century and a half.

The same state of affairs, largely marking time awaiting news from Paris, continued through the winter months of the second session of the Fifth Congress. The President's opening address of 23 November 1797 renewed his recommendations of the previous session. Harry Otis was appointed chairman of the committee on the House reply, and wrote to Sally on the 27th that he had studiously avoided all hard expression, and endeavored to make it as palatable as possible." And he obviously succeeded, since his draft of the Answer was "adopted unanimously with only the change of a *single* word, so that we were in luck at least, to save a fortnight's squabbling." He doubtless saved time, but time was what the Fifth Congress could best afford to squander. Everything hung fire awaiting news from the envoys in Paris.

Amid the excitement over foreign affairs, one act of humanity passed unnoticed. This was a law abolishing imprisonment for debt to the Federal Government. Otis was chairman of the committee that reported the bill, and acted as its sponsor before the House.

Exciting incidents relieved dull routine in the winter months. Matthew Lyon of Vermont, an ill-mannered printer of Irish birth, had managed to make himself the most obnoxious "Jacobin" in Congress. During the last war Lyon had been cashiered for cowardice, and punished by being compelled to wear a wooden sword. On 30 January 1798, before the session for the day commenced, Lyon in conversation boasted of the revolution he would create in Connecticut, could he but bring his printing press thither. Roger Griswold of that state inquired sarcastically whether he would also bring along his wooden sword? Lyon replied by spitting in Griswold's face. The Federalists demanded Lyon's expulsion from the House as the proper punishment for so flagrant a breach of decorum, but he was stoutly defended by his party on the pretext that the spitting took place before the House had been called to order. In the debate that followed, Otis made a speech in favor of expulsion, remarking that "he would challenge anyone to show so shameful an act of assault and battery committed without provocation at any former period or in any country . . . It would not be suffered in a brothel or in a den of robbers!" To his wife he wrote, "Was anything so infamous ever heard of before? Yet I expect the whole party will stand by to protect him, & in that event we cannot expel him; a concurrence of *two thirds* being necessary for this purpose." Such was the case; the vote 52 to 44, strictly on party lines, was insufficient for expulsion. According to Otis, the Republicans shielded Lyon "merely to avail themselves of his *vote* hereafter, while they acknowledge that he was deserving of expulsion. This among other traits serves to shew the character of the party and their disregard of all principle & decency."

Expulsion having failed, Griswold, at the next appearance of Lyon in the Representatives' chamber, attacked him with a stout club. Lyon grasped the congressional fire tongs to defend himself, and the two men rolled over and over upon the floor, striking at each other, until members pulled them apart by the legs. The House was then called to order; but as the combatants renewed their scuffling at intervals, it finally adjourned on Otis's motion.

The Lyon-Griswold fracas indicated the temper of this Congress. While awaiting news from France, members of the two parties gave vent to their feelings in long debates on minor topics, filled with recriminations and bitter personal attacks. William B. Giles of Virginia, on one occasion, accused the Federalists of a determination to make war on France at all costs. When Otis stigmatized these remarks as "bold, ungraceful, and disgraceful," Giles replied that "neither Mr. Otis, nor any other gentleman, durst make that assertion in any other place." A rumor, which gave much anxiety to Otis's family and friends, reported that a duel between Otis and Giles, resulting in the former's death, had followed this exchange of pleasantries; but, since the so-called code of honor was no part of Otis's New England upbringing, the affair went no further than words.

QUASI-WAR WITH FRANCE

On 19 March 1798, President Adams announced that, after an examination and mature consideration of the dispatches from his envoys in Paris, he could perceive no ground to expect the objects of the mission could be "accomplished on terms compatible with the safety, honor, or the essential interests of the nation." He therefore renewed a second time his recommendation to defend our coasts and commerce, and to act with "zeal, vigour, and concert, in defence of the national rights." He promised never to send another minister to France without assurance that he would be "received, respected and honored as the representative of a great, free, powerful and independent nation." This announcement failed to win over the Jeffersonians to national defense. They accused Adams of insincerity, deception, and a desire to drag the country into war with France and into alliance with Britain. John Dawson of Virginia ("Beau" Dawson of Otis's college days) issued a printed letter calling the President's Message "intemperate" and "unconstitutional." Jefferson wished his followers to bring about an adjournment of Congress, in order to gain time to allow the expected French invasion of England — an event which he ardently desired — "to have its effect here as well as there."

This attitude placed the Federalists in an awkward dilemma. Otis, having confidential knowledge of the dispatches, knew that their publication would silence the Republicans; but such a course might not only endanger the lives of our envoys in Paris but prove a bar to future diplomatic negotiations. The opposition demanded publication, foolishly confident that it would expose a Federalist bluff. For a time the Federalists resisted, but they found the temptation too strong. "We wish much for the papers," wrote Jonathan Mason from Boston. "The Jacobins want them. And in the name of God let them be gratified; it is not the first time they have wished for the means of their destruction." On 2 April, Harper introduced a resolution asking for the papers, and on the following day the President sent down to the House the famous "XYZ dispatches."

When a few days later the entire correspondence was published, the people were at last given a firsthand view of the methods of French diplomacy. None of the American grievances had been redressed. The French spoliations continued as before; and after a three months' residence in Paris, the three envoys were still refused an official reception by the Directory. Instead, they had been persistently informed by go-betweens (whose names, in the published dispatches, were discreetly represented by the letters X, Y, and Z) and by Talleyrand himself, that as an indispensable preliminary to negotiation the American envoys must make a loan of $250,000 to the French government, pay over a similar sum as a *douceur* for the Directors' pockets, and apologize. America was threatened with the fate of Venice, and the envoys assured that the Directory was possessed of the means, "through the French party in America," of throwing the blame of a rupture on the Federalists. No set of documents could have served better to open the eyes of the people to the methods and aims of French policy.

The XYZ dispatches, published through newspapers and pamphlets, produced a revolution in American public opinion. As the news spread, a spontaneous clamor of patriotism burst forth in every part of the country. "Millions for defense, but not one cent for tribute!" became the popular cry; "Hail, Columbia" and "Adams and Liberty" the national anthems. The Federal party to a man, and thousands among the former followers of Jefferson, hastened to sign memorials and addresses tendering the government their confidence. Volunteer companies were formed; flags embroidered and presented; Talleyrand hanged in effigy; war vessels purchased or built by popular subscription.

Although dismayed and disheartened, the Republican leaders stuck to their guns. With a consistency that would be admirable but for its lack of patriotism, they continued to preach submission to all-powerful France, our "magnanimous ally"; they even made desperate efforts to prove that Messrs. X, Y and Z were a set of unauthorized swindlers having no connection with the French government; they warned the people that Federalist policy spelled British alliance and monarchy. But Adams, Pinckney and Marshall were the heroes of the day.

By his conduct during this session, Otis won golden opinions. Upon hearing that he was thinking of retiring after one term, Fisher Ames wrote to him on 23 April 1798, flattering him on his letter to General Heath and warning him that he "cannot return to private life yet, without desertion." Jonathan Mason, too, insisted that he remain at his post.

The publication of the XYZ dispatches called for no change in Federalist policy; they simply demonstrated that such measures as Adams and Hamilton and Harper and Otis had been urging for the past year were necessary to defend the nation's commerce and to vindicate its honor. There was no need to declare war on France. The first impulse, indeed, of an ardent Federalist, on reading of the outrageous treatment of our envoys in Paris, and the insolent threats of the "fate of Venice," must have been warlike. We have the authority of Jefferson's *Anas* (his private diary of political gossip), quoting Otis as an indirect source of information, that the policy of declaring war was debated in a caucus of Federalist congressmen, and defeated by a majority of five.

Spurred on by addresses from their constituents, and by spirited messages from the President, Otis and Harper had little difficulty in pushing through Congress a plan of defense and reprisal. "The opposition in our house appears at present so disconcerted," wrote Otis, "that we proceed in business with less difficulty than formerly." With a normal Federalist majority of ten to fifteen votes, Otis and Harper were given full swing. But members from Virginia and Kentucky began to slip away from Philadelphia in order to kindle a backfire of state rights against Federalist nationalism.

An essential part of the Federalist defensive program was to create a navy. Otis, by his oratory and his vote, helped to pass measures authorizing the President to purchase six vessels of thirty-two guns, twelve "twenties," and six "eighteens." A navy department was organized, half a million dollars voted for fortifications, and over a million for arms, ammunition and matériel. The regular army was increased to an authorized total of thirteen thousand "for and during the continuance of the present difficulties with France." Most prominent in the military legislation was the Provisional Army Act of 28 May 1798, although it provided only a skeleton army. Otis helped to pass that bill, and all others of like nature.

In order to meet the necessary increase of expenditure, a direct tax was levied on houses and slaves. The rate of taxation on houses was made progressive — increasing from one fifth of one percent for a house valued at $400, to one percent for a house valued at $30,000. In the debate on this measure on 26 June, we have the interesting spectacle of two Democrats in the opposition, Samuel Smith and Edward Livingston, insisting that the progressive principle was too hard on the well-to-do, whilst Otis, himself a large real estate owner, defended it on the ground that houses are a better criterion of the wealth of their owners than any other form of property. In the end, the bill passed. Although planned to make the burden of taxation on those best able to bear it, this direct tax produced riots in Pennsylvania, and became played up as an engine of Federalist oppression.

The most important part of the Federalist program was retaliation in kind against French spoliations. All vessels flying the American flag, whether merchantmen, privateers, or men-of-war, were authorized to capture French armed vessels and to recapture their American prizes. Commercial intercourse with France was suspended, and the Treaty of 1778, which the French had long since ceased to observe, denounced. Otis defended these policies in debate, the opposition protesting at every step. By the end of the session, 16 July 1798, Congress had created a state of quasi-naval war differing only from an actual declared war in that Frenchmen were not proclaimed public enemies, and the capture of their unarmed vessels was not permitted. During the two and one half years that elapsed before the French Republic came to terms, the infant United States Navy rescued American commerce from the depredations of French privateers, fought several successful actions against French frigates and corvettes, and lost only one small armed schooner. Of this result of their favorite policy President Adams and Otis were justly proud. Their naval policy made the Stars and Stripes a terror to the Tricolor and trained the ships and sea fighters that humbled the Union Jack in 1812.

President Adams thought the army buildup unnecessary, and postponed active recruiting until the spring of 1799, when most of the anti-French fire had died down. By that time the British Navy, by bottling up Bonaparte's army in Egypt, had rendered France incapable of invading America. Consequently, only about 3000 men, whom Washington described as "the riff-raff of the country and the scape-gallows of the large cities," could be persuaded to enlist in the new army, and the provisional force existed only on paper. But one permanent benefit was derived from this army which never fought. The secretary of war promoted the formation of a school for gunners and sappers. West Point was selected as the location, and on his last day of office President Adams appointed the first faculty of the United States Military Academy.

ALIEN AND SEDITION ACTS

John Adams might have been reëlected in 1800 but for the Alien and Sedition Acts which pushed matters too far for the public taste; and Otis was as responsible as any member of Congress for this legislation. First came the Naturalization Act, extending from five to nineteen years the period of residence necessary for aliens to become naturalized. This would have been far more effective than the twenty-dollar tax, objective of Otis's earlier "wild Irish" speech, had it not been repealed in 1802; but it did not go far enough for his taste or Harper's. They wished to exclude the foreign-born from federal office, or even voting. Federalist efforts to do just that continued until 1815.

Whilst the obvious purpose of the Naturalization Act was to deprive the opposition of foreign votes, that of the two Alien Acts of 1798 stemmed from fear of French agents. Some of these actually were stirring up sedition along American frontiers, and on that basis the Federalist party wrought itself into a xenophobia that reminds one of the old Popish Plot in England and the Red scares of 1920 and 1950 in America. It was roundly asserted that the United States contained over 30,000 Frenchmen engaged in intrigues against the government, and ready in case of invasion to rise as one man and murder their hosts. Several would-be Joe McCarthys came forward with tales of horrid plots. President Adams, for instance, was informed anonymously that the Frenchmen in Philadelphia were planning on 9 May 1798 a day of national fast, to destroy Philadelphia by fire, and massacre the inhabitants. How far the paroxysm had affected Otis may be judged by a speech he delivered during the debate on 16 June 1798:

> In my humble opinion, there is greater danger from this source [Aliens] than from any other. I believe that it has been owing to this cause that all the Republics in Europe have been laid prostrate in the dust; it is this system which has enabled the French to overleap all natural and artificial obstructions; to subjugate Holland and Italy, to destroy the Helvetic Confederacy, and to force a passage through rocks and mountains, which have been for ages sacred to the defense of liberty; it is this system which has watered the tomb of William Tell with the blood of widows fighting over their slaughtered husbands, and with the tears of orphans who survive to swell the procession of the victors. . . . In the fate of the European Republics we might read our own. . . . They boasted of their patriotism and courage, they talked loudly of defense and of resisting the invader. . . . Yet when the hour of trial arrived, it appeared that secret corruptions and foreign influence had completed their work; upon the slightest shock, those Republics crumbled into fragments, and the good and the honest citizens were left to stare with stupid wonder, at the ease with which foreign agents and domestic traitors vaulted into place and power.

One remembers sadly the same methods being used in Czecho-
slovakia, Hungary and other countries in our own day, with
similar results.

Neither Otis nor any other prominent Federalist subscribed
to the theory with which the Rev. Jedidiah Morse startled his
Charlestown congregation at the time of the XYZ excitement.
According to him, the French Directory and the American "Jacobins" were agents or dupes of a secret society called the Illuminati, founded in Bavaria by Adam Weishaupt in 1776 and
dedicated to rooting out religion and overturning all existing
governments. Warnings of Illuminati influence are still with us
in 1968.

The Alien Act, passed for two years only, gave the President
power to expel suspected foreigners by executive order. He employed it only to get rid of two objectionable Irish journalists.
Nobody now denies that the safety of the Republic requires executive authority to expel aliens; but the Jeffersonians bawled over
the Alien Act as though it had killed liberty.

Otis also promoted the famous Sedition Act of 14 July 1798.
Few acts of Congress have proved so fatal to their authors as that
unhappy law. In advocating it, Otis made the worst mistake of
his political career, excepting to promote the Hartford Convention. Yet there was a need for this law. There being no common
law of the United States, the federal courts required statutory
authority before taking cognizance of conspiracies against the
government or libels on high officials. The Sedition Act made
proof of the truth of the libel a sufficient defense, and required a
jury trial, which no similar law did in any European country. But
the act was so foolishly enforced as to confound political opposition
with sedition. Under one section, making it a misdemeanor to
speak or write against President or Congress "with the intent to
defame" or bring them "into contempt or disrepute," about
twenty-five men were arrested and ten convicted in an effort to
silence Republican editors. David Brown, who persuaded the

"Jacobins" of Dedham, Massachusetts, to erect a liberty pole, French version of the American liberty tree, on the village green, got the longest sentence, four years in jail. All this seems mild in comparison with the killings and torturings that nowadays are inflicted by tyrants on their critics the world over; but it was too strong meat for American taste in 1800.

On 10 July occurred the principal debate: Otis and Harper against Gallatin and Nicholas. Otis delivered one of the best speeches he ever made in Congress, a defense of the jurisdiction of the Federal Government over seditious libel; a speech distinguished by careful preparation and documentation. Objections to the constitutionality of the bill, he said, might be reduced to two: (1) Did the Constitution give Congress jurisdiction over the offenses described in the bill? (2) Did the first amendment, forbidding Congress to abridge freedom of the press, take this power away? Otis decided the first point emphatically in the affirmative:

> With respect to the first question, it must be allowed that every independent government has a right to preserve and defend itself against injuries and outrages which endanger its existence; for, unless it has this power, it is unworthy of the name of a free government, and must either fall, or be subordinate to some other protection.

He pointed out that Congress had already undertaken to punish crimes against the United States not specified in the Constitution, such as perjury, bribery, and stealing public records. In answer to the second question, Otis insisted that the bill would not abridge the freedom of the press, but merely bridle its licentiousness. He referred to Blackstone's famous definition of freedom of the press — freedom from censorship previous to publication, not freedom from prosecution for libel. Quoting laws and judicial decisions in states which had freedom of the press clauses in their constitutions, he demonstrated that Blackstone's definition had always prevailed.

Otis's speech of 10 July formed the basis of every contemporary justification of the Sedition Act, and his arguments have stood the test of time, whilst those of the Virginia and Kentucky Resolutions, the most powerful on the other side, have not. Like other arguments of the state rights school, the "Resolutions of '98" deny to the Federal Government the necessary means of perpetuating its existence, when threatened by sedition or rebellion. In like manner, Otis's interpretation of the first amendment to the Constitution prevailed until after World War II.

In 1818, when Otis was in the United States Senate, the question came up of indemnifying Matthew Lyon, a victim of the Sedition Act. Otis, the only member in either house who had voted for that law in 1798, took up the gauntlet of Senator Barbour of Virginia in defense of his old principles:

> With respect to the constitutional question, I am content to declare that my mind has always reposed upon a single consideration, detached from all others, as sufficient to uphold the Act. All governments must possess an inherent right to punish all acts, which being morally wrong, tend directly to endanger their existence or safety. This power would be implied in the Constitution, even though no express words had conveyed the authority to make all laws "necessary and proper," to give effect to the instrument. Without such a right, no government is competent to the great duty of self protection.

A few days after this speech was delivered, Otis received from a former political rival a letter that must have given him as much satisfaction as any he ever received. Justice Story of the Supreme Court, the eminent commentator on the Constitution, wrote:

> Salem Decr 27, 1818
>
> Dear Sir
>
> I have the pleasure to acknowledge the receipt of your package covering the Washington City Gazette. I have read your speech with great interest; & equally admire its manner & matter. Such arguments composed in a tone of manliness, urbanity, & candour do honour to our Country. As a citizen of Masssachusetts I feel proud that the redeeming spirit of her elo-

quence is heard with so much effect in the Senate of the Nation. At the time when I first turned my thoughts to political subjects in the ardour of very early youth, I well remember that the sedition law was my great aversion. With the impetuosity & desire of independence so common to zealous young men, I believed it to be unconstitutional. I have now grown wiser in this, & I hope in many other respects; & for many years have entertained no more doubt of the constitutional power of Congress to enact that law, than any other in the Statute book. My present opinion has been forced upon me by reflection, by legal analogy, & by calm deliberation. You may smile at my confession, which I hope you will not call, as Mr Randolph on another occasion did, "a precious confession."

The truth is & it ought not to be disguised, that many opinions are taken up & supported at the moment, which at a distance of time, when the passions of the day have subsided, no longer meet our approbation. He who lives a long life & never changes his opinions may value himself upon his consistency; but rarely can be complimented for his wisdom. Experience cures us of many of our theories; & the results of measures often convince us against our will that we have seen them erroneously in the beginning. I hope I shall never have any pride but to do right, & fearlessly to acknowledge my errors when I perceive them.

With my best wishes for your personal happiness & a sincere interest in your public character I beg the honor of subscribing myself most respectfully

Your obedt friend & servt.

JOSEPH STORY.

Abominable though these acts seemed at the time, to very many Americans they seem insignificant after two world wars, a cold war and sundry legislative attempts to cope with communism. To call the Alien and Sedition Acts a "Reign of Terror," as the Republicans did at the time and as many historians have done since, is a gross perversion of the truth. Nobody was hanged, nobody went before a firing squad, nobody was tortured; the rule of law operated, public discussion remained free, and the writ of habeas corpus ran. A few persons obnoxious to the Federalists were imprisoned for short periods; that is all.

CHAPTER VII

The Republican Court

1797–1801, AET. 31–35

FEDERALIST SOCIETY IN PHILADELPHIA

HARRY OTIS had plenty of amusement during his congressional career. His social standing in Boston and his official position in Philadelphia, as well as his father's, and the Otises' long-standing friendship with the George Harrisons, gave them an entrée to the most aristocratic society America has ever seen, the nearest approach to a court that the Republic has ever tolerated.

Philadelphia, at the end of the eighteenth century, held undisputed leadership among American cities in population, commerce and literature. Her upper class contained two distinct elements: one of Quaker stock, kindly and intellectual but somewhat rigid in social matters; the other, liberal, cultivated and cosmopolitan, descendants for the most part of colonial officials and English merchants. The men were usually educated in the English universities or the Temple; the women, after being presented at the court of George III or of Louis XVI, brought over manners of the English aristocracy and fashions of Paris. Wealth these people possessed through foreign commerce and finance, and they well knew how to spend it. The selection of Philadelphia as the temporary capital of the nation, from 1790 to 1800, added strength and prestige to this society. Members of the Federal Government formed two large clubs of well-bred men from every part of the country, representing our national aristocracy of education and talents which, as John Adams said, will continue to exist "as long as some men are taller and others shorter, some wiser and others sillier, some more virtuous and others more vicious, some richer and others poorer."

The happy combination of a national government, a Federalist administration and a diplomatic corps, with the cultivated native society of Philadelphia, gave this temporary capital the character of a court. It was more cosmopolitan than the smaller courts of Europe, but none could have been more intolerant of political dissent. Republican gentlemen and their families, no matter how high their social qualifications, were ostracized by the best society. The person of most ancient lineage and highest rank in the capital was the Marqués del Casa Yrujo, minister plenipotentiary of the King of Spain. But as Spain had become a French satellite, Casa Yrujo, an attractive bachelor with courtly manners, had to take the French party line. Consequently, one of the few houses that received him was that of Governor Thomas McKean, a Jeffersonian leader who had two very attractive daughters. One of these Yrujo married; their son, later Duke of Sotomayor, was born in Philadelphia. So there were not one but two republican courts: the Federalist led by President Adams, and the Republican led by Governor McKean and Vice President Jefferson, a widower who disliked entertaining. Of this one the Otises knew nothing and cared less.

Harry and Sally Otis found the Federalist society very agreeable. They had already visited Philadelphia during Washington's administrations. Harry, ever witty and convivial, and his wife, whom the historian of this Republican Court describes as "remarkable for beauty and wit, as well as for an intellectual vivacity, tempered always by an indescribable grace," became general favorites. Through Sally's girlhood friend Sophia Francis, who married Otis's friend George Harrison, a protégé of Robert Morris, they became intimate with the Willing and Bingham connection, the ruling oligarchy in Philadelphia society; and Harry was doing business for Senator Bingham in Boston before his election to Congress. Thomas Willing, president of the United States Bank, became chief of a clan which embraced the Francises, Hares, Powels, Byrds, Harrisons and Binghams.

Sally Otis accompanied her husband to the first and third sessions of the Fifth Congress in May 1797 and October 1798; but with the cares of an ever-increasing family she had to remain in Boston during the greater part of her husband's congressional career. Harry felt severely this separation from his wife and children, and mainly for this reason refused to be a candidate for reëlection in 1800. But in Philadelphia he made the best of things among his friends, who seldom permitted him to be lonely; and to amuse his wife he wrote to her a *chronique scandaleuse* of Philadelphia society, from which we can glean many interesting details of daily life at the Republican Court.

Otis's letters to his wife begin at the opening of the dull winter session of 1797–98, when everything in politics hung fire, awaiting news from the mission to France. Vexed at his forced absence from home, Otis was at first inclined to be scornful of Philadelphia and its inhabitants. In this mood was the letter of 17 November 1797:

> Hitherto I have seen or heard of nothing approaching to gaiety or amusement. The theatre is not yet open. The assembly not begun, and the Ladies not yet ready to scald the beau monde with hot tea. I begin to doubt whether the winter is to be what they stile a gay one — and I really feel no disposition to take an active part in the bagatelle of the hour. In short, I am so tranquil in my little chamber, & so constantly in it, that if you could peep in & see me, with my feet nailed to the jamb, & my eyes fixed on my book, you might mistake me for one of Bowens wax figures — though taking my flannel night gown into view I think he has nothing *quite* so elegant.

And again on 20 November:

> Although I have yet heard but once from my dearest friend, I am in full expectation of a line by this morning's post. A complete week has now elapsed since my arrival here, and though

I have long since learnt to realize that my mind can never be tranquil in your absence, yet I hardly expected to be so disconsolate an old Bachelor as I have found myself. The Senators are so dilatory in arriving, that no business has been yet done; & the city so dull that I have seen or heard of no thing that wears the air of pleasure or amusement; so that I have ample time to devote to my books; & with the exception of a quarter of an hour each morning, I have kept my chamber from seven untill three o'clock, & have returned to it again always before nine. Whether it be that commercial derangements, or the effects of the yellow fever, (which may be deep though not visible) have spread a gloom over the city, or whether the very atmosphere is impregnated with Quakerism, & Tom Paine's word gives a drab colour'd cast to the houses and people, I will not pretend to determine, but certainly there is less appearance of the bustle of business, and of the splendour of fashion than I expected to see at this season. Nor can I but admire the readiness with which the people and especially our friend Sophia invent apologies for the procrastination of the public amusements and of the private parties; and if the winter should pass away without either, many fertile expedients will be found to evade the charge of inhospitality, & if every member of Congress should be obliged to mumble his dinner with none but his Landlady, during the session, you may assign whatever reason you please, but the want of a social temper & courteous manners in the inhabitants.

It is not however to be denied with truth, that Quaker and German habits and manners characterise the body of the Citizens. Those who constitute the fashionable world are at best a mere oligarchy, composed of a few natives and as many foreigners. Having none to rival or eclipse them; or contend with them for the right of entertaining strangers, they pursue their own course without interruption. They will tell you that they can give you nothing to eat or drink in summer; because they leave town & reside in the country, & in winter you must wait for their civilities untill the time arrives for commencing the *Parties,* which is sometimes a month or six weeks later than at others, as Mrs. A happens to have finished her new drawing room, or Mrs B. to have gotten up from her last *accouchment.* My experience is yet to inform me wherein consists the pleasure, elegance & taste of

these Parties. As the ladies on these occasions vie with each other
in dress, I presume the eye at least must be gratified, but I fancy
they are often very formal, unenlivened by general conversation
and that the food for the mind contains as little nourishment as
the cold tea which is applied to the dilution of the grosser part of
the system. But it is not just in me to complain. My casual intimacy with a few families places me on a footing of domestic
intercourse which is sufficiently agreeable, and having general invitations to two or three houses, I can partake of the pleasures of
society in a way most conformable to my taste. I do not wish to
enlarge my acquaintance, as I could not cultivate one more extensive with convenience to myself — and while I remain in public
life, my main attention, from duty and choice must be directed
to business. I have dined once with Cutting at Mrs. Grattan's,
once at Yznardis[1] in great stile; & yesterday in the country with
Jonathan Williams.[2] I am engaged for *next Christmas* with Mrs.
Powell, but with nobody for the Christmas *after* next. Rutledge
has brought his wife and three Children, they are at lodgings;
he has dined *once* with an old friend from *Carolina,* but has not
another invitation yet. Mrs. Grattan has a project of hiring the
Government House, for the purpose of a Subscription Assembly.
Mrs. Adams's first drawing room will be on friday; and afterwards once a fortnight. Mrs. Liston[3] is not yet in town; & Mrs.
La Frery sent her husband[4] to enquire about and after you, &
indeed one would think from the numerous enquiries that you
would be in great demand if here.

As the New Year approached these complaints of dullness cease
in Otis's letters; he was asked to more parties than he cared to
accept. "The Binghams and Willings are civil and attentive. I

1 Joseph M. Yznardi, a Spanish gentleman, son of the United States consul at
Cadiz, a resident of Havana, and frequent visitor to Philadelphia. Otis wrote,
5 December, "On friday, Yznardi gave a splendid dinner, at which I was a guest.
It is said he has a very lucrative contract, for supplying flour to Havannah, and he
certainly discovers every disposition to spend at least *a part* of the profits among
his friends."
2 Jonathan Williams, a nephew of Benjamin Franklin, distinguished in various
activities, diplomatic, military, judicial, political, literary and scientific.
3 Wife of the British minister.
4 The Chevalier Cipriano de Freire, the Portuguese minister.

dine with old Square Toes on tuesday — no common favor this"
he writes, the disrespectful epithet referring to old Thomas
Willing.

Another midseason letter has a rich story of Philadelphia's attitude toward the nude in art:

My dear Sally will conclude that I am beginning to get into
a habit of dissipation or some other bad way by my short letters.
It is true — I was last night at Henry Hills with a great concourse
of both sexes, who danced and appeared to be happy. I neither
danced nor supped, but retired at an early hour. Going to these
places I experience but little positive enjoyment, but think it
my duty to cultivate the acquaintance of fashionable and agreeable people who may contribute to your happiness this spring
and next winter. Harry who is a great amateur of the fine arts
& fine women, has a famous Statue of the Venus of Medicis, but
it being intimated to him that the attitude & native beauties
of the fair Goddess would beam too full upon the eye he had
her dressed in a green Silk *Lacedemonian* Dress — much like
Madame Tallien's — & which giving room to conclude that
more was concealed than was really true, only made matters
worse. This Evg there is a teaparty at Phillip's. Monday a dance
at Liston's, Wednesday a dinner at do., thursday a party at Mrs.
Mifflins to all of which I am invited. To some of which I may go.
But I can with good conscience sing, "there's little pleasure to
be had when my dear Girl's away." . . . The weather grows
pleasant, the roads good, and I am impatient to remove all obstacles to your coming to the arms of

Yr affect

H. G. OTIS

Winter seasons in Philadelphia were gay enough for anyone.
Besides subscription assemblies and private entertainments, each
foreign minister gave a dinner and a ball about once a fortnight,
and the President, Vice President, and married members of the
cabinet gave private and official dinners and receptions. Color and
life were everywhere. The "levelling process of France" had not

yet brought the dress of gentlemen to democratic black, and the fair women of the Republican Court dressed like the beautiful subjects of Gainsborough and Sir Joshua. The Duc de la Roche-foucauld Liancourt, who visited Philadelphia at this period, writes: *"Le luxe est, comme je l'ai dit, très-grand à Philadelphie, pour la table dans les jours de cérémonie, pour les voitures et pour la parure des dames. J'ai vu des bals, au jour de naissance du Président, où les ornamens de la salle, l'élégance et la variété des parures rappelaient l'Europe; et dans cette comparaison, il faut convenir que la beauté des dames Américaines aurait l'avantage."*

The President and his lady were the official heads of Philadelphia society. General and Mrs. Washington had been the actual heads, also, but President and Mrs. Adams, although experienced in the society of foreign courts, were not greatly liked in the temporary capital. Otis's stepmother, Mrs. Samuel A. Otis, a cousin and close personal friend of Mrs. Adams, saw to it that the President frequently asked the young congressman to dine. Harry writes to Sally about these visits: "I was last Evg. at the Drawing Room. It was the second evening, but only 16 Ladies were present, perhaps the dullness of the weather was the cause." And on another occasion: "In the morning . . . I went to visit the President. It was nominally grand Levee day, but *really* attended to by a very few persons except the official and diplomatic characters. The weather was bad. Among other Ladies was Madame de Freira who always talks a great deal about you, & who threatens very hard to notice you, when you come next winter."

Obviously the Adamses were being quietly snubbed by capital society. "The Philadelphians are a strange sort of people," wrote Abigail Adams to her sister. "Making pretentions to give Laws of politeness and propriety to the Union, they have the least feeling of real genuine politeness of any people with whom I am acquainted." The occasion for this outburst was the "Birth-night Ball." During Washington's administration Philadelphia annually held a ball on the President's birthday, following English royal

Mrs. John Adams, by Mather Brown.

precedent. In 1798, instead of holding it on John Adams's birthday in June, they announced the usual birth-night ball for 23
February, and sent an invitation to the Adamses as private citizens.
The President and his lady were outraged, and refused to attend,
to the huge delight of Jefferson and his followers, who regarded
birth-night balls as indications of monarchical designs on the part
of the Federalists. Otis sympathized with the President. He wrote
to Sally on 24 February:

> The Birth night ball of last evening was I am told respectably
> attended, tho by no means equal in splendour & numbers to the
> last. . . . The President did not attend, & his refusal has given
> considerable offence, even to some of the federal party. To be
> sure, his apology was rather formal, but I think he acted rightly
> upon principle. As President, he ought to know of no distinction
> among *private* citizens, whatever may be their merit or virtue; &
> having never received from the Philadelphians the slightest mark
> of attention, he was in my mind quite excusable for declining to
> be the pageant, to do honor to another. Many families who
> usually increase the flutter of the beau monde were absent. The
> Morrisites of course. The Binghams who have lately lost a rela-
> tion, & the Chews on account of a Mrs. Pemberton who died last
> Sunday; I am told that the whole house was very damp and be-
> lieve I have not lost much.

Every summer there took place a massive exodus of the *beau
monde* to the country, for fear of yellow fever which usually made
its appearance in July. And Philadelphia was not the only eastern
city to suffer the ravages of "yellow jack." Charlestonians, partly
to escape it, summered at Newport; and Otis vainly tried to persuade John Rutledge to visit him in Boston, which too had been
through an epidemic. He writes thence to Rutledge on 16 October
1798, declaring the "late panic" in Boston to be over — *only* 150
people had died; the Otis family have returned to town, and it
would take the Rutledges only a day and a half to travel from Newport to Boston where everybody is eager to make their acquaint-

ance. But they refused to budge. Again, in August 1799, Otis assures Rutledge that Boston is enjoying a completely healthy summer; he had already received as visitor Elias Horrÿ of Charleston, who suffered no ill consequences. But again Rutledge did not come.

THE BINGHAM FAMILY

Mrs. William Bingham led Philadelphia society during Otis's congressional career. Born Anne Willing, eldest of three beautiful daughters of Thomas Willing, she married at the age of sixteen William Bingham, a successful merchant of humble extraction who had amassed a fortune through privateering and speculating in government warrants. He was elected to the United States Senate in 1795. The Binghams' mansion house, the center of Philadelphia social life, occupied with gardens and stables almost three acres of land, fronting on Third Street at Spruce, and running west to Fourth Street. On the ground floor were a dining room and a library; on the first story the various drawing rooms, to which one ascended by a broad marble staircase. Here were entertained presidents and cabinet ministers, senators and representatives of the Federalist party, and distinguished *émigrés,* the Orléans princes, La Rochefoucauld-Liancourt, and Talleyrand, who took temporary refuge in America. Young Louis-Philippe, future King of the French, courted Mrs. Bingham's sister, but old Mr. Willing refused his consent to the match when that of the dowager Duchesse d'Orléans could not be obtained. At the Bingham mansion were held the "nocturnal caucuses" of the senatorial ring which in 1799 fruitlessly attempted to impose the will of Alexander Hamilton on John Adams.

Mrs. Bingham, young and fascinating, beautiful and wealthy, reigned undisputed queen of the Republican Court. Having passed several years with her husband in England, where she was greatly admired, she imported some of the less amiable traits of English society. Like the Duchess of Devonshire and other great ladies at the Court of St. James's, she besprinkled her conversation with oaths, and spiced it with facetious anecdotes. The following extracts are fair examples of intimate conversations in the Bingham set as related by Otis:

> Yesterday I dined at Clymers, with the Bingham and Willing Party. Sophia not there. It was the first day of the Bingham's return from the country. . . . Dolly then began to rally Clymer on the subject of his *Stomacher,* . . . and mentioned that one of the British Princes (I think the Duke of York) who had lately married the Princess Wirtemburg has so protuberant a corporation that he was compelled to order a semicircular piece cut out of his dining table, to give him access to his plate. Mrs. Bingham expressed a hint of sympathy for the *Dutchess,* and Clymer told his sister Francis that he should soon be able to retort this *excellent jest* upon her. All this, and much facetious matter of the same kind was received with bursts of applause that would have done credit to the national convention especially by Miss Abby & Miss Ann, who did not disguise their delight nor their bosoms.

And in another letter,

> This week, one day I dined at Harrison's, with a family party and Saml Smith & John Brown[1] as Aid de Camps. Old John after rallying Sophia in no very acceptable strain, upon her unfruitfulness, by a natural but not very flattering transition introduced Mrs. Champlin and her want of prolifick qualities as a seasoning for the Canvas Backs. This topic which had a commencement embarrassing to me, whose feelings were excited for our good friends, terminated in a manner most agreeable. Did you never think says Mr. Brown that Mrs Champlin & Mrs. Otis very much resemble each other? Sophia shook her head with dissenting movement. Mr Otis observed that he

[1] Samuel Smith, representative from Baltimore, later senator; the only Democrat mentioned in Otis's letters as present at a Federalist dining table. John Brown, of Providence, prominent merchant and member of Congress.

Mrs. William Bingham, by Gilbert Stuart.

had not perceived the likeness, & that after the encomiums
bestowed on Mrs C. he should hardly venture to make so flattering a comparison, even if he thought it just. Oh the D———l
exclaimed S. Smith, there is no comparison at all. Mrs O with
all the advantages of the other lady, shows in an instant that
she has all her Days been used to Company, her manners are
elegant; but this woman with a pretty face, has the air of a
country girl.

Mrs. Bingham's mannerisms were superficial. For ten years the
focus of metropolitan scandal, no whisper against her good name
has come down the murky channels of historical gossip. But the
story of her children is sad. The eldest daughter Anne married
Alexander Baring of the celebrated London banking house, later
created Lord Ashburton. As Lady Ashburton Anne had the satisfaction of founding a noble house, but a nephew of Otis's friend
George Harrison, who visited the Ashburtons in England, found
her far from happy. "She met with many mortifications," he wrote
in his memoirs, "and from nobody so great as from her son's wife,
Lady Harriet, and her proud family, that of Earl Sandwich.
Certainly Lady Harriet was the most perfect example of insolent
ill breeding I ever saw, treated the poor old lady in her own house,
at the Grange, with great coolness if not impertinence."

The Binghams' second daughter, Maria, furnished scandal for
the Republican Court from an early age. An old beau, who visited
the Binghams with Otis in 1798, predicted that Maria, then aged
fourteen, would not "keep" long. About a year later she fulfilled
the prophecy by making a clandestine marriage with the Comte de
Tilly, a handsome and profligate Frenchman. To quote again the
same memoirs:

It was a shocking and scandalous affair, and created at the time
prodigious sensation in our highest circles. De Tilly was ready,
however, to be bought off. He was bribed to furnish evidence
against himself, and the divorce was obtained by influence with

Marquise de Blaizel (Maria Bingham), by Thomas Lawrence.

the Legislature of Pennsylvania, whether by corruption I am not able to say, but in those days Legislatures were supposed to be unassailable in that way.

Otis commented on the situation in a letter to Sally on 18 January 1800:

> First, then, I just learn that a bill for divorcing Maria Bingham has passed both houses at Lancaster, where Mr. Bingham now is. She was however every day walking with her mother while this business was pending and in a dress which you will hardly believe it possible for a lady to wear at least at this season. A muslin robe and her chemise, and no other article of cloathing upon her body. I have been regaled with the sight of her whole legs for five minutes together, and do not know "to what height" the fashion will be carried. The particulars of her dress I have from old Mrs. F[rancis] who assures me that her chemise is fringed to look like a petticoat.

Abigail Adams was shocked at Maria's appearance "rouged up to the ears," when Mrs. Bingham presented her at a drawing room. But men buzzed about her like flies around honey, especially a young man named Erving, whom Otis thought "conceited, democratical and niggardly." Here is his opinion expressed more fully:

> Thursday evening Miss Peters gave a ball, to which by Erving's special request I procured his admission. Doubtless his principal view was to meet Maria, to whom his attentions were perfectly ridiculous. He scarcely spake to any other Lady, first he danced with her, then sat by her, then followed her up and down when she danced with other persons like a shadow, and in short was so absolutely inattentive to the ladies of the family that I was mortified. It was hinted to me that he has no chance of success, & that Mam'selle is not smitten.

Erving shortly afterward received his *congé,* and the interesting history of Maria Bingham is continued by our same gossipy chronicler:

Maria B. afterward married Henry Baring,[1] was divorced from him on account of an amour with Captain Webster, the son of Sir Godfrey Webster and the lady, afterwards Lady Holland, who was herself an American of the great Vassall family and was divorced from Sir Godfrey after the birth of her first son by Lord Holland, who could not take his father's title. Mr. Vassall's fortune was enormous and the husband of his daughter was compelled to take the name of Vassall. After Maria Bingham's second divorce, she married a Marquis de Blaizel, a Frenchman in the Austrian army and a Chamberlain of the Emperor. I knew her in Paris, then an old woman but quite an amusing one. She had seen the world in many phases and had plenty of anecdotes which she told pleasantly. She was a very amiable, kind-hearted woman and her faults and frailties were attributable to neglect, in some measure, and the bad company into which she was thrown. Her mother was devoted to fashion and incessantly devoted to company, left her daughter to the instruction of a French governess, who had been an Actress and was probably bought by de Tilly. Henry Baring who had no sense of honor or delicacy, threw her into the most dissipated company, was glaringly unfaithful himself, and it is said, laid a plan for her divorce when he had fallen in love with a young lady who became his second wife. Whether Captain Webster knowingly lent himself to his friend's scheme, I know not. The poor lady was unhappy with her third husband who was a gambler and always in want of money which she could not supply in sufficient sums to satisfy him, for Henry Baring had managed to retain the greater part of her fortune. She lived in rather an equivocal position in Paris. She was received at the Austrian Ambassador's but not at the English Embassy. The public trial in England was a stigma which the most notorious profligacy, not certified in Court, did not affix. I think Louis Phillippe refused her the entré of the Palais Royal, though this was probably the act of his virtuous wife, otherwise he would not perhaps, have shunned the daughter of the hospitable house where the exiled French princes were so honorably entertained.

The great Bingham estate, comprising enormous tracts of land in Maine and the West, and future oil lands of Pennsylvania, went

[1] Brother of Alexander Baring who married her sister.

to the two Barings and to the infant son, William Bingham, Jr.,
who, educated in England, came to no good.

> His great fortune was probably his great misfortune. He went
> to Canada afterwards, where he married a very beautiful girl of
> the Provincial Noblesse — a Mademoiselle [de Lothbinière]. She
> was just out of a Convent and the marriage was arranged be-
> tween them; otherwise she could not have married so coarse a
> man as William Bingham. He had sense enough to know he
> could not take care of his estate and was glad to have settlements
> made which put him under control in a measure of his wife —
> who turned out a pretty shrewd manager. They lived for some
> years in the best style at Montreal where their house was open
> to all gay people, especially to officers of the British regiments.
> The opportunities of intrigue were not lost and Wm. Bingham
> admitted that he was only certain of the legitimacy of his eldest
> son. They afterwards went to Paris where Madame, still hand-
> some in mature years and after her hair had become gray, had
> a most scandalous life changing her lovers with the fashions or
> seasons and he sunk into drunkenness or imbecility; was scarcely
> seen and certainly not presentable in his own house.

The brilliant career of the Bingham family in Philadelphia
lasted but a few years. Mrs. Bingham in 1801 developed tubercu-
losis, sailed for Bermuda in the hope of a cure, and died en route.
Her brokenhearted husband went to England where he died in
1804. The Bingham mansion became a hotel where Sir Charles
Vaughan the British minister received "bad accomodation" for
himself and a couple of servants in 1826, and was charged the then
enormous sum of $43 for one night, plus a $2 tip to the waiter.

MISCELLANEOUS OCCURRENCES

Early in 1798 Philadelphia received a shock from the bankruptcy of the great financier of the Revolution, Robert Morris.
Up to that time his entertainments had vied in splendor with those

of the Binghams. Extensive speculations during a number of years brought the first crash, concerning which Otis wrote in February:

Poor Mr. Morris was yesterday compelled to surrender himself to his bail, and was bro't to his house in town, with a design of going to prison. He was either committed yesterday, or will be today, the Sheriff having kept him in custody. I am told that his family exhibited a dreadful scene of distress, that Mrs. M was almost as frantic, and flew upon the Person who was his bail and who bro't him to town and would have committed violence but was prevented. What an example of the folly and vanity of human grandeur. But a few years since he was in wealth and honor, the most considerable man in the United States, & she ruled the world of fashion with unrivalled sway. He will now probably moulder away a few remaining wretched years in prison, and her joys & comforts have probably forever vanished.

Morris was forced to remain in the Prune Street debtors' prison for over three years, and came near dying there. The great man's fall carried others with him, including Otis's friend George Harrison, but he managed to survive the crisis by an appointment to the office of navy agent for the government. Bankruptcies were not uncommon in the fashionable world of Philadelphia, and Otis writes apropos of another sensational affair of that sort in 1800, that of Peter Blight, who had provided one of his merchant vessels with a "corps of marines in brilliant uniform, such as a sovereign prince of rich government alone could equip":

In short everything confirms my opinion that the capital of this country by no means justifies the luxury and style of life affected by so many. Overtrading, & unbounded credit are the mischiefs; bankruptcies & ruin will be the cure, & though I have never thought or called myself rich, I would not exchange my property for that of many who talk of thousands & tens of thousands, as if dollars were needles and pins. Our friends Willing and Francis stand firm; yet am I glad that the notes I hold of theirs fall due from the 9 to the 19 april. They owe me 12500 Dollars, a very serious sum, and such as I will never again suffer to be dependent on any *personal* security whatever.

The most stirring period of Philadelphia's social supremacy immediately followed the XYZ disclosures of April 1798. There were patriotic demonstrations at the theater when the "President's March" was sung to Joseph Hopkinson's new words, "Hail! Columbia," and the Jacobins who called for "Ça ira" were shouted down. There were patriotic dinners and toasts, addresses to the President, serenades, and struggles between men wearing the Federalist black cockade and those wearing the French tricolor. Otis, anxious over an addition to his Boston family, did not refer to these scenes in his letters to Sally, and in May when little Sophia was well enough to be left with a nurse, Sally joined him at Philadelphia. But as she did not attend the following winter season, her husband sent her some fashion hints from the capital:

> Wigs are *out* here, but the hair is dressed like a wig, with the hair of the back part of the head brought forward forming a sort of bandeau ornamented with little *combs,* some of which I will send you if you have none in Boston. Black Velvet great coats made like an open gown are also the rage. Would not my Velvet suit make you one? If not buy a new one. In short let me know all you want, & indulge me in my only real pleasure that of contributing to your wishes and comfort.

The death of Washington on 14 December 1799 is the subject of Otis's next letter of this series:

> My dearest friend,
> The sensation of regret excited by the death of Genl. Washington has suspended all public business, and almost excluded private concerns. Congress will be sincerely engaged for some days in paying honor to his memory. In addition to the measures which you will see detailed in the enclosed papers, the Senate have also agreed to wear mourning during the Session, and the walls of their chambers will be entirely hung with black. A joint committee of both houses have also agreed that a funeral eulogium shall be pronounced, and the orator though not named, will *probably* be Genl H. Lee of Virginia. It is contemplated to turn out all the military and to make a grand

procession, and it was proposed in the Committee that the Universities of America should send in rotation every four years, an orator to commemorate the event by an oration at the seat of government. This last project however has not yet been adopted; but the affection and regret of the people will seek for any possible mode of demonstrating their sense of this truly great and irreparable loss.

On 26 December, from the House of Representatives, he writes:

Before my eyes and in front of the speakers chair lies a coffin covered with a black pall, bearing a military hat & sword. The chair itself & tables shrouded with black. In the background is Washington's portrait. The Members are all provided with black crape for their arms and white scarfs, and in about one hour we shall march attended by the military in grand procession to the German Lutheran Church where funeral obsequies will be performed and an oration delivered by Genl Lee. The day is fine and the streets already so crowded with people that I found it no easy matter to get hither. The concourse will be immense.

At the end of that week comes a long letter, with some interesting comments on Alexander Hamilton and other notables.

I proceed to give my dearest Sally a journal of the last week of my life.

Sunday the 22d. Went to meeting in the morning & heard a young prig of a preacher, who spliced on the end of his discourse a laboured panegyric on Genl Washington which would have been equally suitable to any other sermon. Din'd with Mr. Francis, old Brown eloquent in favor of the slave trade. Passed an hour in the evening at Breck's[1] A good house on a Sunday evening to see *strange* faces. The parties are truly *select,* being congregated from all quarters of Europe and America. Monday dined with Harrison & Sophia only, went home early and passed the evening with some members of Congress who called in.

---

[1] Either "Greenbrier," two miles out of Philadelphia, the estate of Samuel Breck (1771–1862, author of some delightful *Recollections*), or the town house of his father of the same name.

Tuesday Dined at Breck's, with Mrs Church,[1] Miss Schuyler, Genl. Hamilton, Champlin[2] &c &c. Mrs. C. the mirror of affectation, but as she affects to be extremely affable and free from ceremony, this foible is rather amusing than offensive. Miss Schuyler a young wild flirt from Albany, full of glee & apparently desirous of matrimony. After Dinner Mrs. C. dropped her shoe bow, Miss S——— picked it up and put it in Hamiltons buttonhole saying "there brother I have made you a Knight." "But of what order" (says Madam C) "he can't be a Knight of the garter in this country." "True sister" replied Miss S——— "but *he would be if you would let him!"* — Mrs Church took me in her coach to make some visits. Nobody at home but the once celebrated Mrs. Craig, whom I was glad of an opportunity of seeing & conversing with for a few moments. Went to *see* supper at young A McCalls; the party made for the new married couple, Erskine and Miss Cadwallader; returned home in Bond's coach and narrowly escaped being *stretched at full length with Miss Bond,* by the coachman who was drunk & tried to overset the carriage. Happily this truly amiable and well bred virgin escaped the disaster.

Wednesday Christmas day. — Dined at Aunt Powel's,[3] with the Hares, Francis's & Harrisons. The Dowager is really afflicted at the death of her old friend the General, but she thinks it necessary to appear more so than she is in fact, and that she is called upon in decency to shed tears whenever his name is mentioned. She made out very well at first, but Mr. Hare with a maladroit perseverence would talk of nothing else, so that before the cloth was removed, the old Lady's stock of briny element being fairly exhausted, she could only look piteous and at length begged a truce of all conversation on the subject, which being granted she munched her pies with an air of consolation that was truly edifying. I took tea at Bonds, where as well as at Mr Ross' I was invited to keep christmas. — Thursday attended the procession dined at the Presidents, sat near Mrs. Wilson, who astonished me by being very sociable. Evening

---

[1] *Née* Schuyler, sister of Mrs. Alexander Hamilton.

[2] Christopher G. ("Kit") Champlin, member of Congress from Rhode Island.

[3] Mrs. Samuel Powel, *née* Willing, aunt of Mrs. Bingham, of Mrs. George Harrison, and of Charles Willing Hare.

Marquesa del Casa Yrujo (Sally McKean), by Gilbert Stuart.

at Read's with the *Church* party, and passed an hour very agreeably.

Friday dined at the British Minister's — Mrs Champlin the only Lady. Last week Mrs Church dined at Listons & Binghams from the same house, yet the Rhode island beauty was not invited. You may be assured you experienced *more* attention here, than *any other* lady has met with since Congress sat in this city. Kit took occasion to tell me that Hamilton (who cast some liquorish looks at his cara sposa, the day we were at Breck's) appears to him very trifling in his conversation with ladies and that his wife said she did not like him at all. He was evidently *satisfied* with this intimation. Went with Mrs Liston to the drawing room in the evening and led her in. Both rooms were crowded and I missed none of my acquaintance but Mrs Bingham, who burst the gown she had prepared for the occasion Saturday. I dine with my father, drink tea with Betsy Francis, and have not a single engagement on hand untill — tomorrow.

I might here add in a note that I have been every morning before 8 to Schuylkill bridge, and every evening in bed at ten. I might also indulge in a comparison of these scenes, or rather of these vicissitudes of eating and drinking, with the pleasures which I enjoy in your society . . . but I should grow serious, and my object being to amuse you in some small degree I forbear, — and will continue to *kill time.* . . .

20 February 1800:

Since my last we have had an immense fandango at Listons, it was the largest polite mob which I have seen in this city. In other respects it was not distinguished from the ordinary routine of dancing, giggling flirting & eating. . . . A New York party has made its appearance here, consisting of Hammond, his wife & her sister, Mr. Nicholas Low & Lady & her daughter a Miss Fleming, a lady of about 20 or 22, tolerably pretty, & a reigning wit and belle at New York. I dined with them at Liston's on sunday, & was seated next to the said Miss Fleming who rattled and laughed with me so much and so loud, though it was our first interview that Madam Liston, before the whole company called upon Dexter to tell *"Meastress Awtis* how things were going." There is to be a good deal of feasting on their account, the few days they stay, in which I have a share as usual.

PRIMITIVE WASHINGTON

About the middle of March 1800, Otis paired off with a member of the opposition and left for Boston. Philadelphia remained the national capital only a few months longer. During the summer and autumn of 1800 the Federal Government removed to Washington, where the second and last session of the Sixth Congress opened in November. Washington, as Harry and Sally observed it on their approach, was the sharpest possible contrast to Philadelphia. On a hill in the center of the potential city stood the north wing of the Capitol, the only part completed; a mile and a half to the west was the simple Executive Mansion, then euphemistically called "the Palace," now the White House. All else was desolation: tree stumps, brick kilns, workmen's huts, a few mean frame dwellings, a wilderness of mud, were all that met the eye within the borders of the federal city. Beyond were the forest and the broad sweep of the Potomac. No mansion houses, no shops, no commerce, few people; luxuries unobtainable at any price and even necessities such as food and fuel hard to come by. Such is the unattractive picture of Washington in 1801 left by contemporaries, who nevertheless admired the beauty of the site, the noble Potomac, and the wooded background. Comfortable little Georgetown, two miles west of the White House, proved the salvation of transplanted officialdom; without the lodgings it afforded, most of the members of the Sixth Congress must have camped out this first winter, or slept in the Capitol. At Georgetown there were a few good taverns, and a small group of well-bred and hospitable people who did their best to entertain newcomers.

Otis, looking forward to the end of his congressional career and accompanied by his dear Sally, sounded a cheerful note on his arrival. He wrote to his father-in-law William Foster on 25 November 1800:

> We arrived here yesterday without any interruption except one days detention at the Susquehannah river, where we con-

soled ourselves with *canvas backs* for the detention. Sally appears to me in better health than she has enjoyed for a twelvemonth; we are better lodged than we expected and much better than the majority of our neighbours. The place too is more pleasant than I had anticipated, tho' there has been a flight of snow that would do credit to a colder clime and higher latitude.

In January 1801, the Otises made a visit to Mount Vernon, which is described in a letter from Sally to her sister Mary, Mrs. John Trecothick Apthorp:

Washington Jany 13 1801 Monday.

I received my dear Marys letter on friday Evening and notwithstanding her long lectures (as she calls them) I must acknowledge myself much gratified by the whole. On Saturday morning we made up our party for Mount Vernon, Mr Mason, Bayard, Francis Mr O. Betsey[1] & myself in two coaches. The roads are bad beyond the utmost stretch of a new england imagination. We got safe to Alexandria which is eight miles from this place on the opposite bank of the potomack no fine cultivated growns to enliven the scene & not one decent house in this immense space but an unenclosed barren heath it appears to me and what the Virginians call Oldfield — here we were overtaken by Söderstrom, Thornton, Morton (Brother to Mrs Quincy) & Govr Howard[2] who were embarked in the same expedition. We knew Mrs Washington to have ten spare beds — but as that was not sufficient for the whole party, we concluded to remain in Alexandria on Saturday, rise early on the next morning and proceed. The last named Gentn went on & we passed a very pleasant day, walked quite over this little City, which is the perfect Miniature of Philadelphia. In the afternoon Mr & Mrs Callender join'd us, they are on a visit *not being able to exist in Georgetown.* The Evening closed as usual with Cards (the only amusement here known among the men) —

[1] The persons mentioned are Otis's friend Jonathan Mason, then senator from Massachusetts, James A. Bayard, and the Thomas Willing Francises of Philadelphia.

[2] Richard Söderström, consul-general of Sweden; Edward Thornton, British chargé d'affaires; Jacob Morton or his brother Washington, both New York Federalists; and John Eager Howard, formerly governor, then United States senator from Maryland.

Sunday commenced the arduous task. Nine in the morning departed, the first mile out of the city lost our way and in this error came near *stalling* three times besides the loss of one hour. Returned thro the same boggs and set off anew. Mount Vernon is ten miles distant from Alex. The estate is immensely large and inclosed by a high Virginia fence. At the entrance is a gate, after passing which is a thick wood 4 Miles in length: here we were by intricate windings twice led astray. You will imagine by this time we were almost discouraged — a few straggling miserable negroes the only moving objects, now & then a Mule the one & the other alike incapable of giving information in this dilemma. Bayard who is patience *personified* exclaimed "By heaven! this is too bad." A mute dispair seemed to seize us — when a lad more decent than those before seen came in view, we enquired. He said, "you come wrong but you go right" — here we paused; some ingenuity was required to solve this enigma, finding our capacity unequal, a second appeal was more successful. We now learned that we were going to the Mill, but from the Mill was a road to the House: *true* a very bad one. This revived our drooping spirits — the safer way however was to secure this guide, which we accordingly did — and at half past two surmounted all perils by land & by water and had the satisfaction to see on a beautiful emminence the Mansion of the great *Washington* and here description fails me.

I can only tell you tis all that we, in our most romantic moments have imagined of grandeur taste and beauty. I fancy the soil is not very good but all that taste and affluence could affect is here attain'd. The House is antique like the inhabitant: capacious and substantial affording every comfort & luxury. The wings are more modern, they were added some years since by the General; in one is a large Hall hung with the most elegant painting from all parts of europe, (I presume presents) — himself & favorite horse not the least interesting. In the other wing is his own particular apartments his chamber where he died, his study dressing room &c which have nothing to distinguish them from the chambers of any other house: they *reminded me of little Cambridge.* Mrs Washington tells me she has not had resolution to visit these apartments since the death of the General. She received us with the most gracious cordiallity, in her deportment

is that mild benevolence that serene resignation which Charac-
terises the saint — and she speaks of death as a pleasant Journey
which is in contemplation. At the same time Chearful anxious
to perform the most minute civility and unerring in every duty.
The slaves are for the most part liberated in this instance. She
is not so much at her ease (as the training of a young crop, we
all know, is not a small taske) some few quite old domesticks
perferd remaining, these are almost useless. The Stables are
crowded with horses asses and mules, favorites and by the Genls
order exempted from labor.

The morng of Monday was delightful cold for this climate.
I arose with the sun determined to regale myself in these enchanting walks. Mrs Lewis (formaly the beautiful Ellen Custis)
& Bet were already prepared. The house lot & gardens included
cover ten acres the wall is of brick which incloses it but sunk
so that in appearance tis an Open lawn. The walks are irregular
& serpentine cover'd by trees of various kinds but what most
pleased me was a labyrinth of evergreens where the sun cannot
even now penetrate. This must be a little Paradies in summer.
I forgot it was not so even now, seeing the spinach & young
Cabages growing in the open air — the Kitchen gardens are
also beautifully cultivated. On the front of the House is a
gradual declivity to the Potowmac & here the scene is indis-
cribably grand & beautiful.

At the distance of a quarter of a mile is seen the Humble
tomb of the illustrious Washington known only by the little
willows & cypress that wave their melancholy branches over it. I
walked down with a solemn and awful sensation to this sacred
spot. The housekeeper offerd to run & fetch a key but as the
grownd was damp and we perceived Mrs W. walking in the
Piazza we declined. She shewd us into the breakfast Room,
where was a most sumptious entertainment which we did ample
justice to after our long walk. Our visit was now made, but I
assure you it was very difficult to get away. She urged us in the
most flattering manner to remain a few days with her: I sincerely
regretted that it was not in my power as I was facinated with
every thing about me. We dined again in Alexandria and slept
in Washington on Monday night.

And now my dear Mary you will not say I have omitted any

part of this rout, and any deficiencies that you may name I will endeavor to make good. I have been trying to finish this letter since Monday it is now thursday & I declined going to the georgtown Assembly where Betsy my Hub. & all the beaux are, determined to seal it this night. Perhaps you will say better for me when I tell you I was dancing Cotillions till two on Teusday Ngt, and dined at the presidents today with 30 gentlemen and Ladies a select and agreable party — and tomorrow dear Mary we rise at five and depart for Philadelphia from which place I hope to give you an accurate detail of fashion. In the meantime wear your wig with a wreath of flowers thro — or a band of crape folded thick with a long end hanging down on the right side with a silk, or silver, or bead, tassell & two handsome large feathers on the back part, falling forward. A fine muslin trimmed with a fine lace without starch is very pretty if you wear a muslin dress. I advise you to harbour no *evil conjectures* about your sister who is in better health and as good spirits as you generally find her. . . .

Otis's letters which followed his wife to Philadelphia are full of details on the exciting incidents of the last two months of the Federalist era — the attempt to renew the Sedition and the Judiciary Acts, and the choice between Jefferson and Burr for the presidency. They also show that the good people of Georgetown were doing their best to make their guests forget the splendors of Mr. Breck's dinners and Mrs. Bingham's balls. On 1 February 1801 Otis writes:

> Since my last I have dined with Plater and tried my luck once more at a ball at Lingans.[1] The Col & I went together, and the evening being pleasant, we ascended the rock on which the house is situated & returned without danger. Our entertainment consisted first of tea, served out about 8 oclock. Then the dancing continued without interruption untill *twelve. After that* chocolate in cups with dry toast was handed round among the

[1] Thomas Plater, M. C. from Maryland; James M. Lingan, collector of the port of Georgetown, killed by a Baltimore mob in 1812.

ladies, and *after that,* the gentlemen were regaled in a back parlour with a cold ham, mutton & tongue.

I have concluded to go to no more balls, for though the party
here was on the whole agreeable & genteel yet they have all the
strangest way of assorting people in the world. There was 3 or
4 federal members of Congress, together with *Christie Randolph
Dawson Holmes* & *Van Cortlandt,* and I confess I do not enjoy
myself with these people.

The objectionable gentlemen were prominent Republicans from
Maryland, Virginia, and New York. It was natural for one who
had been the target of John Randolph's bony finger and callow
invective to take exception to his presence at an evening entertainment, and John Dawson, Otis's old college friend the "Beau,"
had talked himself out of Federalist society by publicly and violently attacking President Adams. The other three, David Holmes,
Gabriel Christie and Philip Van Cortlandt, were Democratic members of Congress.

On 15 February 1801, Otis describes similar gatherings:

My dearest friend . . .

If I mistake not I mentioned in my last that I was at Johnsons
and at Burrows' balls the last week so that you see the fatigues
of electioneering were diversified by other fatigue. At Johnsons[1] the party was made brilliant by the presence of several
really fine and fashionable Annapolitans. The supper however
was shabby beyond all former precedent. A sideboard with a
round of cold beef & a ham which the dear ladies were obliged
to eat on their blessed knees, presented the sum total of the
appropriation for the craving demands of divers florid and car-
nivorous animals of both sexes. Still the evening was sufficiently
agreeable, and I have since learnt that I made a conquest of a
very charming young lady from the Metropolis of Maryland,
to whom I was not introduced & did not speak. *What a real
misfortune to be so irresistible.*

[1] Probably Thomas Johnson of Frederick, Md., chief judge of the circuit court in
D.C.; Major W. W. Burrows, commandant of the Marine Corps. His quarters, at the
Washington Navy Yard, still stand.

Washington Feby 23. 1801

My dearest friend,

Your patriotic permission to me to remain here untill the 4th instant, has rendered you so popular with the Federal part of the house that I believe they would gladly make you Speaker in the room of Mr S— but I wish to see you in no chair, untill I see you in an easy chair in your own chamber, where I should take the liberty to taste of your cheek — I have no earthly thing, to add, having already written to Sophia this morning, and am (in a great worry to see you) as always

yr truly affect.
H G Otis

Harry's letter of 23 February 1801 to Sally.

We fared still better chez Burrows. Fine music & an elegant supper were among the consolations for disappointment at the absence of many guests who were prevented by weather. Huger[1] danced on his toes as usual with every flirt in the room, while his sedate and venerable lady bedizzened & bejewelled kept a stedfast and deploring eye upon his eccentric follies, and turned a *deaf* ear to the civilities and sighs of those who surrounded her. Mrs B—— took care to apprise me that this party was originally intended for Betsy Francis & yourself. That the cake was actually made while you were here, but that a series of accidents foreign and domestic, and of interferences & disappointments enough to melt a heart of stone compelled them to defer it untill this moment.

Thus you see I continue to trifle away the residue of my wearisome pilgrimage; I will not say here how much I miss you by night and by day. A carriage this moment stops to take me to the capitol and I must close this letter or lose this mail.

God bless my dear wife. H. G. OTIS

The gallant little note of 23 February, here reproduced in facsimile, concludes this series of letters. Obviously the removal of the Federal Government to Washington had cut a rift in the alliance between society and politics, and the Republican victory of 1800 widened the breach. Nothing approaching a court could exist with the materials of the Jeffersonian epoch or in the setting of the backwoods village that Washington remained for many years. Thomas Jefferson, in soiled corduroy breeches and slippers down at the heel, receiving the British minister at the White House, is as typical of the new order as were Washington's stately levees and Mrs. Bingham's balls of the old régime. Aristocracy had been beheaded by the peaceful guillotine of the ballot; and the plain people, led by the Apostle of Democracy, reigned in its place — or at least so they imagined.

---

[1] Benjamin Huger, member of Congress from South Carolina.

CHAPTER VIII

France Backs Down

1798–1801, AET. 33–35

Visits to Adams and Gerry

IN THE INTERVAL between the second and third sessions of the Fifth Congress, July to December 1798, an important change took place in the state of relations with France. The Directory, astonished at the spirit of resentment in the United States, promised to receive an American minister and ordered the destruction of American commerce to cease. On the question whether France should be taken at her word, or a war policy be followed, the Federalist party split.

After the three envoys in Paris sent off the XYZ dispatches in January 1798, they prolonged the quasi-negotiations with Talleyrand and his agents for three months. By April, since Talleyrand refused to talk with anyone but Gerry, Pinckney and Marshall decided to leave Paris. Gerry should have left with them; but, flattered by Talleyrand and fearful of "provoking" France into a declaration of war, he remained in Paris another three months, patiently enduring Talleyrand's alternate bluffing and bullying. Finally this became too much for Gerry, and he demanded his passports. At this point news reached Paris of the rising spirit in America and of the maritime reprisals enacted by Congress. Talleyrand realized that he had overreached himself. The French party in America was not so strong, nor public spirit so humble, as he had been led to expect. He detained Gerry long enough to persuade him that the Directory intended to mend its manners, substituted whining for bullying in his diplomatic notes, canceled all demands for an apology or a loan, and offered to receive any envoy whom the United States might see fit to send.

In the meantime, Gerry's remaining in Paris after the other envoys had departed became an object of bitter attack. John Adams, at first, was mortified by Gerry's conduct; but, when Pickering threatened to expose "not his pusillanimity and weakness alone, but his *duplicity* and *treachery,*" the President rallied to the support of his old friend. His private conversation began to show so alarming a tendency to vindicate Gerry at the expense of Marshall and Pinckney that Cabot, Higginson and other members of the Essex Junto persuaded Otis to visit Quincy in order to tell the President "how much his frankness exposes himself and his friends." This is one of many instances in which Otis's tact secured him the dubious honor of performing some particularly delicate or disagreeable mission. That he succeeded in this case is evident from a temporary cessation of complaints about the President's garrulity; but it is left to our imagination to discover by what means Harry managed to convince proud and irascible Adams that he talked too much.

This visit to the President took place on 28 October 1798. In the meantime, Gerry himself had arrived in Boston. "He landed at Long Wharf," wrote Manasseh Cutler. "The Federalists, by agreement, took not the least notice of him as he walked up State Street; not a hat was moved." Although feigning indifference, the Federalists were fearful lest Gerry vindicate his conduct by attacking their foreign policy. The leaders thought it best to send someone to fathom his intentions; and, of course, Harry Otis was selected. At the interview, according to a letter of George Cabot,

> Mr. Otis intimated to him the state of public opinion concerning him; that the friends of the government were not satisfied, and that its enemies had calculated upon finding in him a character round which they might rally with new spirit. He replied that he was sensible of the predicament in which he

stood, but he thought it an ill compliment to his understanding
to suppose he could be made subservient to the designs of the
opposition.

Gerry was as good as his word. Although the Federalists continued
to abuse him, and Jefferson made a wily appeal to his personal
vanity to air his grievances, he made no complaint, and even issued
a statement endorsing the President's policy.

Reëlection and the French Problem

Shortly after performing these political missions, Otis was reëlected to Congress. His opponent was General William Heath,
to whom his published letter advocating the arming of merchant
vessels had been addressed, and a more popular and formidable
adversary than James Bowdoin had been in 1796. The usual newspaper duel between *Centinel* and *Chronicle* took place. General
Heath, a well-meaning old soldier, was attacked in the *Centinel*
as "the ridiculous, despicable, weak-minded, weak-hearted Jacobin,
commonly distinguished by the appellation of the *Hero of Fort
Independence*," a good example of the insolence of 1798 Federalism.[1] The *Chronicle* made no personal attack on Otis, but charged
upon the Sedition Act and the direct tax, and endeavored to turn
to advantage a rural prejudice against lawyers. There were already
too many of that kidney in Congress; lawyers were responsible for
the Sedition Act and the new taxes, to make more business for
themselves. Let the yeomanry go to the polls and outvote the
foreigners and blacks, who had secured a majority for Otis in the
last election! The popularity of Federalist foreign policy is shown
by the fact that no one ventured to attack that phase of Otis's activity beyond the statement that his calling Frenchmen "pyrates,
rogues, etc." might bar negotiation.

[1] In 1777 General Heath bungled an attack on Fort Independence on the Hudson
and was reprimanded by General Washington. He had been a farmer in Roxbury
since the war.

In the electioneering Otis took no part. In those days, happily
for the peace of mind and the pocketbook of a candidate, personal
participation in one's own campaign was considered highly improper. But that zealous efforts were made on both sides is indicated by the size of the vote — twenty-seven percent greater than
that of 1796, a presidential year. All the increase in Boston went
to Otis — the "wild Irish" evidently did vote for "young Harry" —
but in the rural part of the district, farmer Heath polled more than
twice as many votes as his lawyer opponent.

Otis, as chairman of the House committee on defense from
December 1798 to March 1799, proposed almost every measure that
Alexander Hamilton recommended, and secured the passage of
many. And the Federalists were given an opportunity to show
that they could repel aggression from England as well as from
France. In November 1798 Captain Loring of the British frigate
Carnatic boarded the United States corvette *Baltimore,* took off
fifty-five of the crew, and impressed five. It was a worse outrage than
the later *Chesapeake* affair but attracted less attention owing to the
naval war with France that was going on. In the House of Representatives on the last day of 1798, Otis proposed a resolve calling
for information concerning the outrage, "as we think it necessary
to show Great Britain and the world that instances of abuse of this
kind excite a lively sensibility, and that we are determined to protect our flag against any country whatever." This speech earned
Otis a rare compliment from the French side. According to an
unsigned *mémoire* in the foreign office archives at Paris, "The
member of Congress who moved to demand from the President
information on this insult to the flag by the English, is a Mr. Otis,
a young man whom the government party counted on, and who in
1797 declaimed against France; but who, not being privy to the
ulterior views of the party chiefs, is an independent American in
his politics."

How to treat the changed policy of France became the most absorbing problem of this winter session. Federalists in general
counted on the publication of the XYZ dispatches so infuriating

the French government that it would declare war. The Directory resented having its venality exposed to the delighted laughter of Europe; but it realized that to declare war would throw the United States completely into the arms of England. So, instead of raising the price for peace, it seriously reviewed the causes of American indignation. Before Gerry came home, all letters of marque and reprisal to French corsairs in the Antilles had been canceled.

In the meantime, Dr. James Logan of Stenton, Pennsylvania, a wealthy Quaker and Republican, constituted himself a one-man peace mission. Cordially received by Talleyrand and some of the Directors, he assured them that in case of war no American would support France, and he claimed to have persuaded the Directory to lift an embargo on American naval vessels in French ports. The Federalists, including Otis, were furious with Logan for interfering, and would gladly have put him in jail; but that would have been ex post facto. So they had to content themselves with passing the so-called Logan Act, creating it a misdemeanor punishable by imprisonment to interfere with official diplomatic negotiations.[1] Otis became embroiled in the Logan business because his old college mate Richard Codman, and Joseph Woodward, his partner in Boston real estate, promoted Logan's mission in Paris, where they were speculating in *assignats* and confiscated estates of *émigrés*. Dr. Logan's *mémoire* to the Directory contained certain statements that the Federalists found seditious, such as "the true American Character" would "blaze forth" for Jefferson in the next presidential election if France would but show wisdom. Dr. Logan asserted that the *mémoire* was written by Otis's friend Codman, which Woodward denied, declaring that the doctor merely used Codman's clerk to copy it, and that the only person who altered the doctor's original text was Joel Barlow the Connecticut poet, another speculator then in Paris.

The question of how to receive these overtures became the sub-

[1] The Logan Act "for the Punishment of certain Crimes," of 30 Jan. 1799, is still in effect. It was appealed to in both world wars to check unofficial "doves," but seems to have been no deterrent in the 1960's to "everyone and his dog" talking to Ho or Mao or Kosygin in hope of bringing home an olive branch.

ject of great discussion among Federalists during the following
winter. In his annual address of 8 December 1798, President
Adams indicated that his mind was favorably inclined toward
meeting friendly advances halfway. This gave great umbrage to
the Hamiltonian faction, since an accommodation with France
would ruin their plans. Stephen Higginson, speaking for George
Cabot and the rest of the Essex Junto, wanted a headlong plunge
into the European political system and a British alliance, as the
only sure way to crush the American "Jacobins." Hamilton wrote
to Otis and other members of Congress, demanding a declaration
of war on France, a permanent standing army, and an attack on
Spanish Florida and Louisiana, which he intended to lead himself.

Talleyrand's overtures were sincere in that, wishing to avoid
open war, he had shifted tactics; but his end remained the same,
to gain time to acquire Louisiana from Spain. Even Thomas Jefferson, when he heard of the success of that policy in 1802, wrote,
"The day that France takes possession of New Orleans, . . . we
must marry ourselves to the British fleet and nation." Hamilton's
policy might now be regarded respectfully if Napoleon had not
seen fit, in 1803, to toss Louisiana to the United States "as a sultan
throws a purse of gold to a favorite." Nevertheless, Hamilton's
grand design was chimerical. The United States was no field for
the old-world tactics of foreign war to quell domestic discontent.
Well might Adams feel, as he wrote to Otis, "This man is stark
mad, or I am. He knows nothing of the character, the principles,
the feelings, the opinions and prejudices of this nation. If Congress
should adopt this system, it would produce an instantaneous insurrection of the whole nation from Georgia to New Hampshire."

ADAMS ASSERTS HIMSELF

Hamilton and the cabinet decided to treat Talleyrand's overtures
as insincere and urge Congress to declare war on France. They
counted as usual on the acquiescence of the President; for, in spite

of his peaceful message of 8 December, he permitted Timothy Pickering, the bitterly antigallican secretary of state, to issue a pungent exposé of French duplicity. Not long after, however, there suddenly dawned on John Adams the extent to which he had been "had" by the Hamiltonian junto in his cabinet: Pickering, McHenry and Wolcott. Convinced that the French really desired peace, and determined henceforth to be President in fact as well as in name, he sent to the Senate on 18 February 1799 a message that shattered Hamilton's dreams of glory. This message, which arrived like a missile out of a clear sky, was the nomination of William Vans Murray, minister to the Netherlands, as minister plenipotentiary to the French Republic.

A dramatic story of this announcement by Létombe, the French consul general at Philadelphia, went to Talleyrand in a dispatch. Here it is in translation:

> The debate at this moment was very brisk. The Whigs and the Tories [Republicans and Federalists] were highly animated. They were discussing a bill giving the President eventual authority to increase the army by 24 regiments of infantry. . . . The motion for the second reading of this bill had just been defeated by 45 votes against 37, and Mr. Otis was renewing discussion of a bill concerning the capture of French privateers by vessels freighted or belonging to citizens of the United States, when one of the members, informed by a Senator of what had just happened, notified the House that there was no more reason to work for this bill, since the President had just nominated a minister to the French Republic! The majority acted as if struck by a thunderbolt. The orator Otis, the friend and confidant of Adams, showed embarrassment, grew pale. The House adjourned, and is still adjourned today.

John Adams's move undoubtedly was right, but his manner made it difficult to accept. He had made this radical decision without consulting the cabinet, or anyone else. Hamilton and his powerful following smelled treachery. Words cannot describe the feelings of mingled rage, astonishment and disappointment with

which they received it. "Well may you be in affliction," wrote
Jonathan Mason to Otis from Boston;

> If you have any love of Country, you must feel at so gross a
> departure from principles, so gross a deriliction of position, & so
> gross a desertion of party. From being respectable in Europe,
> from having convinced Great Britain, & from having associated
> with all friends to Order, Property & Society, we must be content
> to sacrifice these advantages & once again to become soothers &
> suppliants for Peace, from a Gang of pityfull robbers, be by
> them despised & finally duped, without attaining in any degree
> the object of these sacrifices. . . . We are not in a situation to
> treat — We are not yet Nationally cloathed. Our Country &
> Govermt is yet assuming & accustoming themselves to National
> Features. Time is wanting to give these Features, stability.
> Great Britain well disposed, & France prostrate — we could creep
> along in our Navy, in our Army, in our Fortifications, in our
> Commerce — & all our permanent establishments, all of which
> would be opposed by the one or other of these nations, & ob-
> structed with success, were it not for the present irregular state of
> things in this Country & Europe.

John Adams, writing on that situation twenty-four years later
in a letter to Otis, recalled to him a conversation at his dinner
table a few days after the nomination of Murray:

> I had invited a small company of ten or a dozen gentlemen
> who had always professed to be my friends, among whom were
> yourself, Mr. Bayard of Delaware, and I think Mr. Sedgwick,
> it is not necessary to recollect any others. It was at the time
> when I had nominated an ambassador to France, a measure
> which produced a real anarchy in the government and infinite
> vexation to me. It was a *sombre diner,* but, unluckily, the sub-
> ject of the embassy to France was brought upon the tapis, I re-
> member not in what manner, or by whom. Mr. Bayard began
> to harangue upon the subject, and, with a dismal countenance,
> a melancholy air, and a Jeremiad tone, began to prophesy ill, as
> near as I can remember, in these words: "Ah! It is an unfortu-
> nate measure. We know not the consequences of it." And he
> went on in this whining strain, in a long harangue, till at last he

said "England would certainly be offended at it, they could not fail to take umbrage and they might declare war upon us."

Upon the maturest reflection, to this hour I am astonished that my patience held out so long. . . . I broke out assertingly upon the occasion, and I said, as nearly as I recollect, in these words or others of a similar import: "Mr. Bayard, I am surprised to hear you express yourself in this manner; would you prefer a war with France to a war with England, in the present state of the world; would you wish for an alliance with Great Britain, and a war with France? If you would, your opinions are totally different from mine." Bayard replied, "Great Britain is very powerful, her navy is very terrible." This put me out of all patience; I broke out, "I know the power of Great Britain, I have measured its omnipotence without treasure, without arms, without ammunition, and without soldiers or ships; I have braved and set at defiance all her power. In the negotiation with France we had done no more than we had a perfect right to do; she had no right, or color of right, to take offense at it, and if she did I would not regard it a farthing. For in a just and righteous cause I shall hold all her policy and power in total contempt." I remember that you, Mr. Otis, afterwards said to me you wondered I had been so severe upon Bayard, for Bayard was my friend; I answered you, I knew him to be my friend, and I knew myself to be his friend, but for those very reasons I used the greater freedom with him — certainly too great for the dignity of my station. But from my inmost soul, I cannot repent it to this day.[1]

Although the Federalists controlled the Senate, they dared not reject the nomination, conscious that public opinion would side with the President. But they extorted from him a compromise: to make Murray one of a commission of three, and not send them to

[1] Otis replied tactfully 12 March 1823, confirming everything that Adams remembered, and concluding, "I consider your great name and the worth of your public and private virtues to be the property of your Country, on which, being tenant in common, if I had the power (which I have not) I should not have the right to commit waste. It will never be my vocation to hold up smoked glasses between the eye of posterity and the softened radiance of the setting sun." A letter from Gov. John E. Howard, also present, describing this conversation, was issued as a broadside.

France until the Directory gave unequivocal assurances of receiving them properly. Adams, accordingly, nominated Governor Davie of North Carolina and Chief Justice Ellsworth as joint commissioners with Murray, and all three were confirmed by the Senate.

Otis's attitude on this occasion was ambiguous. He deplored Adams's action; yet his political sense taught him that the only course now open to the Federalist party was to follow the President. Any attempt to thwart him would render the rift in the party permanent and irreparable. He did his best to preserve harmony and gain adherents to the President's policy by writing a series of articles published in April 1799 under the heading "The Envoy," in *J. Russell's Gazette*. He admits that "respectable and patriotic characters" feel that "Gallic faith affords no basis for a safe or advantageous treaty," and prefer *bellum usque ad internecionem;* but public opinion would never support any such policy in the face of the French offer to negotiate. "In the opinion of many intelligent men," war should have been declared by Congress the previous year and, owing to this "fatal and impolitic omission, the popular zeal and enthusiasm" has subsided "for want of impulse." The only way to repair this error is to convince the people that no means of preserving peace has been neglected. The light and informal character of the French overtures has been taken, says Otis, as a proof of insincerity; but we should "put their sincerity to the touchstone more than once by taking them at their word." Our honor and dignity will not be impaired by the President's policy. England has twice instituted peace negotiations with France during the present war, with happy results on public opinion. "Can we make war with success, if we reject overtures apparently pacific?"

Had the friends of Hamilton followed this sound advice, the fatal split would have been averted; but they did not listen. The orthodoxy of Otis's Federalism had long been suspected by the inflexible gentlemen who composed the Essex Junto. Higginson

wrote to Pickering on 24 November 1799 that, at a dinner at
Jonathan Mason's new house on Beacon Hill, attended by himself,
Cabot and Fisher Ames, Otis, while professing to regard the President's action as unfortunate, "will deprecate and oppose anything
like a disapprobation of the measure; but has pledged himself not
to approve." Pickering put the worst possible construction on
Otis's course, ascribing his endeavors for party harmony to the
unworthy motive of place-hunting. He wrote to Higginson on 23
December that Otis had "two principal objects in view: to please
the President, & *merit his favour;* and *to acquire popularity.*" He
urged Higginson and all his "intelligent friends" to put the heat
on this "vain and ambitious" congressman by threatening "some
things more alarming than his present pursuits are alluring."
Pickering even believed that Otis "is, and for some time has been
the tool of ———[1] and his father, a miserable tale-bearer." Harry's
"insinuating address" and his father's "apparent simplicity" qual-
ify them "for their respective offices." Higginson replied that he
and Cabot could think of no means of putting pressure on Otis
except threatening to deny him a renomination for Congress, or
by persuading the Senate to reject any appointment he might receive from the President. And to do either would create "suspicion." One would think so indeed! Harry, apparently, remained
ignorant of Pickering's enmity, which may have been due to gossip
drifting around Philadelphia.

There exists a document which at first glance seems to confirm
these unflattering estimates of Otis's motives. It is a letter from
him to the President dated 21 February 1799, in which he requests
for himself the appointment of secretary to the Paris legation, "if
it could be accompanied with a provisional appointment to succeed the Minister at the Hague [Murray] in the event of his being
received at Paris." Otis, obviously, hoped to derive personal benefit from the change of policy, but this expectation did not last long.

[1] Name left blank in the manuscript; probably he meant Jefferson, who as President of the Senate spoke almost daily with Samuel A. Otis, the secretary.

The President refused him the desired appointment; and, as he remained loyal to Adams during the presidential election, we may fairly conclude that he acted from principle or, at least, a sense of political expediency, and from no expectation of getting a diplomatic job.

This is also evident from one of Otis's letters to John Rutledge. He observes that, since we never declared war on France or concluded an alliance with Great Britain, and since neither nation "loves us," and either may sacrifice our interests when it concludes peace, we had better come to terms with France at once. He only regrets that neither Ellsworth, Davie nor Murray knows French or is otherwise qualified to negotiate *à la Parisienne*. He hopes, however, that "they will not approach the Directory like Churchill's Pomposo and associates:

> Silent all three went in; about
> All three turned silent and came out."

John Adams did not immediately carry through his new policy. Instead of dismissing the Hamiltonian cabinet members and appointing others loyal to himself, he not only retained them in office but left them in charge of the government while he passed the spring and summer at Quincy. The result was a brief Hamiltonian restoration; and in May 1799, when a definite welcome to the new mission came from Talleyrand and the President ordered his secretary of state to make preparations for the mission's departure, Pickering procrastinated. He hoped that the victorious Archduke Charles of Austria and Marshal Suvorov of Russia would soon overthrow the Directory, restore the French monarchy, and preclude the necessity of negotiating with "Jacobins." Apparently Adams agreed, for he allowed the entire summer to flow by without further action. By October, after an absence of seven months from the seat of government, and also after the French had recovered their military ascendancy, President Adams hastened to Trenton (Philadelphia having been evacuated owing to yellow fever), reasserted his power, and on 3 November packed off Davie and Ellsworth to France in the frigate *United States*.

Henceforth the breach in the party was irreparable. Hamilton and Pickering were not the sort of men to maintain even nominal loyalty to a chief who thus spurned their advice and flouted their policy.

Sixth Congress

Otis was not nearly so active in this Congress as in the last. The novelty of political leadership had worn off, and his letters are full of anticipation of the approaching end to his congressional career. He and Harper as majority leaders were quietly superseded by John Marshall of Virginia. Otis was present at the opening session at Philadelphia on 2 December 1799, and wrote to Sally on the following day:

> Politically speaking, I believe the Session will be agreeable and harmonious. There appears nothing to quarrell about, and I think you will find less asperity in debate and more good-nature between the opposite parties than usual. Old Sedgwick is chosen Speaker, & much delighted with the appointment — We were however obliged to manage a little to secure this object.

As he suggested, the Federalists in the new Congress ceased to be aggressive. The negotiation with France was about to begin, and the majority took its cue from the President's sensible advice in his opening address: "However it may terminate, a steady perseverance in a system of national defence commensurate with our resources and the situation of our country is an obvious dictate of wisdom." Otis, as chairman of the committee on defense, endorsed this policy in a report of early January 1800. He recommended that the 3400 men already enlisted in the twelve new regiments be retained, since "the national honor and interest, in the present posture of affairs make it prudent and necessary to continue prepared for the worst event." As a concession to economy, he advised suspension of the recruiting service until the "approach of danger should compel the Government to resume it." But John Nicholas had already proposed a resolution to repeal the Army Act altogether. The debate, a lengthy one indeed, served as a sort of clearing house for political principles. From the one side we hear of the danger of invasion, the awful fate of Switzerland, Genoa, etc. (the list had grown appreciably longer since the day of Otis's maiden speech); from the other, the bugbear of a standing army, oppressive, expensive, and insulting to France. Democracy's latest acquisition from Virginia, John Randolph of Roanoke, in his shrill voice denounced the United States Army as "mercenaries" and a "handful of ragamuffins."

Otis's only reported speech during the debate was short but significant. He remarked:

> I confess I have indulged mournful presentiments of the effects to be expected from a new treaty. I foresee that, like other nations, we may be compelled to realize that the dangers of peace and amity are the most serious dangers. I know that attempts will be made to demolish the whole defensive fabric which we have erected, and to replunge us into that abyss of debility and inaction from which we shall never escape a second time. With these difficulties I have always thought our Government would be doomed to struggle whenever a treaty should be concluded with France, but I did not expect to see at this time the axe laid to the root of our whole system.

His "mournful presentiments" were well justified, since the history of the next eleven years showed that the American people preferred a foreign policy of "debility and inaction" to the Federalist policy of defense and reprisal.

Nicholas's resolution was finally rejected by the decisive vote of 60 to 39, in favor of Otis's proposal to suspend enlistments. And on 11 January 1800 Otis wrote to his wife:

We buried this baby, last evening, and though the debate was long and animated and your prating husband speechified an hour, there was less acrimony and personal allusion; & in short more decency and attention to feelings than I have ever known on a similar occasion. I am glad it is finished, as it is the most important question that will be agitated; and the only pitched battle that will be fought — and such is the expenditure of ammunition & force that none but slight skirmishes will probably ensue.

If anyone is under the delusion that the present congressional practice of frittering away election year by making political capital is a modern invention, let him read the debates of the Sixth Congress. The Republican party threw out a net for political martyrs and made an excellent catch of bogus ones, who served equally well the purpose of convincing ignorant voters that the Federalists were savage tyrants. Thomas Nash (alias Jonathan Robbins and several other names) was the leader of this noble army; the magic of his name secured countless votes for Jefferson. He was an Irishman accused of murder on a British vessel, who escaped to the United States. His extradition was demanded by the British government and granted by the President, after a claim that Nash had made to American citizenship had been proved false. Concerning this dispute, Otis wrote on 1 March 1800:

> Our Demos are sick of their attempt to inculpate the Executive for his conduct in reference to the pirate Robbins. They wish to postpone or rather to evade the enquiry, but we hold them to it and it will occupy next week. We have begun upon the "ways & means," & when the bills relating to these are passed, I shall consider the main business of the session finished, and hope that three weeks will be sufficient for these objects.

Other details of congressional business are given in Harry's pleasant letters to Sally, one of which indicates that his devotion to her had become the subject of congressional banter — 8 February 1800:

You will perceive by the papers that I have offered a resolution to the house for adjourning the first monday in april. Some of my friends propose to amend it by adding "Provided Mrs. Otis dont come here before that time." . . . I still persist in my intention to be home from the first to the 15 april, "although the heathen may rage and the people imagine vain things."

13 February:

My resolution to adjourn 1st Monday in april, to my surprise passed our house by a large majority. . . . It is my present design to leave them the first week in april. Genl Lee[1] says that if Congress get away in all april he shall tell you when he sees you that you have saved the U. S. thirty thousand dollars at least!

Apparently the resolution to adjourn did not pass the Senate, for on 22 February Otis writes:

Whether they adjourn in april or not, Nicholas & myself have agreed to *pair off* between the 1st and 10th of that month. An event happened yesterday, which saves a full week at least. The Bankrupt bill passed the house by a majority of one yesterday *without debate*. I have not leisure now to inform you how this happened, but so it is, and it will undoubtedly pass the Senate. It is a great important political measure, — I had no idea of its succeeding.

The Bankruptcy Bill, a favorite measure of Otis, had failed at the last Congress. Sedgwick wrote that it was important "as well in a commercial as in a political view," since it was likely to gain Federalist voters among the "discontented." It was an attempt to supersede discordant state definitions of bankruptcy by a nation-wide law. As such it was disliked by state-rights Republicans and repealed in 1803. Otis again promoted a federal bankruptcy law when United States senator.

Throughout this session the air was full of rumors regarding the Federalist presidential nomination. From the moment that John

---

[1] Henry ("Light Horse Harry") Lee, Federalist member from Virginia.

Adams delivered his blow to Hamilton's policy, right-wing Federalists decided on his fall. A letter from Theodore Sedgwick to Timothy Pickering on 22 December 1799 indicates that Otis was already cognizant of this plan, and intended to do his best to thwart it:

> In a mixed company, at Mr. Tilghman's Mr. [Otis] declared that at the next election, whoever might be associated with Mr. Adams, the electors of Massachusetts would not give their votes uniformly, for fear the election of Mr. Adams would, thereby, be endangered. This declaration which a gentleman has since told me he has repeated to him, as far as Mr. [Otis] may be deemed an authority is of the most mischievous kind, and, destroying all means of confidence or concert, will insure, with absolute certainty, the election of the man we dread, to, perhaps, the office of Vice President.

Timothy Pickering was a fanatic. With him, politics and religion were the same thing — a struggle between Good which must be defended, and Evil which must be crushed. The social structure of eighteenth-century New England and the principles of Federalism were the Good; French philosophy and democracy the Evil. He recognized no rules of the game in politics, for politics were to him more than a game; and his zeal to conquer the powers of darkness embodied in the Republican party led him to unworthy intrigues and treasonable correspondence with no consciousness of wrongdoing. On this occasion, Pickering disclaimed Otis's imputations of his heading an "oligarchical faction," but passed out the hint that Ellsworth and Pinckney would be better presidential candidates than Adams and Pinckney.

Thus, Otis's fears for the renomination of Adams were well founded. Hamilton and the Essex Junto were casting about for some candidate to support against the President. John Adams was the only party leader possessing genuine popularity, and his peace policy pleased the mass of voters. It would be a difficult matter to explain to them why he should be superseded.

CHAPTER IX

The Election of 1800–1801

AET. 35

POLITICAL MANEUVERS

IN THE EARLY MONTHS of 1800 the Federalists were talking about ditching Adams for President in favor of Oliver Ellsworth, as Pickering suggested. But a party nominating caucus at Philadelphia in early May 1800 compromised. It agreed that each Federalist elector vote for John Adams and Charles Cotesworth Pinckney, with the understanding that the former should be President, and the latter, Vice President. Hamilton's friends nonetheless continued their intrigue to bring in Pinckney over Adams's head.

Otis at the end of March had paired off with Nicholas, agreeably to his promise to Sally, and returned to Boston. An early departure from Philadelphia enabled him to take care that the Massachusetts Federalists obtained full benefit of their local majority. At that period there was no uniformity in choosing presidential electors. In some states they were chosen by the legislature; in others, on a general ticket by the voters (the uniform practice today); in others, by the voters in districts, like congressmen. Virginia had employed the district method so far, but when the congressional elections of 1798 made it likely that at least five districts would choose Federalist electors, the Republican majority in the legislature abolished the district system and provided for choice by general ticket. It therefore behooved Federalist states to follow the same plan, in order similarly to exclude the Republican minorities within their borders from representation in the electoral college. In Massachusetts, for instance, a continuance of the traditional district method would have given Jefferson at least two votes. Otis and the other Federalist congressmen from Massachusetts wrote a significant letter on that subject on 31 January 1800, addressed to the speaker of the Massachusetts house of representatives and to the president of the state senate. After describing the plan of the Republicans "to democratize . . . the state legislature" and obtain an "antifederal" President, they remark:

> In this critical state of things we feel that it is very important to guard against *one* antifederal vote from Massachusetts; for one vote may turn the election.
> Whether this is to be done by choosing at large thro' the Committees,[1] or by choosing by the Legislature, or by uniting two or more districts for choosing, or in some other mode the wisdom of the Legislature will determine. We presume not to determine the mode, but only to suggest the danger which we apprehend and which we in this place, and in our present employment, are perhaps better circumstanced to observe than our friends in Massachusetts can be. Excuse us for suggesting these ideas; our anxiety for the event of the election must be our apology.

Since the next general court, to be elected in the spring of 1800, would decide, Otis did his best to bring out the full Federalist vote by making a pungent speech on the evening before the state election. The result did not reassure him. The Federalist candidate for governor, Caleb Strong, won by a majority of only one hundred votes. To allow the people to choose presidential electors by a general ticket, under those circumstances, would be to run the risk of total defeat — as actually happened in 1804. The legislature therefore decided to appoint the electors itself. This method, then practiced in five other states, was perfectly legal; but by depriving the people of a privilege they had formerly enjoyed, it aroused indignation and cost the Federalists dear.

The month of May 1800 brought important political events. In

---

[1] Meaning, probably, to use the Federalist caucus committee to nominate a general slate.

New York the Democrats captured the state government, whose legislature chose electors, thus assuring the twelve votes of that state for Jefferson and Burr. John Adams came to the tardy determination to reorganize his cabinet. He forced McHenry to resign on 6 May. Pickering, whom also he requested to resign, refused because he considered that "several matters of importance" made his continuance in office essential for the public welfare! Adams then dismissed him. Pickering disappeared into the wilds of northern Pennsylvania where a land grant was his only means of livelihood. The Massachusetts Federalists missed him so deeply that they took up a subscription to purchase enough of his land to enable him to return to Essex County and reënter politics. Otis's name is conspicuously absent from the list of subscribers. So far as he was concerned, it would have been better for party and country to let "Tim Pick" live out his life in the Pennsylvania wilderness.

With the breakup of the Hamiltonian cabinet cabal (Wolcott, too, had resigned) the adherents of Hamilton and Adams commenced open hostilities, forgetting that their divisions were Jefferson's strength. The Hamiltonians bent their energies to securing the election of Pinckney. It was a miserable policy for, conscious as its authors were of Adams's popularity, they dared not avow their object but sought to attain it by backstairs intrigue such as tampering with state legislatures which chose presidential electors. They relied on the expectation that the Republican South Carolina legislature would cast its vote for Jefferson and favorite son Pinckney, as in 1797. But Pinckney refused to lend his sanction to this shabby betrayal of his running-mate. Hamilton made a journey to Boston in June, stirring things up en route by imprudent speeches, to persuade leaders in the general court to appoint electors pledged to "knife" Adams. In vain the Federalist press attempted to conceal the schism. Some of Hamilton's friends were disgusted. James McHenry considered his party's conduct "tremulous, timid, feeble, deceptive & cowardly. They write private letters. To whom? To each other. But they do nothing to give a proper direction to the public mind."

We search in vain for any indication of steps taken by Otis and other Adams men to thwart their opponents. A rumor reached the South to the effect that "lukewarm Federalists and Adams's private friends," including Otis, Samuel Dexter, Judge Cushing of the Supreme Court, and Elbridge Gerry, were pressuring New England electors to drop Pinckney in order to counteract the extra votes he might obtain in South Carolina. This rumor produced a frantic letter from Robert Goodloe Harper to Otis, begging him in the name of party harmony to see that Adams and Pinckney were voted for equally, and assuring him that there would be no desertion of Adams in the South. The Bostonian, in reply, insisted that no intention was entertained of depriving Pinckney of a full vote in New England.

In a letter to Rutledge of 25 August 1800, Otis expressed typical Federalist pessimism as to the election and the future of democracy:

> My calculations in regard to the Presidential Election are by no means sanguine, though I believe the Federal interest will be perfectly secure in New England. I am forcibly impressed with a belief that the tide of our politics & public affairs is changing, & that the popular current which in governments like ours always sets strong will for *a time* overflow its banks & bear down opposition. The love of change, the *mens novitatis avida* is stronger and more natural than the love of system, & considering that the views and struggles of faction are not less daring & strenuous than they have been in all other republics, & that our claim of universal suffrage removes so many obstacles and legalises so many treasons; the wonder with me is and always has been that the sovreign people have not long since been excited to revolutionary movements. I am no stranger to the ordinary reasons assigned for this forbearance on the part of their majesties, and that they are generally deemed vastly considerate and *the most enlightened* upon earth. This is a very sweet smelling incense which flattery offers to vanity and folly at the shrine of falsehood. *Mais nous verrons.*

Adams himself threw discretion to the winds and inveighed against the Essex Junto "like one possessed." The opposition press naturally did all in its power to fan the flames, and nourished a suggestion that the President was seeking Republican support. The Philadelphia *Aurora* printed a foolish letter that Adams had written several years before, accusing the Pinckney brothers of British influence because they had been educated at Christ Church, Oxford. Hamilton published a severe arraignment of Adams's character, defending the Pinckneys and himself; the President's friends retorted in kind; and the campaign of 1800 closed with the Federal party turned into a Donnybrook Fair, the Republicans as amused onlookers egging on the fight, while Jefferson and Burr captured the presidential prizes.

Jefferson and Burr each received 73 electoral votes, Adams 65, and Pinckney 64. Hamiltonian maneuvers were thwarted by one Federalist elector from Rhode Island throwing away his second vote, and by a second refusal of Charles Cotesworth Pinckney to accept the vote of South Carolina if coupled with Jefferson. So striking an instance of loyalty amid the intrigues, lies and petty bickerings of this campaign is refreshing. If Rhode Island had stood firm and Pinckney had received the eight electoral votes from South Carolina, he and Jefferson would have been tied with 73 each; and there is no doubt that the House would then have elected Pinckney.

Yet Adams and Pinckney were defeated by no accidental or temporary causes. The same wave that swept Jefferson into office swept the Federalist majority out of Congress. Had Otis again aspired to be member of the House, he would have been disappointed, for Josiah Quincy, his successor as Federalist nominee, lost badly. It seems difficult at first to account for the rapid falling-off of Federalist popularity since 1798. In the Sixth Congress the majority had been moderate and discreet; but the source of the Federalists' former popularity lay in the fact that they, in marked contrast to the Republicans, stood for national honor and integrity against foreign insult and aggression. By November 1800 the French peril had passed, and the passions and enthusiasms of 1798 had evaporated. Fruitless sedition prosecutions and the financial cost of a spirited foreign policy had also made enemies for the party. When we consider all these factors, and the disgraceful bickerings and intrigues within the party itself, the wonder is not that Thomas Jefferson was elected President but that John Adams ran so close a second.

On 1 October 1800, the very day after Murray, Ellsworth and Davie signed the Convention of Morfontaine with France, Talleyrand signed with Spain the secret treaty of San Ildefonso, ceding Louisiana to France. Exactly what Hamilton feared, and had hoped to prevent by war.

SIXTH CONGRESS CONCLUDED

Otis's last session in Congress as a representative from Massachusetts began on 30 November 1800, after the popular verdict on his party's performance had been rendered. In the meantime the Federal Government had removed to Washington. Harry, as we have seen in Chapter VII, did not think the new capital too bad — for he had Sally with him and his father had obtained a snug little house in Georgetown. But few of either party shared his views. No room could be found in the half-finished Capitol for the House of Representatives, which was therefore relegated to a temporary brick building disrespectfully known as the Oven, attached to the south wing. It was kept from falling in on the assembled congressmen only by strong temporary shorings.

This third session of the Sixth Congress is of peculiar interest not only for the election of the President by the House, as we shall see, but for the curious spectacle of Federalists maintaining and even extending their system in spite of the rebuke administered in the recent elections. "We shall profit of our short-lived majority," wrote John Rutledge, "and do as much good as we can before the end of this session." President Adams, in his opening address, advised Congress to maintain the navy, advice not needed by Federalists, nor heeded by their Republican rivals. Otis in a long speech expressed his surprise and disapproval of the semi-annual Democratic proposal to reduce the army; he also "hoped his friends would do nothing that might be construed into a death-bed repentance of a conduct that constituted their glory and their pride."

In January of 1801, Otis was appointed chairman of a committee to report on the condition of the treasury, an assignment very important to the party in view of the charges of extravagance and peculation preferred against Secretary Wolcott by the scurrilous Philadelphia *Aurora*. In the course of the investigation there broke out at the treasury building a fire which, according to the Democratic press, was set by Wolcott himself to cover his misdeeds! Otis wrote regarding this matter on 29 January:

> The infamous suggestions to the disadvantage of Wolcot, ought to be punished with any thing but death. They are atrocious and as unfounded as the pretensions of the authors to honor and veracity. Wolcot had done with the office and left it. The examination of the state of the Treasury had been compleated, and in fact no papers are burnt of any consequence except those of Mr Francis and Mr Whelen, in the destruction of which it is palpable Wolcot could have no interest.
>
> The report of our Committee is highly honorable to the Secretary and was *unanimous,* Nicholas, Nicholson & Stone, being *three* of the Committee. This will set all matters right.

It did. Congress exonerated Wolcott, and Otis acquired esteem for the three Republicans, especially Nicholas.

Next, Congress passed a bill for extending and strengthening the federal judiciary. This Judiciary Act of 1801, increasing the number of federal courts, may be looked upon as the last word of the Federalist system. The Republicans regarded it as a scheme to create life offices for their enemies, and repealed it as soon as they could; but the object was fundamentally constitutional. Federalist leaders wished to stiffen the judiciary as an essential branch of the Federal Government and the strongest barrier to state interference. Nevertheless, sundry deserving Federalists hoped to profit. Otis's mail became flooded with applications for the new circuit judge-ships. John Lowell, his former patron, already a district judge, hoped to be promoted, and was. George Richards Minot, known as "The American Sallust" for his history of Shays's Rebellion, mod-estly proposed to receive the district judgeship left vacant by Lowell, to retain his present office of judge of probate, and to "devote any leisure he might have, to literary pursuits, particularly in the line of History." Otis himself aspired to be solicitor general of Massachusetts, but Governor Strong gave that place to another. His letter to Sally, telling of his disappointment, follows:

Washington 4 Feby 1801

"Midst chains and bolts the active soul is free
And flies unfettered Cavendish to thee."

Now if Lord Russell's soul could flie out of jail to the embraces of his friends, it is not extraordinary that mine should escape from the hubbub of a debate about the bill for governing this city to my dearest friend, the companion of my life and the partner of all my joys. It is in this situation now I snatch a moment to reassure you of my own welfare, and what is always more material, to enquire after yours. . . .

My hopes of office are at an end. . . . I was prepared for it, and care not a pinch of snuff for the result. It only confirms my opinion, that I must depend on my own exertions, without favor or affection places or promotion for my own prosperity & the advancement of my family. . . .

You have done well to send for Rush,[1] who I hope however

1 Sally was then at Philadelphia, at the Harrisons'. If she escaped being bled by Dr. Rush, she was lucky — bleeding was his favorite remedy for every complaint from a cold in the head to yellow fever.

will not bleed you, as I am sure that gentle medicine will answer every purpose. . . .

Your affectionate H. G. OTIS

Since the Otises, like other old Whig families, expected to "feed at the public crib," Harry tried another line, with some success. He wrote to Sally on 18 February 1801:

> The President has this day nominated me to be attorney for the United States in the district of Massachusetts. This is the same place which was offered to me by Genl Washington and declined for the *honor* of coming to Congress. It is analogous to the offices of Attorney & Solicitor General, but more eligible for me as I shall be stationary in *Boston*. One circumstance *against* it is I shall hold it during the Pleasure of the President, and though his friends say he will not change any officers but the *heads of departments,* yet I presume in the course of a twelvemonth he will *oust them all.*

As he predicted, Otis's tenure of this office was brief. His father, whom Jefferson did not attempt to remove as secretary of the Senate, pleaded with the new President to retain his son; but Jefferson, considering it no doubt a "midnight appointment," removed Harry before the year was out.

CONGRESS ELECTS JEFFERSON

The most important duty of the House of Representatives in the Sixth Congress was to choose a President. Owing to the smooth working of the Republican machine, and the clumsy method of electoral voting then prescribed by the Constitution, Jefferson and Burr were tied for the presidency with 73 votes each. The duty of choosing between them now fell on the House of Representatives, members voting by states, each state having one vote and a majority of states being necessary for a choice.

Aaron Burr, by Gilbert Stuart.

This exigency had been contemplated by the Federalists since August, and by January the party had decided to promote the election of Aaron Burr over Thomas Jefferson. So great was their dread and detestation of the leader of the Republican party that "little Burr," as Otis called him, seemed less evil to those ignorant of his true character. Even many who knew his unprincipled nature favored him from the unworthy motive of spite, and the expectation that Burr could be kept "right" by influence. Among those who shared these opinions were Theophilus Parsons and Judge Samuel Sewall of the Supreme Court of Massachusetts, who wrote as much to Harrison Gray Otis; and Otis himself, who wrote to Alexander Hamilton 17 December 1800:

> Dear Sir:
> There exists the strongest probability that the electoral votes are equally divided between Messrs. Jefferson and Burr. . . . The question now is, in what *mode shall* the friends of the federal government take advantage of this casualty? Can any terms be obtained from Mr. Burr favorable to the true interest of the country, and is he a man who will adhere to terms when stipulated? Is it advisable to attempt a negotiation with him — and in what manner and through what channel shall it be conducted? We are inclined to believe that some advantage may be derived from it, but few of us have a personal acquaintance with Mr. Burr. It is *palpable* that to elect him would be to cover the opposition with *chagrin,* and to sow among them the seeds of a morbid division. But whether in any event he would act with the friends to the Constitution, or endeavor to redeem himself with his own party by the violence of his measures and the overthrow of the Constitution, is a doubt which you may assist us to resolve. Your local situation and personal acquaintance with these men and the state of parties, enables you to give an opinion upon a subject in which all the friends to the country have a common interest, and if you can venture to repose your confidence in me, I will most solemnly pledge myself that your sentiments shall be reserved within my own breast, or communicated only to those whom you may designate. Should our expectation be realized, which we shall know in a day or two, is it ad-

visable to send a messenger to New-York to confer with *friends there,* or attempt to bring Mr. Burr here? What should be the outlines of an agreement with him, and (alas! it is a difficult question,) what security can be devised for his adherence to it?

I am anxious to act correctly and judiciously. It would be distressing to omit or misdirect an effort which might be beneficial to the country, or preserve the Constitution, and I presume that honor and duty will sanction every endeavor to preserve it, even by an ineligible instrument. The treaty is before the Senate, and I believe will be found another chapter in the book of humiliation. . . .

Hamilton's clear view penetrated this sophistry. By bitter experience he knew, through and through, the character of the man by whose hand he was destined to die. He perceived the lasting disgrace that his party would incur by elevating such a man to the presidency. But his wise counsel was not heeded. Shortly before the election went to the House, a caucus of Federalists decided to support Burr; only four members, not including Otis, opposed. It was decided to commence balloting on 11 February, immediately after the formal count of the electoral vote, and to continue without adjournment until a decision.

No bargain was made; Aaron Burr, to give the devil his due, acted honorably and kept aloof from the intrigue. Suppose the balloting had ended in a tie on 4 March; would the Federalists have usurped the presidency by legislative act? They were accused of so intending and certain hotheads did say or do things to justify this apprehension. Judge Sewall, for instance, wrote to Otis, "It is possible that an election at this time . . . may be wholly prevented. This is most desirable." But nobody in Congress admitted anything of the sort. Otis's letters to his wife, his confidante in political matters, mention no such scheme; they indicate that he expected the election to terminate in the constitutional manner.

In his letter of 4 February, most of which has already been quoted, he says, "It is probable that we shall have no choice the first time of balloting and if the Federalists are all firm, we shall carry our point." But in a letter dated on the 9th, from Congress Hall, he is not so sure of electing Burr:

> . . . We are at this instant debating the rules of proceeding at the approaching election. . . . In this event you see we are to be shut up for God knows how long, though it cannot be longer than the third of march. Our Committee Room must be garnished with beefsteaks, and a few Turkey Carpets to lie upon would not be amiss.
>
> I do not believe however the obstinacy of parties will endure beyond the second day, but I cannot say who will give way.

On 11 February the electoral votes were counted, and the tie between Jefferson and Burr officially announced. Balloting immediately commenced in the House, and that afternoon Otis wrote to Sally:

> We are in Conclave and in a Snow Storm. The votes have been counted in Senate & no choice. We have balloted in the house *seven* times. Thus it stands —
>
> $$\left.\begin{array}{lr} \text{For Jefferson} & 8 \\ \text{For Burr} & 6 \\ \text{Divided} & 2 \end{array}\right\} \text{States}$$
>
> We have agreed not to adjourn, but we have suspended balloting for *one* hour to eat a mouthful. Perhaps we shall continue here a week. No conjecture can be formed how it will terminate, but if we are true to ourselves *we* shall prevail. Poor Nicholson is in the *Committee* Room abed with a fever. It is a chance that this kills him. I would not thus expose myself for any President on Earth, but being in good health & spirits, . . . I have no objection to staying here all night.
>
> I am one of the Tellers and so constantly employed that I cannot write to you at large.

On 15 February:

> The last week has fled rapidly, in spite of the disagreeable and still unfinished business in which we have been engaged, and

Sally Foster Otis, by Gilbert Stuart.

my heart beats higher and my impatience increases as the day
of my departure approaches. If the election should be made,
of which I believe there is little doubt, in a day or two, I shall
probably be off by the 1st of march at the farthest. I shall wait
only for two bills to be passed, the one making the annual appropriation for the support of Government and the other relative to the navy and leave them to wind off the end of the skain.
Yes my beloved angel, with you I shall retire from this scene
of anxiety and bustle, to enjoy the rational and I hope permanent comforts which we have the means of commanding, &
remain a silent spectator of the follies and confusion, of the
strife and licentiousness incident to all popular governments,
and to ours in a most eminent degree.

These letters certainly do not suggest that Otis was conspiring
to prolong the choice over 3 March, and place a Federalist usurper
in the presidential chair.

On 16 February Bayard decided that no more votes could possibly be secured for Burr. He and a few others, who saw no use
continuing the struggle, decided to obtain what they could from
Jefferson before bowing to the inevitable. Samuel Smith told
Bayard that Jefferson had declared that he "considered the prosperity of our commerce as essential to the interests of the nation,"
that the navy should be increased "in progress with the increase of
the nation," and that he "did not think that such officers as the
collectors of the port at Philadelphia and Wilmington" (mentioned
as examples) "ought to be dismissed . . . except in cases where they
had made improper use of their offices." These assurances having
been given, Bayard announced them to the Federalist caucus on
the morning of 17 February after the thirty-fifth ballot had also
been 8-6-2; nine states being necessary for a choice. Jefferson's
assurances satisfied enough Federalists to break the deadlock. On
the next ballot Bayard, to whom the credit for this happy issue is
chiefly due, and several other Federalists, handed in blanks, allowing Thomas Jefferson to be elected President of the United States
by ten states to four.

The Fourth of March 1801 ends an epoch in Otis's life, as in that of his party; it marks the suspension of his career, at the age of thirty-five, as a national statesman. Whether we regard the transfer of national power from Federalists to Republicans as a blessing or a curse, we must admit that the defeated party, in organizing the Federal Government and administering it for twelve years, had laid down a system of administration and followed principles of government by which the Union has been preserved. To quote a contemporary prophecy of Robert Goodloe Harper:

> Names may change; the denominations of parties may be altered or forgotten; but the principles on which the federalists have acted must be adopted, their plans must be substantially pursued, or the government must fall in pieces; for those narrow maxims which apply properly to small communities, and on which speculative men sometimes found their theories, will ever prove in practice wholly inadequate to the government of a great nation.

The "Virginia Dynasty" that followed John Adams found this to be perfectly true, despite their contrary theories.

CHAPTER X

Harry Otis, Friend and Host

1801–1817, AET. 36–52

HARRY AND SALLY

HARRY OTIS the husband, father, friend and host, is even more interesting than the Honorable Harrison Gray Otis, politician and statesman. Among citizens of all classes in Federalist Boston no one was more beloved and respected than he; even in Whig Boston, Daniel Webster never supplanted him in popularity. He owed this widespread admiration more to his well-rounded, vigorous personality than to any outstanding qualities as a public figure. Josiah Quincy, son of Otis's contemporary of the same name, wrote: "Men of the stamp of William Sullivan and his friend Otis were more conspicuous for what they were, than for what they did. They were predominant men, and gave the community its quality, shaping, as if by divine right, its social and political issues." Yet Quincy himself despaired of transmitting Otis's personality by pen and ink. "I wish it were in my power," he wrote in his diary, "to preserve for posterity some traces of the wit, brilliancy, eloquence, and urbanity of Harrison Gray Otis; for when he is gone there is no man who can make good his place in Society."

The relationship between Harry and Sally is the brightest, loveliest aspect of their lives. Her chief concerns were the happiness of her husband and the care and education of their children; she followed, though unconsciously, the pattern of the *haute bourgeoisie* of France. To their old age, in correspondence and in conversation, this couple employed the charming, loving formulas of the eighteenth century. "Dear angel," he wrote to her from Washington shortly before the turn of the century, "but a few weeks and I come to you; never (unless forced by necessity), never again to quit your side for distant & tedious employments. It is my firm resolution not to serve another Congress. . . . If health & inclination should render it eligible for you to accompany me, & suitable accommodations can be procured, . . . I may take you to Washington for one season; but I certainly will never go there without you."

He kept his promise; and when elected to the United States Senate seventeen years later, Sally came with him. She not only directed the Otis household, whether in Boston, Philadelphia or Washington, not only bore him eleven children; she also understood and encouraged her husband, applied her charm to his friends, read with him the books that he liked, cared for him in his frequent attacks of gout or arthritis. She had the quality that the French call *tendresse,* a humorous appreciation of people and sympathy with their shortcomings. Although like Harry she abhorred French politics, she loved French culture, manners and fashion; and like the French she accommodated her dress to advancing age, always retaining a neatness and simplicity which gave her both dignity and elegance.[1]

Harry appeared at his best in family life. In the early nineteenth century it was usual for parents to impress their children that an awful gulf existed between them and their elders. "Honored Papa" and "Honored Mamma" were the proper titles by which to address a parent, and the formalities of a court were exacted in the daily life of the household. With the Otis family it was otherwise. Harrison Gray Otis, like Squire Bracebridge, made each child feel that home was the best place on earth. They

---

[1] When Mrs. Austin Wadsworth, whose family purchased No. 45 Beacon Street after Otis's death, took me over the house around 1910, there were still in the attic the long, coffin-shaped trunks in which Sally Otis's dresses came from Worth or some other couturier in Paris. My grandmother told me that Mrs. Wharton was quite right in stating in one of her novels that the Boston and New York ladies who imported their clothes from Paris had to wait a year or two before wearing them, as the fashion would seem *outré* if they wore them at once.

in turn adored him; and not one gave his parents any unusual trouble or suffered from any incurable malady of mind or body. Except for the drowning of the first Allyne, there were no domestic tragedies at 45 Beacon Street until 1833, and the two youngest boys were born there. These two, the second Allyne and George, were spoiled by their parents, but that cannot be said of their elders.

When absent from home, Harry was apt to send his children presents, mingled with parental admonition. Sally and Sophia, aged fourteen and ten, received each a pair of earrings from Philadelphia. In his covering letter, Papa remarked that he would not say that the young ladies of New York and Philadelphia were prettier than those of Boston, but they were very careful *never* to appear with dirty teeth or fingernails!

The life the Otises led differed completely from that of New England country towns so well described in Harriet Beecher Stowe's *Oldtown Folks*. Nor did they fit into the "proper Bostonian" cliché. Harry and Sally comprehended the most attractive characteristics of the society into which they were born, holdovers from the courts of the colonial governors; and in that society few puritanic traits survived. Although they abandoned the harsh faith of their fathers, they never became irreligious or agnostic; many joined the Episcopal Church, but most, under the guidance of liberal Congregational clergymen, became Unitarians. The Otises belonged to the Brattle Street Church, which John Adams described as the "politest" in Boston, under four successive liberal ministers: J. S. Buckminster, Edward Everett, John G. Palfrey and Samuel K. Lothrop. In taste and manners the Boston Federalist aristocracy were closer to southern gentlemen than to their own country neighbors. When William Wirt, the distinguished lawyer and writer of Richmond, visited Boston, he was astonished to find that his preconceived notions of Yankee society must be cast aside. "This is the most hospitable place in the world," he wrote to Judge Cabell. "Otis has been twice with me, pressing me to dine with him. . . . I think the people of Boston amongst the most agreeable in the United States. . . . I say they are as warm-hearted, as kind, as frank, as truly hospitable as the Virginians themselves. In truth, they are Virginian in all the essentials of character. . . . Would to Heaven the people of Virginia and Massachusetts knew each other better!"

Would indeed that they had! If the gentlemen of Virginia had not "gone a-whoring" after strange gods, they and the gentry of New England and New York might have prevented three wars and solved the slavery problem without fratricide.

At the prime of life Harry Otis was slightly above the average height, well proportioned, with dark brown hair, sparkling, dark blue eyes, a rather broad face, a Roman nose and a florid complexion. His personal appearance, combined with his gracious charm of manner, gave him distinction without stiffness or pomposity. Contemporaries always described his appearance as "elegant" — by which they meant that he dressed with care and fastidiousness at a period when these qualities were not common among American gentlemen. Elder statesmen of New England, refusing any concession to "Jacobin" fashions, continued to wear cocked hats and knee breeches well into the nineteenth century; but Harry always dressed in the latest fashion. Other Federalists were careless and slovenly; Chief Justice Parsons, for instance, returned from a week's circuit wearing, one on top of the other, the seven shirts with which his wife had provided him at the start. Of Otis it is related that he once met on the street a married couple of his acquaintance as the lady was arranging the shirt ruffles of her untidy spouse. "There — look at Mr. Otis's bosom!" said she, pointing to his immaculate linen. "Madam," said Otis with one of his best bows, "if your husband could look within my bosom, he would die of jealousy."

The secret of Otis's popularity lay in his tact, affability, consideration for others, and a natural courtesy that came from the heart. To enumerate his circle of loyal friends would take pages. The fact that he formed as warm friendships among men of the southern and middle states as among his fellow Bostonians was significant. It was impossible for him ever to embrace the extreme brand of New England Federalism affected by the Essex Junto and the "River Gods" of Connecticut. No matter how great the provocation, he could never bring himself to the belief that disunion might be preferable to union.

Enemies Otis had, as any man with a particle of backbone who took part in politics must have had, but he looked on mankind with none of that sour malignity which appears in the writings of puritanical colleagues like Tim Pickering. Considering the political bitterness of that era, his correspondence is remarkably free from illiberal reflections on men and motives. Joseph Story, however, he held suspect for many years on account of his early attachment to Jefferson. After the death of Chief Justice Marshall, someone in conversation said he hoped that President Jackson would say unto this learned judge, as Pharaoh did unto Joseph, "Thou shalt be ruler over my house." "Joseph, indeed! Why, yes, an excellent comparison," snorted Otis. "Pray, was anything said about his coat of many colors?"

THE ADAMS RELATIONSHIP

It was impossible for Otis, with his sunny nature, to carry on one of those lifelong political feuds which were meat and drink to some of his contemporaries. His relationship with John Quincy Adams came the nearest. No two gentlemen could have been more temperamentally unlike: Otis, warm, tactful and pleasure-loving; Adams, cold, tactless, conscientious and, above all, an Adams. "What a queer family!" Otis wrote of them in his old age, apropos of Charles Francis Adams's entry into politics. "I think them *all* (beginning with the grandsire) varieties in a peculiar species of our race exhibiting a combination of talent, & good moral character, with passions and prejudices calculated to defeat their own objects

& embarrass their friends, that would puzzle La Bruyère to describe & which has no Prototype in Shakespeare or Molière."

John Quincy Adams seems to have been under the delusion that
Otis looked upon him as a rival, and a block to his political advancement — "an adder in his path" as he expressed it in Biblical
language. But there is no trace in Otis's writings of any such
feeling. The first break between them occurred when Adams
voted for Jefferson's embargo and joined the Republican party.
Their fathers were old and intimate friends, but during the stormy
years that followed, the clans of Otis and Adams ceased personal
intercourse. The following letter from Abigail Adams to her son,
when minister to Great Britain, describes the characteristic manner
in which Otis brought about a reconciliation:

Quincy, Aug. 27, 1816

My dear Son . . .

In this still calm, and political pause, I must entertain you
with domestic occurrences, one of which is a Family visit,
which we received a fortnight since from Mr W Foster, your
old neighbor,[1] (who lost his Lady about two months since,)
accompanied by Mrs A Otis[2] and daughter, Mr H G Otis
Lady and daughter and son; who all came in a Body to take
tea with us. This visit has been long in contemplation: Mrs A
Otis was commissioned to inquire, if your Father would like
to receive the visit? to which a candid reply was given that he
should be pleased to receive it. Whether the Hartford millstone hung so heavy that it could not be thrown off, or for what
other reason I cannot say, the visit was never accomplished untill a fortnight since, when we past a very pleasant and social
afternoon together. Upon taking leave Mr Otis in his very civil
and polite manner, asked it as a favour that I would dine with
him the next week? I replied, that I had long declined all invitations to dinner, as well as all public company, upon which he
said it should be only a Family party. I then referred him to

[1] H. G. O.'s father-in-law.
[2] Mrs. Samuel Allyne Otis, H. G. O's stepmother.

your Father who promptly accepted his invitation. Accordingly
when the day came, we went, and were most kindly and cordially
received by all the assembled families. Mr Mason [and] Mr
Tudor were considered former appendages to us, and were a part
of the company. All appeared pleased and mutually gratified.
I know not when I have past a pleasanter day, and I could
not but regret the hour of seperation. All this past off very well.
I never expected to hear more of it. But you cannot imagine
what a sensation it has created in the Capital. A Gentleman
from Town yesterday informed me, that it was a subject of speculation in the public offices. Whether the Stocks have risen or
fallen in consequences, I do not pretend to say, but the wise ones
cannot comprehend the phenomenon. Some whisper it was to
obtain a recommendation for a foreign Mission, — now I do
not believe in any such motive I ascribe it to the benevolent
desire of extinguishing all party spirit, and to a desire of renew-
ing former friendship, and Family intimacy. As such I received
it, and in the same spirit returned it.

John Adams had already written to his son on the same event:
"As you live: your Father and Mother & Louisa dined last Tuesday
in Boston with Judge Otis[1] in the neatest Company imaginable;
none but Otis's, Lymans, Thorndykes, Minots, Boardmans and
Fosters, except Tudor and Mason. I never before knew Mrs. Otis.
She has good Understanding. I have seldom if ever passed a more
sociable day. Exert all your Witts to draw Inferences from this
Phenomenon. Do you ascribe it to the Eclipse of 1806, to the
Comet or to the spots in the sun?"

No better description of Otis's social qualities exists than the
letter which John Quincy Adams wrote to his father after receiving
his account of the reconciliation:

   Since beginning this Letter I have received yours of 26. August
   and 5 September, and am highly gratified by your and my
   Mother's Account of your social party at Judge Otis's. Among
   the lights and shades of that worthy Senator's character, there

---

[1] Otis at that time was judge of the Boston court of common pleas.

is none which shows him in higher colours than his hospitality. In the course of nearly thirty years that I have known him, and throughout the range of experience that I have had in that time, it has not fallen to my lot to meet a man more skilled in the useful art of entertaining his friends than Otis; and among the many admirable talents that he possesses, there is none that I should have been more frequently and more strongly prompted to Envy; if the natural turn of my disposition had been envious. Of those qualities Otis has many — His Person while in Youth, his graceful Deportment, his sportive wit, his quick intelligence, his eloquent fluency, always made a strong impression upon my Mind; while his warm domestic Affections, his active Friendship, and his Generosity, always commanded my esteem . . . Mrs. Otis is and always has been a charming woman; and I am very glad you have seen them both in the place where of all others they appear to the greatest advantage — their own house.

His son Charles Francis, some twelve years later, could not figure them out. After calling at the Otis house he wrote in his diary, "Saw all the family. There is something about them which I like very much, and yet what it is, is hardly possible to tell. Mrs. Otis scolded [me] well for my not having been before." What an insufferable young prig! He could not see what his father had perceived, that one secret of the Otises' charm was making every visitor feel that it was a pleasure and a privilege to know him, and that he should come more often.

Houses, Hospitality, and Harvard

The seat of this warm hospitality was Number 45 Beacon Street, the third house built by Otis and designed by Charles Bulfinch, the architectural genius of Federalist Boston. Otis sold his Cambridge Street house in 1801 and built a second (now 85 Mount Vernon Street), which in turn he sold to his friend Benjamin Pickman in 1805, and the same year he built for his father a house on the downhill corner of Spruce and Beacon streets. These, and the

No. 85 Mount Vernon Street, Otis's second house.

No. 45 Beacon Street, Otis's third house.

houses built by Jonathan Mason and others on the south slope of Beacon Hill, helped the Mount Vernon Proprietors to make that part of Boston fashionable. The Otises moved to Number 45 in 1806. It remained Sally's home until her death thirty years later, and Harry's for the rest of his life.

This mansion lay open to Boston Common; from its front windows one could see the Blue Hills across the Back Bay, a broad sheet of water that came within two hundred yards of the door. Courtyards and a garden surrounded it on the other three sides. Built to accommodate a large family, it housed seven Otis children when they moved in: Eliza, aged 15; Harry Jr., 14; Sally, 13; Allyne, 10; Sophia, 8; James, 6; William, 4; and two more were born there. There were no fewer than eleven bedchambers, almost every one with an open fireplace.

From the entrance on Beacon Street one entered directly a vestibule, cannily screened from the stair hall to cut off winter blasts. On the left was Otis's library, where he loved to sit, as he could see through the windows everyone who passed along Beacon Street. On the right was an "office" — meaning the room where home accounts and such business were done; and in the rear, a storage room which eventually became Otis's upstairs "wine room" to supplement the wine cellar in the basement. An ell, extending to the stables, contained the main kitchen, a "wash room" (laundry) and a woodshed. By a typical Bulfinch spiral stairway one ascended to the *piano nobile,* the main or second floor. Here, in front, were two handsome square rooms, the "dining parlour" and the "saloon." The latter opened into an "oval room," the second drawing room, whose bow extended into the garden. Behind the dining parlor was a china closet; and, behind that, across a landing on the back stairs, the "upstairs kitchen." Three bedrooms were eventually built behind that, making a second floor over the ell.

Passing a beautiful Palladian window on the stairs, one reached the third floor. The sunny Beacon Street side was taken up by two large square chambers, Harry's and Sally's, separated by a charming dressing room finished with carved woodwork. In the rear were two big chambers and a dressing room for the older girls. The fourth floor had seven chambers, three of them in front, for the younger children and five or six maidservants.

These were either New England country girls or girls from the Maritime Provinces. The Otises lived without ostentation; they did not go in for liveried butlers or footmen or French chefs, but always kept a coachman and groom and a stout houseman or two to lug in the fuel, polish boots and keep the steel knives bright. The menservants lived over the stable and coachhouse at the foot of the cobblestone yard. There was no central heating; wood or cannel coal had to be manhandled to keep a dozen fires burning, and the house was not piped for gas in Otis's time; all the lighting came from candles and Argand sperm-oil portable lamps imported from France. Since plumbing did not exist, water had to be carried upstairs, for drinking, bathing, washing and cooking, from a capacious cistern in the garden. My grandmother, who passed twelve of the first sixteen years of her life at 45 Beacon Street, told me that she and her brother and sister were marched to the Tremont House weekly for hot tub baths — but there was no Tremont House when her father and aunts and uncles were growing up. On the northern end of the ell, reached from the main floor, was a privy for the family; and, below, opening off the shed and the stable, another for the servants. These were pumped out every week or so into a horse-drawn tank truck, to be discharged in Brighton to manure truck gardens. The rumbling of these trucks on the cobblestoned streets accounts for their nickname, the "Brighton Artillery."

Whilst there was a certain amplitude in the Otises' way of living, it was neither extravagant nor aristocratic; for a contemporary parallel, a *hôtel* of the *haute bourgeoisie* in Lyon, Toulouse or Saint-Malo would be much nearer than anything in England.

The Otises never moved out of Number 45 Beacon Street, but they did acquire a country house. In the winter of 1808–09 Harry

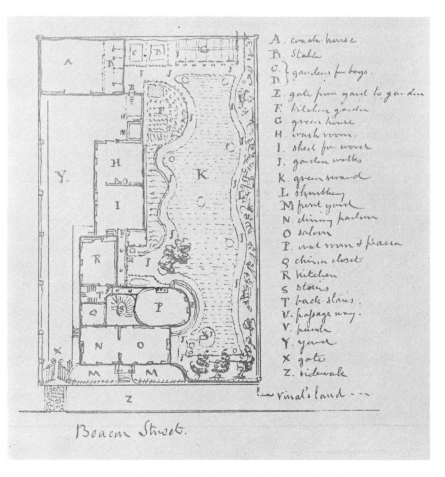

A. coach house
B. Stable
C. }
D. } gardens for boys.
E. gate from yard to garden
F. kitchen garden
G. green house
H. wash room.
I. shed for wood
J. garden walks
K. green sward
L. shrubbery
M. front yard
N. dining parlour
O. saloon
P. oval room & piazza
Q. china closet
R. kitchen
S. stairs
T. back stairs.
U. passage way.
V. privie
Y. yard
X. gate
Z. sidewalk
⌐—⌐ Vinal's land - - -

Beacon Street.

45 Beacon Street. Otis's plan of main floor and garden.
"H" and "I" are ground floor; two or three bedrooms were late·
built over them.

45 Beacon Street. Yard and coach-house, in 1968.

purchased a twelve-acre farm in Watertown, and by extensive additions and improvements to the grounds turned it into a country estate of some 38 acres, named Oakley. On the hilltop, whence one had a beautiful view of the Charles River valley, Bulfinch built for him a stately country house complete with spiral staircase and oval dining room. Otis wrote to John Rutledge at Charleston on 13 May 1809, asking him to lay out "five or ten dollars" on "a little assortment of seeds of any kind of shrubbery or plants which are not indigenous to this cold climate." To which Rutledge replied genially on 6 June:

> Having settled the affairs of the State, & put Democracy "in a Hole," as that queer gentleman John Adams quaintly said, it seems you have bought a Villa, & are going to indulge in a little rural felicity. This I presume is the *Ton* at Boston, & Mrs. Otis & the President[1] are at the head of the fashionables, getting this Country seat was, I presume, quite "en regle." But it really seemed to me that having such a House as you have, with the whole Common of Boston as an Apendage, & open & improved grounds all around, might have satisfied any man of ordinary ambition. I will with very great pleasure send you an assortment of Seeds of Shrubs & Plants which may subsist in your frozen region — but this, my good friend, is not the season. I have spoken to a Mr. Champneys who is the President of our Agricultural Society, & has in this neighbourhood a prodigiously fine garden, & he promises to make an assortment of plants for you in the season, which will not [be] before the month of December. He says that altho' you are an Oracle in Politics & in law, that you are in the very horn book of Botany & Gardening in supposing that Plants can be removed at this Season. As Mr. Robert [Rutledge] has determined to make a visit to Boston, I shall have the pleasure of seeing you *deo volente* about the beginning of August. . . . I pray of you to present me affectionately to Mrs. Otis, Miss Eliza, Sarah & the young folks. I request you would give my affections to Mason & say to him that I shall be in Boston in August — in the meantime God bless you & yours —

---

[1] Otis was then president of the state senate.

Rutledge did send him some copper beech trees which were still flourishing in 1968, and some cuttings for Black Hamburg grapes which reached prodigious size in a greenhouse, long since torn down.

Yet Oakley was not altogether a success. Both Otises were town bred; Harry knew nothing of horticulture, and Sally (so her granddaughter told me) used to say, "Better an attic in the city than a palace in the country!" And the children, too, preferred Boston to Watertown. Unable to lease part of the land to farmers, and warned by John Lowell that any attempt to go shares with a gardener would be disastrous, Otis sold the place in 1825 and thereafter spent part of each summer at Nahant, Newport or Sharon Springs. The estate eventually became the Oakley Country Club, but the Bulfinch-designed mansion burned down in 1961.

The Otises never left Boston for an entire summer, because they loved to entertain visitors from other cities. John Rutledge and other Carolinian friends made a practice of spending the summer at Newport and passing a week or two at 45 Beacon Street coming and going, especially at the time of Harvard Commencement — the last Wednesday of August. Harvard families made a point of being in town at that time, not only to enjoy the festival rites at Cambridge, but also to entertain friends from Philadelphia and the South who had sons in college. There was seldom a year after 1805 when Harvard contained no member of the Otis clan and Harry himself served on one or both of the governing boards from 1810 to 1825. Although not a great benefactor, he subscribed $100 toward the Massachusetts Chair of Natural History established in 1807, and twenty years later gave $500 toward the founding of the Harvard Divinity School.

Harvard students during the early nineteenth century used to express their disapproval of the college government by the modern methods of strike, boycott and sabotage. In 1805 occurred the "Bread and Butter Rebellion." As a protest against the quality of food provided, the student body refused for ten successive days to attend commons. The authorities suspended regular exercises and threatened to lock out the entire student body. The lads were too spirited to submit. A committee of the Board of Overseers presided over by Levi Lincoln, President Jefferson's former attorney general, reported in favor of a general pardon and promise of improved commons. This led to a prolonged debate in the Board (which then included the entire state senate) along strict party lines. A majority upheld the Federalist Harvard Corporation and defeated Lincoln's "jacobinical" report by 29 votes to 26. Two distinguished alumni, Samuel Dexter and Harrison Gray Otis, were then called upon to arbitrate. This they did to such good purpose that both sides accepted Lincoln's original proposal and peace was restored to the banks of the Charles.

Many of the Harvard students from outside New England, who rose to twenty percent of the total under the benign presidency of Dr. Kirkland, were introduced by their parents to Otis. He thus became an unofficial mentor to several young southern gentlemen in the college. One of these, John Lee, son of Governor Thomas Sim Lee of Maryland, was the first Roman Catholic to enter Harvard. Some of these young Southerners were rather a trial owing to their casual attitude; they would disappear from college without leave, spend weeks or months away, and cheerfully return when they felt like it, expecting to be received back into their class — and usually were. Thus, John Rutledge's son Robert, in and out of college since 1801, was finally dropped in 1809, "not for any vice or meanness, but for negligence," wrote Otis, who advised the father to put him into business; and John's cousin, Hugh Rutledge, not only dropped out but went home leaving his last term bill and about $500 in debts for classmate Charles Cotesworth Pinckney II to collect, and Otis to pay. Robert Smith, a younger son of the Bishop of South Carolina and uncle to the Rutledge boys, dropped in and out for years, but made Phi Beta Kappa as well as the Porcellian Club, and graduated in 1805. John Rutledge, Jr., however, was a model student "and conducts himself like a gentleman," said

Otis. With Harrison Gray Otis, Jr., he prepared for college at a private school kept by the Reverend John Sylvester John Gardiner, Rector of Trinity Church, Boston; and the two boys became "chums" — the old word for roommates — in college. Otis feared they would not get along, "John being of a mild and even temper, and Harry ardent and choleric to a degree that gives me concern, though a fellow of fine heart and as yet addicted to no species of dissipation or excess." But they did become good friends. The elder Rutledge wrote to Otis from Charleston early in 1808 on behalf of John Jr., to "pay him monthly Fifty Dollars, or, if it would be more agreeable to him, one hundred & fifty once in three months. With a due regard to economy (which I hope he will observe) Six hundred Dollars a year will be a sufficient allowance during his residence at Cambridge." That was a generous allowance for those days, assuming that father also paid for board, lodging and tuition.

On 26 March 1809 Rutledge wrote about both his sons, with a typical parental caution that they typically disregarded:

> I enclose a Bill of Exchange for the use of my Boys. Pray my dear friend, discourage as much as possible their visiting Boston, frequenting Taverns, driving carriages &c &c. It is using a great freedom I know to draw upon your Charities in this way — I also know it is not "Othelo's occupation" to be lecturing & ordering Boys. I know how much, & how well, "he serves the state"; but my friend unless you have the goodness & humility to condescend to advise these fellows, &, by your parental attentions, give some correction to their aberations, I fear that the objects of their residence at Cambridge will not be realized. John writes to me of the brilliance of Mrs. Apthorpes Ball, Mrs. Otis's Parties, &c. This is all wrong, & these Boys must not be permitted to have any engagements but with their Books.

POLITICS AND SOCIAL LIFE

Social life in Boston in the first decade of the nineteenth century
became more elaborate as a natural result of material prosperity.
"Private balls are numerous, and little cotillion parties occur every
week," wrote one of the Quincy girls in 1807; and in addition to
private parties there were club cotillions at Concert Hall, which
continued through the War of 1812. At the Samuel Welles ball in
November 1807, music was furnished by a "Turkish band," and the
supper, including peaches and melons, served three hundred people. "All went off with éclat," noted Miss Quincy, "except the
toasts, which were rather flat. The gentlemen were not prepared to
be either witty or sentimental, and impromptus suit the genius of
the French better than that of the English or their American descendants. Mr. Otis alone was happy on this occasion; his wit is
ever ready." Eliza Quincy left a good description of a house dance
at the Quincy town house on Summer Street in 1817, which would
hold good for any similar party before the war. The 150 or so
guests, including the entire Otis clan, "began to appear at 8 o'clock.
The ladies were all in full dress, gold and silver muslins, lace &
jewels of all descriptions. . . . We took care to have plenty of beaux
invited; all our Cambridge acquaintances, Josiah and several of his
friends, collegians, were of the party, in addition to the Boston
gentlemen. . . . Anna was much admired as a little girl of 7 years,
and danced a cotillion with Mr. H. G. Otis jr. — who took a fancy
to the young lady."

It will be observed that all ages from seven to seventy were
represented. That was the old-world custom, now unhappily done
away with in every eastern city except Baltimore, and replaced by
parties of the same age group. "Plenty of beaux" from Harvard
now swamp every Boston ball. As Santayana caustically remarked,
"The young [in America] were simply young, and the old simply
old, as among peasants."

Almost every visitor of distinction to Boston brought a letter of introduction to Harrison Gray Otis and received abundant hospitality. "We have kept tavern for John Bull these thirty years," Harry once wrote; and he loved to relate the answer of his victualer, when pressed to tell whether he had any customer as good as himself. After scratching his head, the tradesman, a noncommittal Yankee, replied that he guessed he sold about as much to the Hotel Albion — the second largest hotel in Boston. Less formal entertainment than the dances for both sexes were so-called tea parties, precursor of cocktail parties, from about 5 to 7 P.M.; and evening parties, especially Sunday evenings. These were *conversazioni,* followed by a supper of scalloped oysters, many hot and cold dishes, and Madeira wine. Men's clubs, of the London pattern, with their own houses and restaurants, did not appear in Boston before Otis's old age, but in his time there were several men's dinner clubs. These were formed among Harvard classmates and other congenial friends who met weekly or fortnightly at a member's house. Otis, with William Sullivan, Thomas Handasyd Perkins, Benjamin Joy, General David Cobb, President Kirkland of Harvard, and other choice spirits, belonged to one of these coteries known as the Saturday Fish Club, of which little more than the name is known; presumably the excuse for it was to eat an old-fashioned New England salt fish dinner, which the Yankees always consumed on Saturday night in order to be different from the Catholics. When General Cobb, deposed from his agency for the Bingham lands east of the Penobscot in 1822, returned to Gouldsborough for the last time, each member of the club contributed two bottles of Madeira and shipped them to him Down East. Two years later, Sullivan in a Sunday letter to Otis told about the club's previous dinner:

> The club dined yesterday at Mr. Joy's — *wine* from 20 to 45 years old — and no better for being more than 20. Besides the members we had Mr. Henderson of N. York, Pres. K[irkland], Brother Rufus [King or Amory?] who complained to Mr. J. that

the women wear no *pockets* nowadays — that his House keeper
takes the keys out of her bosom, when he wants them, and that
they are so *warm* that he likes to let them *cool* before he uses
them. — Joy broke the sober rules of the club, by bringing
oysters from the shell, to give a *gout,* and a market, for his wine;
— it certainly needed no such aid.

Until after the end of the second war with Britain, Federalists
and Republicans kept rigidly separate in Boston, as we have already seen they were in Philadelphia. Theophilus Parsons tells us
in the memoir of his like-named father, the Chief Justice, that he
never saw a "Jacobin" in their house until 1807 when his Uncle
Cross, a Maine Democrat, came to dinner on a visit to Boston. The
children examined him attentively, as specimen of a new and
strange breed. In the course of the meal the Chief Justice remarked pleasantly, "Mr. Cross, pray take a glass of wine with me,"
and handed him the decanter; when to the consternation of the
company young Theophilus called out, "Why, he is not a Jacobin,
after all!" "No, my young friend, I am not a *Jacobin;* at least, I
hope not," said Uncle Cross; "did you think I was?" "Yes, sir!"
said young hopeful, "but I see you are not, for I have heard father
say, again and again, that nothing on earth would make him drink
wine with a Jacobin!" At which point the conversation was broken
off by young Theophilus being sent away from the table.

Yet Otis and his friends, who dreaded democracy in theory, were
in some respects more democratic socially than the bloated billion-
aires of today. They lived on terms of friendly intimacy with
servants, tradespeople and country neighbors. J. W. Hale tells us
how "almost any morning might be seen Col. Thos. H. Perkins,
Harrison Gray Otis, William (Billy) Gray, Ben. Bussey, Peter C.
Brooks, Israel Thorndike and other wealthy townsfolk, trudging
homeward for their eight o'clock breakfast with their market bas-
kets containing their one o'clock dinner." Harry always did just
that, when not laid up by arthritis, with this difference: he ate the
hearty breakfast first and a manservant carried the basket.

A story of Theophilus Parsons may give us the key to this seeming inconsistency. When a Salem man asked his father why the Newburyporters were forever quarreling about religion, he replied, "Because we look upon religion as having a real importance. We think it worth quarreling about; you don't." The situation was the same in politics. Federalists and Republicans alike, at the period of which we speak, took their politics with a grim earnestness that the present generation can hardly comprehend. To a Federalist, a Jacobin was an anarchist who would pull down the entire political and social structure; Jacobinism was a disease to be avoided and proscribed. Dance with a Jacobin? Drink wine with a Jacobin? Of course not! Would a daughter of Jefferson Davis have danced with Wendell Phillips? Would Pius IX have invited Cavour to dinner?

Otis, as we have seen, took offense from finding Jeffersonians at a social party in Washington, but he never allowed political differences to sour family relations. He always remained intimate with the James Warrens and with Sally's father William Foster, ardent Jeffersonians. Presumably, when Aunt Warren or Father Foster dined at Number 45, Eliza, Harry, Sally, Sophy, Jimmy and Willie were firmly warned not to mention the word Jacobin. Otis loved his "Aunt Warren" but did not approve of her. In sending to John Rutledge in 1805 the prospectus of her *History of the Rise, Progress and Termination of the American Revolution,* he warned his Carolina friend that "her political opinions will exhibit the tincture of democracy. Though well born & a real lady, and as proud a woman as lives, she is the wife of a disappointed patriot of seventy-five and is too much under his influence altho' vastly his superior in every sort of literary attainment. She assures me however that she has been strictly impartial, and it is at her request that I send you the prospectus. . . ." The book turned out to be anything but impartial, containing cracks at John Adams which aroused his ire, and afforded the reading public vast amusement.

Otis found his brother-in-law, William Foster, Jr., a bit hard to take. William, one of the American speculators in Paris in the 1790's, enlisted in the French Republican army, married a cousin of General Moreau, and in 1809 returned with her to Boston, there compounding his "Jacobin" villainy by writing pro-French articles for the Democratic press. Nevertheless, Otis promoted Foster's candidacy for the new Smith Professorship of French and Spanish Literature at Harvard in 1815. Fortunately for Harvard, George Ticknor received the chair.

EATING, DRINKING, AND SCANDALS

Every Thanksgiving there took place a huge family reunion of the numerous Otis, Foster, Apthorp, Lyman, Ritchie and Thorn- dike connections. In the winter season there were frequent parties of a hundred or more, and breakfast parties such as the following, related in one of Otis's letters, were not uncommon:

> Night before last, Sophia undertook to ask Mrs. I. P. Davis and Miss Lovell to eat buckwheats, and the party swelled to between twenty & thirty, — all the 2nd & 3d generation of Fos- ters, my sisters, Thorndikes, Callanders, Holleys, and half a doz Codmans, Grays, Brooks' &c to fill up chinks.

Those old Bostonians unashamedly enjoyed eating and drinking. While the Otis family were in residence at Number 45 Beacon Street, a blue and white Lowestoft punch bowl, with a capacity of over two gallons, sat every afternoon on the landing halfway to the drawing rooms, filled with punch for the benefit of visitors. Otis became famous as a gourmet and connoisseur of wines, although how he managed to indulge in the good things of this world on the scale that he did through forty gouty years is hard to imagine. Family tradition is positive that his usual breakfast dish, even at the age of eighty, was a moderate-sized tureen of pâté de fois gras.

After beginning the day in this fashion, Otis would walk to the State House if the general court was in session; and, if not, to his law office on Court Street, or to the courthouse if a case in which he was involved needed his presence. At noon or shortly after, the merchants, lawyers and other professional men left their offices for " 'Change," which meant strolling up and down State Street in fair weather, or meeting in the Exchange Coffee-House or an insurance office if the weather were cold or inclement. For an hour or so the gentlemen exchanged gossip, made deals, wrote insurance for ships going foreign, and damned the Democrats. At about two o'clock 'Change broke up; everyone walked or drove home for a two-thirty or three o'clock dinner, which lasted until candlelight in winter. At other seasons, dinner ended in time for the family to drive out to the country — maybe to Oakley, or to Tom Perkins's house in Brookline, Jack Lowell's Bromley Vale in Roxbury, or Theodore Lyman's The Vale in Waltham — to take tea. Once home, a hearty supper was enjoyed at eight or nine o'clock, "and so to bed."

The punch bowl on the stairs prevented the male members of the Otis family from becoming thirsty during the afternoon, and tradition assures us that a special ice chest, within easy reach of friends and family, provided jellies, whips and syllabubs for whoever might be attacked by hunger between meals. At the dinner table there was none of your modern false modesty about looking at food — joints and pies were spread out to regale sight and nostrils; no great variety, to be sure, and no French cooking; but good honest food in unstinted abundance. "I wish you could get here by dinner time," Harry wrote to Sally one 30 May while she was at New York and most of the children at Oakley. At a few hours' notice he got up a dinner of twenty Federalists in honor of Theodore Lyman, and this sketch of the dining room is added by way of explanation. All are eating their soup; James and William, aged fifteen and fourteen, are seated at a side table. A large saddle of mutton adorns the center of the main table, and its periphery is

garnished wtih a leg of lamb, a Virginia ham, a meat pie, chickens
and a salmon. "Brants & chickens for second course," a note informs us; vegetables and dessert are left to the imagination. The
wine, we may safely guess, was Madeira.

There was a fabulous consumption of that wine in nineteenth-
century Boston. Otis's old friend George Harrison of Philadelphia
became agent for the house of Gordon Duff & Company, and received orders from Harry and his Boston friends for that king of
wines. Here is a sample consignment of "choice particular old
Madeira" at £46 the pipe (a double hogshead containing one hundred and twenty-six gallons), which arrived in the schooner *Lark*
in 1807, just in time to escape Jefferson's embargo:

Jonn. Mason	£46
Ditto	82.10.
Gardiner Green	46
Ditto	46
I. P. Davis	82.10.
John Lowell Junr.	60

Thomas Perkins	46
Lady Temple	46
William Phillips	46
Jeremiah Allen	46
Andrew Allen	46
Benjn. Bussey	46
Danl Davis	46
Commodore Preble	46
E. H. Derby	46
John Phillips	46
P. C. Brooks	46
Andrew Seaton	92
John Philips Junr.	23.10.
Prentess Mellen	23.10.
Saml S. Wilde	23.10.
H. G. Otis	46
	£ Stg 1077.10.

In addition to his quota in the above consignment, Otis procured another pipe direct. The previous year, he had received
"2 pipes choice particular Madeira wine in strong iron-bound casks
at £45 Stg. p. pipe, mark'd H G O branded I A G," and "1 pipe
ditto wine"; but in 1809 (the embargo having lifted) he considered
it time to lay in a new stock, for in that year George Harrison
writes, "I will order 'H G O — G H' of very superior wine for you,
& God grant that I may partake of it when ripe 7 years hence."

Madeira was always imported in the wood, preferably in a vessel
that had sailed around the world, which was supposed to have a
favorable effect on its flavor and bouquet. After resting a few years
in the owner's house — in the attic rather than the cellar if he
wished it to mature quickly — the wine was drawn off into bottles,
and given the name of the ship in which it had been imported, as
well as the vintage year. Naval officers commanding ships and
frigates made a practice of bringing home pipes of Madeira for

their friends, which not only saved them freight money but also gave their wine a peculiar distinction. In my youth in Boston a generous host would open a bottle of "Constitution," "Constellation," or "Macedonian" Madeira; and the last bottle of the "Constitution," owned by Russell Codman, was drunk at my house in 1967. Bostonians never cared much for port wine; claret, burgundy, hock and champagne they drank only at mixed parties or on gala occasions. Otis, however, was always ready to give a new wine a try, as this letter to him from A. F. Humphreys of Boston, in 1812, indicates:

> Do not be surprized, my dear Mr. Otis should you see a cask of *Bucellas* wine walking into your yard today. . . . I wrote to Lisbon for it immediately after I heard you express a wish to try that wine, & behold! it is already here. . . . A light white wine, between *Vin de Grave* & *Vin du Rhin*.

By 1835 Otis apparently was running low on old Madeira, since he commissioned his youngest son Allyne to shop around for a fresh supply. Allyne's application to Judge William Prescott, father of the historian, produced the following reply, from Nahant:

> Dear Sir
>   I have not an entire pipe of *Juno* wine. Many years since I had imported, on my private order, a pipe of *Juno* and another of *Essex* jr., which have been bottled and part of them used. I have understood high prices have been given or offered in N York for these wines, $50 a dozen for *Juno* and nearly as much for *Essex* jr. I did not think of disposing of any part of mine, but if I have as much remaining as I suppose, such high prices would tempt me to part with 10 or 12 dozen of each at say $45 for *Juno* and $35 for *Essex* jr. They cost considerably more than the wine on cargo and I believe are of superior quality. If you wish to try them, after this explanation, I will send you samples when I go to Town, which will be in a few days.
>   I am Dear Sir, very respy. Your Obedt. Servt. Wm. Prescott

Otis loved small informal parties as well as the big affairs to which scores of people of both sexes were invited. His little longhand notes of invitation were so amusing that the recipients were apt to preserve them. Here are two samples from the Harvard collection of autograph letters. The first is evidently to a state senator:

Dr Sir,
    I intend asking a few of the Senate to take punch &c at 1 o'clock — Will you come & if you please ask Thatcher & any ½ Doz. you think best —
                                    Yrs H G O
June 1 1810

The second, to John P. Bigelow of Boston, contains a zodiacal pun which has evaporated, although it evidently means that Federalists only will be welcome:

Dr Sir,
    Would it be too much to ask you to take Mr. Fuller or any other friend whose heart is in the right sign of the political Zodiac (Sagittarius I suppose) to call & pass a half hour with me tomorrow P.M. after Service — If you will, & will go to church without your wine, I will give you a glass of mine, & take one with you —
    Dont trouble yourself to reply —

A natural consequence of the high living then prevalent was arthritis or gout, with which Otis was afflicted during the last forty years of his life. This irritating disease soured the temper of many an old gentleman, but Otis's temper and constitution were proof against it. Although he lived to the age of eighty-three, he retained until the last his wit, good nature, and every quality that endeared him to his fellow men.

Scandals, especially illicit love affairs, were rare in this close-knit society which honored the puritan ethic after moving away from the Puritans' religion. Occasionally, however, they did occur. Otis early in 1803 received a distressing letter from Newport written

by his friend Rutledge, who had just discovered the unfaithfulness
of his wife, daughter of the Bishop of South Carolina and mother of
his three children. Otis offered to place his Boston house at Rutledge's or Mrs. Rutledge's disposition if a physical separation were
desirable, and undertook to deny publicly malicious gossip "which
I foresaw would be propagated from Newport, that Pandora's box
& fertile source of public and private vice." With Otis's approval,
Rutledge challenged the lover, also a southern summer visitor at
Newport, to a duel. They fought in Georgia; Rutledge killed the
lover and obtained a divorce by special act of the South Carolina
legislature.

A similar case occurred about the same time in Boston; and since
the only record of it omits the names of the parties, we shall call
them Mr. and Mrs. Smith, and Mr. Jones, Smith's partner and
lodger. Jones was caught in *flagrante delicto* with Mrs. Smith.
Again there was a duel, this time in Canada; the lover fell dead
and the injured husband sought a divorce *a vinculo* from the
Supreme Judicial Court of Massachusetts. Mrs. Smith's friends
persuaded her to resist, and she retained Harrison Gray Otis and
William Sullivan as counsel. As our one informant describes it,

> Mr. Otis was himself, that day; elegant in his person and car-
> riage; his voice appeared more than usually melodious, as
> though he had adapted it to that tone of supplication, which
> seemed to be the only resource for his miserable client; and he
> poured forth a profluvium of that characteristic eloquence,
> which was ever so captivating in promiscuous assemblies, and
> with the softer sex. When he sat down, there were, doubtless in
> that dense assemblage — for the court room was literally packed
> with excited and deeply interested listeners — some persons, who
> had a vague impression that the adultress must be innocent; or,
> if guilty, that there was nothing, after all, so very terrible in the
> little slip that she had made!

But the litigant's counsel, the great Samuel Dexter, had not been
heard. Evidence against the naughty lady was so complete that he
easily disposed of Otis's arguments. Dexter had the reputation of

displaying "that kind of eloquence which struts around the heart without ever entering it." But in this case he drew a picture of domestic happiness tarnished by sordid adultery that pulled tears from the same audience which had been almost persuaded by Otis that the lady's sin (if it were a sin) was venial. Smith won his divorce.

THE OTIS WIT

Otis became famous for that "sportive wit" which Adams mentions among his attractive characteristics. We look in vain for it in his political correspondence and speeches, for politics of the Federalist era were so intense and seemed so vital that to season them with humor was considered almost blasphemous. But Otis, who in private intercourse was always bubbling over with spontaneous fun and good nature, was the life of every assembly of men or women where he appeared. At public and private dinners he was the favorite toastmaster. Josiah Quincy gives an equally pleasing impression of him at a cattle show in Worcester:

> The speeches by Otis and Everett were in the happiest vein; and a grand ball concluded the day. No, it did not conclude it, after all; for near midnight some gentlemen from Providence, who had arrived by the newly opened Blackstone Canal, invited a few of us to adjourn to a room they had engaged and taste some of "Roger Williams Spring," which they had brought all the way from the settlement he founded. Now this same spring, as it turned out, ran some remarkably choice Madeira, and this beverage, served with an excellent supper, furnished the material basis for brilliant displays of wit, flashing out upon the background of hearty and genial humor. Mr. Otis fairly surpassed himself. He was wonderful in repartee, and his old-fashioned stories were full of rollicking fun. I well remember the account he gave of the first appearance of champagne in Boston. It was produced at a party given by the French consul,

and was mistaken by his guests for some especially mild cider of foreign growth. The scene was beneath the dignity of history, to be sure; but taken as a sort of side-show, it was very enjoyable.

Then there were the lawyers' stories. Otis wrote to Hamilton that the 1800 treaty with France, according to which all ships captured by each side were to be returned and nothing done about spoliations, reminded him of the fictitious case of Bullum *v.* Boatum. Farmer A owned a bull, Farmer B owned a flatboat. The second farmer's scow, laden with turnips, was moored to the river-bank by a grass rope. Farmer A's bull climbed into the boat to eat the turnips and then, for good measure, ate the rope. The boat floated downstream, hit a rock, the bull was drowned and the boat smashed. The owner of the boat sued the owner of the bull, and the owner of the bull sued the owner of the boat. After hearing extended arguments by both common and admiralty law, the learned justice non-suited the parties; upon paying all costs, they were allowed to begin again *de novo.* As the French spoliation claims consumed time and effort in Congress for over a century, this comparison was very much to the point.

Another story that Otis told illustrated the fact that a big lawyer from a small town might not appear so distinguished in Boston. Squire Waldron of Newburyport, having business to transact with Governor Gore in springtime, procured a Merrimack river salmon as a propitiatory gift, packed it with ice in the boot of his chaise, and started for Boston along the Newburyport turnpike. When he broke the journey at Salem to dine with brother lawyers, a couple of wags removed the salmon from the chaise and substituted a common codfish. The Squire innocently continued to Boston where, after stabling his horse, he was astonished to find a cod in the boot, a fish he dared not offer to a gourmet like Governor "Kitty" Gore. So he left it there; but not wishing to waste it, applied more ice to take it home fresh. Returning next day, he again lunched at Salem, where the same two jokers removed the codfish and put back the salmon. Upon returning home Mrs.

Waldron greeted her spouse with, "How did His Excellency like the salmon?" "Why, 't wa'nt no salmon," said the Squire, "you made a mistake!" "No mistake at all! That was one of the finest salmon I ever did see, and I packed it in ice myself!" "Well, let's take a look at it." They did. The Squire, dumbfounded, burst out with, "Maybe 'tis a salmon in Newburyport but in Boston 'twas nothin' but a goddam codfish!"

Many surviving examples of Harry Otis's humor consist of puns — a form of witticism now out of fashion. We are told, for instance, how he won a case from a Mr. Gee who was trying to acquire land to which he had no good title. Since $\gamma\hat{\eta}$ in Greek means the earth, Otis played about with geography, geology, geometry, perigee, apogee, until the jury was roaring with laughter and poor Gee was utterly confounded. A more convincing example of his ready wit — although to appreciate it requires some knowledge of Massachusetts topography — was told to me by Frank B. Sanborn, who heard it from Wendell Phillips. It seems that one of the colleagues of Otis and John Phillips in the state senate about the year 1808 rejoiced in the curious name of Salem Towne. On one occasion, when the Democratic minority offered a "joker" resolution, drawn up for the express purpose of trapping unwary Federalists into endorsing Democratic principles, Mr. Towne alone of the Federalists swallowed the bait and voted yea in the roll call. Otis came to him after the vote had been taken and remarked in a solemn tone, "Mr. Towne, your parents were four miles out of the way, more or less, in naming you." "Four miles, Mr. Otis! What do you mean, sir?" "Instead of *Salem Towne,* they should have christened you *Marble Head!*"

CHAPTER XI

Business, Oratory, and Family Affairs

1800–1828, AET. 34–63

BOSTON REAL ESTATE

ON 4 FEBRUARY 1800, with one year of his second term in Congress still to go, Harry wrote to Sally the letter already quoted, declaring that he would quit federal politics and never leave home without her. And he kept his word; but that did not preclude state politics, and the State House was less than ten minutes' walk from his home. Pressure from friends and his own sense of duty forced him into it. Every year from 1802 to 1817 he served in one branch or another of the general court (the state legislature), requiring much hard work and no compensating glory. "I have not yet had a chance of living for myself," he writes to Aunt Warren in 1809, "nor for the pleasures and advantages of sweet communion with any particular connections. I sometimes am so sanguine as to hope that these blessings are not forever alienated from me even in this world, but the hours fly, and my white hairs become daily more discernible."

The first decade after Otis's return, Boston expanded marvelously. The population increased from 24,000 in 1800 to 34,000 in 1810, and the import and export trade increased in even greater proportion. Boston vessels were taking the American flag to every part of the globe. The China and India trade, in which Otis's lifelong friends, Theodore Lyman and Thomas Handasyd Perkins, made fortunes, expanded; and through Boston enterprise trade routes were opened to India, Russia, and the Oregon country. Otis never owned a ship or engaged in commerce, but he played a major role in the development of Boston itself. A long head for business he evidently had, since mainly by wise investments in real estate his estate grew from nothing at all in 1786 to a considerable fortune in 1810. There were few forms of local enterprise with which he was not connected. It was owing largely to his foresight and energy that Beacon Hill became a fashionable residential district, and that several other enterprises were pursued. "Through all these moves," write the historians of Bulfinch's Boston, "shines the kind, intelligent and happy face of Harrison Gray Otis — the most successful man in Bulfinch's town. . . . He combined good breeding and sufficient wealth with a thirst for the pleasantest ways of life." To which one should add that the architectural genius of Charles Bulfinch, operating on Otis's good taste and financial acumen, gave Boston her most distinguished buildings prior to the age of H. H. Richardson, Robert S. Peabody and McKim, Mead & White.

In 1799 the Mount Vernon Proprietors first laid out streets on their Beacon Hill property. Following Philadelphian precedent, they named most of them after trees — Chestnut, Walnut, Cedar, etc., commemorating good Federalists on the longer ones — Mount Vernon, Pinckney and Revere. A formidable bar to the development of the Hill was its high, three-peaked summit. Two of these peaks, Cotton Hill on the site of Pemberton Square, and Sentry Hill behind the State House, did not impinge on Otis's land, but the westernmost, on the site of 77–85 Mount Vernon Street, decidedly did. This eminence was commonly known as "Mount Whoredom," a Bunyanesque name dating from the colonial era when a disorderly collection of wooden buildings, the town's red-light district, straggled up the northern slope. Between 1800 and 1802 the Mount Vernon Proprietors leveled this unsavory peak and chastely renamed it Mount Vernon. "We are taking down Mt. Whoredom," wrote Harry to a friend. "If in future you visit it with less pleasure you will do so with more profit!" A little railroad carried gravel from the condemned hilltop down across the future West Cedar Street to the river, where branches distributed the fill to make Charles Street. This primitive gravity railroad, on which the laden cars, attached to the empties by a cable running through a pulley on the hilltop, hoisted them back up, attracted such crowds of idlers and small boys that Otis humorously remarked that one would think it an engineering feat equivalent to Bonaparte's building a road across the Alps. By laying out Charles Street, Beacon Hill became more accessible, the Proprietors had scores of new house lots to sell on both sides of the filled-in street, and the building of the Third Baptist Church (now the Charles Street Meeting House) on the edge of the river, designed by the distinguished architect Asher Benjamin, helped keep Charles Street respectable for another century and a half.

The biggest holdup of the Mount Vernon Proprietors was a threatened suit from the heirs of one Cunningham for the western half of their estate, including the site of Otis's own house on Beacon Street. Copley had bought this pasture in the 1760's but no deed could be found; and the artist, who still considered himself swindled, refused to furnish evidence of his title until Otis had settled the suit by other means. Mrs. Susanna Cunningham, the heir and claimant, got into the hands of two unscrupulous lawyers who in 1810 tried to shake down the Proprietors for the modest sum of $750,000! The lawyers sequestered Susanna at a country estate in New York so she could not be "got at," but Otis found her just the same and bought a release of all her claims for a mere $10,000.

The development of Beacon Hill received a rude check from Jefferson's embargo and the War of 1812; but not long after, the old Copley pasture began to make handsome returns to the Mount Vernon Proprietors (now Otis, Mason, Joy and William Sullivan) on their original investment and the large sums they had to expend for improvements and payoffs.

Boston felt cramped on its narrow peninsula as early as 1801, when Otis initiated several enterprises for obtaining more room by artificial means. The Broad Street Association which he organized extended the shoreline near Fort Hill, transforming an area of small dilapidated buildings and rotting wharves into one of broad streets and brick warehouses, including the noble India Wharf designed by Bulfinch. Otis, Bulfinch and Uriah Cotting, another energetic city developer, formed the Mill Pond Corporation which filled in the pond behind Causeway Street, the city taking one eighth and they seven eighths of the reclaimed land. This mill pond drained into the harbor by Mill Creek across the neck of the North End, the difference in tide levels furnishing power for grinding corn. The proprietors cut down Sentry Hill, the highest summit of Beacon Hill, to obtain gravel fill for this particular development.

The same three entrepreneurs were responsible for extending Beacon Street from Charles Street across the Back Bay to Sewall's Point, Brookline. The "Mill Dam," as this extension was called, had a tide mill at about the site of Exeter Street. The Mount Vernon Proprietors, wishing to extend the character of Beacon Hill to the Mill Dam, built in 1828 a block of handsome residences faced with Chelmsford granite, below Charles Street and facing what later became the Public Garden. These, designed by Asher Benjamin, are now Numbers 70–75 Beacon Street. Otis himself built the first two and gave Number 71 to his son William upon his marriage to Emily Marshall in 1831; the other four were built by his associates Mason, Joy and Sullivan. One or two have been converted into flats, but the entire block in 1968 is still in the "premium" class. Otis, it will be observed, had a genius for choosing desirable sites and buildings so well that his houses are being lived in more than a century after his death. That also applies to Louisbourg Square, for which he was responsible. The lots were divided equally between the four Mount Vernon partners, who formed a special proprietorship, to which purchasers were admitted, to maintain the greensward and protect themselves from encroachment. The first houses, erected in 1834, have been as jealously held as any residential properties in the United States;

The Otis and Sears mansions, c. 1817, reconstructed by Ogden Codman.

The Granite Block, now 70–75 Beacon Street, in 1968. Nos. 70 and 73 retain the original roof line; two stories have been added to No. 71.

and although some have been converted into apartments, almost every house built there in Otis's day is still used for its original purpose.

Otis shared responsibility for the earliest development of Dorchester Neck, which became South Boston. He and four friends were incorporated as the South Boston Association in 1803, when there were only ten families living on the Neck and communication with Boston required a long detour. After considerable resistance from the town of Dorchester, the Neck became a part of Boston in 1804. The Association then built Dover Street Bridge across the channel. The influence of commercial interests in South Bay prevented its being built where it would have been most convenient to South Boston, and this retarded the area's growth; but the bridge became the favorite promenade of the belles and beaux for some thirty years after the War of 1812. Others besides Otis and his associates reaped the profit of South Boston's later development. The bridge, which never paid a dividend, was sold to the city in 1833 for a song. About the time of the Civil War, the mid-century wave of Irish immigrants, who had first settled in the North End, Fort Hill and South Cove, moved *en masse* into South Boston, and "Southie" is now said to be the biggest Irish town after Dublin.

The outward appearance of Boston became very much changed for the better. John Howe, a former loyalist who returned in 1808, wrote, "The great number of new and elegant buildings which have been erected in this Town, within the last ten years, strike the eye with astonishment, and prove the rapid manner in which the people have been acquiring wealth." Another visitor eight years later declared that Boston could boast more splendid private dwellings than any other city in America or Europe of four times its population. Several blocks of four- and five-story buildings had been erected, intruding upon the pleasant gardens and open spaces; and the Exchange Coffee-House in State Street, built by a corporation of which Otis was president, rose to the dizzy height of seven

The Exchange Coffee-House.

India Wharf, c. 1855.

stories. For ten years (it burned down in 1818) this was the largest hotel and office building in the country. India Wharf, designed by Bulfinch, with brick stores and warehouses from which shipping magnates could lade their vessels lying alongside, was the most magnificent wharf structure in America. Otis did a good part of the financing, and acted as agent for selling the individual stores, at prices ranging from $7000 to $9000.

MAINE LANDS

Otis did not confine his land investments to Boston. He invested a small sum in the famous Yazoo speculation in the Delta country of Mississippi, but unloaded early, to his subsequent relief. His principal real estate holdings lay in New England.

On the map of the State of Maine you will find today a Harrison, a Gray and an Otis; but only the first was named after our Harry. Otis, a poor little farming town in Hancock County north of Ellsworth, had been granted to Colonel James Otis before the Revolution for some real or imagined service to Massachusetts — of which Maine was a part until 1820. His son, Harry's Uncle Joe, inherited it and sold the land gradually, but made very little profit. The town of Gray, settled before the Revolution, was named after Thomas Gray, an uncle or brother of the old treasurer. Harrison was definitely named after Harrison Gray Otis when it separated from the town of Otisfield; and that town was named after the entire Otis family which owned most of it.

During the provincial period Massachusetts enlarged her area of settlement, and afforded nascent capitalists an opportunity for profit, by the amiable fiction of bestowing land on veterans of colonial wars. Otisfield originated in a grant to Shubael Gorham and others of Barnstable in 1736, on behalf of survivors and heirs of a Cape Cod militia company which took part in the abortive Canada Expedition of 1690. It followed the usual pattern: six miles square, divided into sixty shares to as many veterans, most of whom promptly sold out to a few leading citizens — in this instance to Gorham and Colonel James Otis. The general court located their grant near Lake Ossipee, in the hope of nailing down its claim to all New England north and east of the Merrimack River, but the Privy Council of Great Britain, in a boundary decision of 1740, awarded that section to New Hampshire; and New Hampshire refused to honor Massachusetts grants. Accordingly, in 1771 Colonel Otis and Shubael Gorham applied to the general court for compensation. They got it, in the shape of a township in Cumberland County, Maine, about thirty miles north of Portland. The surviving proprietors — mostly Otises with a Gorham or two and a few Prescotts — met at the Bunch of Grapes Tavern in Boston, elected Samuel A. Otis their clerk, adopted the name Otisfield, and offered the land for sale. After the war they began to do business, and Otisfield, with over 200 inhabitants, became a full-fledged town in 1798. The proprietors built the first meeting house, presented the first settled minister with a lot for his parsonage, hewed out a few rough roads, and sold land on easy installments. A settler named Barzilla Howard wrote to Harrison Gray Otis in 1822, after paying a final installment on land bought from his father, praising the Otises' "kindness and forbearance." Although absentees, the Otises obviously were popular, the towns where they had interests consistently voted Federalist.

Otisfield, as an unusually big township, suffered amputations. Parts were set off to the exotically named towns of Naples and Oxford, and a substantial southwestern section became the town of Harrison in 1805. This was definitely named after Harrison Gray Otis, who was then doing a "land office business" selling lots. Harrison, more populous than her parent town, became during Otis's lifetime the northern terminus of the Cumberland and Oxford Canal. The canal boats, rigged as bald-headed schooners with folding masts like those of Thames barges, were towed by horses through the canal from Portland to Sebago Lake, sailed

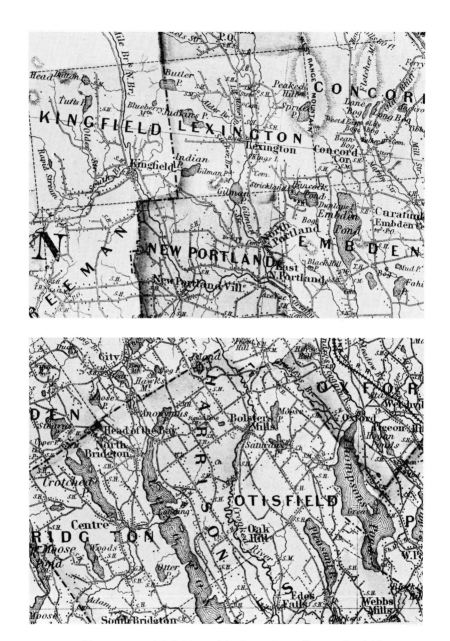

Two groups of Otis Townships in Maine. *Above:* Kingfield,
Lexington and Concord. *Below:* Harrison and Otisfield

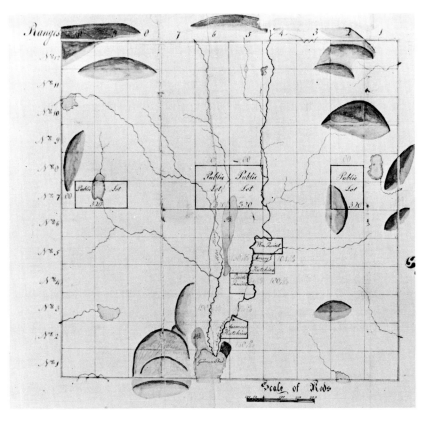

Map of "No. 2" (Lexington), 1808.

across that beautiful body of water, were poled up the connecting river to Long Lake, and sailed again to Harrison Landing. On the return trip, if they found no good market for a cargo of country produce and lumber, they made sail and continued along the coast, sometimes as far as Boston. By 1860 both Harrison and Otisfield had each attained a population around 1200. After the Civil War both towns steadily declined. Otisfield center, situated where a stream empties into Thompson Pond, in 1967 consisted of a general store and two houses; but there is a pretty white-painted village called Bolsters Mills, half in each town. Harrison's center village, at the old canalboat terminus at the north end of Long Lake, is a thriving center of the summer camp business.

A different story is that of Otis's connection with the vast Bingham holdings in Maine. These were born of the speculative movement in northern New England land that set in after the War of Independence. Senator William Bingham of Philadelphia, whose family we have pleasantly encountered in the "Republican Court," bought three million acres for $311,250 from the original speculators, Colonel William Duer and General Henry Knox. One million were on the upper Kennebec; the other two million, east of the Penobscot, comprised 52 six-mile-square townships and included almost the entire mainland between that river and the St. Croix, south of the Bangor-Calais road. Not content with this princely domain, Bingham added a few bits and pieces such as the eastern half of Mount Desert Island and the Fontaine Leval holdings in nearby Trenton, relics of a defunct French colony. Otis's first business for Bingham, in the early 1790's, was to clear his title to the Leval tract. After the senator's death, Otis as a prominent member of the Massachusetts legislature became the Bingham estate's number one political protector.

General David Cobb, the Binghams' agent in eastern Maine and a state senator, wrote in 1805 that "malignant spirits" (i.e. Democrats) were threatening an inquiry "for party purposes" into the Binghams' non-performance of their legal duty to bring in so many settlers. As rich absentee proprietors and Federalists at that, the Bingham heirs feared they were in for confiscation or a terrific fine, when Otis shrewdly enlisted William King of Bath, Republican state senator from Lincoln County, to promote a compromise. King and Otis in 1807 became bondsmen for future performance of the settlement requirement; and for saving this immense property from confiscation, the Bingham trustees deeded them, for the nominal sum of $5000, three townships totaling some 65,000 acres on the southernmost, the most desirable range of the Kennebec tract. Situated about ninety miles north of Portland, thirty miles east of Rangeley Lake, and fifty miles southwest of Moosehead Lake, they were named Kingfield, Lexington and Concord. Each took one half — the "Federalist moiety" and the "Republican moiety." Senator King actually lived for a time in Kingfield, picturesquely situated on an intervale in the Carrabasset valley. That town, with lumber and other mills, attained a modest prosperity; and, owing to its nearness to the skiing centers of Sugarloaf and Saddleback, now has a population approaching one thousand.

Lexington and Concord, rugged townships with more rocks than soil, gave Otis and John Richards of Gardiner, his partner in this speculation, little satisfaction. To fulfill the settlement requirements, they and King managed to procure 1976 settlers, each family receiving a hundred-acre lot free and a bonus of $30. In 1809, after selling only $1500 worth of land and laying out five to ten times that sum on roads, bonuses and other improvements, Otis petitioned the Bingham estate for the grant of an extra half-township. They refused; but King came to his partner's assistance by purchasing the Federalist moiety and assuming all settling duties; and Otis was happy to get clear. Lexington and Concord attained their maximum population of 538 and 736 respectively in 1850. Too poor and sparsely settled to maintain town government, they eventually became "wild land" governed by the county. The latest censuses give these two patriotically named towns a combined population of 285 souls.

Otis also succeeded in persuading Henry Knox's executors to relinquish the general's legal claim to certain "residuary profits" on the Binghams' Penobscot tract, and to settle for other encumbrances. But not until 1835 did these Maine lands yield their proprietors enough revenue to pay taxes; and their subsequent profits were due to marketing timber instead of trying to sell land for farms. This vast speculation was based on two suppositions, both of which proved groundless: that the land and climate of interior Maine were suitable for mixed farming, and that settlers would flock thither from Europe and other parts of the United States instead of moving westward.

Harry also had a town named after him in the Berkshire hills of western Massachusetts. In 1810 two little settlements called Loudon and Bethlehem petitioned the general court to combine and be renamed Otis after the speaker of the house, whom they evidently admired for his efforts to defeat Jefferson's embargo. This was done, raising the combined population to 1111 souls; but less than half that number lived there in 1960. Their eponym owned no property in the town, and his only recorded connection with Otis, Massachusetts, was to present the meeting house with a bell. Berkshire, although the poorest county in Massachusetts proper, usually went Federalist; Otis and almost every other hill town voted for Governor Strong in 1814 against the pro-war candidate Dexter.

LITERATURE AND ART

Expansion in Boston during this first decade of the nineteenth century was not wholly material. The intellectual ferment of the age, penetrating this conservative town, produced a new interest in literature which prepared the way for the great movement of the eighteen-thirties that made Boston the literary center of America.

Little was produced, but much was read. Suspicious Federalism tabooed the romanticism of Jean-Jacques and his countrymen who were lumped together as "infidel philosophers," but it welcomed the corresponding movement in Great Britain, since British approval vouched for the fact that no "disorganizing principles" were concealed therein. The well-worn Popes, *Spectators* and Johnsons were laid aside; everyone read Walter Scott, Wordsworth, Miss Edgeworth, and Byron.

Otis had few literary interests. Although the first scholar in his class at Harvard, he always loved men so much better than books that he found little time for reading. A passage in one of his letters of 1820 to Mrs. Otis indicates his taste in literature:

> I have employed myself in reading two volumes of the memoirs of the Margrave of Bareith sister of Frederick 2d, which, as far as I have gone, . . . is more interesting than any romance I have ever read. I advise you to enquire for it. It contains nothing which a married lady may not be known to have read. . . . I worried thro' [Scott's] *Abbot,* as I began it with Gorham. As illustrating an incident in the life of poor Mary Stuart not generally known (supposing it to be founded on fact,) it is worth reading, but I think little of it as a romance.

He took part, however, in promoting literary activity, especially the preliminary phase of founding libraries, literary clubs and magazines. He befriended and encouraged William Tudor, a leader in this movement, and skilled in many other activities as well. Tudor in 1805 founded a club which published the *Monthly Anthology,* one of the earliest American literary magazines, and led to the Boston Athenaeum, of which Otis became one of the original stockholders. In the financial distress incident to Jefferson's embargo and the War of 1812, the *Monthly Anthology* perished for want of support. After the peace of 1815, Tudor and his friends took up their work with fresh zeal and founded the *North American Review.* Otis's interest in this new enterprise is shown by the

following letter from him to Robert Goodloe Harper of 31 May
1816:

> My Dear Sir
>   I transmit to you a subscription paper for the N American
> review. The work has hitherto been conducted in a mode quite
> satisfactory to the subscribers. The Editor William Tudor
> Esquire is a gentleman of highly respectable talents & principles
> and it is believed that with the encouragement of a small addi-
> tional patronage, the work will be found deserving of a dis-
> tinguished rank in the literary annals of our Country. If with-
> out too much trouble you can procure a few names, you will
> promote the cause of literature.

A letter from Tudor to Otis, dated 2 September 1815, shows the
beginning of the movement that led to the Boston Museum of Fine
Arts, as well as the writer's aspirations for the literary and artistic
preëminence of his native city:

> My Dear Sir,
>   A few individuals, (Dr. Warren, I. P. Davis, S. Wells, T. Ly-
> man, D. Sears jr. R. Sullivan, C. Codman &c) have met together
> once or twice to talk over the possibility of getting up an institu-
> tion, for the Fine Arts, the enclosed is a hasty first sketch of the
> paper that was drawn up to form the heading of a subscription
> paper, & enclose it to you for your perusal, and to draw your pen
> across what you may think too *broad,* or if there [are] any other
> ideas will you suggest them. If certain men could be induced to
> put their hands in their pockets, 30,000 Dolls. might be raised
> without inconvenience. The *interest* of the sum would at once
> enable us to make a very great *shew* in two years it would give
> us copies of all the casts in the Louvre, and some paintings. The
> income arising from such an exhibition would pay for its
> charges, and we should have after the first two years 2000 $ to
> give away to artists, this sum would be a sufficient inducement
> to bring Allston, Morse & one or two other young men here, and
> would give us the start of New York & Philadelphia, and strange
> as it may seem, yet so far as my recollection goes we should have

a more complete collection, than any *permanent, public* collection that I know of in London.

Some of the inducements mentioned in the paper, as you well know cannot weigh with me *"per la mia disgracia."* But others do. I wish most heartily the prosperity of the town, and the enlargement of polished society in it. I have heard a good deal of talk this summer, from the circumstances of my residence, among southern people & foreigners, and the general opinion of all these people was that Boston does & must decline, that New York, Baltimore, & Philadelphia must run away with our population & capital. This I do not believe but I believe that exertion is at this time very necessary to secure our standing & future increase. They are straining every nerve in Phila. & Balt. in rivalship, so in New York. The object here contemplated, may with a bold effort at first, go at once beyond them, and will produce permanent advantages. If we can make ourselves the capital of the arts & sciences, and we have already so many powerful institutions that we may do it, our town will increase in that sort of society which is principally to be desired. I think the present state of Europe, will drive many to this country. Other events may happen which will keep up the emigration from England of persons who are not mere laborers & mechanics. An object of this kind trifling as it may be in reality will tend more than ten times the sum employed in any other way to give us our share of this increase of population.

Less than five thousand dollars was raised for the proposed art collection, and the project languished. In the meantime, Otis, David Sears, T. H. Perkins, Samuel Eliot and other affluent Federalists had become art collectors in a modest way. Believing that the walls of a gentleman's mansion should have more decoration than family portraits, they commissioned Washington Allston, the young artist from Charleston and Newport whom they had met during his earlier residence in Boston, to purchase "old masters" and other paintings for them in Europe; and by 1827 there were enough of these in private hands to stage an exhibit. The Athenaeum gave (as the catalogue reads) "The First Exhibition of Paintings in the Athenaeum Gallery: consisting of Specimens by

American Artists, and a Selection of the Works of the Old Masters. From the Various Cabinets in this City and its Vicinity. Admittance 25 Cts. Season Tickets 50 Cts. Catalogue 12½ Cts." The show succeeded so well as to be repeated the next year, with fresh loans from Boston "cabinets" and even a few borrowed from other cities. The curious who paid a quarter to see what the Bostonians collected could gaze on the following lent by Harrison Gray Otis:

> Copley's portrait of his Grandfather Otis
> "A Wild Landscape" by Tempesta
> "A Mountainous Landscape" by Both
> "Near Sunset" and "Landscape, Cattle and Figures" by Pynacher
> "Landscape" by Waterloo
> "Dutch Merry-Making" by Jan Steen (1636–89)
> "Fording the Brook" by Sybrecht (1625–1703)
> "An Interior, Rembrandt."

The last item is the only one that has descended to your author. Unfortunately for him, it is not a Rembrandt (as Otis had been led to believe), but "The Music Lesson" by Willem de Poorter (1608–1648), one of Rembrandt's pupils.

It is evident that Boston had become a provincial center of the arts, and Otis one of the *cognoscenti*. The Athenaeum's second catalogue, of 1828, listed the following resident artists who were taking orders: Francis Alexander, Washington Allston, Chester Harding, Rembrandt Peale and Gilbert Stuart. Part of this exhibit consisted of the collection of paintings owned by Thomas Jefferson, which his heirs had sent for sale to Boston, rather than to New York or Philadelphia. Otis did not buy!

Apart from a fellowship in the American Academy of Arts and Sciences since 1804, Otis had little or no contact with the New England literary movement of his day. No Harvard professors except George Ticknor, Edward Everett, and John G. Palfrey, who had been Otis's pastor in Boston, and no prose writer except William H. Prescott were included in

Otis's "Rembrandt" — De Poorter's "Music Lesson."

his circle of intimate friends. His only recorded personal contact with Ralph Waldo Emerson was fellow membership on a municipal committee to visit the Latin School.

OTIS ORATORY

Young Emerson attended a meeting at Faneuil Hall on 12 or 13 May 1822 in which Otis delivered a speech which he described as a "prodigious display of eloquence"; it "astonished and delighted" him above any other oration he had ever heard. Otis's eloquence, the most conspicuous of his many talents, gave him fame in an era of great orators, who conspicuously helped to mold American public opinion. Otis possessed that gift to the highest degree. We have already seen what a prodigious sensation was produced by his first public speech of importance, on Jay's treaty. With the growing years his mastery of the spoken word increased until he became the favorite speaker at Boston town meeting, and in Judge Story's opinion, the best popular orator in the country. Not only to the cultured but to all classes of people his word was an electric impulse. It used to be said that Otis excited his Faneuil Hall audiences to such a degree that had he called on the people to follow him to burn the town, they would have obeyed.

Otis's eulogy on Alexander Hamilton, pronounced at King's Chapel, on 26 July 1804, is the only speech of his to be published in a collection of America orations; yet it was not his most effective utterance. It opens with a turgid apostrophe to "insatiable death," and the remainder, a somewhat dry outline of Hamilton's career, errs rather on the side of simplicity. To a Republican, Otis seemed "the least objectionable of these eulogists, because the least false and fulsome." In the opinion of many Federalists, he did not do the subject justice. For Otis was never at his best in a formal oration. He had to extemporize in the swift give and take of the bar and the public forum, to show his full powers.

Contemporaries speak of his "voice of silvery sweetness," so modulated as to express every emotion, of his fine features and graceful gestures, of his self-possession and tact. The same personality that won him friends, charmed his audiences. The qualities which most impressed his audiences were spontaneity, the apparent lack of effort, a rich and varied vocabulary enhanced by happy choice of words. Take this sentence as an example, from his speech in Faneuil Hall after Hull's surrender in 1812:

> Our political orb has almost completed its revolution; it is about to set in the cold and dreary regions of Canada, where night and chaos will brood over the last of desolated republics.

No one could better have expressed the sentiment of gloom, disaster and grim foreboding with which Federalists regarded the second war with England.

Otis had neither the lusty strength of Daniel Webster, nor the keen reasoning powers of Samuel Dexter; but he surpassed even the former in the power of felicitous and spontaneous expression. He was once seated on the platform in Faneuil Hall when Webster, speaking in favor of the Maysville Road Bill, remarked in the course of his speech, "I am in favor, Mr. Chairman, of all roads, except . . . except . . ." Here he stuck fast for a word until Otis, who sat near, whispered, "The road to ruin!" Webster adopted the suggestion and inserted Otis's happy phrase as if he had merely paused to make it more effective.

Of this same happy and extemporaneous generosity A. B. Muzzy gives in his *Reminiscences* another example:

> Harrison Gray Otis was, in the year 1828, a candidate for the mayoralty of Boston. . . . Hon. Josiah Quincy was the opposing candidate. . . . Mr. Otis speaks first. His personal appearance is most striking: a large frame, tall, and well proportioned, with a bearing dignified and courteous. . . . his complexion florid, with bright eyes, and a pleasing and gracious expression, he prepossesses general favor as he rises from his seat. This effect

is enhanced by a voice mellow, flexible, and admirably modulated. His gesticulation is graceful, his whole manner per-
suasive. . . . He is applauded at frequent intervals, and resumes
his seat amid deafening cheers. It is a trying moment for Mr.
Quincy. . . . With a constitutional hesitancy of speech, he feels,
it is manifest, an unusual embarrassment. Mr. Otis, seeing
clearly what he is attempting to utter, rises, and in a few flowing
periods, gives an eloquent expression to the thought of his rival.
The effect is electric. His noble magnanimity brings out cheer
upon cheer; and it is followed by a speech from Mr. Quincy,
comprehensive, logical, worthy of the man and of the occasion.

Another story confirms Otis's readiness in debate, and ability to
get out of a hole that he dug for himself. In the darkest period of
the second war with England, in late August 1814, there was a
meeting in Faneuil Hall to consider measures for the defense of
Boston. Otis offered a set of resolutions which were eventually
adopted, although they included a covert attack on the government
at Washington. His rival Samuel Dexter, who had left his Federalist colleagues to support the war, argued that the resolutions were
not strong enough and deprecated opposing the national government. Otis, more than usually excited, said, "We shall not be
turned aside from our course, which we believe to be the path of
duty, by any fear of the rulers, at Washington, on the one hand,
nor by that of apostacy, on the other," accompanying these words
by a fling of his arm toward Dexter who sat a few feet away. Dexter
half rose and cried out, "If he does not retract those words, I'll
wring his nose, in spite of his popularity!" A third party interrupted Otis and spoke a few words in his ear. Otis resumed; and
as a witness remembered, "Never was oil more skilfully poured
upon the waters of strife: — Nothing could have been more remote
from his intention, than the slightest allusion of disrespect to any
member of that assembly; especially to one, the purity of whose
patriotism was above all suspicion. He should as soon think of
doubting the existence of his God. He exceedingly regretted to

Samuel Dexter, by Gilbert Stuart.

have been so entirely misapprehended." This calmed the rising
storm and prevented what might have been an unseemly scuffle on
the floor of the "Cradle of Liberty."

BOSTON SOCIETY AND POOR RELATIONS

An English traveler who visited Boston shortly after the Civil War
remarked that Boston society seemed to be divided into family sets
or clans, each of which established its own standards, unlike the
London sets who aped the higher aristocracy. Grandchildren,
mixing constantly with cousins in family parties and outings, were
apt to marry within the clan despite meeting other young ladies
and gentlemen at dancing assemblies, Harvard Commencements
and private balls. This pattern, already true of Otis's Boston, lasted
even into the twentieth century. Outstanding in his day was the
Essex County circle, social background of the Essex Junto. As
Colonel Henry Lee wrote, "The Jacksons came up from Newburyport to Boston, social and kindly people, inclined to make acquaintances and mingle with the world pleasantly. *But they got
some Cabot wives, who shut them up.*" To which Lee's biographer
added, "Lees, Cabots, Jacksons and Higginsons knew each other
well in Essex County, and had a satisfying belief that New England
morality and intellectuality had produced nothing better . . . so
they contentedly made a little clique by themselves, and inter-
married very much, with a sure and cheerful faith that in such
alliances there could be no blunder." And he might have added
the Lowells of Newburyport to the list; Judge John Lowell married, first, a Higginson and, second, a Cabot; and his grandsons
married a Jackson, a Lowell and a Putnam. Then there were the
Adams-Brooks-Quincy-Cranch set, the Forbes-Perkins set, and the
Lawrence-Peabody-Loring set. Mrs. Marian Lawrence Peabody, in
her charming reminiscences, observed that it was almost inevitable
that she marry a Peabody, since three of her grandfather Peabody's

children married Lawrences and a fourth married a Peabody cousin; and marriages of double first cousins between Lowells and Lawrences, Higginsons and Cabots, were not infrequent.

The Otises, with roots in Boston before the Revolution, during which they lost most of their relatives in the loyalist emigration, had to start from scratch. Harry and Sally made their own set, first by friendship with other pre-revolutionary Boston families such as Perkins, Mason, Sullivan, Russell, Sears and Eliot. They quickly enlarged their "circle of friends" (as Mrs. Otis called them) and founded a veritable clan through their children's and grandchildren's marriages with Lymans, Thorndikes, Appletons and the like. This gave them a central position in Boston society, having friendly contacts with all others — excepting, of course, the "Jacobin" Gerry-Austin-Eustis clan — and their relations with the presidential Adamses were subject to political interruptions.

Otis was the patron saint of poor relations, especially of the ever impecunious Grays. Until 1830 Harrison Gray, Jr., lived a grumbling existence in London, supported by a small pension from the crown and the American property that his nephew had managed to save from the old treasurer's estate. The reader may remember Jack Gray, the young loyalist of 1775, entrusted to the Otises in Barnstable for safekeeping during the siege of Boston. His capacity for getting into trouble did not decrease with age, judging by the following letter of 1804 from Harrison Gray, Jr., describing Jack's departure for Demerara to seek his fortune:

Dear nephew —
. . . Your Uncle saild from Falmouth the 3d of April with a fair Wind. . . . The very Evening before he intended to leave Town he was arrested and taken to a Spunging House by a Man he had conceived to be his good Friend. I had to borrow the money the next day to get him liberated the debt was twenty pounds & the Damn infamous Charges £9.5.7. . . . After he was discharged from this execrable & infamous place, which is a disgrace to the Government, I was determined to get him out of London & the

next morning he went & arrived at Portsmouth in the Evening
& he wrote me the day After to say the Ship from the Downs
had not got round and the next Sunday following as I was at
Breakfast a Knock at my door was Announced, and as Usual I
said walk in, and to my Utter *Astonishment*, when I turned my
head round, I found it was your Uncle. . . . I said in the Name
of God what has happened have you lost your passage, he said
no but as he was going to embark he was Arrested for £13.10 by
a Hair dresser who he did not owe one farthing to, and who he
saw every day before he left Town, the Scoundrel took the
Advantage of his situation as he knew all his movemts and swore
to his debt.

    Being Sunday I did not know where to apply for the money as
all Banks were shut & most all my Friends in the Country. fortunately the Man of the House where I lived had twenty pounds
by him which I borrowed and added two more as the Charges
was £7.15.6 & immediately sent to take his place for that Evening
& after I made him eat a Beefsteak & a pint of Wine I accompanied him to the Coach & saw him off once more After paying
£50.11.1 which to a *positive Certainty* would have been saved,
if he had left Town the day I urged him. . . . I heard from him
on Tuesday dated 3 o Clock on Monday saying he Arrived at
8 o Clock very much fatigued not having his Cloaths off for 48
hours & that the infamous Scoundrels did not discharge him
until 3 o Clock & he was then going on board as the Convoy
was Under Weigh with a fair wind.

Yellow fever in the West Indies soon put an end to the troubles
of happy-go-lucky Uncle Jack, and on nephew Harry fell the duty
of helping to support two orphan daughters left destitute. He thus
acquired a reputation for benevolence too great for his comfort.
In June 1812 he received a letter from a prominent lawyer of New
Orleans informing him of the sudden death the previous October
of "Judge Turner and his lady," the former a Boston man who had
acquired a sugar plantation in Louisiana, the latter a niece of Jack
and daughter of Harrison Gray, Jr. After giving a few details with
regard to the property, which seemed likely to be wiped out by
debts, the writer coolly announced:

I proceed to inform you, that I now send you their seven children by the brig *Juno,* Capt: Arnold, accompanied by an old Negro woman named Dolly . . . to whom the children are extremely attached. . . . You will be satisfied, I presume, Sir, with my addressing these unhappy orphans to you, in preference to any other person of Mr. Turner's family, whose names have come to my knowledge. I know by letters I have found among the papers of the deceased, that he had a Mother & a sister living, but neither of them in a situation to take such a charge upon them. . . . But sir, having heard on all hands, that your fortune & respectability render you the only person to whom I can with propriety send them, I cannot hesitate at so doing; and I do it in the full confidence that you will receive and act by them, as I am persuaded our poor deceased friend wou'd have done by yours under like circumstances.

The writer goes on to request that Otis see to the maintenance and education of these seven children, without any likelihood of procuring a penny for their support from their father's estate. Harry, as may be supposed, was somewhat taken aback by this extraordinary announcement. He threatened to send the seven unfortunate orphans back to New Orleans if the lawyers refused to relinquish sufficient funds for their support from the estate. They finally produced the money, and Otis was relieved from the painful alternative of adding seven children to his own family of eight, or of letting them become objects of charity. Two of the Turner girls grew up in Boston, and Otis busied himself with trying to obtain a legacy from one of their cousins for their further support.

CHAPTER XII

Federalist Reorganization

1801–1814, AET. 35–48

Caucus System and Central Committee

THE PRESIDENTIAL ELECTION of 1800–01 demonstrated to younger Federalists like Harrison Gray Otis that if their party were to survive it must have more organization than leaders "writing private letters to each other" (as James McHenry had said), or taking orders from the Essex Junto as if it was the admiral, and they, his captains. There was a problem of nominations for elective office. Should they take over the convention system from the Republicans, or adopt a different method? As Federalists had consistently denounced conventions as Jacobin or Shaysite, something different it must be. The second problem was education of the voters, which could no longer be left to chance. New Federalist newspapers were established, old and tottering ones shored up, pamphlets published to supplement them. And, as the Jefferson party had profited immensely from the social, get-together, free handout activities of Tammany societies in New York and elsewhere, the Federalists countered with the Washington Benevolent Society.

Otis led his party in setting up one of the neatest political organizations in America prior to the Albany Regency. Thoroughly centralized, it operated from the top down, making no concession to popular rights, frankly based upon the theory that the leaders knew best. Voters were indeed asked to attend caucuses at the local level, but these were nothing more than rallies where men appointed from higher up told them whom to nominate and what resolves to pass.

The starting point of Federalist reorganization in Massachusetts was a caucus consisting of the party members in both branches of the general court, to nominate governor and lieutenant governor. The 1800 caucus did a master stroke in persuading Caleb Strong to run for governor. Member of a pioneer Northampton family, a graduate of Harvard before Harry Otis was born, Caleb made his living by the law, but looked and talked like a farmer; and he had already been in public life for a quarter century, member of the Federal Convention of 1787, and United States senator. A simple, homespun, unpretentious man, he won votes by honesty and frugal habits. The Democratic newspapers (now that Jefferson had set the fashion of high living) used to poke fun at the simple fare of salt codfish and hasty pudding that Canny Caleb put before his guests; but that made the voters love him the more, and as Federalist standard-bearer he disproved the charge that all political plums in the Bay State went to Boston aristocrats or Essex County autocrats. Caleb was the prototype of his fellow townsman Calvin Coolidge; he had firm conservative principles, with the reputation of a middle-of-the-road moderate. Eleven times elected governor and only once defeated, annually increasing his vote, Caleb Strong may be considered the most popular governor in Massachusetts history.

The legislative caucus chose a committee, consisting of one member from each county, which initiated the nomination, and its recommendations were usually adopted by the whole body. But either the legislative caucus, or the caucus committee, elected annually a smaller permanent body, the state central committee. Consisting usually of seven Bostonians, not necessarily members of the legislature, this was the keystone and executive head of the Federalist organization in Massachusetts. It appointed the local committees which initiated nominations for the general court. It published an annual address to the people, distributed literature, kept local leaders up to the mark, and saw to it that Federalist towns were fully represented. Its very existence, however, was supposed to be a profound secret.

A few copies of printed circular letters have survived, signed in manuscript, by which the central committee communicated with the county and town committees. Since Otis's name invariably stands first, he must have been chairman. Associated with him were Thomas Handasyd Perkins, William Sullivan, Daniel Sargent, John Welles, and John Phillips, all politicians and members of leading Boston families; Israel Thorndike (whose son married Otis's daughter), as well as other Boston merchants; Artemas Ward, son of the general of the same name; and Francis Dana Channing, a brother of William Ellery Channing. Although the Essex Junto were not represented (probably because they considered the routine party work infra dig) they still profoundly influenced Federalist policy, and the committees which managed the presidential campaigns of 1808 and 1812 were chosen almost exclusively from Junto ranks.

Circular letters were issued by the central committee at least twice a year: before the governor's election, and between that date and the election of state representatives. A page of stock remarks on French influence and Jacobin intolerance, with stress upon the particular need for exertion that year, was followed by a confidential communication on methods and organization. The circular of 9 February 1810, for instance, states to the county committees:

> You will impress the several town committees, with the necessity of dividing their towns into sections, of appointing committees for every district, of confirming the doubtful, and exciting those who are firm; and of sending the full number of representatives. The means of information must be placed in the hands of all who will make a right use of them.
>
> You will recommend to the committees frequent meetings with the inhabitants, and the prompt distribution of any political papers they may receive, and communications of any intelligence they may obtain.
>
> A correspondence should be maintained between the several county committees, and information given of the arts that may be resorted to by our opponents, in season to frustrate them.

A circular of 19 February 1811 shows the central committee ordering a change in the form of county and town committees. It is signed by Otis, Phillips and Welles, and addressed to "Samuel Crocker Esqr., Nicholas Tillinghast Esqr., John Seabury Esqr., Taunton," who had been "selected at a numerous and respectable meeting of Federalists" (the central committee) which had decided to appoint a committee of three in each town to "give vigour and effect to all measures, that may promote the election of the Federal candidates." A circular letter of 19 April 1811 to all town committees followed this up, with such detailed instructions for getting out the vote that it is difficult to see how a single Federalist voter escaped being dragged to the polls. These documents reveal a highly centralized party machine in a surprisingly advanced state of development: a hierarchy of committees, district, town and county, all controlled and set in motion by the state central committee in Boston.

Methods of Nomination

Let us now turn to practical workings. The county committees summoned a county caucus every March to nominate a slate of state senators. This caucus, theoretically a mass meeting open to every voter in the county, was usually swamped by those living in the county seat, and rigged by the committee. In Boston, both town and county, the machinery was controlled by a central committee of Suffolk County appointed by the state central committee and, to some extent, influenced by the ward committees. These last were elected by ward caucuses, the only popular feature of the Federalist organization. Twice a year (thrice in even years), about two weeks before the elections for governor (first Monday in April), for state representatives (first Monday in May) and for Congress (first week of November), the Suffolk central committee called a primary or initial caucus composed of itself, the ward committees and a carefully selected list of invited guests — a very congenial little affair. Primary caucus met in Concert Hall or Exchange Coffee-House, and the Federalist press respected its privacy. At the March meeting a slate of state senators was agreed upon; and at the October meeting, in even years, a member of Congress was nominated without, it appears, taking any notice of the country towns which were in the same district with Boston. In May this initial or primary caucus selected a slate for the "Boston Seat" in the general court. Every town had a right to one member in the lower house for every 225 ratable polls, but Boston never sent more than seven members until 1805. Up to that year the courts insisted on a literal application of the constitutional provision that "every member of the house of representatives shall be chosen by written votes," which made the writing of ballots an onerous task. After printed ballots had been allowed, the initial caucus availed itself of the town's full privilege, and nominated annually between twenty-seven and forty-five representatives, who were invariably elected, and made a powerful Federalist bloc in the general court.

Nominations made by the initial caucus were announced in the newspapers as being "recommended" from some mysterious source, and were formally adopted by a general or "Grand Federal" caucus at Faneuil Hall on the Sunday evening before the election of governor, to which every Federalist was invited. This was the great political occasion of the year, the scene of brilliant forensic displays by Otis and lesser Boston orators. John Quincy Adams wrote in his diary for 5 April 1807:

> I attended the federal meeting at Faneuil Hall this evening. The hall was nearly as full as it could hold. Mr. Quincy was speaking when I went in. Mr. Otis and Mr. Gore succeeded him, but there was no diversity of opinion. The vote was put for supporting Mr. Strong as Governor, at the election tomorrow, and Mr. Robbins as Lieutenant Governor, with the last years list of Senators. They were all unanimously carried. Walking home with Mr. Dexter, I was remarking upon the questionable nature

of this party organization, and its tendency under our Constitution. It is perhaps unavoidable, but it is not altogether reconcilable to the freedom of the elective principle.

Shortly after this, Adams defected to the Republican party, which, as he discovered, paid even less respect than the Federalist "to the freedom of the elective principle." The ideal of the founding fathers that every voter would make his free choice without a party nomination or any sort of management showed a deep misunderstanding of human nature.

Election Day in Boston was an exciting affair, under the old régime. All the polling took place in Faneuil Hall. All day its steps were lined with young men of both parties, offering written or printed ballots to the voters as they arrived, and taking a last opportunity to strengthen the wavering and alarm the timid. Every man had to show his colors or abstain, and vigilant ward committees made life miserable for stay-at-homes. Otis was loath to give up the old methods in 1822, when the city charter was adopted in favor of separate polling places in the wards. Federalist supremacy, he wrote to William Sullivan,

depends upon the influence and example of the most respectable persons in the various walks and professions who have long been habituated to act together. — The force of these persons is increased by the sympathy and enthusiasm of numbers, and by a feeling of shame or self reproach which attends the consciousness of a *known* dereliction of duty — The class which is *acted upon* by this example and influence realize a pride and pleasure in shewing their colors upon a general review, which they cannot feel when trained in a gun house. — The old leaders have learned the art of giving a salutary impulse to the whole body when collected together. — This impulse ought to be a unit, to procure unity of action. — It is easier to manage the town of B—— by a *Lancastrian* system of political discipline than to institute numerous schools.

Judged by results, this "Lancastrian system" had been a complete success. While the Federal party existed, Boston was its pocket borough. Between 1788 and 1828 it never failed to give a majority to the Federalist candidate for Congress. A Democratic candidate for governor carried the town only twice (1800 and 1801) between 1797 and 1825; and the Democratic ticket for representatives succeeded but once (1800) in the same period. No wonder, then, that Federalists called Boston "The Headquarters of Good Principles."

In spite of the scurrility and personal abuse with which newspapers of both parties were filled; in spite of the perfervid speeches of night-before caucuses; election days in New England prior to the Jacksonian era were never sullied by disorder or violence. New England had a rigid code of etiquette regarding political campaigns, in which stump-speaking, spellbinding, and whirlwind tours were taboo, and candidates were forbidden by public opinion to electioneer in their own behalf. It was even considered improper for them to make a statement. Samuel Dexter in 1814 apologized for publishing an explanation of his attitude, when unexpectedly nominated by the Democrats; and Otis's friends dissuaded him from publishing a denial of his opposition to war loans, when he was a candidate for governor in 1823. But political conversation and newspaper campaigning never abated during the feverish period between 1807 and 1815. The State Street insurance offices became informal political clubs at which leading Federalists dropped in during the morning to discuss the latest French outrage or Jacobin delusion. "The office of the Suffolk Insurance Company," wrote Lucius Manlius Sargent, "was more noted for its daily political harangues, than for its semi-annual dividends. . . . The voice of Mr. Parsons, then Chief Justice of the Commonwealth, was often heard in those conventicles; not in his official capacity, of course, but as the Magnus Apollo of the Assembly."

Nevertheless, both parties got a lot of fun out of electioneering. Formal dinners, especially those of the Fourth of July, were occasions for the display of piquant political toasts, for which Otis was famous. Twenty formal toasts, accompanied by a band of music and discharges of artillery, were not unusual on these occasions, and informal toasts followed until most of the diners were under the table. The following are a few of the *formal* ones at the Federalist dinner in Salem on 4 July 1812, just after war had been declared:

July 4th, 1812. — We hail it as the commencement of a new Independence.
    2 guns. "Yankee Doodle."

Embargo. — A base *retreat*, treacherously *beat*, while commercial prosperity was in full *march*.
    1 gun. "Austrian Retreat."

Non-Importation. — A vile measure calculated to introduce smuggling, deprave the public morals, and sap the foundation of *Northern* liberty.
    1 gun. "Jefferson's Delight."

The Existing War. — The Child of Prostitution, may no American acknowledge it legitimate.
    1 gun. "Wapping Landlady."

Democratic Office Holders: — They draw *double rations* and never go on *fatigue duty* except on days of election.
    1 gun. "Faith! The world's a good thing."

Thos. Jefferson. — May we never cease to continue to idolize the man who *copied off* the Declaration of Independence.
    1 gun. "Dicky Gossip is the man."

Physical and Moral Strength. — the STATE is favored of Heaven which sees itself STRONG in the field, STRONG, in the cabinet, and STRONG in the hearts of the people.
    3 guns. "Gov. Strong's March."

EDUCATING THE VOTERS

To return to the functions of the central committee, we find one of its most important duties was that of educating the voters. It produced (and Otis usually composed) an Address to the People which filled the front page of the *Centinel* in the latter part of

March. Members of the committee wrote political essays and stimulated others to express their ideas. Newspapers were more ex-
tensively employed as a party weapon by the Federalists than by
their opponents. As late as 1810 there were Federalist newspapers
in every state, and in two Territories. Among Otis's manuscripts
is a list of northern New England newspapers containing pithy
comments, such as:

> The *Watchman* printed at Montpelier, Vt. by Samuel Goss;
> though Federal — this watchman appears to be asleep on his
> post — if roused to his duty and made acquainted with the im-
> portance of his trust, he may prove as serviceable to his country
> as the winged biped that saved Rome.

> *The Hampshire Federalist* — printed in Springfield by Thomas
> Dickman; zealously federal — but destitute of talent, and with-
> out any literary assistance.

> *The Farmers Cabinet,* printed at Amherst, N. H., by Joseph
> Cushing — a no-sided or two-sided paper — its editor boasting
> an intolerable degree of Independence with considerable in-
> genuity and industry. The paper has a large circulation, and
> may be made beneficial by requiring for every democratic alle-
> gation, a federal reply.

When the Boston *Weekly Messenger* ventured in 1812 to criticize the party's presidential nomination, Otis wrote to William
Sullivan, sputtering with rage against the "perfidy" of the editor
"in thus perverting a paper set up with great pains trouble and
expense by the Federal Party." Central committee, knowing that
pamphlets reached many who refused to read Federalist newspapers, circulated them in large quantities. "Electioneering
opened. Pamphlets flying like wild geese in a storm," wrote Dr.
Ames in 1808. Five thousand copies of Timothy Pickering's pamphlet on Jefferson's embargo were distributed within the state that
year.

In the Washington Benevolent Societies the Federalists possessed a powerful auxiliary corresponding to modern political clubs. The first society of that name, founded in New York City in 1808, was copied in Massachusetts in 1812; and as indignation rose against the War of 1812, within two years almost every town of any size in New England, and many points outside, had established branch societies. Each applicant for membership took an oath to support the Constitution of the United States, to use his exertions to preserve it "against the inroads of despotism, monarchy, aristocracy, *and democracy*," and to be faithful to "those political principles which distinguished the Administration of Washington." He then received a pamphlet containing Washington's Farewell Address and the Constitution of the United States, with a certificate of membership on the flyleaf.

The ostensible objects of the Washington Benevolent Society were "to support the Constitution of the United States in its original purity," and "to supply the wants and alleviate the sufferings of unfortunate individuals within the sphere of our personal acquaintance." It gave the Federalist party a social bond. The Society not only dispensed charity; it also appealed to that universal human weakness, the desire to belong to something. Annual dues were only a dollar; there were badges, dinners, meetings and elaborate processions; and in a period when the wealthy and powerful were looked up to, it was a desirable privilege to sit down at table with Harrison Gray Otis or Thomas Handasyd Perkins and to be hailed by them as "brother." A directory of the Boston society in 1813 contains over 1500 names — half the Federalist vote of the town — and includes men in every walk of life. Officers for the most part were chosen from the younger generation; Harrison Gray Otis, Jr., for instance, served as secretary.

The Democrats, who had profited through Tammany and similar societies since 1793, were outraged at Federalists doing the same thing, and accused the Washington societies of plotting secession. The Democrats also employed ridicule — a satirical pamphlet of 1813, "The First Book of the 'Washington Benevolents,'

otherwise called the Book of Knaves," is dedicated "to the 'Beloved
Harry,' otherwise 'the man of the People,' " and assigns Otis the
following role in the organization:

> 1. Now it was far past the going down of the sun; and Harry
> who was surnamed the "beloved," proposed that the council
> should make preparation for the great feast of the political
> passover.
> 2. Moreover he said, that albeit the name of *Tory* had become
> a bye-word, and a scoff among the people, he did propose that
> the tribe of the tories should forthwith be called *Washington
> Benevolents*.
> 3. And the council applauded Harry for his wisdom and cried
> out with one voice, who is like unto the grand contriver?

This pamphlet poked fun at the colorful ceremonials in which
every Washington Benevolent Society indulged on 30 April, the
anniversary of Washington's inauguration. On 30 April 1814, at
a critical period of the war, brightly uniformed militia companies
with fifes shrilling, drums beating and colors flying, led the Washington Benevolents' procession. Behind them marched the officers
of the society mingled with "public characters and strangers of distinction," and honored members of the clergy. Next in line were
four hundred children dressed in white, bearing wreaths, garlands
and, hanging from a necklace, a little book containing excerpts
from the sage's sayings. They were followed by twenty-one youths
carrying silken banners commemorating Washington's victories in
the War of Independence, and other events of his life, or representing sentiments such as independence, union, commerce, peace, and
national glory. Next — borne reverently on a satin cushion — came
George Washington's gorget which he had worn in the French and
Indian War. Martha's granddaughter Mrs. Peter presented this to
the society, on the ground that Boston cherished, while Virginia
had befouled, the memory of Washington. Behind this sacred relic
marched the main body of the society four abreast, stretching for
a mile and a half. All this took place in an April downpour which

pious Democrats considered a "judgment of Heaven," but it failed to discourage the participants or to extinguish their patriotic ardor.

There is no doubt that the Washington Benevolent Societies increased the strength and furthered the solidarity of Federalism during the War of 1812. After the end of that war they languished and died for want of any exciting issue.

The Secret National Conventions

The Massachusetts leaders cooperated with Federalist organizations in other states in calling secret meetings of delegates in 1808 and 1812, hoping to agree on candidates for the presidency. A peculiar problem of the Federalists in 1808, repeated in 1812, produced this premature appearance of the modern party showpiece, the national nominating convention. In each year an insurgent Republican, one of the New York Clintons, entered the race in protest against the anti-commercial policy of Jefferson and the war policy of Madison. Should the Federalists run their own candidates, or, with greater chance of success, support the insurgent already in the field? To reach a decision, a conference of leaders was called from all parts of the country.

Harrison Gray Otis broached the idea to leading New York and Philadelphia Federalists during a visit to those cities in May 1808. Shortly after his return to Boston he received a letter from Charles Willing Hare[1] of Philadelphia, alluding to these conversations with him and suggesting that it was high time to do something about the presidential nomination. The hint was taken; Federalists in the Massachusetts legislature appointed a committee of correspondence, with Otis chairman, to concert measures with party mem-

---

[1] Charles Willing Hare, 1778–1827, a prominent lawyer and Federalist leader in Philadelphia at this time, a member of the state legislature and a candidate for Congress. He was a close relative of Otis's friends the Harrisons, and trustee of the Bingham estate.

bers elsewhere. Timothy Bigelow, speaker of the house, Senator
James Lloyd, Jr., and two members of the Essex Junto, George
Cabot and Christopher Gore, were the other members. This committee on 10 June decided to call "a meeting of Federalists, from as
many states as could be seasonably notified, at New York." It
notified Hare in Philadelphia and Rufus King in New York of the
decision, and Hare wrote to Otis on 19 June:

> I received yours of the 11th on the 16. I immediately took
> measures for convening a few of our most active firm and dis-
> creet friends. A Meeting of about a dozen was held yesterday —
> at which your objects and reasoning were stated — and so far
> as regards the propriety of the proposed convention, immediately
> and without hesitation acquiesced in. A Committee consisting
> of Messrs Fitzsimons, R Waln, Latimer, Morgan and myself,
> were appointed to correspond with you — and in obedience to
> your suggestion to 'organise for the South.' We shall immedi-
> ately write to some of our friends in Maryland and Delaware,
> and after having heard from them I shall again address you.

Judge Egbert Benson of New York, who happened to be in
Boston shortly after the committee meeting, communicated with
the leading Federalists in Connecticut and New Jersey on his way
home, and suggested that they set up committees of correspondence
in their states. The Massachusetts committee sent Otis and Bigelow on special missions to Vermont, New Hampshire and Rhode
Island, in order to obtain their cooperation.

Thirty-five delegates from eight states, chosen by exclusive committees of the Boston type, met at New York in the third week of
August. The Federalist journals breathed no hint of it, since the
very existence of the convention was supposed to be a profound
secret; but the assembling of so many prominent persons did not
escape the impudent Democratic press. Among the delegates were
Otis, Gore and Lloyd from Massachusetts; Hare and Thomas Fitz-
simmons from Pennsylvania; Robert Goodloe Harper from Mary-

land, and John Rutledge from South Carolina. No record has been found of the discussion, but the question between supporting Clinton and making separate nominations was so thoroughly threshed out in Otis's correspondence, that we may fairly assume the line of argument that prevailed. Otis believed that it was hopeless to expect the success of a Federalist candidate and that, to elect Clinton, a course which he strongly favored, would not only dethrone the Virginia dynasty but take the Federal Government out of the hands of dangerous ideologues and secure an administration favoring the commercial interests. He was supported by the intellectual leader of the party, George Cabot, who saw that a page of democratic evolution had been turned; that Federalists had better give up hope of capturing the presidency and ally themselves with the better element among the Democrats. Otis enlarged on this in a letter to John Rutledge before the convention assembled. To elect a Federalist president, he said, would not serve the country or the party "if by any other means the Virginia snake can be scotched. The mischief to be expected from the system already adopted will be of a nature and extent beyond the power of any administration suddenly to remedy." Thus it would be better to have a New York Democrat to clean up the mess. As a clincher, Fisher Ames "impressed this opinion upon me with his almost dying breath."[1]

But the New York Federalists ruined Otis's plan because they regarded the Clintonian dynasty as bad as the Virginian. "We have condescended twice to tamper with Democratic Candidates," wrote Abraham Van Vechten to Otis, "and in both instances have been subjected to severe self-reproach. . . . Our experimental knowledge of the Clintonian System is a powerful Antidote against affording it any facility here." And to coalesce with Clinton Democrats would be a dereliction of principle. As Judge Theodore Sedgwick wrote to Otis on 6 June, "I cannot endure the humiliating idea

---

[1] Otis to Rutledge 3 July 1808; a P.S. dated the 14th says, "Ames is no more, he died this morning at 5 o'clock."

that those who alone from education, fortune, character and principle are entitled to command should voluntarily arrange themselves under the banners of a party in all respects inferior,
and in many odious, to them." The proposed coalition with
the Clintonians was rejected, and Charles Cotesworth Pinckney
and Rufus King were nominated for the presidency and vice
presidency.

The Philadelphia committee, to which the convention confided
the task of announcing the Pinckney and King nominations, did
not even dare to do so. "We were led to this conclusion," they
wrote to the Massachusetts committee, "from having observed
something like a Jealousy, in our friends at having a Nomination
so Important decided on by so small a Number as we were, and
without any Special authority for the purpose." So the nominations were published hypocritically as the result of "information
collected from every part of the Union . . . without the aid of any
Caucus, or other preliminary." Some Federalist journals never
even published the nominations but announced that their state
Federalist electoral ticket was "unpledged," leaving it possible to
switch to Clinton at the last moment. Otis favored this plan, and
Theophilus Parsons attempted to seduce the Connecticut electors
into the same course. Obviously the first nominating convention
did not succeed in impressing its members with party loyalty. And
the Pinckney-King ticket ran a bad second, carrying only New
England, except Vermont, and Delaware.

Again, in the presidential election of 1812, the Federalist party
had to decide between making separate nominations and supporting a Clinton; De Witt Clinton had come out for the presidency,
as his Uncle George had done earlier, as an insurgent. A Federalist
national convention at New York was decided upon in June 1812,
and organized, as in 1808, by irregularly chosen committees of
correspondence in the several states. Otis was chairman of a committee which elected the Massachusetts delegates, including himself, at a meeting consisting only of Cabot, Gore and Sullivan. On

the eve of the convention, Samuel Dexter wrote a very sapient and eloquent letter to Otis:

> . . . The great object is to prevent our annihilation as a commercial Nation. It is to me of little importance whether the rulers be of one party name or another. Every expedient will of necessity be temporary & only a choice of evils. Such indeed is Government itself. The great question is how can we escape with as little suffering as possible & for as long as possible. If these objects can best be obtained by a coalition with a portion of the opposite party why should pride or passion prevent it? An honorable peace is the present object; & I hope the Country can bear it & the prosperity that might attend it. Tho' sometimes I indulge gloom eno' to think that we are so corrupt as to need war. Everything that ought to be honorable in our Country seems to be at market as much as butcher's meat. To allude to the Roman history . . . ; when no formidable enemy remained corruption made them a fit prey for barbarians. While they were warlike they suffered, but they were magnanimous. The Greeks produced patriots, for posterity to admire, in the midst of War & Revolution. They have left a blaze of light behind them, but it was because their Country was on fire. . . .

Dexter later changed his mind and supported the war, earning the nickname "Mr. Ambi-Dexter"; but Otis remained implacable. "Our first and greatest effort," he wrote John Rutledge on 31 July 1812, "will be to extricate ourselves in a regular mode, by changing the administration. . . . It is impossible for us to elect a Federal President. D. W. Clinton will receive the undivided support of New York, and as I have every reason to think, of all New England. . . . For God's sake bestir yourself and endeavour to operate upon some of the republican leaders who will be likely to impell others. . . . I have satisfactory evidence that upon the great points of War, French Alliance, and Commerce, he will adopt a course perfectly in unison with *our* views and wishes."

About sixty-five delegates from eleven states were present at the New York convention on 15–17 September. The arguments of

1808 were repeated; and, as a clincher, no Federalist candidate was available. Pinckney refused to run again, and John Jay, as Samuel Dexter observed, "could no more play president than Seneca could Emperor," whilst John Marshall would not leave the Supreme Court. Although Clinton promised if elected to administer the government in a manner satisfactory to the Federalists, and to sue for peace with Great Britain, Rufus King, unconvinced, declared that his election would merely substitute Caesar Borgia for James Madison. King's speech, according to William Sullivan, produced a deadlock between Clinton's friends and enemies which lasted until the convention was about to break up without result. Then,

> Mr. Otis arose, apparently much embarrassed, holding his hat in his hand, and seeming as if he were almost sorry he had arisen. Soon he warmed to the subject, his hat fell from his hand, and he poured forth a strain of eloquence that chained all present to their seats; and when, at a late hour, the vote was taken, it was almost unanimously resolved to support Clinton. This effort was unprepared, but only proves how entirely Mr. Otis deserves the reputation he enjoys of being a great orator.

It is a pity to spoil this dramatic picture, but more trustworthy sources than Sullivan's memory thirty-five years after the event show that Otis's speech failed to produce a decision. The convention adjourned after passing a set of ambiguous resolutions that left the delegates in a state of muddled incertitude. According to Rufus King's diary, it was voted (1) inexpedient to nominate Federalist candidates, but (2) proper to support candidates who "would be likely to pursue a different course of measures from that of the now President," and (3) a committee of five Pennsylvanians be appointed "to ascertain the results of the elections for Electors, and the Candidates whom they would be likely to support, and to communicate the same as expeditiously as practicable to the Electors of the several States." No two members agreed as to the precise meaning that these resolves were intended to convey — and no wonder. In most of the states a "Clintonian" or "Peace" ticket of electors was supported by dissident Republicans and Federalists; Otis was a presidential elector in Massachusetts. De Witt ran much better than his uncle had in 1808, winning 89 electoral votes from four New England states, New York, New Jersey, Delaware and Maryland; but Madison, with 128 votes, won.

These rudimentary national conventions were typical of the Federalist party. A few well-born and congenial gentlemen who could afford the time and expense of travel were chosen by their friends to settle, in a quiet and leisurely manner, the matter of nominations. From the body of voters neither authority nor advice was asked, and profound secrecy sheltered the convention's deliberations from vulgar scrutiny. Like the Federalist state machinery, the two New York conventions were based on the right and duty of leaders to settle party matters without popular co-operation. The voter was expected to vote for candidates nominated by "those who alone from education, fortune, character, and principle are entitled to command." But unfortunately these gentlemen could neither decide what they wanted nor impose their ambiguous wishes on their colleagues. So the whole thing, like so many other attempts of the Federalists, ended in futility.

CHAPTER XIII

Conspiracy and the *Chesapeake* Affair

1801–1807, AET. 35–41

OTIS IN THE STATE HOUSE

WE MUST now turn back to the events of this crucial decade and a half. In 1801 Otis expected the worst from Jefferson. When John Rutledge wrote to him from Charleston asking what he thought of the political situation, he answered (15 December 1801):

> Let me ask what you can expect from the administration of a government in the hands of its uniformly implacable foes? What but the application of its powers to the purposes of its destruction? What but the selfish tyranny of the most profligate and contemptible portion of society, and the exclusion of honest men either by direct force or by disgust from all the offices of State? Like tenants of a decaying estate the present men may be willing to patch up the walls of the buildings and to gather in the crop during the continuance of their lease, but they will leave at the end of their time, the foundations undermined, and the soil exhausted. Yes my friend, the Tobacco worms will destroy all that is flourishing and verdant, stalk and stem, and the Federal constitution in our time will I fear become literally a Virginia *"old field."*

Nevertheless, the inauguration of the Virginia Dynasty brought a brief breathing space. Peace in Europe suspended those questions of foreign policy which had convulsed the country for the past seven years, and removed the principal cause for dissension between Federalists and Republicans. Jefferson governed with a moderation that vexed many of his old friends and made converts from the ranks of his former enemies. Federalist leaders in vain

sounded the note of alarm at the infiltration of "disorganizing principles." The people were tired of politics; they approved Jefferson's policy of retrenchment; they saw no reason for change. Otis
and his friends had to fall back on a sarcastic enjoyment of the
President's difficulty in carrying out his promises. Particularly they
enjoyed what they called the New Haven Remonstrance, the protest of expectant officeholders in Connecticut against Jefferson's
keeping too many Federalists in power.

Apropos, Otis wrote to John Rutledge on 18 October 1801:

> The answer to the Newhaven remonstrance is a recantation of
> the Speech, and probably an expiatory sacrafice to the *resent-
> ment* of many who made no secret of their disapprobation of the
> tolerant and specious language of that instrument. Jefferson is
> not the first chieftain of a party who has realised that the hour
> of success was also the hour of the decline of his personal influ-
> ence among his own adherents. By proclaiming himself the head
> and champion of a party, he secures the continuance of their
> zeal and exertions. By affecting to be the President of the nation
> he would forfeit all claims to their confidence & support. He has
> chosen his part, and it remains to be tried whether a government
> by *acclamation* can maintain itself for years in opposition to the
> sober sense of the virtuous and intelligent part of the com-
> munity, which I agree with you ought to be manifested in every
> mode and upon all occasions, or whether its blunders and its
> vices will precipitate its fall into the hands of its legitimate
> proprietors.

And on 2 August 1802:

> I would gladly accompany Mason upon his present tour to
> Newport, and join with you in laughing at events which we
> cannot controul, & in reprobating those men whom we cannot
> correct; but I am tied by the wing for the residue of the fleeting
> summer; My new house, my old clients, my wild lands will either
> retain me at home or propel me to move in an opposite direction
> to Newport, & to plunge into dull but necessary affairs. What

records of infamy, selfishness, corruption and folly are daily de-
velopd by the ruling party.

The persecutions of Diocletian, the proscriptions of Scylla,
and of Robespierre were far more sanguinary but not more inveterate than those of the chief who now commands. The
temper of the Roman people in their decline and of the French
in their prosperity and decline also were more abject but less
fitted for the impositions & deceptions of bad men than that of
our people.

When he wrote this letter, Otis had already accepted an election
to the Massachusetts house of representatives, thus beginning the
second and most characteristic phase of his political career. For
the next fifteen years he sat in one branch or the other of the general court, and during six years served as speaker of the house or
president of the senate.[1] Throughout this period Otis was the most
popular, though not the most powerful, leader of the Federal party
in Massachusetts. The Essex Junto, distrusting him on account of
his refusal to take part in the intrigue of 1800 against Adams, never
admitted him to their secret councils; but he usually led whatever
branch of the legislature in which he happened to be serving.

In the political revolution of 1800, Massachusetts almost slipped
through the fingers of the Federalists. Caleb Strong, their (for
once) brilliant choice as candidate for governor, got in by a very
narrow majority, but was annually reëlected by an ever-increasing
vote. Under Strong's guidance, the general court turned its attention to internal reforms and commercial development.

In 1802 the penitentiary system was instituted, and the application of capital punishment restricted. Otis had a good deal to do
with the principal reforms between 1803 and 1805 relating to the
state judiciary, a department much in need of reorganization.
Even with more courts and judges than were necessary, the division

---

[1] From 1802 to 1805 in the house of representatives, and speaker the last two years;
from 1805 to 1813 in the senate, and its president 1805–06 and 1808–11; again in the
house, 1813–14, and once more in the senate 1814–17. The political year began on
the last Wednesday in May.

of labor between them was so unequal, the circuits so clumsily arranged, the procedure so complicated, that the cost of justice had become a serious burden. The first reforming impulse came from the bench itself, which seems to have had a realistic conception of its functions and of the proper relations between judiciary and people. Judge Theodore Sedgwick of the Supreme Judicial Court wrote to Otis on 7 February 1803:

> The absolute and uncontrouled independence, of any branch of the judiciary, tends to the establishment of a judicial despotism; and if there has hitherto been no appearance of it, in this state, we are more than indebted to the peculiar *mildness* of temper, and *politeness* of manners of the gentlemen who composed the courts, than to the wisdom of the system.

In a second letter to Otis, he calls the Massachusetts judicial system "the most barbarous and absurd that was ever endured by an enlightened people." Evidently the judges of that day were under no illusions as to the inviolability of their privileges and functions.

Otis gave the exponents of reform all possible aid. A beginning was made in 1803 by depriving the county courts of session, composed of justices of the peace, of criminal jurisdiction. The ideas of Otis and the judges themselves were then substantially adopted in two acts of 1804 and 1805, in which *nisi prius* sessions of one or more judges of the Supreme Court were established in addition to the regular sessions of three or more. One judge alone could exercise jurisdiction over all questions "whereof the Supreme Judicial Court hath hitherto had cognizance," excepting capital offenses, divorce, and alimony. Regular circuits were rearranged, in order to expedite matters; the Supreme Judicial Court was reduced from six to five members, and the judges for the first time were given a fixed compensation instead of annual grants. Theophilus Parsons, who was appointed to the vacant chief-justiceship in 1806, proved most efficient in enforcing the spirit of reform.

The banking facilities of Boston, which the expansion of com-

merce had rendered inadequate, also required attention. John
Quincy Adams records in his diary a project of special interest to
Otis, the Boston Bank, which he desired to get through the senate
as quietly as possible. The bill provided that no one could own
more than fifty shares of stock, except the original proprietors,
"about twenty gentlemen," including Otis, who could own up to
two thousand shares apiece. Otis did not wish to have the subscription paper made public, and to have his name "bandied about" the
legislature. Adams, having heard rumors that certain shares were
set aside for the purpose of corrupting the legislature, refused to
give the bill his support. It finally passed, without the neat provision for keeping control in the hands of the original proprietors,
and with a considerable part of its capital subscribed for by the
Commonwealth. Several other banking schemes became issues in
local politics at this time; and throughout the period of Federalist
rule in Massachusetts the connection between the banking interests
and the Federalist party was close. Otis's name frequently appeared
on boards of directors.

STATE RIGHTS AND SECESSION PLOT

"The Federalists must entrench themselves in the State governments, and endeavour to make State justice and State power a
shelter of the wise, and good, and rich, from the wild destroying
rage of the southern Jacobins." So wrote Fisher Ames in 1802, only
three years after he and his party had denounced as unconstitutional the attempt of the Virginia and Kentucky Democrats similarly to protect themselves against the Sedition Act. With these
words Ames struck the keynote of the policy followed for the next
twelve years by his native state.

The Louisiana Purchase of 1803 gave the signal for a renewal
of the old party bitterness, and caused the "wise, and good, and
rich" of Massachusetts to take a definite step away from national-

ism. By the Republican newspapers of New England the cession of Louisiana was received as "glorious intelligence"; by the Federalist press, coldly and without comment. Although nothing emanating from Jefferson could expect Federalist praise, there must have been some difficulty in finding fault with a treaty which thwarted the steady policy of France since 1793 and carried out to its logical conclusion the Federalist policy of 1798. Jefferson acquired peacefully what Hamilton and his friends had dreamed of securing through war with France and alliance with England. There were, however, just grounds for criticism of the Louisiana Purchase. It was by no means certain that we had not paid $15 million for a revocable permission from Bonaparte to hold Louisiana against all comers, if we had the strength. The colony had been ceded by Spain to France in 1800, but the transfer had not yet taken place. France had never paid for the territory, and its cession was contrary both to French treaty obligations and to her own constitution. The boundaries on the east and on the west were indefinite. The position, then, that we had been cheated, was tenable in 1804.

But the real cause of Federalist opposition lay deeper than flaws in the title; it was based on the realization that the acquisition of this vast territory threatened the economic and political interests of the Federal party. It would lower the value of eastern lands. It would enable Jeffersonian Democracy to expand westward, and keep Federalism in a perpetual minority. "This seems to me a miserably calamitous business — indeed I think it must result in the disunion of these States — and yet such is the force of prejudice & popular delusion that the measure cannot yet be even brought to the bar of argument," wrote John Rutledge to Otis on 1 October 1803. Eastern leaders were already conscious of the lack of expansive force in their party, which by 1804 existed only as a sickly exotic in the West. Ohio, in spite of the fact that a considerable element of her population was from New England, had just entered the Union with a constitution embodying the most advanced ideas of democracy, and looked to Virginia, not Massachusetts, for leadership. It was practically certain that new states to be formed from Louisiana would manifest the same spirit. "Virginia will soon become the Austria of America," wrote a Federalist pamphleteer, referring to the old quip that A.E.I.O.U. means *Austria Est Imperare Orbem Universalem.*

Future prospects for the New England Federalists, with their shipping and mercantile interests, were rendered the more alarming by the expectation that the new trans-Mississippi states would be slaveholding and send representatives to Washington according to the federal ratio. The constitutional provision by which representatives and presidential electors were allotted to the states in proportion to the free population *plus* three fifths of "all other persons" had long been a rankling sore to New England Federalists. It gave Virginia, a state with a free population slightly less than that of Massachusetts, five more representatives and electoral votes; without it Jefferson would not have been elected. Hence arose a proposal to abolish slave representation. A constitutional amendment to this effect was introduced in the Massachusetts general court by William Ely of Springfield and passed by a strict party vote in 1804. Otis, then speaker of the house, no doubt gave this his full approval. The resolution, commenting upon the unjust provision in the Constitution by which "a planter with fifty slaves has thirty votes," states that the purchase of Louisiana makes these provisions more injurious to New England and "will contribute . . . to destroy the real influence of the Eastern states in the National Government"; therefore, *"Resolved,* that representatives and direct taxes be henceforth apportioned on the basis of free population only."

With this, Massachusetts entered the road of sectionalism that she followed for the next ten years. Striking, as it did, at one of the sacred cows of the Constitution, Ely's amendment was rejected by every state except Connecticut and Delaware, which took no action. Nevertheless a similar proposal appears in the Report of the Hartford Convention.

Whilst the Massachusetts legislature contemplated this initial step in sectionalism, the extremist leaders of the Federal party, boldly spanning the successive stages of state rights, were secretly planning secession. The conspiracy originated with extreme Federalists in Congress, of whom Timothy Pickering of Massachusetts and three Connecticut members, James Hillhouse, Uriah Tracy and Roger Griswold, were the leaders. These — and the same might be said of the Essex Junto and of Gouverneur Morris of New York — were men of one idea and one object, to suppress democracy, which to them meant atheism, destruction of property, and mob rule. "The principles of democracy are everywhere what they have been in France," wrote Fisher Ames in 1803. "The fire of revolution . . . when once kindled, would burrow deep into the soil, search out and consume the roots, and leave, after one crop, a *caput mortuum,* black and barren, for ages. . . . Our country is too big for union, too sordid for patriotism, too democratic for liberty." Looking on current events from this standpoint, extreme Federalists saw in Jefferson's attacks on the judiciary, his removals in the civil service, the adoption of the twelfth amendment to the Constitution, and the annexation of Louisiana, a prelude to universal chaos. "My life is not worth much," wrote Pickering, "but if it must be offered up, let it be in the hope of obtaining a more stable government, under which my children, at least, may enjoy freedom with security."

The South, they observed, and to a certain extent the Middle States, were already violated by democracy; New England was yet chaste — but every day Pickering and men of like mind saw new barriers to her virtue prostrated. "And must we with folded hands wait the result? . . . The principles of our Resolution point to the remedy — a separation." In their minds arose the picture of "a new confederacy, exempt from the corrupt and corrupting influence and oppression of the aristocratic Democrats of the South," a confederacy with New England as its nucleus, the British provinces as possible adherents, and New York, to be brought in through the influence of Aaron Burr, a barrier against Virginia, the source of corruption. Much as southern leaders demanded secession in 1861 to exclude the poison of abolition, so Pickering and his friends wished New England to secede in order to exclude the poison of democracy. Each assumed that a frontier line could stop a world force.

This wild scheme was cautiously broached by its authors to the Essex Junto in Massachusetts, and to Federalist leaders in Connecticut and New York. Ames, Cabot, Parsons and Higginson all replied that secession, although desirable, was impossible — there was no public sentiment to support it. The people were altogether too contented and prosperous. But in New York the plot found a leader in Aaron Burr, "The Catiline of America." His candidacy for the governorship was supported by Griswold and Pickering, with the understanding that if he won, he should lead secession. Burr's defeat at the polls ended all chance of even getting it off the launching pad. Hamilton had already expressed disapproval and done his best to prevent it. Burr's demand for an explanation, Hamilton's defiance, and the fatal duel followed in swift succession. On 11 July 1804, Alexander Hamilton paid the penalty, on the dueling ground of Weehawken, for having stood between Aaron Burr and the presidency of a northern Confederacy.

With this dramatic ending, the disunion conspiracy of 1804, first serious plot against the integrity of the Union, dissolved. It never had the remotest chance of success, and the fact that Pickering, Tracy and Griswold could seriously believe it practicable and, above all, intrigue with Aaron Burr to carry it out, shows how thoroughly devoid they were of political morality and how completely out of touch with public opinion.

Our chief concern in this affair is to find out whether Harrison Gray Otis had any part in it. As speaker of the house of the leading state in New England, he was the first leader outside the Essex Junto to whom the conspirators would naturally have turned. John Quincy Adams believed that they had. In the course of the

Timothy Pickering, by Charles Willson Peale.

presidential campaign of 1828, Adams published a statement to the effect that the object of the Federal leaders in 1803, and for several years, had been the dissolution of the Union. Otis and twelve other old Federalists challenged him to publish the evidence of such a design, and to name the leaders. Otis declared that he had not so much as heard of the 1804 plot until 1828. His statement was un-doubtedly correct. Adams himself, in the lengthy reply which he prepared to the Federalist challenge, acknowledged that the 1804 project was "in its nature secret," and admitted, "Mr. Otis is not one of those whom I ever heard or believed to have been engaged in the project of 1804." We may safely conclude, then, that he had no connection with the 1804 project of a northern Confederacy. Rumors of the plot must have leaked out, because the Boston *Democrat* on Christmas Day 1805 declared, "When the United States come to be divided, [the] President of this Eastern Empire" will probably be "The Honorable H. G. Otis, Esquire."

Federalists made the iniquity of the Louisiana Purchase a lead-ing issue in the elections of 1804, but the people were obstinate enough to regard it as a national triumph in which they shared. When the presidential election approached, the general court dared not repeat the unpopular expedient of 1800, itself choosing presidential electors. Trusting, however, that the Federalist ma-jority in the spring state election would continue, it provided for the choice of electors by general ticket, as is done in every state nowadays. This "squeamishness," as the *Centinel* called it, re-sulted, to the Federalists' profound dismay, in a victory for Jeffer-son by a substantial majority. For the first and last time Massa-chusetts voted for a President opposed to the Federalist party. Connecticut and Delaware alone remained faithful to Federalism; Jefferson was reëlected President in 1804 by 162 votes out of 176.[1]

The Democrats had good reason to believe that Federalism was in its death throes. Otis thought so himself; in a letter to John

[1] Not again until 1932 did Massachusetts and Virginia vote for the same presi-dential candidate — Franklin D. Roosevelt.

Rutledge he predicted, "The total prostration of federalism in our state . . . the dreadful torrent will finally overwhelm and perhaps destroy us." According to a political satire, *The Hamiltoniad:*

> Boston, that royal hot-bed of the States,
> Now sinks in grief — now menaces the Fates;
> Ot-s, melifluous Ot-s, cannot please;
> His silver accents only charm the Breeze.

FEAST OF SHELLS AND SELFRIDGE-AUSTIN AFFRAY

The late Charles Warren, who worked through the Boston press of this period, agreed with me that never has political partisanship been so virulent, or language so vituperative, as in the press of this era, when Federalists fought desperately to retain power, and the Democrats as desperately to capture the state government. Dr. Johnson's and Noah Webster's dictionaries were combed for pejorative adjectives and adverbs. Violent pamphlets rained from party headquarters, and the records of leading candidates were raked to discover incidents to their discredit. Partisanship extended to every class in the community, and entered every occupation — even horticulture; as Jefferson imported Lombardy poplars, Democrats planted that tree in front of their dwellings, while Federalists stuck to the good old American elm. To accommodate commuters, Hingham maintained rival Federalist and Republican sailing packets to Boston; and if a member of one party missed his packet home he would spend the night on Long Wharf rather than patronize the other. The annual Forefathers' Day celebration at Plymouth every 22 December, nicknamed (after Ossian) "The Feast of Shells" owing to the traditional menu of clams and lobsters, became a Federalist clambake in 1805. According to the Boston *Democrat,* Otis defended a recent British court decision and joined the crowd in roaring out "Rule, Britannia!" For this

"riotous festivity," as that newspaper called it, and for the "malignant, dirty, and abusive toasts" drunk at the dinner, Otis was bitterly attacked by "Henry Trimsharp," and another scribbler contributed an "Impromptu":

> They've hung young HARRY up so high
> And drest him out in gauze so thin,
> That common people passing by
> Can see his very flesh and skin.
>
> 'Twas cruel, in the open air,
> To hang young Harry up so bare.

This squib was the worst ever aimed at Otis; his popularity protected him from the most vicious attacks of the Republicans, and
his nickname — "Young Harry" or "Sir Harry" was gentle compared with "Duke of Braintree" for John Adams, "Crazy Jack"
for John Lowell, and "Sly Kit" for Christopher Gore. Dr. Benjamin Waterhouse, who flaunted his democracy with a row of Lombardy poplars, wrote to Jefferson that Chief Justice Parsons was
"the Ahitophel of the high federal party, while H. G. Otis is the
Absalom."

In 1806 the Democrats finally secured a majority in the general
court, but Caleb Strong won again by a narrow margin after a
violent hassle over the returns. Otis, defeated for the presidency
of the senate that year by a majority of one, wrote on 20 May in a
tone of bitter jocularity to his old friend, Robert Goodloe Harper:

> I believe at length *c'est une affaire finie* with Massachusetts.
> The old Governor is elected, but a systematic plan has been
> adopted by the democratic towns to fill the legislature with their
> complement of members. Our H. of R. will therefore literally
> be a council of 500, and you may expect to see us disgraced by a
> fulsome address to the weakest of possible administrations. If
> Bonaparte had time to examine our affairs with minute atten-
> tion, he would think we were making too much haste; we shall
> be ready for him before he has leisure to take us under his pro-

tection. Would your Baltimorians vote for Prince Jerome? I think however we cannot expect to share the honors of the *first line* of Princes. There is not enough of them to distribute among the fallen & falling powers of Europe. A few years will produce a new mongrel breed from the German and Italian alliances, either of wives or mistresses and a few years may probably fit America for the sway of any abortion which it may be convenient to transport. Till then God bless you.

A murderous affray on State Street intensified political bitterness. Benjamin Austin, a Democrat belonging to a patrician family, had made himself particularly obnoxious to the ruling class by his vitriolic articles over the signature "Honestus," for which Jefferson rewarded him with the position of federal commissioner of loans for Massachusetts. As such, he was chosen by the Boston Republicans to conduct their Fourth of July celebration in 1806, held on Copps Hill since the Federalists had preëmpted Faneuil Hall. The Republicans had the star attraction, a visit by Sidi Soliman Mellimelni, the Tunisian Ambassador to Washington, but had no more sense than to build their banquet around roast pig. Scores of succulent porkers, with gallons of green peas and innumerable plum puddings had been laid out in a tent by the landlord of the Jefferson Tavern on Prince Street, headquarters of the local Democracy. But so great became the press of citizenry eager to view the Barbary coast envoy in his native silks and turban, that the ticket taker was overwhelmed, hundreds crashed the banquet free, and Austin's committee refused to pay for surplus food provided at the last minute by the publican. He, furious with his Democratic patrons, employed Thomas O. Selfridge, a Federalist lawyer of high repute, to collect the balance due from the committee. Austin, ill-tempered and irascible, and red-faced at a Jeffersonian's employing a Federalist lawyer, publicly accused Selfridge of having instigated the suit himself. That meant barratry, a high offense against legal ethics. Selfridge proved the charge to be completely false and called upon the man who brought it to retract. Austin made an evasive retraction, shifting the charge to a friend whom he refused to name, and proposed to do nothing further about it. Selfridge, whose irascibility at least equaled that of his accuser, then posted Austin in the Boston *Gazette* of 4 August 1806 as "a COWARD a LIAR and a SCOUNDREL," and Austin, having advance knowledge of this libel, posted Selfridge in the *Independent Chronicle* as unworthy of a reply, so "insolent and false" was his accusation.

That very afternoon Austin's son Charles, an eighteen-year-old Harvard student, purchased a stout hickory stick, took a few stiff drinks, and lay in wait for Selfridge on that part of State Street called 'Change, where Boston lawyers congregated at the noon hour. Selfridge, having been warned what to expect, provided himself with a loaded pistol. As he walked down the center of State Street from the Old State House, at a point halfway between Devonshire and Exchange streets, young Austin rushed out at him from the sidewalk and dealt him a blow which inflicted a severe contusion, even through his hat. Selfridge (a small, weak man in comparison with the Austin lad) staggered back, drew and cocked his pistol and, just as he received a second blow from the stick, shot Austin dead through the throat.

The trial of Selfridge for manslaughter became a trial of strength between the two political parties. Christopher Gore and Samuel Dexter were principal counsels for the defense; Otis too was employed but did not appear in court, probably because of the recent drowning of his son Allyne. James Sullivan the attorney general and Daniel Davis the solicitor general prosecuted. The venerable Paul Revere, foreman of the trial jury, and the trial judge Isaac Parker, were Federalists, and the jury is said to have been too. They acquitted Selfridge as having acted in self-defense. The Boston Democratic press compared this affair with the Boston Massacre of 1770, and Selfridge was so hounded and insulted that he decided to spend the following winter in South Carolina. He carried a letter of introduction to John Rutledge from Otis describing him as "a gentleman of talents . . . of a character impeached only by the malice of political Enmity. . . . I hope he will be received with the attention due to one who has done nothing to forfeit the claims of a gentleman."

No trial prior to that of Sacco and Vanzetti caused so much rage and rancor as the Selfridge-Austin affair. Public opinion divided strictly along political lines. At the next spring state election, a few months after the trial, James Sullivan the prosecutor was elected governor of Massachusetts, and his party obtained control of every branch of the state government. All signs pointed to the coming disappearance of the Federalist party. Vermont succumbed the same year; New Hampshire and Rhode Island had already yielded; only Connecticut, "the land of steady habits," resisted the advance of Jeffersonian Democracy. Had the European peace endured, or had Thomas Jefferson been able to cope successfully with a European war, the party might have died out for want of an issue. But the gods willed it that no permanent peace could be made between England and France, or between Federalists and Republicans in America, until Napoleon should conquer the British Isles or be driven into exile.

BOSTON AND THE *CHESAPEAKE* AFFAIR

Europe having resolved herself for the third time into coalitions around England and France as nuclei, Federalists and Republicans resumed their former positions on the outer edges of the warring circles. Questions other than foreign affairs sink out of sight; and, as Harper wrote to Otis, "The affairs of our own country make a sort of underplot, which engages the attention only because it is near, and in which the miserable actors . . . excite no other emotions than those of pity and contempt." Throughout the long struggle that ended at Waterloo, the Federalists continued to regard England as the "advanced guard of our country," the exponent of rational liberty and well-ordered government; whilst the Republican party, although somewhat embarrassed at Bonaparte's assuming an imperial crown, defended the cause of France while she crushed liberty and republicanism in one country after another.

In 1807 occurred an incident which for a few weeks obliterated party lines in the United States and brought forth the only united expression of American patriotism between the XYZ disclosures and the battle of New Orleans. Off Hampton Roads the commander of H.M.S. *Leopard* spoke U.S.S. *Chesapeake* and demanded that certain deserters from the Royal Navy, said to be on board, be given up. Upon being refused, he opened fire, killed or wounded twenty-one of *Chesapeake's* crew, and after she had struck, impressed three American citizens and one British subject.

News of this outrage to the American flag reached Boston on the last day of June. All newspapers, even those regarded as organs of the Essex Junto, reprobated the British government, but the leading Federalists, wishing to await further information, refused to call a town meeting. The Republicans then took the lead, and called a public meeting for 10 July. Their organ, the *Independent Chronicle,* announced that the "Federal leaders" responsible for the outrage by their "display of disaffection" should be excluded from the meeting, and after that insult, no Federalist cared to attend, except John Quincy Adams . The Federalists then called a regular town meeting for 16 July. This was attended by the great body of citizens, some two thousand strong as opposed to two hundred at the Democratic meeting. Harrison Gray Otis, the most prominent speaker, delivered a spirited denunciation of the British outrage. He also served on a committee, composed chiefly of Federalists, that drew up a set of resolutions promising the government their support.

Nevertheless, he warns his friend Rutledge that among Boston Federalists there was neither desire nor disposition for war: "It would ruin us. . . . How miserable and deplorable is our condition, to have our fortunes, our prosperity, our comfort and our honor dependent on the blunders and perverseness of a cabinet. . . . This whole controversy respecting sailors, was practically to us not worth mooting, we have always had ten to their one, and it was a farce for a government who disregarded national honor in all the essentials to make such a bustle upon a secondary question." He approved the treaty which James Monroe and William Pinkney had recently negotiated with Great Britain — it was humorously similar in terms to the much-denounced Jay Treaty — but Jefferson would not even submit the Monroe-Pinkney treaty to the Senate. John Rutledge replied in a more patriotic strain on 3 August:

> You are so cool & dispassionate a people in Boston that you seem to have escaped the passion which enflames us, in consequence of the outrage on one of our frigates. Altho' I deprecate war quite as much as any of my friends can, yet, I think, a War (even with Great Britain) would prove more honourable prosperous & safe, & less costly, than a state of Peace in which a foreign Nation is to exercise the right of searching our National Ships. The general business of impressing American seamen was to be sure not worth mooting — where G. Britain has in her service one of our sailors we have twenty of hers on board our Merchantmen, & this is so well known in that section of the Union where Mariners & navigation belong (New England) that complaints have ceased. The complainings come from Virginia, where there are neither sailors nor ships, & where this is contrived to aliment & concentrate the angry passions floating through our Country against G. Britain, Altho' this disgraceful Spirit has brought upon us our present deplorable condition, & this miserable state is chargeable to the Errors & Vices of those Empirics who administer our government, still my friend we must support this government. With our Commerce so extended as it is, & our Keels fretting every sea, we must have a navy; & that will be impossible if our Ships of War are to be searched — we must kick against this & fight against it, & fight as we should *pro Aris & focis*.

Although Otis ignored party lines in this crisis, unfortunately it was the last time he could be impartial. For the administration soon embarked on a policy which made it impossible for a Massachusetts man to support Jefferson and, at the same time, be loyal to his state.

After the *Chesapeake* affair, Jefferson lost his chance to obtain a "consensus" (to use modern political jargon) for war against Great Britain. Looking back at the year 1807 after a century and a half of wars and revolutions, Jefferson's moderation and restraint, like Woodrow Wilson's "too proud to fight," impel a certain admiration. But the sequel proved that his expedients could not prevent a war, which might far better have come in 1807 with the nation up in arms over an insult to the flag, than in 1812 after one section of the Union had become disaffected by four years of commercial restriction. Instead of commencing reprisals or encouraging the war spirit, Jefferson on 2 July 1807 issued a proclamation closing American ports to British men-of-war, and expressing his confidence that Great Britain would apologize for the *Leopard's* action. The British government did somewhat ungraciously acknowledge that mistake, and sent a special envoy to the United States to make reparation, but with so many strings to it that Jefferson refused to accept the offer.

Before this envoy arrived, European affairs assumed an alarming aspect for the United States. The British government and Napoleon seemed to have determined to eliminate all neutrals. In September 1807, after neutral Copenhagen had been bombarded by a British fleet, Denmark surrendered her fleet to England. The lesson applied to the United States like the earlier overthrow of Venice and Switzerland by France. In December, information arrived of a new and sweeping British order in council forbidding all trade between the United States and continental Europe, unless the cargo were first landed in Great Britain and there inspected. Next came official notice of a royal proclamation ordering naval officers to exercise the right of impressment to its fullest extent, adding insult to the injury of the *Chesapeake* affair.

Jefferson felt that the moment had come for prompt and vigorous action, both to protect American shipping and to coerce the two powerful belligerents into abandoning their anti-neutral systems. He wished at all hazards to avoid war. Here was an opportunity to try an experiment he had long dreamed of — forcing Europe to yield by prohibiting commercial intercourse. At his dictation, the Republican majority in Congress passed the famous Embargo Act, which from 22 December 1807 until 4 March 1809 forbade the American merchant marine to engage in foreign commerce, and placed burdensome restrictions on coastwise traffic.

CHAPTER XIV

Trip to Montreal

July 1806, AET. 40

BOSTON TO MONTREAL BY CHAISE AND BOAT

A PLEASANT INTERLUDE in this era of perfervid politics was a summer journey which Harry and a party of friends made to Montreal in 1806. It assuaged his chagrin over having been defeated for the presidency of the state senate, and afforded a change from the strain of moving from the Mount Vernon Street house to 45 Beacon Street. His traveling companions were his boyhood friend Thomas Handasyd Perkins, Thomas C. Amory, a Boston commission merchant, and James Bowdoin.[1] Although made under conditions that would daunt recent visitors to Expo 67, it was not without interesting incidents. Extracts from Harry's journal of the trip, and his letters to Sally in Boston, tell the story.

They left Boston early in the morning of 2 July, in a hired "shay," with two servants. Their first amusing occurrence was an encounter with General William Eaton, hero of the capture of Derna in the war with Tripoli. The general had been recalled from active duty by President Jefferson, whom he then denounced, greatly to Federalist joy; in that Plymouth dinner of 1805 in which Otis starred, one of the toasts was "A Soil like Egypt for Eaton's laurels; a Sandy Desert for *theirs* who tried to stop him."

> Just before our arrival at Brookfield we met Genl Eaton on horseback, going to Boston to join in the celebration of inde-

[1] Not the James Bowdoin whom Otis had defeated for Congress, and who in 1806 was U.S. Minister to Spain, but James Temple Bowdoin, the son of Sir John Temple, who had added Bowdoin to his name after his widowed mother married a member of that family.

pendence. The dress, and air of the General appeared to be better adapted to a second attack upon Derne than to a Solitary excursion to Boston; but the impatience of our driver had nearly disqualified him for active service of any description. Having thrown both legs on one side of the horse, as he was carelessly conversing with us, our driver without any warning cracked his whip & the General's horse started and nearly threw him from his ballance. He however recovered and went off *à grande gallope*. . . .

July 4. Breakfast at Merrick's, a decent house, and great preparations making to celebrate the anniversary of independence. From the quantity of pigs prepared for the Spit, it would have been fair to presume a swinish taste in the guests, had we not known them to be Democrats with fierce cocked opera hats.[1] An awkward company of artillery, with a drunken fifer, and solitary fourpounder afforded a presentiment of the noise, fire & smoke which doubtless tested the Sincerity of these good patriots. . . .

5 July. . . . The only peculiarly interesting occurrence in this day's ride was a view of *Glens falls* which are formed by the whole Hudson river, which is here compressed into a very narrow bed, by high perpendicular rocks, & rushes over a ledge which entirely crosses it with tremendous violence, exhibiting a variety of picturesque & beautiful cascades, & forming above and below eddies, whirlpools & currents, which render the river innavigable except for rafts — and one of these as we were informed about two years since approaching too near to the falls, was forced into the Vortex with two men who were instantly overwhelmed & did not rise again until they were carried five miles by the fury of the stream when their bodies were taken out broken and mangled by the rocks. These falls, judging from inspection merely, are about 40 feet in height. A number of mills are placed by the margin of the river on each side of the falls, and one of them carries 25 Saws. Large quantities of board lumber are here collected for the Troy, Albany & New York markets.

[1] It is surprising to find an opera hat mentioned so early, but the *Oxford Dictionary* quotes it from the nursery rhyme "A frog he would a-wooing go."

The same day, he wrote to Sally:

Ballstown July 5 1806

You will be surprized, my dearest love, at a letter from this place as nothing was more remote from my intention than to visit it. We found however upon enquiry and calculation that we could not perform our journey to Quebec by the way of Niagara and Lake Ontario within the utmost period limited for our absence without being in constant hurry & fatigue, and perhaps not at all within less than eight or nine weeks. We therefore unanimously agreed to turn off, and resume our first plan of going by lake Champlain, and being at Albany, it is but a few miles out of our route to pass thro' this place which T. C. A[mory] was desirous of seeing. We arrived at 5 this afternoon and shall leave it by 5 tomorrow morning for Skeensborough, where we embark for Montreal. Our journey has been pleasant, and my health is fine. . . .

Write to me to the care of William McGilvray Esqr. Montreal, *and see that the postage be paid,* & so marked, or I shall not get it.[1] Sam[2] will do this for you. Receive for yourself and my children my most affectionate regards & believe me, dearest and best of women, always

Yr H G OTIS

Skeensborough July 7. Monday

My dear Sally,

We arrived here last evening; this is a small village at the head of lake Champlain whence the principal intercourse is preserved between the States and Canada. We have chartered a fine little sloop to take us to Montreal and are waiting only for a wind which though fair on our arrival has now subsided. Our jaunt has been as pleasant, as any excursion of the kind can be to me without your society. . . . Tell my dear children how much I think of them when absent, and particularly repeat to Harry my

[1] William McGillivray, Scots fur trader, rose to be chief director of the North West Company. Fort William, the company's chief inland depot, was named in his honor in 1807.

[2] Harry's brother Samuel A. of Newburyport, who seems to have made a practice of coming to stay whenever Harry went on a journey.

hope that he will be governed by his good sense, and do whatever he can, to promote the happiness of his mother and brethren, which is the only way to ensure his own; and my approbation. ... I trust you will improve every hour of this *belle saison* in exercise and occupations calculated to amuse the mind and to confirm health. I hope to find my dear Elisa a fine jocund hearty country girl, *mais avec les graces, l'aisance et les manières de la bonne compagnie.* I will please myself also with the hope that Sal will water *no plants* but those of my green house; that Master Allan will leave off shrugging his Shoulders, That Sophia will keep her place, and that the urchins will be good boys.

Remember me to my father and family, as also to yours. Adieu my love, untill I write from the other Side of the Lake.

Otis's journal takes up the story from this point:

Here on monday 7 July we embarkd in a sloop of about thirty tons Capt Smith, on Lake Champlain which at this place and for twenty miles below is merely a continuation of Wood Creek, & thus far the land on each side is covered with bushes and low trees, and the morasses are unfit for cultivation, producing only sedge & nourishing nothing but mosquitoes. Soon after the lake expands, and the prospects of improvement & cultivation on each Side become more interesting. Our passage this day was pleasant & agreeable, but the wind being light, we made but little progress.

Tuesday 8. We were still on the lake this day with light & variable wind, & before sunset, stood into the harbour of Charlotte a small village on the East side of the Lake, in the State of Vermont, and there remained during the night. In the evening a canoe arrived with 2 men & a young woman the daughter of one of them & an infant child bound to Mirriske bay, about 70 miles from this place in the British dominions. The woman expressed a perfect confidence & satisfaction in this mode of navigation, & the men informed us that they were regardless of the Shore but ventured the nearest way across the lake. The country in this neighbourhood is remarkably fine and produces abundant crops of wheat & corn, the orchards are fine and the settlements

already wear the aspect of age and comfort, tho more than 20
years have not elapsed since they were commenced.

[July] 10. Arrived at St. Johns & proceeded to the guard house
& gave in our names to the Serjeant of the Guard, we were then
announced to the Capt., who gave us leave to proceed. We obtained a carriage to take us to Lake Prairie (9 miles) and for the
first time I found myself in a french village, the novelty of which
was in no small degree interesting to me. We remained here only
while the boat was preparing to take us over the ferry, & had only
time to stroll thro' the streets, and stop a few moments at the
window of the first convent that I had ever seen, & to saunter
thro' the aisles of the Church.

[Upon arrival at Montreal] we went immediately to the Hamilton Hotel which we found to be a house kept in a style by no
means usual in this country. After dinner we sauntered thro
the town & I found myself greatly interested in the novelty of
the scene. Manners, habitations & employments appeared to be
suddenly changed since we left the United States. By far the
greater number of the inhabitants are french, their homes are
principally built of rough stones & plaistered; many of them occupy extensive fronts, but they are mostly of one or two stories in
height, and provided with iron shutters and tinned roofs, & are
frequently situated in the rear of other houses or behind high
walls, which totally intercept the view of the streets.

[July] 11. This morning was occupied in visiting the Court
house, one of the Convents of the grey Nuns, the gardens of the
Monastery of St. Sulpice, and the great store of Mr. McGillvray
which is appropriated to the holding of the birch canoes which
are employed in the North West traffic, & which must be renewed every year. A whole fleet of these canoes was moored at
anchor on the floor of this store forming [blank] lines each containing six canoes. They are about 30 feet in length and appear
to be slight vessells for a navigation of many thousand miles; yet
are the best and perhaps the only ones which can be employed
in going to the N. West Coast, and discending over the rapids
of St. Lawrence with heavy and valuable cargoes of furs worth
from 1 to 3000 £ sterling.

In the evening we went to Mr. Frobishers a mile from the

city.[1] his house is delightfully situated on the acclivity of of [sic] the great mountain, & commands a highly picturesque view of the town of montreal, of the St. Lawrence, which here expands to seven miles in width, and of the mountains around and beyond lake Champlain. Mr. Frobisher has a spacious and handsome kitchen garden, filled with vegetables, and with such fruit trees as can be brought to perfection in this climate which are but few. Apples pears & plums we are told succeed well, but cherries we know are few and miserable and peaches there are none. His hothouse is indeed well stocked with a variety of plants & contains a passion flower which is truly a curiosity. It is planted against the back wall which it covers with its extended branches, and the smaller shoots are conducted in every direction. The main flower is probably [blank] inches in circumference, and it was in full & luxuriant bearing. Except this, there was nothing which is not seen in every green house, and nothing but what demonstrates the pains & expence necessary to contend with the rigors of this climate.

Montreal July Sunday 13

My dearest friend, . . .

It is impossible to describe to you the *violent* manner in which the gentlemen of this place impose upon us their hospitality. From *sunrise* till night we are not permitted to be alone, and walk the Streets, attended by a patrole or retinue of the first people here. To these attentions are added the usual accompaniments of *la bonne chère*, &c., the unusual ones of the most perfect cordiality & sincere pleasure on the part of those who receive us. The appearance of this city, the mansions of its inhabitants, and many of its institutions, are to us objects altogether novel and interesting.

What think you of our going to Quebec 180 miles in an open boat? This is the usual & most eligible mode of conveyance. It is unattended with the smallest degree of danger. The boats run along by the banks of the river, are well manned, & as large as *your oval room* & go ashore whenever we see fit. We shall be three days going. We shall be at Quebec four or five days, and

---

1 Joseph Frobisher, a wealthy fur trader who had retired and lived at "Beaver Hall," his Montreal mansion.

return hither by land. It is therefore not probable that I shall write to you again unless I find a private conveyance.

On my return I hope to hear that you are well & happy at this date. My old impatience to be at home is I am sure an incurable disorder, & who can wonder that I deem every hour of separation from the best of wives, & from my loved & interesting family absolutely mispent, whatever may be the substitutes for their society which are offered by the hospitalities or civilities of Strangers! It is indeed a long time since "my love and I parted" for weeks together, & I find myself, if possible less than ever reconciled to the Separation. . . .

To Quebec and Back

[July] 13. Embarked at 6 in the morning in a batteau, with 4 oars & a pilot for Quebec. We had provided ourselves with good stores and proceeded down the river with the current but ahead wind, at the rate of 4 or 5 miles an hour, and reached Berthier (about 40 miles) by sunset. The passage was pleasant and the prospect from the river enchanting. The country on both sides is level, and opens at a small distance to be on a [k]nol elevated above the surface of the river. The settlements or concessions extend back generally about thirty acres deep & are skirted with a thick wood, so that the eye is confined to a small extent of inhabited or cultivated ground. But this teems with population & is covered with houses. It appears indeed to be an entire village, varying in some places in the number and frequency of the houses, but everywhere abounding with them in call of each other. These houses are very generally plaistered or whitened on the outside, and impress the eye as being much more neat and elegant than an approach to them will justify. At the distance of every six miles on each side of the river, you behold the Spire of a church which is covered with tin, & which reflecting the rays of the sun upon the surrounding houses and objects, give to this whole scene an indescribable brilliancy. You have scarcely ceased to admire the dazzling brightness of one of these, which upon approaching it "sheds intolerable day" upon the beholder, when another appears sparkling in the blue mist which hangs over a distant promontory, and which mitigates the brightness so that it can be endured by the eye. We advanced only 45 miles this day and lodged at *Berthier,* a French village.

[July] 14. Again made sail, but the wind being adverse and our progress slow Mr. Perkins and myself took a *calash* and proceeded about 30 miles to the *point du lac* which forms the end of Lake St. Francis, which is a part of the river St. Lawrence about 5 miles in width upon an average and twenty miles in length. Here we again took boat and proceeded about one league below *Trois Rivières,* where we again went ashore to lodge. The Distance from Montreal being 93 miles.

[July] 15. Attempted to proceed down the river but found it tedious with the wind ahead, and accordingly left the Servants and baggage in the boat and took calashes for Quebec, & arrived at Point au Tremble where we slept.

[July] 16. Resumed our carriages and arrived at Quebec about 9 in the morning to Breakfast.

[July] 17. We dined with Col. Sheaffe[1] at his mess in company with Mr. Gore, a young gentleman just arrived to take upon him the Government of Upper Canada. He seems to be a well bred, affable man. The number present was about thirty. The dinner very good & the music afterwards from the band belonging to the 49 regiment was very fine.

Quebec, Thursday 17 July

My dearest friend, . . .

It is literally true, that neither at Montreal or in this place, have we been permitted to be alone from the hour of rising till late in the evening. The good people to whom we have been introduced think they can never do enough for us, and put us completely in requisition. . . .

Col. Sheaffe is at our elbow tho' only 7 o'clock to take us out of town to the falls of Montmorency. I shall endeavor to take such notice of them as will enable me to describe them to you.

---

1 Sir Roger Hale Sheaffe, veteran of the British Army in the American Revolution, later C. in C. British forces in Upper Canada, created baronet for his services at Queenston Heights battle.

I hope Harry takes good care of my family and will enable me to embrace him as my eldest Son upon my return, and that all my children strive who shall give most pleasure to their dear mother.

Adieu yours most affect'y, H G Otis

[July] 18. We this morning embarked us a batteau, accompanied by Mr. Craigie, Col. Sheaffe & Mr. Natl Coffin and proceeded three leagues up the river, to visit the falls of Chaudière. We took a rural breakfast & walked thro the woods one league, to the falls. The view of them repaid us for our fatigue. The height is about 90 feet, yet they are more romantic and interesting than those of Montmorency. The river is wider, and the rocks, are more abrupt and majestic in their appearance. The quantity of water here was comparatively small, but imagination may easily conceive of the effect when the rocks we saw bare are covered by the rushing torrent.

We returned down the river to young Mr. Caldwells to dine.[1] This gentleman is son of a large & respectable land holder and old settler & is a member of the house of commons in Canada. He is the owner of various mills upon an extensive establishment, which he is occupied in improving and enlarging. His house is pleasantly situated on the river. Col. Sheaffe had bro't his band of music which were stationed in a grove near the house and entertained us while dining with a variety of airs. The evening we passed with Mr. Craigie.

[July] 19. This morning we visited the two convents of the Ursulines and Hotel Dieu, the first of these is consecrated to education. we were received with great politeness and ceremony by the Sisters (having obtained permission from the Bishop to visit them) & were conducted thro' the various apartments. The chapel is richly decorated; but the other apartments are plain and gloomy. On each side of the Spacious passages are placed the cells or chambers of the sisters; Several large rooms are appropriated to their boarders and scholars, in one of which we saw about 20 or 30 young girls, who were engaged in reading, writing & embroidery. The Sisters exhibited several specimens of needle-

---

[1] Son of Henry Caldwell, administrator of provincial finances, who "lived in almost feudal splendor at Belmont Manor."

work upon bark, some of which we bought. In one room, we saw several statues of Paris plaister as large as life which one of the Nuns was engaged in gilding. The work appeared equal to the best we had seen. This nun is much employd in painting and gilding for the churches and for any who choose to employ her. Another room was shown to us completely panneld with wood by one of the Sisters who is a joiner. Many of the sisters are constantly employed in various mechanical trades, such as the making of shoes, of soap & candles, of bread &c, & those attentions with those of gardening & others which are indispensable to their dress, all the articles of which they make, & to the cleaning of their rooms & furniture give them constant & laborious employment.

In the building of the Hotel Dieu we saw nothing materially different from the other. There is a general style which pervades them all. Heavy and gloomy external walls; large & numerous apartments destitute of all internal ornament & not even plaistered, extensive passages running throughout the buildings, but the cells on each side for the lodging rooms of the Sisters, chapel, &c coated with the usual ornaments of Catholic Churches, give to all these huge and Gothic piles a uniformity of external & internal aspect. In this convent, we were shown various relics of Saints, &c, among others the bones of the first Sisters who came hither from France. They were deposited with pious care in a gilt mahogany case with glass pannels. We also saw the relics of a Jesuit who had been most horribly massacred by the Indians, and a painting exhibiting a scene of the inhuman butchery of a member of that order, & we were told of a tradition, that this massacre was perpetrated by wretches who had professed to be converted to the Christian faith & were baptised, & who afterward with dreadful mockery pretended to requite the service by baptising the Jesuits with boiling oil poured into their gaping wounds inflicted by pincers and other diabolical instruments of torture.

The most interesting object, however which we saw here, was the body of a sister who had died yesterday of a consumption. She was laid out upon a long table in the robes of the order, her feet naked and her hands raised & united above her breast, & in them were placed a crucifix & a written paper which we found to be a copy of the vow originally taken by her in assuming the

veil. Her feet & hands were of alabaster whiteness, her countenance serene and tranquil. Candles were burning near the body
& a Sister on her knees, with the aspect of mingled grief & resignation watched the Corps, & this last duty, we understood was
performed by them in rotation.

We passed through the hospital in which were several sick
persons. The necessary attention to the sick becomes a very arduous occupation for these kind & charitable women. Ample
provision is made for the comfort & cleanliness of the Patients.
A complete and well arranged assortment of drugs and medi-
cines is under the superintendance of a female apothecary. A
regular Physician attends every day, & prescribes for each patient,
and as the name of a Saint is written on each bed, the Physician
without knowing his patients name, needs only to order a blister
for St. Andrew or a cathartic for St. Genevieve. In the admission
of patients, the right of priority is determined by the degree of
poverty & distress, & the most wretched are deemed to have the
best claims. They are however frequently exposed to great impositions, from which they ought to be protected by a Government
which makes no provision for the poor, except by a grant of
1000 £ annually to be divided among all the convents, which
does not by half indemnify them for the medicine alone, & which
is a miserable Substitute for the revenues which they lost first
by the Conquest of Canada by the British & since by the Revolution in France.

On the whole these institutions, far from being nests of idleness or vice, are highly useful, and could not be abolished without some substitute for the relief of poverty and sickness. All the
women appeared to be past 30, & most of them older. Several
were quite advanced in years. Their countenance in general
sallow, but expressive of content & tranquillity either real or
affected, except in a few instances & their bills of mortality prove
that their mode of living is not unfavorable to longevity. The
term of novitiate is 2 years, and the admission is with the approbation of a majority of voices.

We went to dine at an Indian village called Loretta, accompanied by Mr. & Mrs. Craigie, Mr. Coffin & family & Col. Sheaffe.
The village consists of about 50 wretched hovels, & contain nothing worthy of remark. The natives unite in their persons &
characters all the vices of the savage and social states and dirt,

idleness & misery are their constant Companions. We purchased a few trinkets & left them with disgust.

[July] 20. The city of Quebec contains by estimation about 10,000 Souls, of which at least 3/5 are French. Though its Site is lofty & commanding and the prospects around it highly magnificent and picturesque, yet it is not so well built a city as Montreal nor does it possess the same natural advantages. The climate is also more severe than at Montreal, vegetation is later & less luxuriant, and everything indicates the dominion of long and tedious winters. Their ships make but one European voyage in the year. Their exports like those of the whole province consist of furs, wheat lumber & potashes, which last come principally from the United States. The effects of the war are felt and complained of by their merchants. The trade is carried on in the regular ancient channels, and there is neither the capital or disposition for new enterprise. They have no books, no insurance companies, & no canals or turnpikes. The commerce is almost exclusively confined to a few of the English & Scots, and the native Canadians are of consequence becoming more and more depressed & dependent.

[July] 21. We yesterday left Quebec at 5 oclock and arrived by 8 at Trois Rivières, a distance of 90 miles, & this day crossed the ferry into town which we left at 7 oclock & arrived in Montreal also 90 miles by 1/2 past 8. We travelled in the common vehicle of the country which is a thing called a calash, an ordinary sort of horse cart made of wood with a seat behind calculated for two persons. The front part of the body is hung upon hinges & opens to admit the passengers; it is then closed & fastened with bolts, & forms the Seat for the driver. The harness is made of ropes or untanned leather, & the horse of the little Canada breed perfectly docile & conscious of the task he is to perform.

Montreal 23d July Wednesday.

We returned to this place, my dearest friend, last night, having perform'd the jaunt by land 180 miles in two days. . . . We are all disappointed in receiving no letters from our friends, which we impute entirely to the want of arrangement between the Post office of the British Government and ours. . . . Our

A Canadian calèche. From a drawing by Cornelius Krieghoff.

journey has been interesting and pleasant, tho a little too rapid for Bowdoin, who does not feel the incentives to dispatch which operate with the rest of us.

As to yourself, I do not bear absence better than I used to. Though perfectly well, and constantly occupied, I am dead to pleasure, when separated from a companion always loved and cherished as the partner of my heart, and now endeared and become necessary to my happiness, by sixteen years of habitual intimacy and love. I feel also the want of my little groupe, I think no employment interesting, or hardly justifiable that is not connected with views to their prosperity. In short these 3 weeks appear to us longer than the Shadows of evening, & yet they have been incessantly employed in scenes both novel and interesting.

We cannot with decency leave this place before Saturday or Sunday. If our passage over the lake to Burlington should be short, I may be at home by next Saturday sen'night. This however depends on circumstances. The passage is Sometimes 12 hours, & some times 3 days, and the Stages from Burlington are irregular.

Adieu my dear. You will hardly hear from me again, untill you see me.

When Harry returned home from this interesting tour, about 9 August 1806, he heard for the first time of a domestic tragedy. The previous month his ten-year-old son Allyne, bathing in the Back Bay off one of the new wharves at the foot of Boston Common, drowned almost before his mother's eyes. The Otises had already lost two children in their infancy; but in those days that was to be expected. Allyne, however, was a lusty young boy, the image of his father, who wrote to Uncle Harrison Gray, "The loss is never to be forgotten. As our affection for him was unbounded, so is our grief, and all the troubles of my life have been small in comparison with this."

A second Allyne soon filled this gap in the "little groupe," and many years elapsed before this loving family circle was again broken by death.

CHAPTER XV

Embargo to War

1807–1812, AET. 41–46

JEFFERSON'S EMBARGO

Our ships all in motion once whitened the ocean,
They sailed back and forth with a cargo;
Now all laid away they fall into decay
From Jefferson, worms and Embargo.

So JINGLED a Federalist newspaper poet early in 1808. It was all very well to laugh at Jefferson's theory that his embargo would be a perfect substitute for war, without the attendant cost and loss of life; New England did not care to sacrifice her leading interest to prove a presidential theory. Practically, the embargo proved the greatest failure of any political experiment ever tried in the United States — excepting national prohibition. It protected ships, but destroyed commerce; it produced no effect on either belligerent, but threw the carrying trade into other hands; it could be enforced only by measures which violated popular ideas of liberty. And it revived the declining power of the Federalist party.

The Federalists had experimented with a temporary embargo in Washington's second administration to coerce England, and rejected it as a failure. When again proposed in 1798 to counter the French spoliations, Otis in his *Letter to William Heath* pointed out that it would protect neither commerce nor navigation, "but destroy both." This prediction was amply fulfilled in 1808, especially in Massachusetts which owned over one third of American merchant tonnage, and where the shipbuilding and fishing industries were still paramount. It was useless to tell shipowners that the embargo protected their property, since the orders in council had left loopholes for trade under British protection which they longed to enjoy. Nor did seamen and laborers in maritime industries see the advantage of an embargo, throwing them out of work, over war which would have increased the demand for their labor. Before the embargo had lasted many months, stagnation, bankruptcy and distress were the rule along the New England coast. Farmers of the interior, now that exports had ceased, found their products a glut on the market and prices of imported goods greatly enhanced. Otis felt the pinch in his real estate interests; the embargo put a stop to building in Boston, forcing him and Bulfinch to modify materially their original plans for the development of Beacon Hill, and also throwing carpenters and bricklayers out of work.

"The affairs of our Country are overspread with gloom," wrote Otis to Rutledge on 13 February 1808. The President, in conversation with an unnamed member of Congress from Massachusetts, had said that France was certain to win the European war, and Otis suspected that Napoleon, bent on "exterminating Great Britain," had required his friend Jefferson to pass the embargo. "I pray that I may be mistaken," he adds; he was, of course. In a somber letter to Rutledge six months later he refers to the "inveterate & implacable hatred of England" by Jefferson and Madison, their "blind attachment to France with a servile fear of her power," as well as "a sincere hostility to our own Commerce." He and other Federalist leaders believed that the embargo was intended as a mere prelude to war with England. How else could one explain why every administration newspaper extolled Napoleon and decried England, denounced the orders in council and apologized for Napoleon's far more sweeping Berlin and Milan decrees? The French Emperor, to the Federalists, had become a living embodiment of forces that threatened liberty, property and good order worldwide. They would grant England's every reasonable demand in order to aid her battles; she had been forbearing and magnanimous, argued Timothy Pickering. "Although Great Britain, with her thousand ships of war, could have destroyed our commerce, she has really done it no essential injury."

That last clause became "fighting words" in the next few years, with which Democrats taunted Federalists, who retaliated with James Madison's remark, "France wants money and must have it," shrilly repeated on sundry occasions by John Randolph of Roanoke.

NEW ENGLAND WRECKS THE EMBARGO

"The Embargo will touch their bone and their flesh, when they must curse its authors," wrote Pickering, paraphrasing Job ii.5. Election returns proved him correct.

To understand the furious opposition of New England to the embargo, one must remember that shipping with all its ramifications (shipbuilding, spar-making, ropewalks, sail lofts, anchor foundries, etc.) was that section's prime industry, the one thing that had enabled the Yankees to lift themselves out of a penury incident to poor soil and a harsh climate. And they were justly proud of it: of *Columbia's* voyage around the world; of the nor'-westers who sailed around the Horn to Vancouver, Hawaii and Canton; of the Salem ships which traded with the East Indies and the South Pacific; of the whalers whom the great Edmund Burke had praised; of the Baltic, Mediterranean and West Indies traders. Other parts of the United States owned shipping, to be sure, and they did not care much for the embargo; but in New England, shipping was paramount. Its influence extended far inland since it gave a foreign market for products of soil and forest; and there was not a farming town in New England that did not contribute stout lads to ships' crews, whose take-home wages and little speculations enabled them to acquire a family and a farm. So, for a southern president and majority in Congress to tell New England "Thou shalt not sail!" was as if a Yankee president and Congress had said to the South, "Thou shalt plant neither tobacco, cotton, nor sweet potatoes!"

In the spring of 1808 the Federalists recovered their majority in both houses of the general court and reëlected Harrison Gray Otis to the presidency of the senate. Their victory would have been complete had Otis been nominated for governor instead of Christopher Gore, a nomination dictated by the Essex Junto who distrusted Otis. "Kit" Gore, a gentleman of means and culture, lacked Otis's popular appeal. His manners were stiff and formal, and he displayed his wealth to no political advantage, prancing around the countryside in a handsome coach with liveried servants. So it is not surprising that the Republican candidate, James Sullivan, won the governorship.

The general court had been in session barely a week when they felt obliged to do something about the apostasy of John Quincy Adams. Elected to the United States Senate in 1803 as a Federalist, Adams went completely over to Jefferson, voted for the embargo, and attacked Pickering's arraignment of it in a published *Letter to the Hon. Harrison Gray Otis on the Present State of our National Affairs*. The Federalists got rid of Adams by choosing a successor to the United States Senate more than a year before his term expired; he took the hint and resigned. Otis was chairman of the legislative caucus that nominated as Adams's successor James Lloyd, Jr., a Boston merchant and banker whom the Essex Junto trusted; yet Otis himself did not favor that action. Adams later recorded a conversation with Harry's father at Washington in 1808. Samuel Allyne Otis said that his son "was mortified at the electing of another person in my place; that his son had done everything in his power to prevent it, but could not; that the tide ran too strong; that '*the Essex Junto were omnipotent.*' "

If Otis felt that way, argued Adams, he too should have supported the embargo, especially since he had promised in the July town meeting of 1807 to support any measures judged necessary by the administration for the safety and honor of the country. Otis might have replied that his pledge in the town meeting related to the *Chesapeake* affair, for which England had apologized

Christopher Gore, by John Trumbull.

and offered to pay compensation. But the embargo fell with undue weight on New England interests, and compromised both national honor and dignity.

In the summer of 1808 a turn in European affairs made commercial restriction even more irksome to New England than before. Spain having revolted against Napoleon and King Joseph, Great Britain supported her, and only the embargo prevented New England ships from supplying allied armies in the Peninsula. In a special Boston town meeting on 9 August, a motion requesting the President to remove the embargo either wholly, or partially in regard to Spain and Portugal, passed by a strong majority despite opposition by prominent Democrats. The inhabitants express their willingness "to endure any privations which the public welfare may require," and apologize for not awaiting the meeting of Congress, on the ground of the change in European affairs, and their pressing desire for "relief from the pressure of this great calamity, which bears with peculiar weight on the Eastern States. — Denied by nature those valuable & luxuriant Staples which constitute the riches of the South, they necessarily owe much of their prosperity . . . to their own enterprise & Industry on the Ocean." These Boston resolutions set an example. By the end of September, at least seventy Massachusetts towns, and fifteen or more elsewhere in New England and New York, had petitioned the President to modify or repeal the embargo. Jefferson refused.

When state elections in the last days of August and early September swung the rest of New England back into the Federalist column, the prospect of electing Charles Cotesworth Pinckney, presidential nominee of the Federalist national convention,[1] appeared excellent to Otis's correspondents. But Pinckney obtained only 47 electoral votes to Madison's 122. All chance of removing the embargo by a change of rulers now ended. With the people of New England facing another winter of privation and distress, Presi-

---

[1] See above, Chap. XII.

HIS EXCELLENCY CALEB STRONG, LLD
* elected in April 1814
GOVERNOR of MASSACHUSETTS
for the TENTH time
by the

FREE SUFFRAGES of his FELLOW CITIZENS.

dent Jefferson could hardly expect them to confine their opposition within prudent or constitutional bounds.

By the time that Congress assembled for its winter session, on 7 November 1808, no sensible man in the United States doubted that the embargo was a failure. Nevertheless, on 9 January 1809 Congress passed a bill to tighten it up, by a law compared with which the old Sedition Act seemed a mild piece of legislation. This "Force Act," as the Federalists called it, required coasting vessels to give bonds to the amount of six times the value of vessel and cargo before their freight could even be loaded. Customs collectors were given power to seize and confiscate goods on land or sea, "in any manner apparently on their way toward the territory of a foreign nation, or the vicinity thereof, or toward a place whence such articles are intended to be transported." They were declared immune from legal liability for their actions. Jefferson now exercised a power that no later president has wielded except in wartime. When a shortage of flour occurred in Massachusetts, Governor Sullivan had to beg the President for permission to bring a supply from Virginia. So palpable was the failure of the embargo that almost every Democrat from the northern states now favored repeal. John Quincy Adams wrote to his friends in Congress that the embargo must go, or New England would be up in arms against the national government. The legislature of Massachusetts warned Congress, "The evils which are menaced by the continuance of this policy . . . must soon become intolerable, and endanger our domestic peace, and the union of these States."

One week after the Force Bill was introduced in Congress, although before it passed, Otis wrote to Josiah Quincy, the member from Boston, a letter which reveals, six years before its accomplishment, a plan for a New England Convention, complete even to the place of meeting:

Boston 15 Dec. 1808

. . . Our General Court will soon meet, and I doubt not the majority will require the bridle rather than the spur. If I am not mistaken, there will be found among them a fullness of zeal and indignation which can be mitigated only by giving them a direction and an object. This temper you are sensible must not be extinguished for want of sympathy, nor permitted to burst forth into imprudent excess. We must look to our friends in Congress for advice. You are together and can best decide on such a course as would probably be agreed to, by Connecticut, New H. &c. and no other ought to be adopted. You are sensible how obnoxious Massachusetts for a thousand reasons, has already become, and perceive more plainly than any of us the efforts which are made to mark and distinguish this State as the hotbed of opposition, and this town as the citadel of a British faction. Perhaps our Legislature have said as much as is expedient for them to say, unless they are to be supported by a correspondent spirit in the other States. It would be a great misfortune for us to justify the obloquy of wishing to promote a separation of the States, and of being solitary in that pursuit. . . . On the other hand, to do nothing will expose us to danger and contempt, our resolutions will seem to be a flash in the pan, and our apostate representatives will be justified in the opinions which they have doubtless inculcated of our want of union and of nerve.

What then shall we do? In other words, what can Connecticut do? For we can and will come up to her tone. Is she ready to declare the Embargo and its supplementary chains unconstitutional, to propose to their State the appointment of delegates to meet those from the other commercial States in convention at Hartford or elsewhere, for the purpose of providing some mode of relief that may not be *inconsistent with the Union of these States,* to which we should adhere as long as possible? Shall New York be invited to join? and what shall be the proposed objects of such a convention? . . .

Let me know whether you think any good effect would be produced in *Congress* by hints of this kind, in the public papers. Sometimes I fear that we are so neutralized by our accursed adversaries, that all efforts will be ineffectual and that we must sit down quietly and count the links of our chains, but then again this system appears so monstrous, so unprecedented, so ruinous, that I think the time will come that must make resistance a duty. . . .

This letter has given Otis the credit for fathering the Hartford Convention of 1814. A strong advocate of it he certainly was; but the project had already been a matter of common conversation in Washington. And the vital question with regard to the proposed New England Convention of 1808 is not its paternity, but its object. What was the mode of relief, not *"inconsistent with the Union of these States,"* that Otis had in mind?

"Secession" is the answer supplied by John Quincy Adams; but secession was completely inconsistent with union. Adams knew that Pickering had plotted disunion in 1804, and so readily believed that the same scheme was on foot. Secession talk was common enough in New England during the embargo. President Dwight of Yale preached on the text of 2 Corinthians vi.17, "Come out therefore from among them and be ye separate, saith the Lord"; and the Boston *Gazette* announced, "It is better to suffer the *amputation* of a Limb, than to lose the *whole body*. We must prepare for the operation." But threats of secession, common enough throughout the first century of the American Union, do not imply the existence of a definite plot, plan or policy to secede. Nor was secession talk confined to New England. The Washington *Monitor,* an administration organ edited by J. B. Colvin, recommended "an immediate severance of the union, the Southern States putting themselves under the protection, or in union with France, and the Northern States being suffered to do as they would."

Otis's letter to Quincy distinctly states that in no case must the Federalists "justify the obloquy of wishing to promote a Separation of the States," and that the "mode of relief" to be provided by the New England Convention must not be *"inconsistent with the Union of these States."* In 1828, declaring that he had never even heard of a northern Confederacy plan, he insisted that he had proposed a New England convention in 1808 as the most effective method of obtaining a united New England demand to get rid of the embargo, and to draft constitutional amendments to protect New England's commercial interests. To John Rutledge he wrote

on 9 January 1809 that after the spring state elections "the Legislatures of the 5 Eastern States will recommend a convention . . .
for the purpose of procuring amendments to the Constitution."
But, he added sinisterly, if the southern states refuse to accept these
amendments, there will probably be "consequences" which he
cares not "to contemplate, much less to put in black and white."

Obviously a situation was shaping up like that of 1861 when
Virginia and the border slave states demanded constitutional
amendments to protect and extend slavery as the price of union.
The New England Federalists' project was very similar: a concerted demand for amendments protecting the commercial and
shipping interests — or else! Circumstances, fortunately, brought
a very different outcome from that of 1861.

From the passage of the Force Act, the people of New England
bombarded President and Congress with anti-embargo resolutions.
In a Boston town meeting of 24 January 1809, following an exciting debate between Otis and Samuel Dexter on one side, and
William Eustis and George Blake on the other, a petition was
drawn up to the general court of Massachusetts for "means of relief against unconstitutional measures of the General Government." On the following day the legislature opened an attack on
the embargo and the Force Act, details of which were printed in a
pamphlet entitled *Patriotick Proceedings*. As Otis was then president of the state senate, he may be presumed to have had much to
do with this. Its tone was more moderate and unionist than that of
contemporary town resolutions. These "Patriotick Proceedings"
were, however, sufficiently alarming to that staunch Old Roman,
Mercy Warren, to bring forth a query to nephew Harry as to
"what he was about?" Otis answered her somewhat flippantly:

Boston, 4 feby 1809.
My dear Aunt,

    If I could allow the right of any person to interrogate me as to
"what I am about," you may well suppose that there is no individual of your political party, whom I would prefer for a confes-

sor to your much respected self. But it certainly must occur to you that if I have really turned conspirator against the State, I ought not to put it even in your power to hang me; nor even to write a letter which under the present arbitrary government, might by a forced construction, if found by accident, be construed into evidence of treason. . . .

To be serious, my dear Aunt, my respect and affection for you, are so utterly at variance with the political views & party attachments which to my great sorrow & mortification, you have been led to embrace; that I have for twenty years, studiously evaded all discussions of the last, lest the former might be brought into jeopardy. And from this determination I cannot consent to be diverted, at this late period of your existence, when my duty and your afflictions equally require, that all the sentiments which I have an opportunity to express to you, should breathe nothing but tenderness consolation & respectful love. To mingle with these the acidulating, corrosive ingredients of political creeds, would be to turn the milk of human kindness into poison. I will not engage in such a process. . . .

My family all unite with me, in the sincere assur[ances] of regard and duty to you and yours, with w[hich] I am dear Madam,

Yr dutiful Nephew, H. G. Otis.

And on the very next day Samuel Allyne Otis assured Mercy's son Henry that

> The President of your Senate . . . writes but little on political subjects; Enough however, to convince me that, altho he ardently wishes to guard against unconstitutional and oppressive restrictions, he as ardently wishes to prevent things going to extremities and confusion. For indeed he hath many valuable articles afloat, "on the tempestuous sea of liberty."

The *Patriotick Proceedings* reach a climax in two resolutions of 15 February 1809. The Force Act is "unjust, oppressive, and unconstitutional." The people are advised "to abstain from forcible resistance, and to apply for their remedy in a peaceable manner to the laws of the Commonwealth." The remedy suggested is constitutional amendment.

All through January 1809, memorials from Connecticut and Massachusetts towns came pouring in on Jefferson. Their language was extreme: immediate repeal of the embargo and reversal of the administration's foreign policy were imperatively demanded, and in many instances accompanied by threats of forcible resistance and even secession. "I felt the foundation of the government shaken under my feet by the New England townships," Jefferson afterward wrote. "The organization of this little selfish minority enabled it to overrule the Union." Northern Democrats in Congress joined the Federalists, and on 1 March 1809 President Jefferson signed an act repealing the embargo. Three days after this enforced act of humiliation, his reign ended.

As Henry Adams has well said, the cost of his experiment "exceeded all calculation. Financially, it emptied the Treasury, bankrupted the mercantile and agricultural class, and ground the poor beyond endurance. Constitutionally, it overrode every specified limit on arbitrary power and made Congress despotic, while it left no bounds to the authority which might be vested by Congress in the President. Morally it sapped the nation's vital force, lowering its courage, paralyzing its energy, corrupting its principles, and arraying all the active elements of society in factious opposition to government or in secret paths of treason. Politically, it cost Jefferson the fruits of eight years' painful labor for popularity, and brought the Union to the edge of a precipice."

Anyone who honestly and thoroughly studies this period will agree that Henry Adams's indictment is valid. But Jefferson has become such a god to American liberals and radicals that articles and books have been published to defend the embargo, claiming that it really protected shipping, and that it would have succeeded, but for those nasty Federalists. And the embargo idea has been embraced again and again by the American people as a panacea. The southern Confederacy embargoed cotton in 1861, hoping thus to coerce England into recognition. The United States embargoed war materials in 1935 and exports to Japan in 1940, hoping to prevent Europe from fighting and to force Japan to change her policy. There are embargoes on Red China and Cuba as I write. Yet not one of these has ever attained its objective.

Jefferson's embargo forced the Federalist party to abandon nationalism in favor of state rights. Until the world peace of 1815, the party in Massachusetts was anti-federal, gaining its ends by methods, and sheltering itself under theories that were finally used to break up the Union. The convention project fell through in 1809 merely because the embargo was repealed. But it was not forgotten.

The simultaneous retirement of Jefferson and repeal of his embargo brought a short breathing space in American politics. Congress replaced the embargo by an act of non-intercourse with Great Britain and France which did not prohibit the supplying of provisions to British armies in the Iberian Peninsula, an exceedingly profitable trade. And in April 1809 came an event which temporarily reconciled New England Federalists with the Madison administration. This was the Erskine Agreement in which the British minister at Washington promised, on behalf of his government, to revoke the offensive orders in council if the United States would repeal the Non-Intercourse Act against Great Britain and maintain it against France. Madison and Congress at once carried out their side of the agreement, and the Federalist press showered praises upon the President. Otis was delighted. "Democracy here is thrown up in the wind," he wrote to John Rutledge on 22 June. "The confusion & embarrassment in [our] approbation of Madison's conduct, are ludicrous. They cannot rally again this year, if an accommodation with G. Britain should be sincere."

Alas, it was not sincere on the other side. Before Otis wrote that letter, Erskine's agreement had been repudiated by Foreign Minister George Canning in the most summary fashion. He then added insult to injury in replacing Erskine as minister to Washington by Francis J. ("Copenhagen") Jackson, his favorite instru-

ment for bullying weak neutrals. When Jackson formally accused
Madison of bad faith in accepting Erskine's agreement, the President properly replied that no further communication would be
received from him. Congress in November renewed the Non-
Intercourse Act against Great Britain, and every disputed question
between the two countries boiled up again.

The Federalist party, with reprehensible folly, now took the
part of Canning against their own insulted government, and Otis
was one of the worst. As president of the Massachusetts senate he
promoted resolutions denouncing the Erskine Agreement as unfair
to England, and accusing the administration of dismissing Jackson
in order to create a crisis. Senator Pickering opened correspondence with Jackson, and received with delight his disparaging
remarks on President Madison. Jackson himself made a trium-
phal tour northward, receiving flattering attention from Federalists in every city en route. His reception in Boston became an occasion for pro-British demonstrations. Since Elbridge Gerry had
been elected governor, Jackson could not be officially received,
but Otis and his friends made up in warmth what was lacking in
official sanction. The dismissed English minister on 4 June 1810
attended the annual dinner of the Ancient and Honorable Artillery Company. He swaggered late into the hall, and without
taking the slightest notice of Governor Gerry, seated himself at
the same table. Upon being called upon for a toast, Jackson had
the impudence to offer the following:

> Perpetual harmony between Great Britain and the United States
> — May the swords of this Ancient and Honorable Artillery Com-
> pany be drawn against those who would interrupt it!

This sentiment created a sensation which Harrison Gray Otis only
partly effaced by a gracious and non-committal response:

> May our prejudices against the British Nation, like those against
> her minister, vanish upon a more intimate acquaintance.

We have no record of the private party that the Otises gave for Jackson, except that Chief Justice Parsons was one of the guests; but we know plenty about the "superb public dinner" that almost 300 Federalists tendered to the dismissed minister at the Exchange Coffee-House. Here Senator Pickering, called upon for a sentiment, boldly flung out a challenge to Madison and Napoleon:

> The World's last hope — Britain's fast-anchored Isle!

These words, which summarized the Federalist platform for a decade, were greeted by the company with a roar of approval. Pickering afterward exclaimed, "I am willing the sentiment should be inscribed on my tombstone!"

MADISON AND GERRY

No Federalist president could have done more than Madison to obtain the good will of the British government. Since Canning had blocked his attempt, he now sought an opening in France, where Napoleon met him with a Machiavellian change of policy which so completely outwitted and deceived the President as to give color to the Federalist charge of French influence. This was, in effect, a fictitious repeal of the French anti-neutral decrees, provided the United States would cease commercial intercourse with England. Madison swallowed the bait, announced that the French decrees were repealed, and that commercial intercourse with Great Britain would again be suspended on 2 January 1811, since the "national faith was pledged to France."

Boston Federalism, already stirred up over the admission of Louisiana to the Union, an act which Josiah Quincy stated in Congress to be sufficient cause for secession, expressed its opinion of Madison's new policy in the grand caucus rally at Faneuil Hall on 31 March 1811. John Lowell, Jr., presented a resolution in favor of nullification as official doctrine of the party — to "oppose

by peaceable but firm measures the execution of laws, which if
persisted in must and will be resisted." Otis seconded the motion,
and in the debate that followed, according to the *Columbian
Centinel,* "He proved that the plans of the present administration
are in perfect conformity with those of *Napoleon,* and that the
Continental System which *Napoleon* has established through
Europe is now in operation on our own merchants at home."
Expressions of surprise from Democratic critics at finding Otis
supporting extreme measures, indicate that his position as a moderate was well understood. "Leolin" (pseudonym of James T.
Austin, Elbridge Gerry's son-in-law and biographer) addressed a
series of letters to Otis in the Boston *Patriot,* in which he deplored
that "that splendid eloquence, which always animates and charms
— which on every subject is equally ready and brilliant," should
be raised in support of resistance to the laws. Otis also received
several lines in an amusing Hudibrastic poem on the Boston
caucus by "Tristram Trap'em Esq.":

> We now shall say a word or two
> Of Harry O. Ben P. and Q.
> The *first* with tongue as smooth as oil,
> Address'd the gaping crowd awhile;
> Told a long train of sad disasters,
> (No doubt to please his tory masters)
> Which never came into existence;
> And closed with threats of stout resistance.
> Alas! poor Harry, where are now
> The honors which once on thy brow
> Began to bud? — O fie! for shame!
> That thou shouldst tarnish the bright name
> Of ——, and become the tool
> Of every factious, meddling fool!
> Believe me, friend, you ne'er will share
> The honors of the Gov'nor's chair;
> No doubt but still the tory party
> Will stuff your ears with praises hearty —
> But all that you can hope to be,
> Is a mere *imp of drudgery.*

These last six lines went straight to the mark, for Otis had not yet received the Federalist nomination for governor, in spite of his long public career and his continual drudgery on their central committee.

There is no doubt that the party intended to nullify the Non-Intercourse Act, if returned to power, or to resist its enforcement, if defeated. But, since the economic effects of this act were mild compared with those of the embargo, the people rebuked Federalist extremism at the polls by giving the Republican ticket a clean sweep, reëlecting Elbridge Gerry governor and obtaining a majority in both branches of the legislature. Otis was deposed from the presidency of the senate.

In his speech at the opening session on 7 June 1811, Governor Gerry, castigating the Boston caucus of 31 March and its leaders, imputed to them with some justice such conduct "as would beguile peaceable and happy citizens into a state of civil warfare." The senate drew up a suitable reply, from which Otis proposed to strike out "all that part of the answer which was a mere echo of the Governor's denunciation of the 'assemblage' of Bostonians," and proposed a set of sarcastic amendments, such as, "We are sensible that this species of invective was a familiar expedient with some royal governors, the use of which compelled some of them to exile themselves and to spend the residue of their mournful days in foreign climes."

John Lowell in June and July 1811 published a series of articles signed "A Boston Rebel" in the Salem *Gazette* and other Federalist journals, which were a scathing indictment of Governor Gerry. He even suggested, by means of a quotation from Sallust, that during the Revolution Gerry had prosecuted the tory Oliver in order to obtain his Elmwood estate in Cambridge! As everyone knew that Lowell had written these articles, he became known as "the Boston Rebel."

Having secured the executive department and both branches of the legislature, the Massachusetts Democracy pushed through a series of "reforms," the objects of which were to crush the Federalist establishment and to entrench itself in power. Even the incorporation of the Massachusetts General Hospital, proposed by two Federalist physicians, got kicked around the political arena. It did not pass the general court until Republican leaders such as Gerry, Eustis, Crowninshield, Varnum and Perez Morton were added to the original list of incorporators, which included only Federalists such as Otis, Cabot, the Perkins brothers, Jack Lowell, President Kirkland and William Phillips. The famous gerrymander, typical of this short-lived regime, has become embalmed in political vocabulary.

Governor Gerry began his administration with high ideals, but could not resist his party's hungry office seekers, and lost popularity by showing intense sensitiveness to criticism. Otis, now minority leader, passed the pleasantest session of his legislative career watching the "Jacobins" rushing to their own destruction, and furthering the process by turning upon them his rich fund of humor. And in the spring elections of 1812 the Federalists, under the lead of their old standard-bearer Caleb Strong of Northampton, recovered power on the eve of war. Not until 1823 did the people of Massachusetts again venture to trust their government to a party bearing the stamp of Jeffersonian Democracy.

The years 1810–1811 were very happy for the Otis family. Elizabeth Gray, the eldest daughter, married George Williams Lyman, son of Theodore Lyman of Waltham, a leading China merchant allied to the Essex Junto. Sally Jr., their second daughter, married Israel Thorndike, Jr., whom Otis regarded as "the most uniformly well bred and respectable young man of his age that I have ever seen." Receipted bills in the Otis manuscripts indicate that the girls were given French lessons, drawing lessons and dancing lessons; and, both boys and girls, riding lessons at Mr. Roulstone's fashionable school of equestrianism.

In the summer of 1810 the Otises' third daughter, Sophia, aged twelve, was sent to a fashionable boarding school with the odd name Mansion of Truth, kept by a Mrs. Brenton in the then rural

THE GERRY-MANDER.

A new species of *Monster*, which appeared in *Essex South District* in Jan. 1812.

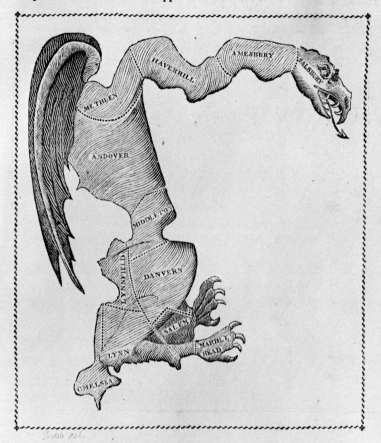

" *O generation of* VIPERS ! *who hath warned you of the wrath to come ?*"

THE horrid Monster of which this drawing is a correct representation, appeared in the County of Essex, during the last session of the Legislature. Various and manifold have been the speculations and conjectures, among learned naturalists respecting the *genus* and origin of this astonishing production. Some believe it to be the real *Basilisk*, a creature which had been supposed to exist only in the poet's imagination. Others pronounce it the *Serpens Monocephalus* of Pliny, or single-headed *Hydra*, a terrible animal of pagan extraction. Many are of opinion that it is the *Griffin* or *Hippogriff* of romance, which flourished in the dark ages, and has come hither to assist the knight of the ruefcl countenance in restoring that gloomy period of ignorance, fiction and imposition. Some think it the great Red Dragon, or Bunyan's *Apollyon* or the *Monstrum Horrendum* of Virgil, and all believe it a creature of infernal origin, both from its aspect, and from the circumstance of its birth.

ROULSTONE'S
Riding School,

LADIES & GENTLEMEN taught the polite Art of Riding on the following terms

Ladies Twelve Lefsons including Horse Twice a week, days & hour when convenient	12.	0
Lefsons on the Road	2.	0
Gentlemen in clafses Sixteen Lefsons two Lefsons a week days and hour when convenient	16.	0
Single Lefsons	1.	50
Horse for each Lefson	.	50
Lefson on the Road	2.	0
Military Gentlemen taught the Horse Exercise from the drill to the attack in Speed 18 Lefsons	50.	0

Ladies & Gentlemens Horses & Officers Chargers Broke and Completely managed on Reasonable terms.

RULES FOR
Mr. R's Riding School.

1. EVERY Gentleman will pay, in advance, for entrance, ten dollars.
2. Every Lady, do. five dollars.
3. Every Lady and Gentleman will attend the day and hour agreed upon, sickness excepted, for lessons.
4. A class is not to consist of more than Eight Gentlemen.
5. Ladies after going through their lessons complete, will be admitted to ride in the school for amusement and practice, for fifty cents, Horse included.
6. Gentlemen after going through their lessons complete, will be admitted to ride in the School for amusement and practice, for seventy-five cents, Horse included.
7. No spectator will be admitted when the scholars are riding.

☞ Application for admittance of Scholars, apply at the School, Sheafe's Lane, near the bottom of the Mall.

N. B. Well broke Horses for Ladies and Gentlemen, may be had by applying at Mr. R's School, or his Dragoon Stable, Essex Street, Boston.

village of Harlem, New York. Affectionate and admonitory letters from her father followed Sophia to Harlem. She must pay particular attention to music, French, and "a dignified deportment," which with a "cultivated mind" will give her an advantage "over the slatternly habits which characterize the manners of many of the Misses of the present age." She spends a long summer vacation with the Harrisons at Philadelphia where (says Papa, evidently remembering Maria Bingham) the ladies "range through the streets on foot by night and day, sometimes with very light draperies underneath. These are liberties which you must take in moderation." Papa visits her at the school in November. His carriage breaks down between New York and Harlem, he has to spend a night in a tavern. He finds Sophia "perfectly well" and a favorite with the headmistress, but her letters are unsatisfactory and Mama is surprised (as hundreds of thousands of parents have been since), "that one who talks so fluently should be at a loss to know how to compose a letter." This young lady had a mind of her own; she endorsed one of her father's admonitory epistles, "In an ill humour and tipsy when he wrote this!" After winning three prizes in school, Sophia returned home in the summer of 1811, just in time to see her eldest brother Harry Jr. graduate from Harvard in company with young John Rutledge, and to attend the commencement parties.

THE APPROACH OF WAR

Events were now moving stumblingly but inevitably toward the war that Otis dreaded. The British government, refusing to take Madison's word that Napoleon had revoked his anti-neutral decrees, in view of continued French captures and condemnations of American vessels, maintained the orders in council. An accidental sea fight occurred in May 1811 between an American frigate and an English corvette. Ominous was the appearance in the Twelfth

Congress, which convened on 4 November, of a formidable group
of young Southerners and Westerners who had been elected on a
war platform: Henry Clay of Kentucky, John C. Calhoun and
William Lowndes of South Carolina, and Felix P. Grundy of
Tennessee. Josiah Quincy described them as "young politicians,
half hatched, the shell still on their heads, and their pin feathers
not yet shed"; but they were no younger than Otis, Harper and
Rutledge had been when leading the Fifth Congress. These men
represented sections which had lost faith in the Jeffersonian system
of commercial restriction, and resented the contemptuous attitude
of the European belligerents. The West demanded war; and that
war must be against Great Britain to accord with sectional interests and prejudices. Every Westerner believed that the British
government had been pressuring the Indians to resist the advance
of white settlement. The only way to end this state of affairs, it
was thought, was to conquer Canada. That was supposed to be
easy. Henry Clay boasted he could do it with Kentucky troops
alone; Jefferson wrote Duane after the war began, "The acquisition of Canada this year, as far as . . . Quebec, will be a mere
matter of marching"; and William Eustis, Madison's secretary of
war, predicted even that would be unnecessary: the government
need only send political commissars to the Canadians, who would
"rise as one man" and "throw off the British yoke." How wrong
they all were!

The "war hawks," as the exponents of hostilities were first called
by John Randolph of Roanoke, chose Henry Clay speaker of the
House. In the face of this new state of affairs, Josiah Quincy,
minority House leader, attempted to persuade his fellow Federalists to outscream the war hawks. Believing that the Republican
majority "could not be kicked" into hostilities, Quincy broached
this strategy in two long letters to Otis, written from Washington
after the winter session opened. He besought his friends to
abandon "British ground," and developed the startling idea that
war with Great Britain would not be too bad, since it would be

so incompetently managed that the people would turn the war hawks out and vote the Federalists in.

Had this party brought itself to support Quincy's policy, there would have been no unpatriotic opposition and no Hartford Convention. It might have profited by Madison's mismanagement of the war, as the Whigs profited by the Mexican War, and obtained a new lease on life. But Quincy's strategy was both unsound and insincere; unsound because based on an assumption of Madison's inveterate pacifism, and insincere because the Federalists abhorred war with England above everything. So, to ask their leaders to blow war trumpets against "Britain's fast-anchored isle" was to expect them to belie past records and their own consciences. Otis wrote cautiously to Quincy that Boston approved his strategy only on the assumption of the administration's inveterate pacifism. In the showdown Quincy's support vanished, and he voted against the declaration of war.

Otis, although accused by Christopher Gore of having "hatched" this strategy with Quincy, actually never did support it. On the contrary, he made an earnest behind-the-scenes effort to prevent war with England by persuading the British government to be reasonable, through correspondence with his loyalist uncle in London, Harrison Gray. The first letter in the series that has been preserved, dated 30 April 1811, contains this sensible résumé of the situation:

> You cannot be more afflicted than I am at the state of the political relations of the two countries; in which I expect no change for the better. The Government of this Country is unquestionably intimidated though not corrupted by France; and the mass of people are infected with strong prejudices against G Britain. The most intelligent and respectable men in the country are not however of this description. They tremble for the prosperity and fate of Britain, and consider her justly as the Bulwark of the liberties of this country and mankind. Unfortunately however, your Cabinet has not adopted a course of measures which without injury to themselves, would have enabled the wise men of

this country to become an overmatch for the knaves & fools who have always too great a share of influence in democratic governments. I doubt not, that your Government, by repealing your orders in Council which have produced no benefit to the nation, and by such partial concessions as the times would justify, in favor of American Commerce, might have enabled the real friends to your prosperity, to have given a direction to the policy and measures of this administration, which would have cemented the friendship of the two countries, without any sacrifice of your principles of maratime law, or any abandonment of our just pretensions. But my fears for the event are daily augmenting. The American Cabinet is doubtless weak and perhaps not very well affected towards your Country. But you must allow in return, that John Bull, though a good sailor, soldier, and in fact on the whole a good fellow, is a bad negotiator and politician.

Harrison Gray, pleased with this letter, presented a copy of it to an opposton newspaper, the London *Morning Chronicle*, where it was printed on 24 June 1811, as "from a Gentleman high in office and of great respectability in America." Otis, apparently, had no objection to having his letters so used, for he continued writing in the same strain to his uncle. Another letter of the same series is dated January 1812:

You will perceive by the papers by the *Sally Anne*, that our Government professes the intention to assume a very warlike attitude, and that the sentiment of indignation throughout the country, at the continuation of the Orders in Council; is loud and universal from both parties. The motives which induce your Government to continue them, are quite incomprehensible to the best friends of Great Britain in this country; and the effect will be, to make every man odious who dares to express a wish for your success and prosperity — a sentiment still common to our best men, but which an adherence to this system will impair and destroy. It is too true that the repeal of the Berlin and Milan Decrees are merely nominal; and that our Administration have become willingly the dupes to the insidious policy of Napoleon. But why should your Cabinet mind that, why should they not embrace any pretence for restoring harmony between our countries, especially *as it will, of consequence, be followed by hostility on the part of France.* Napoleon will renew his outrages the moment we are friends, and the natural ties which connect Great Britain and America would be drawn closer. On the contrary, the scrupulous adherence of your Cabinet to an empty punctilio, will too probably unite the whole country in opposition to your nation, and sever for generations, perhaps forever, interests that have the most natural ties of affinity, and men who ought to feel and love like brethren.

This was excellent advice for the British government, which, if followed in time, would have prevented the War of 1812. The language is a refreshing contrast to that used by the Federalists in Washington to the British minister, and to the tone of Pickering's contemporary correspondence with his English friends. Harrison Gray gave the letter for publication to the London *Evening Star,* and also sent a copy of it to the Prime Minister, Spencer Perceval. In reply he received the following cold and caustic note, written in the third person in Perceval's hand:

Mr. P's compliments to Mr. G — and thanks him for his note and its enclosure from his American correspondent. It is impossible for Mr P to enter into the subject of that enclosure in a note to Mr G, but he begs to assure him that the Order in Council is not grounded on *extravagant and fancied punctilio* but that whether wisely or not, it is deem'd by those who advise it, to be of absolutely essential and indispensable necessity to the hopes of maintaining the independence and security of the British Empire.

Downing Street 22 Feby 1812

This was not the end of the matter. Within a few days, much to Harrison Gray's astonishment and his nephew's subsequent disgust, an incorrect copy of one letter, wrongly dated, appeared printed on a handbill headed "Extract of a Letter from the Honorable H. G. Otis, Esq. of Boston, to his friend in London, dated

January 14, 1812." Published by a friend, to whom Gray had given a copy of the letter, it was circulated by the opposition who desired a repeal of the orders. Republished in the *Centinel* on 25 April 1812, it caused Otis considerable embarrassment. For the letter states that England's motives for a continuance of the orders in council "are quite incomprehensible to the best friends of Great Britain in this country," whereas the leading Federalists had loudly defended the orders as necessary to Great Britain in her struggle with Napoleon. The printers of the handbill, moreover had twisted Otis's statement that the repeal of the French decrees was "nominal," into "less formal than it should have been."

According to the London *Evening Star* of 13 July 1812, Otis's letter had "great weight in hastening the repeal of the obnoxious Orders in Council," and "Mr. Otis and his relative are therefore certainly entitled to the best thanks of both Countries." But the force of this tribute is impaired by the naïve disclosure of Harrison Gray that he wrote the leader himself and paid the editor of the *Star* "the enormous sum of one pound for putting it in."

Revocation of the orders in council actually had been decided in principle as early as April. Unfortunately the assassination of Perceval on 11 May, consequent shakeup of the cabinet, and the absence of an American minister in London, delayed the announcement until 17 June; otherwise there would have been no War of 1812. About twenty-four hours later, Congress passed a declaration of war against Great Britain.

CHAPTER XVI

Mr. Madison's War

1812–1814, AET. 46–48

OUR MOST UNPOPULAR WAR

THE SECOND war with England, which began in June 1812 and lasted into 1815, was the most unpopular war that this country has ever waged, not even excepting the Vietnam conflict. The war declaration on 18 June passed by a vote of 79 to 49 in the House, and 19 to 13 in the Senate. Eight out of ten New England senators, 11 out of 14 New York representatives, voted against it, and twenty-five percent of the Republicans in Congress abstained, for there was a strong anti-war faction in Madison's party, led by John Randolph of Roanoke. Although the South and West were keen for the war when it began, their enthusiasm soon evaporated, judging from recruiting statistics. The war department could never build up the regular army to half its authorized strength, and obtained only 10,000 one-year volunteers out of 50,000 authorized. Even Henry Clay's Kentucky furnished only 400 recruits in 1812. Interestingly enough, the loyal minority in New England more than made up for the discouraging stand of the Federalist state governments; those five states provided the regular army with 19 regiments as against 15 from the middle states and 10 from the southern states. The truth seems to be that after Hull's surrender had shown that the war would be no walkover, it became disliked throughout the country, and only recovered popularity after it had ended.

The notion that only Yankee Federalists opposed the war is pure myth. Robert Smith, a Maryland merchant-shipowner who

served in the cabinets of Jefferson and Madison, issued a public
address against the war and sent a copy to Chief Justice Marshall
who replied in part: "All minor considerations should be waived
. . . and the great division between the friends of peace & the advocates of war ought alone to remain. . . . All who wish peace ought
to unite in the means which may facilitate its attainment." Marshall's biographer admits that the Chief Justice opposed the war
as bitterly as did Otis or Pickering, and that most of the southern
Federalists were of the same mind. General William Heath,
whom Otis had defeated for Congress in 1798, denounced the war
as "unwise and improper," and with Otis served as presidential
elector in 1812. But the Yankee Federalists called down most of
the postwar odium on themselves because they alone controlled
state governments and turned state rights against the nation.

Massachusetts led off with an address to the people by the lower
house of her legislature, one week after Congress declared war:

> Organize a *peace party* throughout your Country, and let all
> other party distinctions vanish . . . meet and consult together for
> the common good in your towns and counties. . . . Express your
> sentiments without fear, and let the sound of your disapproba-
> tion of this war be loud and deep. Let it be distinctly under-
> stood, that in support of it your conformity to the requisitions of
> law will be the result of principle and not of choice. If your sons
> must be torn from you by conscriptions, consign them to the care
> of GOD; but let there be no volunteers except for defensive war.

And a day or two later, Governor Strong issued a proclamation
for a public fast to atone for a declaration of war "against the
nation from which we are descended, and which for many generations has been the bulwark of the religion we profess."

There was no "economic influence" on the New Englanders'
opposition — even the late Charles A. Beard could find none.
Hostilities affected Massachusetts much less than the rest of the
country, and enriched many individuals — as the Federalists refused to admit. Privateering furnished Yankee sailors, shipowners

and beachcombers with profitable employment, which the embargo had not done. A British blockade of the coast south of New York gave Yankee merchants a monopoly of the importing business, besides opportunities for smuggling. The cutting off of legitimate trade with England stimulated the infant manufacturing industries of New England; in Massachusetts proper, 34 new cotton and woolen mills were incorporated during the war, and at least twice as many sprang up elsewhere in New England. Specie flowed into Boston banks to such an extent that they were charged with deliberately attempting to bankrupt the rest of the country. Moreover, if the West had effected her dearest object of conquering Canada, the northern, non-slaveholding part of the Union would have been fortified.

None of these considerations moved Otis and his friends. To them it seemed unchristian and downright wicked to attack England when she was "the world's last hope" against the tyrant Napoleon. As Otis wrote to his uncle, "The most intelligent and respectable men in the country . . . tremble for the prosperity and fate of Britain, and consider her justly as the Bulwark of the liberties of this country and mankind." That belief happened to be correct in 1812. Napoleon had brought his continental system almost to perfection. He had suppressed every vestige of liberty in Western Europe save in England, Portugal and recalcitrant Spain. Within a week after America declared war on Great Britain, his grand army entered Russia. England's cause in 1812 as in 1914 and 1939, was that of the free world.

John Lowell, Jr., published a bitter, scurrilous tract against the national administration called *Mr. Madison's War* which had a countrywide circulation and great influence. But the Federalists' violent opposition to the war and their spiteful hatred of "that little man in the Palace," as they called James Madison, cannot be understood without knowledge of two incidents that took place, one shortly before, one shortly after the declaration of war: the so-called "Henry Plot," and the Baltimore riots.

The Henry affair was an attempt on the part of the national administration to fasten on Otis and his friends a stigma of disloyalty and treason. An Irish adventurer named John Henry visited Boston during and shortly after Jefferson's embargo, as a volunteer spy, to find out whether disaffection in New England could be turned to account by the Canadian or British governments. He carried good letters of introduction to prominent citizens such as Otis, who, after having been lavishly entertained in Montreal, felt obliged to give the visitor a party. Henry then proceeded to England to claim a reward for his services, which amounted to nothing more than writing letters to the Governor of Canada retailing Boston dinner-table gossip. The British government turned him down. Poverty-stricken and resentful, Henry took into his confidence a Gascon adventurer who styled himself the Count de Crillon. Together they conceived the scheme of betraying to the American government, for a consideration, Henry's copies of his correspondence with Governor Sir James Craig, and returning to France to enjoy the proceeds.

Their plan succeeded admirably. President Madison and Secretary of State Monroe evinced such eagerness to obtain assured evidence, as the sellers presented it to be, of an Anglo-Federalist plot to divide the Union, that Henry was able to hold them up for $50,000, the entire secret service fund at the government's disposal — almost the cost of a warship in that era. The documents changed hands on 7 February 1812, and on 9 March the President transmitted them to Congress, together with a message stating that they proved a deep-dyed plot between a British secret agent and the Boston Federalists "for . . . destroying the Union and forming the Eastern part thereof into a political connection with Great Britain."

The sensation felt by Otis and his friends on finding themselves accused of plotting disunion with a young man whom they had entertained as a gentlemanly tourist may well be imagined. Otis's half-sister Harriet, a romantic young lady of twenty-four, in Washington when the Henry papers were printed, commented in her diary, incidentally coining one of the wildest mixed metaphors on record:

> Monday March 9th. The Senate were detained until a late hour reading the base and unexpected disclosures of John Henry!!! the vain self-sufficient but as I had imagined noble minded friend of the enthusiastic H. C. this man has so lowered his proud spirit as to become the base agent of the british government in spying out the dissentions of the country to which he had sworn allegiance and on being dissapointed of a reward equal to his expectations has had the shameless effrontery to betray the transactions of his employers to our government. This is now presented to the public to implicate the northern federalists in a view of severing the union and becoming attached to G Britain. but I trust the aim will be fruitless, for what has it discovered but that the british ministers are on the watch to take advantage of querelous murmurs of men who when they see their interests neglected will scold and complain as every man in a free government has a right to do without being suspected of traitorous designs. But how astonishing does it seem to me that this rolling stone who fluttered about without any other apparent aim than his own amusement should have been harbouring in his breast such views and the romantic generous spirit that seemed too sublimated to "grub this earthly hole, in low pursuit" should degrade itself to such baseness. I now recur with curiosity to every interview I ever had with him and every word I have heard him utter to discover some mark of treachery.

Josiah Quincy promptly forced an investigation of the transaction. Madison, in transmitting the documents to Congress, had included a letter from Henry dated 20 February 1812, in which the spy affected, as a penitent patriot, to make a gift of them to the government. By tracing treasury warrants, Quincy discovered not only the price paid to Henry but the fact that the transaction had been completed much earlier. And he forced Madison to acknowledge publicly that he possessed no names of any "traitors." A careful reading of the documents proved that Henry had not disclosed to anyone in Boston his Canadian credentials, and that suggestions he had made for New England to secede had received no encouragement. Henry himself, having been given by Madison free passage to France in U.S.S. *Wasp,* could not be questioned.

From the newspaper controversy that followed, the Federalists emerged with flying colors and succeeded in shifting the obloquy of the affair from themselves to Madison. Nevertheless, the Massachusetts Democrats attempted to incriminate Otis. On 26 June 1812 the Democratic state senate of Massachusetts passed a resolve stating that whereas Henry claimed to have influenced the "Patriotick Proceedings" of Massachusetts in 1809, it be ordered that Harrison Gray Otis and Timothy Bigelow, president of the senate and speaker of the house at that time, lay before the legislature copies of all letters or documents connected with those proceedings. The lower house, still Federalist, denounced this resolve as a base insinuation, passed a vote of confidence in Otis and Bigelow, and pointed out that the dates of Henry's letters showed that he reached Boston after the "Patriotick Proceedings" were over and the legislature had adjourned. The administration press, however, published the senate's charge without the answer; consequently it became an article of Democratic faith that Otis and Bigelow had been hand and glove with Henry. Amos Kendall in his *Autobiography* records an incident that he witnessed in a state debate in 1813. The question under discussion was whether officers of the United States Army could hold elective office. Otis pointed out that they could not, as contrary to the state constitution. A Democrat then replied "that he thought those who were ready to fight the battles of their country were quite as much entitled to seats in that body as those who had been closeted with British spies. Otis sprang to his feet and said that any man who charged him with having been closeted with a British spy was a scoundrel. He sat down amidst the applause of the spectators and cries of order."

On 18 June 1812, war was declared. Within six weeks occurred the Baltimore riots. The Baltimore *Federal Republican* which, like other Federalist journals, had opposed the war, was threatened with violence by the local Democracy. After one attack by the mob, unhindered by the city authorities, the editors prepared to resist. In the printing office gathered Generals James Lingan and "Light Horse Harry" Lee, veterans of the Revolution, together with several young men of the best blood in Maryland, to defend the rights of free speech and a free press. A mob surrounded the building on 27 July and became so menacing that the editors and their friends submitted to being locked up in the city jail for protection. That night the mob broke open the jail, beat and tortured the prisoners, and on the prison steps left nine mutilated bodies. Lingan was killed and Lee crippled for life.

To comprehend the profound sensation of horror and fear that this event caused in Federalist circles, we must remember that for eighteen years Federalism had been prophesying that democracy would produce the excesses of the French Revolution. Here they were! A war of conquest against England, ranting demagogues in control of the government, mob rule and massacre of prisoners, within fifty miles of the capital, condoned by the administration press; a perfect parallel between France of 1793 and America in 1812. A Boston town meeting on 6 August adopted hysterical resolutions to the effect that "the mob erects its horrid crest over the ruins of liberty, of property, of the domestic relations of life and of civil institutions; until satiated or fatigued with slaughter it resigns its bludgeons and its pikes at the feet of a dictator, and raises its bloody hands to worship some God of its Idolatry, to whose more tolerable despotism all ranks of men become ready to submit."

BOSTON DURING THE WAR

Boston let her opposition to the war be heard "loud and deep" as
the lower house suggested, in a Faneuil Hall meeting of 15 July
1812. War-hawk Republicans called it, but to their dismay Federalists turned out in such numbers as completely to overwhelm
them and to pass resolutions that breathed war on Madison instead
of on George III. According to the *Centinel,*

> The debate was closed by the "man of the people," the Hon.
> Mr. Otis. It is unnecessary to say more than that he renewed,
> by his glowing and pathetic eloquence, that enthusiasm which
> has been so often excited in the breasts of his fellow-citizens, by
> his patriotic and masterly speeches; *orations* they ought to be
> called; for, like DEMOSTHENES, rousing the Athenians to watchful-
> ness against PHILIP, his addresses have awakened the citizens of
> *Boston* to a virtuous jealousy of the intrigues of *France,* and of
> those who are co-operating with her ruler to destroy the liberties
> and happiness of mankind.

"The town meetings held in Boston during the war of 1812,"
wrote George Ticknor half a century later, "were more like the
popular meetings in Athens than anything of the kind the world
has ever seen. Commerce and trade were dead; the whole population was idle, and all minds intent on the politics of the day, as
affecting their individual existence and happiness. Faneuil Hall
could be filled with an eager and intelligent crowd at any moment
of day or night. Town meetings were often continued two or three
days, morning and evening. . . . All the speeches were extemporaneous; it would have lowered a man's reputation materially if
it had been supposed that he had prepared and committed a speech
to memory. . . . Mr. Otis was a very captivating speaker; hand-

some, gesticulating gracefully, with a beautiful voice and fervent manner. . . ."

The vivid impression made by one of Otis's speeches was thus described many years later by one who had heard him, Francis Bassett:

> When Bonaparte was making progress in his military conquests, news arrived that he had gained a great victory over the allies, and that the killed and wounded on both sides was terrible. Notice was given that there would be a meeting in Faneuil Hall, in the afternoon of the next day. There was a great gathering of citizens, and Mr. Otis took his seat on the platform. When he arose to speak, he commenced by stating the effects the war between this country and England had produced in Boston. He said industry was paralyzed, the music of the saw and hammer was no longer heard, and a general gloom seemed to hang over the town. He had sought retirement in the country, for a while, to avoid meeting the sad countenances of his fellow-citizens. In coming into town that morning, as he looked at the grass covered with dew and saw the farmer mowing it down, he thought he perceived in the instrument which he used, a type of that despotism which mows down nations.

The Massachusetts Federalists maintained throughout a policy of giving the war minimum support consistent with obedience to the laws (as interpreted by themselves), in the hope of promoting a speedy peace. No obstacles other than hostile public opinion were placed in the way of recruiting, but Governor Strong, advised by three judges of the highest state court, and by Otis, that he had the constitutional right to decide whether or not to honor presidential requisitions for militia, refused most of such calls during the war. So did every other New England governor except Gilman of New Hampshire. There was a certain justification for this localism. In July 1812, almost every regular unit garrisoning coastal forts marched off to invade Canada, leaving the New England coast defenseless except for militia. Distrustful as the state administrations were of the Washington government, they feared that any militia placed under federal control would be withdrawn for purposes of conquest; and the "citizen soldiery," who elected their own officers, balked at being placed under regulars. That, too, is not surprising. General Winfield Scott of Virginia wrote in his *Memoirs* what nobody dared to say during the war, that the administration refused commissions to Federalist gentlemen who wanted to serve, and in New England "there were but very few educated Republicans." Hence the Yankees selected for commissions "consisted mostly of coarse and ignorant men. In the other States, . . . the appointments consisted, generally, of swaggerers, dependants, decayed gentlemen and others 'fit for nothing else' which always turned out *utterly unfit for any military purpose whatever.*"

Otis took a spectacular part in this militia controversy. In November 1813, when Governor Chittenden of Vermont attempted to recall his state's militia from national service, certain congressmen proposed to indict him for treason. Otis then offered from the floor of the Massachusetts house (14 January 1814) a resolution offering to support her sister state. He believed it to be "the duty of . . . Massachusetts to aid the Governor of Vermont & the people of that State, . . . to support their constitutional rights whenever the same shall be in danger of infringement from any quarter." And, if Vermont or any other state calls for "effectual support," to grant it. Since Congress never carried out the threat against Vermont, Otis's resolve remained *vox et praeterea nihil.* But it created a tremendous sensation. The legislature of New Jersey officially expressed its "contempt and abhorrence" for the "ravings of an infuriated faction, either as issuing from a legislative body, a maniac governor, or discontented and ambitious demagogues," meaning Otis. But John Randolph of Roanoke wrote to Josiah Quincy:

> I have seen Mr. Otis's motion, and I assure you that no occurrence since the war has made so deep an impression upon me. It has had the like effect upon all seriously thinking people with

whom I have conversed. What a game of roundabout has been played since I was initiated into the mysteries of politics! I recollect the time when with Mr Otis *States rights* were as nothing in comparison with the proud prerogatives of the Federal government. *Then* Virginia was building an armory to enable her to resist *Federal usurpation.* You will not infer that I attach the least blame to Mr. Otis; far from it. I rejoice, on the contrary, to see him enlisted on the side of the *liberty of the subject and the rights of the States.*

Boston Federalists shared the enthusiasm aroused by the exploits of the United States Navy. Otis's name headed the committees that got up public dinners in their honor, and presented a service of plate to Commodore Perry, victor of the Battle of Lake Erie. For, they felt, the Federalist navy effected the saltwater triumphs in spite of its neglect by Jefferson and Madison, and the freshwater navy on Lake Erie was organized and largely manned by Yankees. On 5 September 1812 both parties united in giving a dinner of 500 covers in Faneuil Hall to Commodore Isaac Hull to celebrate the victory of the *Constitution* over the *Guerrière.* The Hon. John Coffin Jones presided; Otis, Dexter, Perkins and other Federalists were among the vice presidents, and some twenty toasts were drunk, to the accompaniment of salvos from the Washington Artillery, fortunately outside the hall. Although most of the toasts were to naval heroes, the one that aroused the most enthusiasm was Dexter's, "To the Downfall of the Iron Colossus" — Napoleon. Again, on 9 March 1813, a "splendid ball" was organized by a committee of the younger Federalists and Republicans at the Exchange Coffee-House in "honour of the late naval victories achieved by our gallant little Navy." Quoting *The New England Palladium:*

At 7 o'clock the ball-room was opened, and shortly was completely filled — . . . four elegant transparencies, from the pencil of Mr. Corné were displayed, representing the captures of the *Guerrière, Frolic, Macedonian,* and the destruction of the *Java.*

In the centre of the room, opposite the orchestra, was a full length portrait of WASHINGTON; and national flags, the banners of the Washington Benevolent Society, evergreen and flowers, rendered the scene truly magnificent. At 8 o'clock the dancing commenced, which, at about 11, was suspended to give place to a sumptuous supper, at which, by judicious arrangement, the whole company (about seven hundred) were able to sit at once. . . . The splendor of the ball was never equalled in this town, and we believe never was surpassed in the United States. Commodores Rodgers and Bainbridge and Capt. Hull, with their respective ladies, . . . and most of the other naval officers in town, augmented the brilliancy, as much as they increased the enjoyments of the evening.

The Federalists even capitalized on naval victories in their ballots.

Otis always stood in well with the navy. Officers were frequently entertained by him at 45 Beacon Street, and two of the most eminent elected him arbitrator in a curious dispute over prize money. Captain Charles Stewart, newly appointed commander of U.S.S. *Constitution* in 1813, badly wanted Captain Archibald Henderson USMC to be with him on his next war cruise. He offered to share with this future commandant of the Marine Corps one fifth of his prize money. Henderson, however, insisted on an additional bonus of merino sheep, a flock of which, apparently, Stewart had obtained from an earlier prize; and he was under the impression that Stewart consented. At the end of this cruise, in April 1814, Henderson demanded twenty sheep in addition to his cut of the prize money; Stewart denied he had ever promised him anything on the hoof and, just before the Hartford Convention met, the two officers called Otis to arbitrate. He took varying testimony from several officers, but his papers do not reveal the decision, or why a captain of marines wanted a flock of sheep.

The Federalists, having determined that the war was unjustified and wicked, regarded trade with the enemy as natural and virtu-

"Ships of the Line," Federalist ballot for
the state election of 1814.

ous. It became common for New England-owned vessels to accept protection licenses from the British admiral at Halifax and happily to trade between British ports and the Spanish Peninsula as though there were no war on. Otis became principal counsel for the defendants in a celebrated case which had a very fishy look. His clients, unemployed sailors of Portland, in the fall of 1814 fitted out a "shaving mill," as small privateers were called: the 24-ton schooner *Washington,* with one gun and a crew of fifteen. Cruising off the mouth of Chedebucto Bay, these merry mariners hit the jackpot, capturing two vessels right out of Halifax, brig *Jahnstoff* and schooner *Bothnea.* New England-built, both vessels were provided with false Swedish papers and laden with British goods intended to be run through the blockade into New London. The *Washington* put a prize crew on board each vessel — and some prizes they were, ships and cargoes being worth $100,000 — and sailed them into port. At Salem the federal district attorney (a nasty Democrat!) libeled both prizes for the United States, alleging that their capture was a put-up job to acquire British goods illegally. Justice Story, sitting as federal circuit judge in Massachusetts, so held. The privateer's owners then appealed, appointing Otis chief counsel, and he retained Robert Goodloe Harper to argue the case before the Supreme Court, twice. In the second appeal, in 1817, Justice William Johnson observed "that the voyage of these vessels was loaded with infamy," that both vessels had earlier in the war freighted provisions from New Haven to Halifax, and he strongly suspected that the capture was collusive; but "the evidence is not sufficient to fasten on the captors a participation in the fraud." So the Portland privateersmen kept their jackpot.

In celebrating American naval victories, Otis and his friends spent far less energy and enthusiasm than over two European events, the retreat of Napoleon from Moscow, and the entrance of the Allies into Paris. Russia had already become very popular because of the Emperor's attempted mediation in "Mr. Madison's

War," when news arrived of the Battle of Borodino and the utter rout of Napoleon's grand army. A committee of Federalists, Otis chairman, "determined to have a public religious celebration of thanks" for these "glorious and important events." On 25 March 1813 the festivities began with "religious solemnities" in King's Chapel. A choir sang Handel's Hallelujah Chorus, the Reverend William Ellery Channing offered a prayer which "united the elegance, and what the French call the *onction* of Fénelon, with the simplicity of the Apostolick Age," and the Reverend James Freeman delivered an extraordinary discourse composed of passages from the Old Testament so cunningly woven together as to appear a prophecy of the war and recent events. After the religious ceremony Otis presided at a public dinner in the Exchange Coffee-House. Here President Kirkland of Harvard invoked the Lord's blessing, and Otis "before the first toast . . . addressed the company in a speech replete with sound sentiments, expressed with that felicity both of style and manner, of which those only can form an adequate idea who have been witnesses of his eloquence." Of that portion of his speech reported in the press, the significant passages repeat the Federalist myth that Congress had declared war on England to please Napoleon; hence the Emperor's defeat would be America's salvation.

> Who indeed could remain unmoved by the miseries of the French people (to whom we have no enmity) by their oppressions, their conscriptions, their privation of the most estimable enjoyments? . . . But if there be any whose exclusive patriotism rejects all interest in the welfare of other nations they may also find cause of rejoicing, in the influence which these events will produce at home. We have nearly been victims to the delirium which has occasioned the destruction of other states. The history of our government, for several years, has exhibited a coincidence in the measures and a conformity to the plans of Napoleon too plain to be mistaken. . . . We have sacrificed our resources by embracing his Continental system, and we have exchanged a state of unprecedented prosperity for that of voluntary and ruinous

war. It is of secondary consequence now to ascertain, whether
our unhappy condition has arisen from obedience to his suggestions, fear of his power, sympathy in his policy, hatred of his
rival, or a mere respect for his example. . . .

By the check now given to this formidable power, the basis of
the disastrous policy, which is big with ruin for our country, is
undermined, and *we are rescued from our greatest danger.* The
rage of the passions which have produced the present war, will
not be suddenly assuaged; but they are deprived of their chief
aliment. Probably we have great sufferings to endure, but the
bitter experience which we yet undergo, *has now a chance to
make us wise, before it makes us slaves.*

Let us then hail these glorious events, as the prelude to better
times for our country!

At the first toast, to "Alexander the Great," a transparency representing the Emperor as "The Deliverer of Europe" was unveiled,
and an orchestra played the imperial anthem. Among the other
toasts were:

The Madman of France — The Russian regimen, iced-water and
phlebotomy, till *reason* be restored.

Our Navy — the brilliant star of glory shedding its beams on the
disastrous night of this once-favoured land.

The Russian consul made a speech; and after Otis retired, an
extempore toast was drunk:

Our beloved Otis, President of the Day — Boston may boast a
luminary that warms and delights at home, and enlightens
abroad.

This celebration infuriated the war party — as the Bostonians
intended it should — but Federalists in other parts of the Union
highly approved, and some put on similar pro-Russian shows.
John Randolph of Roanoke wrote to Josiah Quincy, "The festival
does honor to those who planned and presided over it, and, as
primus inter pares, I beg that you present my best respects to
Mr. Otis."

Similarly, in 1814, Boston sang no hallelujahs for the few and far-between American victories, but held a "Splendid and Solemn Festival" on 15 June in order to commemorate the "downfall of the Tyrant" — Napoleon. An appropriate sermon by Channing, an oration by Christopher Gore, and a turgid ode recited by Lucius Manlius Sargent diverted the afternoon audience; and in the evening the State House was illuminated, a band played in the colonnade, red-hot shot and "carbonic comets" were fired from Boston Neck, and the John Hancock mansion was adorned with transparencies showing fleurs-de-lys and "Honor to the Allies." Doubtless Otis and his friends were right in deeming the fall of Napoleon more significant than American victories; but the mere fact that they did indicates their wide diversion from the mainstream of American life. And their June celebration was singularly ill-timed, as the British blockaders were raiding Massachusetts harbors; more than twenty sail had already been destroyed before the festival.

Whatever Boston Federalists were able to effect by resolutions and celebrations paled in comparison with the results of their financial policy. Various factors resulting from the war — privateers bringing in English goods, smuggling, setting up of textile mills — gave New England a monopoly of manufactured and imported goods, and a large part of the specie in the country migrated to Boston banks. These institutions, with one exception, were controlled by Federalists — Otis directed several — and Philadelphia financial circles were similarly constituted. A good understanding existed between the financial powers of both cities (New York, apparently, did not count), to withhold subscriptions to government loans until assured of peace, hoping thus to force Madison to abandon his policy of conquering Canada. And they nearly succeeded in bankrupting their government at a very critical period.

On 4 April 1814 Congress authorized a new loan of $25 million. Otis and the Philadelphia bankers, David Parish and Charles

Willing Hare, were eager to subscribe. The original purpose, to force the government to stop the war, had failed. Dollars were now plentiful and hard to place; Washington would obtain the money somehow, probably in Europe; in short, they hated to miss this opportunity for safe and lucrative investment. They urged that subscribing to loans was no greater encouragement of the war than importing goods and paying duties on them, and pointed out that Federalists would not be exempt from the consequences of a total prostration of public credit. The leading merchant-financiers of Boston, including George Cabot, John Phillips, Samuel Eliot, Theodore Lyman and Thomas Handasyd Perkins, thrashed the matter out at a private meeting. Otis argued the Philadelphia case but Cabot countered (so he remembered five years later) "on the ground that the war was *absolutely unjust";* hence "we ought never to *volunteer* our services in a cause which we believe to be morally wrong." The meeting then voted to help the government financially only upon receiving definite assurances from Washington that satisfactory instructions had been given to the peace commissioners. Like any self-respecting government, it refused to give this information, and the loan proved a failure without Federalist support. Otis later declared that no attempt was made to compel those present at the meeting to follow the majority; and since the name of his friend Perkins is found among the subscribers, this statement is undoubtedly correct. But Otis, I regret to say, did not subscribe, and Boston took up only $1 million of the $15 million loan. This, however, compares pretty well with the $200,000 subscribed by Virginia.

INTENSIFIED OPPOSITION

Boston did not stand alone in anti-war agitation. On 14 July 1812 a convention of delegates from over fifty towns in "Old Hampshire" — the three Massachusetts counties that crossed the Connecticut River, Hampshire, Hampden and Franklin[1] — convened at Northampton for the express purpose of peace-mongering. Besides issuing an address to the people, the convention appointed twelve delegates "to meet in a State Convention provided such a measure shall become necessary and be adopted in other parts of the Commonwealth." Within two weeks conventions in Essex and Plymouth Counties took similar action, and the project was next taken up in the same Boston town meeting of 6 August that adopted resolutions on the Baltimore riots. There Otis delivered a strong argument in favor of a state convention, but opposition suddenly appeared from an unexpected quarter. Samuel Dexter, a moderate Federalist who had stated publicly his intention to support the administration during the war, reminded the meeting of the mischievous effects of popular conventions at the time of Shays's Rebellion. He argued that a state convention, in the then excited state of popular feeling, might incite insurrection against the national government and justify the Democratic imputation that the Federal party was seeking to disrupt the Union. This speech wrecked the state convention project for the time being, but unfortunately the sound common sense of Dexter's arguments did not convert Otis or any other Federalist leaders.

Both Otis and Dexter, as we have seen, attended the Federalist national convention at New York in September 1812, as principal exponents of coalition with the New York Clintonians. De Witt Clinton appealed to Federalists by promising a speedy peace, and to the Republicans on the ground of Madison's incapacity to wage war. He carried all New England (except Vermont), the middle states, and half of Maryland. But Madison's victory meant that all hope of ending the war by a change of rulers had gone. So the New England Federalists fell back on state rights.

The tide of Federalist reaction against "the war made upon *us*, by our own Government," as Otis put it in a letter to Rutledge,

---

[1] The two last had been set off from Hampshire County within a year. "Old Hampshire" was the strongest Federalist district in Massachusetts.

continued unabated in the state elections of 1813. In Massachusetts, Governor Caleb Strong, who had just squeaked in over
Gerry in 1812, won his ninth election by a plurality of 13,965 votes
out of some 100,000 cast. In the lower house, to which Otis now
returned, the Federalist contingent rose from 130 to 247; and in
the state senate the gerrymandered Democratic majority of 14
now became a Federalist majority of 16. New Hampshire and
Vermont also went Federalist, so for the first time New England
presented a united front in opposition to the war.

Stimulated by success, the tone of remonstrance rose in Massachusetts. Governor Strong in his opening address of the spring
session unearthed the old grievances of slave representation and
the admission of Louisiana to the Union. Otis, chairman of the
house committee to which this message was referred, endorsed
the governor's remarks in words which need little comment:

> We are duly impressed by your Excellency's suggestion, that
> the extension of territorial limits was never contemplated by
> the framers of the Constitution. If the President and Senate
> may purchase land, and Congress may plant States in *Loui-
> siana,* they may with equal right establish them on the *North-
> west Coast,* or in *South-America.* It may be questioned here-
> after, whether after this formation of new States, the adherence
> of the old ones which dissented from the measure, is the result
> of obligation or expediency. And it is evident, that this multi-
> plication of new States, not parties to the original compact, must
> soon be regarded as fatal to the rights and liberties of some of the
> present members of the confederacy, and consequently as an in-
> supportable grievance. This extension of territory has already
> excited a spirit of cupidity and speculation, which is among the
> causes of our present troubles. By means of power thus acquired,
> and the operation of the Constitutional provision, whereby
> three freemen in certain parts of the Union enjoy the same priv-
> ileges in the choice of Representatives, which in other states is
> divided among five; the influence of *Massachusetts,* and of the
> Eastern States, in the National Councils, is lost, and systems of
> commercial restriction, of War, and conquest, fatal to their in-

terests, and outrageous to their feelings, are founded on its ruins. We are aware that the expression of these truths, which are wrung from us by the tortures of an unfeeling and unmerited policy, will be imputed . . . to disaffection to the Union. . . . It is not true, as your Excellency is aware, that the good people of this Commonwealth, or of the metropolis, cherish views inimical to the continuance of the Union. . . . We know that the affinities of interest, which ought to unite us, are natural, and predominate over the artificial collisions which tend to detach from each other the members of the great family. . . . But on the other hand, we regard the Union as only *one of the objects* of the Constitution. The others, as expressed in the instrument, are "to establish justice, ensure domestic tranquility, provide for the common defense, promote the general welfare, and secure the blessings of liberty to ourselves and posterity." So long as the Union can be made the instrument of these other Constitutional objects, it will deserve the support of all the friends of this country.

Substituting slavery for commerce and the scoldings of abolitionists for the "tortures of an unfeeling policy," this document might have emanated from any southern legislature between 1850 and 1861. Otis and the New England Federalists, like Calhoun and the southern Democrats, valued the Union, but on their own terms. Otis wrote, 5 May 1813, to John Rutledge whose state profited by slave representation, that it "must be reformed at all hazards, and I shall be mistaken if a most serious effort is not made to rectify the error. . . . I doubt whether we should cohere [to the Union] upon any other terms m[uch long]er. *Mais nous verrons.*"[1] What terms Massachusetts had in mind are indicated by the conclusion to Otis's house committee report: "It was not betraying an indifference to the Union, to protest against measures as weak and mischievous, which their authors afterwards abandoned as mischievous and weak. . . . The portion of the Union which

[1] Otis to Rutledge 5 May 1813, a damaged and almost illegible letter, at Chapel Hill.

lives by Commerce, is plunged into war by those who exult in
their means of living without it, claiming, however, to be its best
friends, and most competent to its regulation."

And Otis wrote to Rutledge that the legislature was disposed
"to go to great lengths" but he trusted "they will not be intemperate." If the extremist line prevailed, "the State would declare
itself neutral at least, if it did not secede from the Union. But
these measures I trust will not be resorted to at present." The
measure Otis wanted and worked for was a New England, or,
still better, northern, convention. Unfortunately, he got it.

By the close of 1813, another act of government enhanced the
woes of maritime New England. Contraband trade, especially in
Maine and Georgia, had assumed such proportions that Congress
passed a general embargo act even more severe than Jefferson's,
prohibiting coasting trade or fishing outside harbors, and permitting transportation on inland waterways only by presidential
permission. "Madison's Embargo" aroused the most indignant protests in the normally Democratic district of Maine, especially the
eastern part where the only way to get about was by water. Deer
Isle regarded Madison's embargo as "the utmost stench of despotism"; Belfast declared that the down-easters' sufferings, injuries
and oppressions "under the present Dynasty, are tenfold greater"
than those of 1775–76; Ellsworth compared Madison to Bonaparte;
the voters of Gouldsborough complained that even sleighs carrying food for their families were stopped and searched for contraband by Madison's minions; Castine asked, "Shall Massachusetts
be . . . obliged to carry on this war forever to gratify the malignity
of a few individuals directed by 'an unseen hand'?" — Napoleon,
of course. Maine was the hottest part of the Federalist bloc in
1813–14. Cyrus King, Federalist brother to Otis's Democratic
partner in the Bingham deal, ran for Congress and won, on an
extremist platform. In a widely quoted speech he said, "If a
simple king of England, by his corrupt servants, chastised New
England with whips, the administration here chastised her with

scorpions. . . . The states of New England can never be satellites."
Only because leaders such as Otis, Quincy and James Lloyd
acted as brakes did the general court escape an attitude of open
hostility toward the Union during the winter session of 1813–14.
Timothy Pickering, stung by the sneers of his Washington colleagues that Massachusetts might bluster but dared not act,
spurred on his followers. Francis Blake, state senator from
Worcester, delivered a glowing eulogy of Great Britain, declaring
that if our Constitution permitted embargoes, he preferred the
British, "monarchy and all." Samuel Fessenden of New Glouces-
ter, Maine, announced that "it was time to take our rights into
our own hands. . . . We ought to establish a custom house by law,
and the sooner we come at issue with the general government the
better." One who heard this speech wrote that "these ravings of
a political maniac were received with manifest applause." But, he
says, Harrison Gray Otis "rose immediately after, and dispelled
the illusion. He had listened, with great pleasure, to the stirring
eloquence of his friend from Maine. He admired the spirit by
which he had been actuated; but he thought we were not yet ready
to proceed to those extremities, indicated by his honorable friend."
Otis's stand against this imprudent proposal, which went no
further than the demands of the towns, revealed his policy. A
quarter century later he wrote of this session: "The leading members in the legislature had on hand an embarrassing task. It was
impossible for them to say, 'Thus far may ye come but no further,'
without refrigerating the popular zeal in opposition to the ruinous
system of Government." But, on the other hand, popular demands "could not be afforded by the Legislature, unless by
avowed *nullification;* for which those leading persons were by no
means prepared or desirous."
By the spring of 1814, so violent had become the feeling against
war and embargo that Massachusetts Democrats dared not go before the people on a platform of unqualified support of the administration. They nominated for governor Samuel Dexter, who

in an open letter proclaimed himself still a Federalist, announced
that on the policy of commercial restriction he "differs radically
from the party called Republican, and *he desires that they should
know it*," and that his only quarrel with the Federalists arose from
their aggressive pacifism. Thus the war became the sole issue in
the state campaign. Should Massachusetts bury her grievances and
pitch in against England, or strengthen her opposition by calling
a New England or northern Convention? Every voter, whether
Federalist or Republican, who favored "Mr. Madison's War" or
opposed the Convention, must have voted for Dexter; and the outcome proved that they were in a decided minority. Caleb Strong
won his tenth election easily; and, more significant, 360 Federalists
and only 156 Democrats were elected to the lower house of the
general court.

Otis, reëlected for his thirteenth consecutive term, returned
again to the state senate. Other honors came to him that year
besides the dubious one of leading the Hartford Convention.
Governor Strong appointed him judge of the Boston court of
common pleas; Harvard conferred on him the degree of LL.D.
At Commencement he shared the honors with Judge Isaac Parker
who had advised the governor to disregard federal requisitions for
militia, with Jack Lowell the inflammatory Federalist pamphleteer, and with Chief Justice Tilghman of Pennsylvania who had
upheld the sovereignty of his state against the United States Supreme Court. The Harvard Corporation obviously had gone all
out for state rights.

THE CRISIS OF 1814

Before the general court assembled for the spring session of 1814,
Congress had repealed Madison's embargo, removing the immediate grievance. The Federalist leaders then decided to defer the
Convention, which the more vociferous members of their party
had been demanding. Governor Strong's opening address of 30

May, and the replies of both houses, showed a conciliatory disposition, calling repeal of the embargo a "harbinger of a better day,
auspicious to the interests of commerce." This short session passed
off uneventfully, and to all appearances the New England Convention movement had been indefinitely postponed.

Presently there developed a situation far more critical and
alarming to New England than that of the previous winter. The
British government, relieved in Europe by the collapse of Napoleon and the Peace of Paris, prepared to overwhelm its only
remaining enemy by invasions and raids at every vulnerable point
of the coast and frontier. Hitherto New England had not been invested by sea, but in June 1814 British men-of-war blockaded her
ports and began minor raiding attacks on several points along her
coast. On 7 July, armed barges from a warship off Boston Light
raided the harbor and carried off five small sloops. Moose Island
and Eastport, Maine, were captured on 11 July, and the inhabitants forced to take an oath of allegiance to King George. The
United States Army forestalled one British invasion at the battles
of Lundy's Lane and Fort Erie in July and early August; but the
last week of August and the first week of September brought a
startling series of military and naval disasters. On 24 August
Boston newspapers announced that a great British fleet had entered Chesapeake Bay, and on the twenty-sixth that the enemy was
moving on Washington. On 30–31 August came details of the
Battle of Bladensburg, the rout of the Virginia militia, the capture
of Washington, and the burning of the Capitol. The capitulation
of Alexandria was announced on Saturday, 3 September; and on
the following day Sir George Prevost invaded New York at Lake
Champlain, with the finest British army ever sent to America. On
the same day it became known in Boston that a formidable am-
phibious expedition (three ships of the line, two frigates, three
more warships and ten transports lifting 3500 soldiers) under
Lieutenant General Sherbrooke had occupied Castine, raided
Bangor, and taken possession of eastern Maine. It was a natural

assumption that this expedition would proceed to attack Boston. With the Federal Government a fugitive from Washington, national integrity threatened at every point, the regular army undermined by desertion, and several states forced to provide for their own defense, the Union has never been so weak, or national prestige so low, as in that first week of September 1814. Ominous was the increasing disaffection in New England, exposed to the overwhelming sea power of Britain, yet left to her fate by Madison's administration. There was a certain rough retribution, it is true, in this sad plight. "You complain that Massachusetts is left defenceless," said John Holmes, Democratic leader in the state senate. "You took the defence of the State out of the hands of the general government. You would not permit them to decide on the danger. You refused them the means to repel it, and now, forsooth, you complain that you are left defenceless." Although the war department offered to keep the Massachusetts militia within the state if it were placed under the command of regular army officers, Governor Strong refused. Similar offers from the war department to Connecticut, Rhode Island and Vermont met with similar refusals; hence the war department refused to pay the militia. Fair enough; but the New England Federalists were incapable of taking a judicious view of this subject. They knew that Massachusetts had paid more war taxes than any other state of the Union, and furnished more troops by voluntary enlistment than any except New York. To be told that she must also find men and money for her own defense, because her governor resisted "unconstitutional" demands of the national executive, seemed the last straw.

Even in this hour of danger, some Boston Federalists were so blinded by prejudice as to neglect local defense. Men were heard to say that the town should capitulate if attacked, since the magnanimous British would respect private property. Finally, some of the younger men of the party called a town meeting for 3 September to consider local defense. It would be a pleasure to find Otis employing his eloquence at the head of this movement, but he took the opposite course. As chairman of a Federalist committee appointed to draft an agenda for the town meeting, he promoted resolutions which simply approved what Governor Strong had done, or not done. This was the meeting we have earlier described, in which Otis called Samuel Dexter an "apostate," and Mr. Dexter audibly expressed a desire to pull Mr. Otis's nose. The meeting finally adopted Otis's resolutions, which made a slight concession to patriotism by promising that the citizens of Boston would, by manual labor and pecuniary contributions, promote any measure of defense which might be "devised by the proper authority" — the state, of course.

Next day, 4 September, news arrived in Boston which changed the picture. The citizens of Alexandria, as Federalist as Boston itself, had surrendered their town on the Potomac to the enemy in the hope of protecting private property. Nevertheless, they had been forced to hand over everything — shipping, merchandise, flour and tobacco. This dispelled a few Bostonian illusions. The state committee on defense, including Otis, now adopted a program recommended by Commodore Bainbridge. Individuals, organizations and nearby towns vied with one another in offering their services. In the official statement of voluntary labor on the fortifications we find the Hibernian Society and the Suffolk Bar, Importers of English Goods and the African Society, Bishop Cheverus's Roman Catholic congregation and Harvard students working side by side. Captain Stewart of U.S.S. *Constitution* afterward said "he never saw more determined resolution of resistance than was exhibited by the people of Boston. Men of the first respectability, some among the proscribed traitors,[1] working, with their coats off, like common laborers."

Thus, "Mr. Madison's War," a grievance in itself, had sharpened and hardened all other grievances formulated by New England Federalist leaders since 1801. These grievances proceeded from

[1] I.e., members of the Hartford Convention.

fixed ideas which crop out again and again in letters, speeches and state papers: the fetish of seaborne commerce, without which New England would sink; fear of democracy as a solvent of society; and the conviction that Jefferson's and Madison's policies were dictated by hatred of England, jealousy of New England, and subservience to Bonaparte. These ideas had become ingrained in the average New England conscience of 1814 as, in the South of 1860, were a similar set of pernicious *idées fixes,* which caused that section to secede from the Union. And Federalist prejudices were stimulated by an angry conviction that New England was paying for the war but getting no protection. These fixed ideas were primarily responsible for the Hartford Convention.

CHAPTER XVII

The Hartford Convention

1814–1815, AET. 48–49

WHY A CONVENTION?

THE HARTFORD CONVENTION of 1814 was the central event in the life of Harrison Gray Otis, and the most important event in his country's history upon which he had a paramount influence. Thrice during the past six years had he promoted the calling of a New England Convention, and he acted as chairman of the committee which finally brought it into being. He assumed leadership in the Convention itself, and probably wrote the Report. In after years, the burden of defending the Convention against charges of disloyalty fell on him. He wrote, or was directly responsible for, five formal vindications of the Convention; and so often did he refer to it in his speeches that John Quincy Adams said with truth, "Whatever subject" brings Otis before the public, "his exhibition always ends with a defence of the Hartford Convention." It remained a millstone around his neck for life; and just as (in that old game of allusions) if you say "Cotton Mather," everyone responds "witchcraft," so the name of Harrison Gray Otis inevitably evokes "Hartford Convention." As Republican election doggerel put it, "Honest men frown whenever they mention the names of Sir Harry and the Hartford Convention!"

Otis always insisted that the Convention was not his baby, but popular in origin and conception, that its objects were to "let off steam,"[1] calm popular indignation, provide for the defense of New England against the British, and save the Union; and that its

---

[1] After the public had become familiar with fatal boiler explosions, Otis wrote that the Convention "was intended by those who voted for it as a safety-valve by

leaders represented "whatever of moral, intellectual, or patriotic worth is to be found in the character of the New England community." Adams, his most eminent critic, summing up a myth created by the triumphant war party, declared the Convention to have been the result of a secession conspiracy, that its objects were to "inflame to madness" the already feverish Federalists, to organize resistance against the national government, and break up the Union; that its members were desperate political gamblers, and that the whole movement was disloyal, treasonable and abominable. My aim has been not to defend Otis or attack Adams, but to find out from contemporary sources how the project originated, what it was expected to accomplish, and what actually happened.

One may say this with confidence: the Hartford Convention was the normal product of a recurring situation. When a sectional minority in a federal government becomes conscious of grave oppression by the central government and wishes to recover its supposed rights by some method short of secession, there is no better method of airing grievances and formulating demands than a convention of delegates from the regions that deem themselves oppressed. American tradition pointed to it: the Albany Congress in 1754, the Stamp Act Congress of 1765, the First Continental Congress of 1774 were conventions of delegates seeking redress for sectional oppression within the British Empire. Nor did the convention method end in 1815. The Nashville Convention of 1850 was a southern Hartford representing nine states, whose resolutions were rendered useless by the compromise of that year, just as Hartford's were by the Peace of Ghent. Again in 1861, a Peace Convention was called by the border slave states in the hope of agreeing on constitutional amendments to perpetuate slavery, and its resolves were rendered abortive by the outbreak of civil war.

---

which the steam arising from the fermentation of the times might escape, not as a boiler in which it should be generated." Emma Willard, *History of the U.S.* (1842), p. 357n.

A New England or northern Convention to air grievances had, as we have seen, first been proposed by Otis in 1808. It then came to nothing because of the embargo repeal. During the War of 1812 there were three such movements. The first, for a northern Convention to force "the Southern States either [to] submit to what is just or break up the Union," was promoted almost single-handed by Gouverneur Morris. This never got started because it had no base; the Republican party then controlled the State of New York. The second, stimulated by Madison's embargo of 1813, began in the Connecticut Valley and jumped, like a cancer infection, to eastern Maine. A meeting of Old Hampshire Federalists, including Noah Webster the lexicographer, called for "a convention of all the Northern and Commercial States" to consult upon "procuring . . . alterations in the federal constitution." Otis, then in the lower house, had to use all his arts of persuasion to defeat extremist proposals like those of "monarchy and all" Blake, which we have already quoted. He also succeeded in postponing the convention. The committee (James Lloyd, chairman) to which the town memorials were referred reported that the best way "to prevent that hostility to the Union, the result of oppression, which will eventually terminate in its downfall" would be "for the Wise and Good, of those states which deem themselves oppressed, to assemble with delegated authority." But they declined to recommend so momentous a step before consulting their constituents. The lower house adopted Lloyd's Report, as this document was named from the committee chairman, by a vote of 178 to 43, and the state senate confirmed it, 23 to 8. Thus the convention became the leading plank in the Federalist platform in the spring state elections of 1814.

The popular verdict was unmistakable. Federalists won 360 seats in the lower house as against 156 Republicans, and 27 out of 40 seats in the state senate. Governor Strong handsomely defeated Dexter, the pro-war Federalist. The mandate to "do something" could hardly have been stronger. Yet, owing to repeal of Madison's embargo, the immediate grievance, six months elapsed before anything was done.

In the meantime came the startling series of events in the summer of 1814 which we have already related: British occupation of eastern Maine, raid on Washington and capture of Alexandria, threat of conscription, hasty, last-minute measures for the defense of Boston, and the failure of the latest war loan. Governor Strong, on 7 September, summoned the already elected general court for a special session on 5 October 1814.

Prior to that date (wrote Otis a quarter century later) "a few influential members of the legislature" held meetings to prepare a program. In this caucus Otis, according to Rufus G. Amory's account of a conversation with him at the time, opposed the calling of a sectional convention as unwise, untimely, and certain to be misconstrued. He was overruled on the ground that "our country friends" wanted a convention and would not be denied; so it had better be called, to concert state defensive measures if for nothing else and, "in any event, for restraining the tendency to excess manifested in some of the petitions." Otis then decided to go along. Why had he hung back? I frankly do not know. Maybe the timidity which Jack Lowell ascribed to him, maybe political instinct, the feeling that something might happen, such as peace breaking out, which would leave a sectional anti-war convention out on a limb. Anyway, that is exactly what happened.

The effect of his decision to go along became evident in the rapidity with which the legislature acted under Otis's leadership. Governor Strong in his opening speech described the state's situation: coast blockaded, capital threatened, two Maine counties occupied by the enemy, resources exhausted by the double strain of paying federal war taxes and supporting her own defense. His speech was referred to a joint committee of which Otis was chairman. "Otis's Report," submitted in three days' time, exhorted all citizens to unite "in repelling our invading foe," but deplored "the destructive policy by which a state of unparalleled national felicity has been converted into one of humiliation, of danger, and distress." After repeating the historic Federalist grievances, the committee recommended that "a conference should be invited between those states, the affinity of whose interest is closest." There followed a series of resolves, the fifth being a definite call of the Hartford Convention:

> *Resolved,* That twelve persons be appointed, as Delegates from this Commonwealth, to meet and confer with Delegates from the other States of New England, or any of them, upon the subjects of their public grievances and concerns, and upon the best means of preserving our resources and of defence against the enemy, and to advise and suggest for adoption by those respective States, such measures as they may deem expedient; and also to take measures, if they shall think proper, for procuring a convention of Delegates from all the United States, in order to revise the Constitution thereof, and more effectually to secure the support and attachment of all the people, by placing all upon the basis of fair representation.

Otis's Report became the subject of a long-winded, acrimonious debate which the press of both parties fully reported. When the Report was read, Francis ("monarchy and all") Blake leaped to his feet and proposed an additional resolve prohibiting the Federal Government from collecting duties, excises or other taxes in Massachusetts. Otis declared he was "extremely sorry for this," believed it to be "very injurious to our national government," and persuaded the Worcester senator, much against his will, to withdraw his proposition. Otis also "disclaimed" any idea of "raising an army against the General Government." Leverett Saltonstall, the young member from Salem, made an able speech defending Governor Strong's stand on the militia problem. He attempted to answer the charge of poor timing by quoting 2 Corinthians vi.2: "Now is the accepted time; behold, now is the day of salvation." Saltonstall admitted the Union to be in danger, but that was the administration's fault. Unless *we* make an effort, the

Union "will soon as naturally fall asunder, as ripe fruit falling from our trees." John Holmes of Maine, ablest orator on the Republican side, answered Saltonstall in a speech that took two and a half hours to deliver, and in which he called Otis "the flippant orator, the pretty man."

After everyone had had his say, Otis's Report passed the senate on 12 October by a vote of 22 to 12, and the house four days later by 260 to 20. Next day the general court directed the governor to forward copies of the report, together with a letter of invitation (also drafted by Otis) to the other New England state governors. A convention of both houses on the 18th, boycotted by the Republicans, elected twelve delegates to represent Massachusetts at Hartford on 15 December 1814.

Harrison Gray Otis appeared second on the list. He accepted the appointment with reluctance. He well knew it might mean political suicide. When Sally Otis's brother Charles told their father that Harry had been elected, William Foster put on his greatcoat and hat, called on his son-in-law, and said to him, "Harry, if you are going to be such a fool as to go to that Hartford Convention, you will never get over it as long as you live!" And, I dare say, Sally added her tears to Father Foster's warnings, since her husband was receiving threatening letters. But Harry could not honorably refuse. He had fathered the convention idea; he had acquiesced in the caucus decision to call it; he had written the legislature's report setting it up; he could not get out of it now. And the argument that his influence was necessary to guide the Convention into moderate channels appealed to his vanity as well as to his sense of responsibility.

THE "WISE AND GOOD"

That smug description in Lloyd's Report of the kind of men who should be sent to a New England convention does happen to fit. Number one of the Massachusetts delegation was not Otis but

George Cabot, 62 years of age, whose white locks, impressive stature, and air of calm dignity reminded young men of the traditional picture of George Washington. Although he always kept his finger on the party pulse, Cabot hated responsibility and preferred to brood over national problems in retirement in Brookline — the Cabot capital since the family left Beverly. "Why can't you and I let the world ruin itself in its own way?" he said to Tim Pickering in 1813. A charter member, as it were, of the Essex Junto, Cabot had so mellowed with years that his presence at Hartford was a guarantee of moderation; when an extremist asked what he expected to accomplish he replied, "We are going to keep you young hot-heads from getting into mischief." Old John Adams never judged a fellow man more unjustly than in December 1814, when he exclaimed to the astonished young Ticknor, "Thank God, thank God! George Cabot's close-buttoned ambition has broke out at last. He wants to be President of New England, sir!"

The states and counties which sent delegates to Hartford chose highly respectable citizens, experienced in public service. For instance, Nathan Dane of Beverly, legal scholar, author of the Territorial Ordinance of 1787 under the Confederation and later founder of the Dane chair at the Harvard law school; Judge Joseph Lyman of Northampton whom even the opposition called "mild"; Judge William Prescott, son of Colonel Prescott of Bunker Hill fame and father of the historian; Stephen Longfellow of Portland, father of the poet. The only Massachusetts delegate besides Otis who had been active in politics since 1800 was Timothy Bigelow of Medford, now serving his ninth term as speaker of the house, and the only member on whom the extremists counted.

Connecticut, "Land of Steady Habits," felt herself no less wronged, deserted and cheated than her sister state. She too had suffered from British raids on an exposed and undefended coast. The same controversy over the command and pay of the militia existed as in Massachusetts, and Governor John Cotton Smith recalled the only detachment of state militia in national service on the very day the British burned Washington. The Connecticut

general assembly became greatly alarmed over two measures before Congress: a bill for filling the regular army by conscription,
and a proposal to enlist minors over seventeen years of age without
the consent of parents or guardians. During the October session
of 1814 the assembly threatened to nullify these offensive bills,
should they become law. A resolution to send delegates to Hartford "for the purpose of advising and recommending such measures for the safety and welfare of this State, *as may consist with our
obligations as members of the National Union,*" passed the assembly by 153 votes to 36.

Connecticut's seven delegates were of the same stamp as the Bay
State's. There were James Hillhouse and Lieutenant Governor
Chauncey Goodrich, both former United States senators; former
governor John Treadwell; Zephaniah Swift and Nathaniel Smith,
both judges of the state supreme court; Calvin Goddard and
Roger Minott Sherman,[1] both members of the council. Rhode
Island came next — and last — with four delegates. Colonel Samuel Ward,[2] who had held no political office since membership in
the Annapolis Convention of 1786, headed her delegation. Following him were Chief Justice Daniel Lyman and his son-in-law
Benjamin Hazard who looked like a wild Indian, but as Newport's
favorite son had represented her in the Rhode Island legislature
since 1809.

Governor John Taylor Gilman of New Hampshire, although a
Federalist, played coy with Governor Strong's invitation. His
legislature was not in session; to Otis he wrote that he feared "the
consequences of a call" for the "especial purpose" of sending delegates to Hartford, "even if a Majority of the Council would consent to it." A good part of the Granite State nevertheless became
represented in the Convention. Citizens of the strongly Federalist
Connecticut River counties called local conventions which sent

---

[1] Son of Roger Sherman of Federal Convention fame.
[2] Son of Gov. Samuel Ward the "signer," father of Samuel Ward, New York
banker, and grandfather of the famous "Sam" Ward and of Julia Ward Howe.

the venerable Benjamin West, hitherto a persistent refuser of public office, and Mills Olcott, treasurer of Dartmouth College, to Hartford. In Vermont the party had a clear majority in the general assembly, and Governor Chittenden too was a Federalist who had recalled militia from the United States Army. But Prevost's invasion of the state, and the battle of Plattsburg, aroused a spirit in Vermont Federalism different from anything their Massachusetts brethren had yet exhibited. On 19 September Chittenden proclaimed that since the war had become almost exclusively defensive, all party animosities should be laid aside; a principle which Otis, unfortunately, did not embrace. For it cannot be denied that a convention of sectional malcontents at such a time tottered on the edge of treason by giving "aid and comfort" to the common enemy. Windham, the southeastern county of Vermont, did not agree; a mass meeting chose William Hall, Jr., a member of the state council, as delegate to Hartford. Arriving late, on 28 December, Hall raised the number of the assembled "wise and good" to twenty-six.

In the face of their records, Jefferson's stigmatizing of Otis and his colleagues as "Marats, Dantons, and Robespierres" seems rather wide of the mark. John Adams rightly called them "intelligent and honest men who had lost touch with reality," and he maliciously reminded Jefferson that they were "servile mimics" of the southern Republicans who had pestered the Adams administration.

The Convention well represented the ruling class of New England. Twenty-two of the twenty-six were college graduates and lawyers, and nine of this number were jurists. They were not old men. Ten, including Otis, were under fifty years of age, and none as old as seventy. And all, with the exception of Bigelow, were moderate Federalists. Jack Lowell, in a letter to Pickering, bewailed the fact that not one "bold and ardent man," such as Daniel Sargent, William Sullivan and Israel Thorndike, Jr., had been included in the Massachusetts delegation; and he judged the Rhode Island and Connecticut delegations to be equally wishy-washy. The legislatures had taken care not to choose extremists.

Extremist Demands

Exactly what were these "wise and good" expected to accomplish at Hartford? The official objectives — drafting of constitutional amendments to protect New England interests, and an agreement with the Federal Government to let the states conduct their own defense — we have already noticed. But was that really all? The New England Democrats at the time, and ever thereafter, charged that the whole thing was a secession plot, to be initiated by concluding a separate peace with Great Britain. We may confidently deny that charge, since all evidence points to the fact that Otis and his colleagues wished to avoid secession at all costs; and a separate peace was never discussed or even mentioned. How far secession sentiment had then gone in New England we have no means of knowing. The administration press exaggerated it in order to damn the Federalists as traitors and rebels, but one gets the distinct impression from the three Republican papers in Boston that the local Democrats were "running scared." They had suffered another bad beating at the congressional elections in early November. Every district in Massachusetts proper, and six out of seven in Maine, had elected Federalists. Even Varnum's ordinarily safe Middlesex district, despite a ringing appeal by Samuel Hoar to show its "indignation" over the Hartford Convention, went Federalist. Even John Holmes, the administration's champion in the state senate, went down to defeat. Never had the Federalists enjoyed so near a clean sweep. A writer in the Republican *Patriot* of 7 December admitted that at least half the people of Massachusetts were for disunion, and warned that if it came to that the Bay State, ruled by "Blakes, Quincys, Pickerings and Saltonstalls," would have to live off the export of "potash, mules, grindstones and pine boards." *The Yankee* featured a long and turgid dialogue in blank verse between Otis and Satan, but the *Patriot* recognized Otis's moderate position, in a jingle on the members:

> And Otis will rise all so modest
> To recommend lenient measures,
> Which will call up old Timothy Pickering
> As sharp as a long pair of scissors.

Fortunately "Tim Pick" was not there. But an earthquake shock in Boston on 30 November, first since 1783, convinced many of the godly that the Almighty felt the "Headquarters of Good Principles" needed a good shaking up.

Most of the proposals which Otis regarded as dangerous, and which he hoped would whistle out to sea when the Convention met, were for seizing the customs houses, impounding federal revenues, declaring neutrality, nullifying conscription, and the like. Action of this kind — portending the firing on Fort Sumter — would certainly have brought a direct confrontation between state and federal governments, which he wished above all to avoid. A threat which he knew nothing about was Governor Strong's secret mission to lay the grounds for an armistice, or separate peace, with Great Britain. This intrigue seems to have been the personal diplomacy of the supposedly simple, straightforward sage of Northampton, whose speeches had been published under the title *Piety and Patriotism*. Canny Caleb was too cagey to put anything down in writing, but he sent Thomas Adams, Federalist member of the general court from occupied Castine, to General Sir John Sherbrooke at Halifax in mid-November 1814, with oral instructions to ascertain the "views" of the British government in the event of a direct clash between himself and Madison. Sir John wrote to Lord Bathurst, the Colonial Secretary, on 20 November that he hoped His Majesty's government would profit from any such opportunity to break up the Union. Bathurst replied from London

(13 December) that if Madison did not ratify the peace treaty, which he expected would shortly be signed (and was signed on Christmas Eve), and the war went on, Sir John had authority to sign an armistice with the New England states and to furnish them with logistic support to help defend themselves from the expected "resentment of the American Executive." But he must not promise troops.

Here was a potentially dangerous situation if the war continued. But, by the time Sir John received his reply from London, the war was over.

A third extremist proposal was so idiotic that it would hardly be worth serious consideration, had it not come from a high source and been promoted in the Federalist press. This was a plan for a pistol-point reorganization of the Union, initiated by Jack Lowell, "the Boston Rebel," in 1813, at a time when every eastern state down to Virginia, except Pennsylvania and New Jersey, had elected a Federalist or Peace Democrat administration.

Lowell's plan — unrealistic to the point of imbecility — took the form of the New England Convention's drafting a new federal constitution so drawn as to safeguard maritime and commercial interests, and presenting it as an ultimatum to the original Thirteen States only. In other words, kicking the West out of the Union! He argued that the admission of Louisiana had broken the original "compact," that a separation of the West "*must* take place, and the sooner the better"; but he hoped we might "soon again embrace our elder sister Virginia." To unite "the original Thirteen States . . . appears to be the last hope of our country." Timothy Pickering, then in Congress, took up the idea with enthusiasm, as did Gouverneur Morris, Charles Willing Hare and Charles Carroll of Carrollton. Assuming that General Pakenham's expeditionary force would defeat Jackson, Pickering wrote, "From the moment that the British possess New Orleans, the Union is severed." The West would embrace British sovereignty — or at least protection — to secure a Mississippi outlet, as it had

John Lowell, by Gilbert Stuart.

often threatened to do in the past. Thus, if the Hartford Conven-
would but draft a new federal constitution protecting commercial
interests and offer it for ratification only to the "good old Thirteen
States," they would damn well have to accept! Jack Lowell was so
puffed up with sectional pride and arrogance as to predict in a
letter to Pickering of December 1814 that the other eight eastern
states would dare not interfere — the lamentable performance of
the Virginia militia in defending Washington proved that they
could not if they would. As for the loyal Yankee Democrats,
Lowell fatuously predicted that they would go along in order to
be relieved from paying Madison's war taxes!

This wild scheme, the only near-secession proposition to be discussed in the Federalist press, was no mere brain wave of "Crazy
Jack" and "Tim Pick." Every Federalist paper of Boston but one
promoted it as a platform for the Hartford Convention. The
Boston *Gazette* on the 17th predicted that by 4 July 1815, "if
James Madison is not out of office, a new form of government will
be in operation in the eastern section of the Union." "The people," said this paper when the Convention was in session, "expect
decisive measures not only for their present relief but for future
security." The *Columbian Centinel,* oldest and most respectable
of the Boston Federalist press, promoted Lowell's scheme in a
series of violent articles called "The Crisis" by "A New-England
Man," and before they were finished, started another series by a
writer who chose the pseudonym "Epaminondas" — the Theban
general who had detached several states from the Athenian Confederacy. "Epaminondas" begged the Hartford Convention "not
to be entangled by the cobwebs of a compact which has long since
ceased to exist." Number 2 of "The Crisis," published during the
Convention sessions, declared that the Union, once a blessing, had
become a curse under Madison; that New England was not afraid
of secession — look at how a little country, Holland, "threw off
the yoke of Spain (our Virginia)." The *Centinel* announced Connecticut's and Rhode Island's acceptance of the invitation to
Hartford as "Second" and "Third Pillar of a New Federal Edifice

Raised," accompanying the text by a cut of two or three columns. The significance of this metaphor lies in the fact that the *Centinel* in 1788 had thus announced state ratifications of the Federal Constitution. A witty writer in *The Yankee* said that the *Centinel's* three pillars looked like snuff bottles in an apothecary's window, and for the Republicans the Hartford conclave became the "Snuff Bottle Convention."

Otis never showed any interest in this idiotic scheme for an eastern republic, and the official call of the Convention, drafted by him, authorized it only "to take measures, if they shall think proper," for procuring a constitutional convention of *all* the states. Nevertheless, Otis toyed with an equally dangerous plan, for the Hartford Convention to assume that the Washington government had abdicated. That is the theme of the following extraordinary letter that he wrote to Senator Gore on 3 December 1814:

> As the period of the Hartford meeting approaches, and the public expectation augments, I feel the weight and responsibility of my appointment press heavily upon my mind. . . . I do exceedingly mistrust my own skill and talents as a pilot in a revolutionary storm, and I fear for myself the more, because my impulse is strong and increasing towards a very decided and energetic course of measures. You know that I require a great deal of screwing to work me up to the plan of a Convention, but a greater power will be necessary to get me down. My present propensity is to consider and to treat the administration as having *abdicated* the Government. . . .
>
> It is the opinion of my best informed friends from the Country that a reliance upon some effectual suggestions from that body [the Convention] alone prevents a violent ferment and open opposition in many places. It is dreadful to reflect that the sentiment in Maine and on our South Shore is hourly gaining proselytes, that the people at Castine and Nantucket are the happiest and most prosperous part of the Union.[1] With these feel-

---

[1] It is true that Castine and Eastport were "making hay" from British military expenditures, coasting trade with the Provinces, and enjoying a prosperity they had not known since 1807. But Nantucket, short of food, was far from happy.

ings predominating and armies and detachments quartered in different parts of the Country, what awaits us, but to be conquer'd piecemeal and to be exhausted and ruined before we are conquered.

He adds a rumor that John Quincy Adams had written to his father from Ghent that the British had "no tho't of peace" and that old John Adams anticipated a seven years' war. Bad news or no news from Ghent undoubtedly helped the Federalist extremists. The last lot of dispatches to be published prior to Otis's letter of 3 December were those dated 19 August, which were printed in Boston papers about two months later. These showed the two peace missions to be at loggerheads, the Americans demanding that Britain abandon impressment and evacuate occupied territory, and the British requiring sundry rectifications of the northern frontier in favor of Canada, and the cancellation of fishing and other rights. The American demands seemed so preposterous in view of military realities as to justify the title of one of Jack Lowell's pamphlets, *Perpetual War the Policy of Mr. Madison*. And the truculent attitude of the *Chronicle* did not help matters; this principal administration organ in New England wished Madison to insist that he would negotiate peace only in Washington, and it demanded a fresh attack on Montreal and Quebec. Nobody, even in Washington, anticipated the sudden collapse of diplomatic pretensions on both sides which resulted in the "Peace of Christmas Eve."

Important men on the spot in Washington felt that President Madison's government was tottering on the verge of dissolution. A Virginia visitor to Madison in his temporary White House reported, "He looks miserably shattered and wo-begone. In short, he looked heart-broken." Senator Jeremiah Mason of New Hampshire on 24 November reported "alarming indications of approaching dissolution" and predicted, "If the war goes on the States will be left in a great degree to take care of themselves. What this will end in it is impossible to foresee"; probably it would end in "a

HARTFORD STATE HOUSE.

dissolution of the Union." Daniel Webster, on the 29th, expected "a blow-up soon. . . . Everything is in confusion. . . . If Peace does not come this winter, the Govt. will die in its own weakness." And on 22 December he predicted that "the Govt. *cannot last,* under this war, and in the hands of these men another twelve month. Not that opposition will break it down, but it will break itself down. It will go out. This is my sober opinion."

Jack Lowell had no hope of anyone in the Convention endorsing his radical program. He wrote to Pickering on 3 December 1814, "Mr. Otis is naturally timid, and frequently wavering, to-day bold, and to-morrow like a hare trembling at every breeze. . . . He is sincere in wishing thorough measures; but a thousand fears restrain him." A few of those thousand fears may have been excited by the minatory attitude of the administration press and spokesmen. Spencer Roane of Virginia, later a leading state rights advocate, took "a severe attitude toward New England, and advocated harsh measures." The Richmond *Enquirer* hoped that Madison would order the army to attack New England, and in its issue of 1 November declared:

> No man, no association of men, no state or set of states *has a right* to withdraw itself from this Union, of its own accord. The same power which knit us together, can only unknit. The same formality, which forged the links of the Union, is necessary to dissolve it. The *majority of states* which form the Union must consent to the withdrawal of *any one* branch of it. Until *that* consent has been obtained, any attempt to dissolve the *Union,* or to obstruct the efficacy of its constitutional laws, is Treason — Treason to all intents & purposes.

One only regrets that the *Enquirer* abandoned this excellent doctrine and became the literary spearhead for "Southern rights" and secession.

Where the Hartford Convention Met.
Council Chamber in the State House.

SESSIONS AND REPORT

Presumably Otis and his Boston colleagues traveled to Hartford, about a hundred miles distant from the Yankee metropolis, by a stagecoach which left Boston at 4 A.M. and, by changing horses every ten miles or so and traveling by the "middle road" through Dedham, Uxbridge, Pomfret and Wilmington, reached Hartford at 8 P.M. the same day — if the weather was good.

The Convention met on the morning of Thursday, 15 December, in the council chamber of the Connecticut State House, a beautifully proportioned edifice designed by Charles Bulfinch and built in 1795. Otis, in a letter to his wife, described the council chamber as "a tremendous Hall — sixty feet square, and two stories high, in which though our labours may be gigantic, we look like pigmies." On the center of the wall opposite the chair hung a full-length portrait of Washington, a good reminder of the value of the Union. At the first session Theodore Dwight, brother of the president of Yale College, was appointed secretary; neither he nor the members received pay or mileage. Otis moved that the Convention be opened with prayer (the only motion, sneered J. Q. Adams, of which the mover is recorded!) and the Reverend Nathan Strong of the First Church invoked the divine blessing. The members met for dinner that evening or the next at the house of Lieutenant Governor Goodrich. His nephew Samuel G. Goodrich ("Peter Parley"), staying there at the time, made this observation of Otis in a letter printed in his *Recollections:*

> The impression he made on my mind on the occasion I am describing, was deep and lasting. He had not the lofty Washingtonian dignity of George Cabot, nor the grave suavity of Chauncey Goodrich; he was in fact, of quite a different type — easy, polished, courtly — passing from one individual to another, and carrying a line of light from countenance to countenance, either

by his playful wit or gracious personal allusions. He seemed to know everybody, and to be able to say to each precisely the most appropriate thing that could be said. He was one of the handsomest men of his time; his features being classically cut, and still full of movement and expression. To me — who had seen little of society beyond Connecticut, and accustomed therefore to the rather staid manners of public men — Mr. Otis was an object of strange, yet admiring curiosity. I knew him well, some years after and when I was more conversant with the world, and he still seemed to me a very high example of the finished gentleman of the assiduous and courtly school.

That afternoon, rules were adopted, including preservation of "the most inviolable secrecy" by each member "as to all propositions, debates and proceedings." This was natural enough — the Federal Convention's sessions had been secret, as were those of the Peace Convention of 1861; the "wise and good" did not wish to waste time by speaking to the gallery, or to be disturbed by untimely speculations in the press. And there was the possibility of local Democrats making themselves obnoxious. They did not go so far as to picket the State House with placards reading "Cabot Go Home!" or "Hang Harry Otis!" During one session, however, Jemmy Lamb the town crier, dressed in a fantastic uniform, led a body of soldiers around the State House playing the "Rogues' March" — the tune to which malefactors used to be led to the gallows. Delegate Stephen Longfellow's wife wrote to her husband protesting against "a secret consultation" as likely to "give more plausibility to the cry of treason that will be raised." Thus the mother of Henry Wadsworth Longfellow was wiser than the members. Secrecy was assumed by the Convention's enemies to have been adopted in order to conceal talk of secession and a separate peace.

Also on the opening day, the Convention appointed a committee of five consisting of Goodrich, Otis, Daniel Lyman, Swift and Dane, to report on "what subjects will be proper to be considered by this Convention." Otis, in the only speech that anyone particularly remembered, proposed to recommend that the New England legislatures petition Congress for official permission to "unite in defending themselves against the public enemy"; that federal revenues collected within the five states "be appropriated to the expense of that defence," "and that the United States should agree to pay whatever should be expended beyond that amount." So the committee recommended; and, in addition, that the Convention consider the constitutional conflict over the militia, the threatened conscription bill, and expenditure of federal revenue for purposes of conquest.

These were leading grievances, to be sure; but where were those constitutional amendments which had been the object of every sectional convention proposal for the last six years? If this committee wished the Hartford Convention to forget about them and concentrate on defense, they were soon overruled; for a second committee of five, consisting of Smith, Otis, Goddard, West and Hazard, appointed on the 19th, brought amendments into discussion.

On the 22nd Longfellow wrote to his wife, "We are progressing very pleasantly, & with great unanimity; & shall, I am confident, arrive at a result which *ought* to satisfy every reasonable man & true friend of his country." And the same day Harry Otis wrote to Sally:

> My dear Soul, I have been *here* a week, & from home nine days, and not a line from your dear hand. It was not so in days of yore, and I hope I shall no longer be under this privation. It is very dull work in which we are employed, I have been in no one house but our lodgings, except the Lieut Governor's and I shall this day dine with Wadsworth, as an excepted case. But as a general rule we decline all invitations. As usual in my own State, a full share of work will fall upon my Shoulders here, but this I am easy about. We sit *twice* a day Connecticut fashion, and in the evenings talk politicks over the fire, and hear Bigelow tell stories, though the old Stock is nearly exhausted. I cannot

yet see beyond the *Horizon* of this place but shall keep hoping that Saturday week, will enable us to come to a conclusion. We have great unanimity, but still a great deal of discussion. All is secret. We shall probably gratify nobody at first, but believing as I do that we shall do the very best *practicable* thing, we shall do good, and ensure final approbation from the wise and good and from our own Consciences. . . .

That day the second committee of five proposed, and the Convention on Christmas Eve decided, that in addition to action on the militia controversy it "recommend to the several State Legislatures, certain amendments to the Constitution of the United States." A committee of seven, Otis chairman, the other members being Smith, Sherman,[1] Dane, Prescott, West and Hazard, which had already been appointed to draft the report of the Convention, received the additional assignment of drafting the proposed constitutional amendments. On 30 December Otis's committee presented a first draft of the final Report. After considerable debate, this was adopted on 3 January 1815. The Convention adjourned *sine die* on the 5th, and next day its Report was published in full as an extra number of the Hartford *Courant*. It was reprinted by almost every newspaper in New England, and by many elsewhere.

Thus, the real work of the Convention was done by three committees consisting of ten of the oldest and most eminent members, Otis alone serving on all three. Timothy Bigelow, the one member trusted by Lowell to advocate bold measures, had no committee assignment; and in a later letter to Otis he admitted disagreement with the moderate Report. George Cabot, or some other guiding spirit, obviously maneuvered committee assignment so as to keep wild proposals off the agenda, and there is no reason to doubt Otis's oft reiterated statement that neither a separate peace nor secession was even discussed.

Viewed as a literary production, the Report takes a high rank

[1] Swift was substituted for Sherman, who had to leave Hartford for unexplained reasons.

among American state papers; politically one can only say that it is "good in spots," like the curate's egg; chronologically, it came out at the worst possible time.

Tradition assigns the authorship to Otis. He never claimed or disclaimed the honor, but since it issued from his committee, we may assume that tradition is correct; and in any case, the Report expressed his views and he never failed to defend each and every word of it. The opening paragraph strikes the keynote — a mellow one in the middle register:

> The Convention is deeply impressed with a sense of the arduous nature of the commission which they were appointed to execute, of devising the means of defence against dangers, and of relief from oppressions proceeding from the acts of their own Government, without violating constitutional principles, or disappointing the hopes of a suffering and injured people.

Respect is then paid to the violent wing of the Federalist party, by acknowledging that

> a sentiment prevails to no inconsiderable extent . . . that the time for a change is at hand. Those who so believe, regard the evils which surround them as intrinsic and incurable defects in the Constitution. . . . This opinion may ultimately prove to be correct. But as the evidence on which it rests is not yet conclusive, and as measures adopted upon the assumption of its certainty might be irrevocable, some general considerations are submitted in the hope of reconciling all to a course of moderation and firmness, which may save them from the regret incident to sudden decisions, [and] probably avert the evil.

The Convention recognizes that the Federal Constitution, "competent to all the objects of national prosperity" under a "wise and virtuous Administration," has been perverted to an instrument of misgovernment and oppression under a weak and wicked one. "But to attempt upon every abuse of power to change the Constitution would be to perpetuate the evils of revolution." Wise words!

Most of New England's troubles derive from "the fierce passions which have convulsed the nations of Europe" having "passed the Ocean" and entered "the bosoms of our citizens." Right again! These causes of discord have vanished; Democratic and southern hostility to maritime commerce is burning itself out, and extremist action on the part of New England would be the worst thing "to accelerate this propitious change." Good prophecy!

"Finally, if the Union be destined to dissolution, by reason of the multiplied abuses of bad administration, it should, if possible, be the work of peaceable times, and deliberate consent. . . . A severance of the Union by one or more States, against the will of the rest, and especially in a time of war, can be justified only by absolute necessity. These are among the principal objections against precipitate measures tending to disunite the States, and when examined in connection with the farewell address of the Father of his country, they must, it is believed, be deemed conclusive."

After thus politely throwing overboard Essex Junto extremism, the Report proceeds "to a consideration, in the first place, of the dangers and grievances which menace an immediate or speedy pressure, with a view of suggesting means of present relief." Prominent among these is the administration's militia policy which, "by placing at the disposal of the National Government the lives and services of . . . the people, enable it at pleasure to destroy their liberties, and erect a military despotism on the ruins." Similar consequences are predicted if the bills for conscription and the enlistment of minors should pass. These infractions of the Constitution are so "deliberate, dangerous, and palpable, affecting the sovereignty of a State and the liberties of the people," as to make it (in the language of Madison's Resolutions of 1789) "the duty of such a State to interpose its authority for their protection." In the resolutions at the end of the Report, the New England states are advised, in case the conscription acts do pass, to "adopt all such measures as may be necessary effectually to protect the citizens of said States" from their operation. Thus for the third time within six years New England Federalism advanced Jeffersonian principles of state interposition or nullification, in direct contradiction to the Federalism of Washington and Hamilton.

The next subject to be taken up is the military defense of New England. Defenseless and impoverished by administration policy, the people will presently find themselves "reduced to the necessity either of submission to a foreign enemy, or of appropriating to their own use, those means of defence which are indispensable to self-preservation. . . . This Convention will not trust themselves to express their conviction of the catastrophe to which such a state of things inevitably tends." As a way out, an arrangement is suggested, at once "consistent with the honour and interest of the National Government, and the security of these States," by the terms of which Congress may permit the states to assume their own defense, and to pay into the treasury of each state for that purpose a portion of the national taxes there collected. This was Otis's own proposition, described in his opening speech.

After drawing a comparison between the Hamiltonian and Jeffersonian periods of our history, highly unflattering to the latter, the Report leads up to the subject of amending the Constitution by outlining the causes of "this vicissitude." These were sectionalism, political intolerance, hostility toward the federal judiciary, corrupt use of patronage and of "malcontent subjects of the old world," admission of new states in the West, animosity toward Great Britain, partiality toward France, and "Lastly and principally. — A visionary and superficial theory in regard to commerce, accompanied by . . . a ruinous perseverance in efforts to render it an instrument of coercion and war."

Seven amendments are now proposed, with the avowed object "to strengthen, and if possible to perpetuate, the Union of the States, by removing the grounds of existing jealousies, and providing for a fair and equal representation, and a limitation of powers, which have been misused." All these amendments had been suggested before the Convention met in town resolutions, public speeches, and in the newspapers. Yet Otis and his colleagues must now have proposed them more to please constituents (as suggested in the "keynote" paragraph) than with any hope of getting them adopted. The only possible way to get that done was to threaten secession, as the border slave states did with their pro-slavery amendments in the Peace Conference of 1861. Otis and his colleagues having already rejected "precipitate measures tending to disunite the States," they could hardly have expected their propositions to be accepted by any state outside New England.

So, the proposed constitutional amendments represented what the New England Federalists wanted, rather than what they thought they could get; but we may briefly glance at them nevertheless:

1. The old Ely Amendment of 1804, abolishing the 1787 compromise of allowing slaves to be counted partially in allotting members of Congress, presidential electors and direct taxes. Nathan Dane, who drew up a report on the subject, asserted that a slave representation had been responsible for electing Jefferson president, and for passing sundry undesirable bills. But he was candid enough to add that the proposed amendment would increase the free states' share of a direct tax, such as had been laid in 1798 and during the current war.

2. No new state to be admitted to the Union without the concurrent vote of two thirds of both houses of Congress.

3. Duration of embargoes limited to sixty days.

4 and 5. A two-thirds vote of both houses necessary to pass a non-intercourse act, or a declaration of war.

6. No naturalized citizen to be eligible for elective or appointive office under the Federal Government.

7. No President of the United States to enjoy more than one term, or the same state to provide a President twice in succession. This slap at the "Virginia Dynasty" is obvious; but a similar

amendment was formally proposed more than ninety times between 1815 and 1892, and even found a place in the Democratic
platform of 1912. A constitutional restriction to two terms was
finally adopted in 1951.

These amendments exhibit a woeful disregard of realities, and
mark a low point in the retreat of Federalism from its position of
1790. Their adoption would have weakened materially the Federal Government and stimulated other sections to demand amendments in their own behalf.

Although the Convention adjourned *sine die* on 5 January
1815, it gave Cabot, Goodrich and Daniel Lyman power to con-
voke a new session, "if in their judgment the situation of the
Country shall urgently require it." Cabot, a few months later,
explained to Christopher Gore that this was passed in order to
have some sort of organized body in existence in case the Federal
Government should collapse. As we have seen, that calamity
seemed possible at the close of 1814. And the Convention recommended that in case peace should not be concluded and their
defense be still neglected, the New England States call another
convention to meet at Boston in June 1815, with powers compatible to a "crisis so momentous." That was the most radical
suggestion to issue from the "wise and good."

The Report of the Hartford Convention has been criticized as
variously as every other aspect of that unfortunate assembly. John
Quincy Adams read into it an insidious attempt to ripen New
England sentiment to the point of sustaining secession. Otis, on
the other hand, apostrophized it as "a manual of elementary principles; — a commentary on WASHINGTON's Farewell Address — by
which . . . the most zealous friend to the Union may be content
to live or die." Each estimate is extravagant. The Report was an
attempt to satisfy enraged Yankees and to persuade or frighten the
administration into ending the war and treating New England
more justly in the future. It failed to satisfy extremist demands
to consider the Union already dissolved, or to start the eastern

states on the road to reunion with the West left out. It did not even carry out all the suggestions of Otis's Report of 8 October. Amendments to the Constitution are requested, not demanded; and no revolutionary mode, such as summoning a nationwide constitutional convention, is suggested for their adoption. This restraint surprised the Convention's bitterest enemies and disgusted some of its most zealous friends. Gouverneur Morris openly ridiculed the Report — the mountain had labored and brought forth a mouse. But it certainly had the intended soothing effect.

Two weeks after the adjournment, Otis wrote from Boston to Senator Gore in Washington, "The proceedings of the convention, though generally approved, are adopted rather to appease than to produce excitement." There is "probably some secret disappointment, though very little is expressed." The Federalist press without exception assured readers that the Report met with their entire approval, and admitted no more violent suggestions to their columns; the Democratic press was so taken aback by the mild tone of the Report as to comment upon it in terms of qualified praise. *The Yankee* of Boston called it "very weak." The Washington *National Intelligencer,* semi-official organ of the Madison administration, remarked: "The proceedings are tempered with more moderation than was to have been expected, from the contemporaneous expositions, in the Eastern papers, for the views and objects of the Convention. A separation from the Union, so far from being openly recommended, is the subject only of remote allusion."

Before long the administration press recovered sufficiently from its surprise to construe the Report's moderation as indicating pusillanimity, not patriotism. And if the Report quashed secession talk in New England, it did not do so elsewhere. Within five years of the date of the Hartford Convention, threats of secession were heard from southern Republicans on the floor of Congress on the Missouri question. "Is it not a queer world?" wrote Otis in 1820. "Just as I have demonstrated that Massachusetts did not mean to

break up the Union . . . it is about to be shown by Virginia that
the thing itself is no crime." Even John Quincy Adams wrote in
his diary of that year remarks indicating that he contemplated a
policy similar to Jack Lowell's, in comparison with which the
Hartford Convention's recommendations were indeed a "commentary on Washington's Farewell Address." Said Adams: "Perhaps it would have been a wiser as well as a bolder course to have
persisted in the [slavery] restriction upon Missouri, till it should
have terminated in a convention of the States to revise and amend
the Constitution. This would have produced a new Union of
thirteen or fourteen states unpolluted with slavery, with a great
and glorious object to effect, that of rallying to their standard the
other States by the universal emancipation of their slaves."

CHAPTER XVIII

The Mission to Washington

February 1815, AET. 49

"Three Black Crows"

From the East came three wise men
    Rump ti dity!
They went to Washington and back again
    Higgledy piggledy!

These three wise men, they went to the South
    Fiddledum diddledum —
They came home again without opening a mouth,
    Diddledum fiddledum![1]

THE GENERAL COURT of Massachusetts, meeting in mid-January 1815, congratulated the Convention on its "most satisfactory proofs of attachment to the Constitution of the United States, and to the national Union." The subject of defense required immediate attention. Enlistment of a state army and a loan of a million dollars to support it, recommended by Otis's Report of 8 October, had been authorized by the general court; but Governor Strong, finding Boston banks as unwilling to lend money for war purposes to their state as to the United States, had been forced to suspend recruiting and fortification for lack of funds. In the meantime the British continued to occupy eastern Maine, apparently with no intention of giving it up, and to threaten a descent on Boston. On 27 January 1815 the general court authorized the governor to appoint three commissioners to

[1] *Hector Benevolus, Or, the Hartford Convention in an Uproar* (Windsor, Vt., 1815), p. 21.

" *Three wise men of Gotham*
Went to sea in a bowl.—"

A TRIP TO WASHINGTON CITY.

Tune—" JOHNNY BULL BEWARE.

1.

When shall we away,
Says Harry, to the City?
We must not lose a day,
'Twould be a dreadful pity.
Harry, Tommy, Bill
Set out for a frolick,
Said they, we've got a pill,
'Twill give 'em all the cholic.

2.

Better try 'em quick,
They're fairly in the traces;
No matter if they kick
We're ready for their places.
' Tom, Dick and Harry'
Never mind the rabble,
We our point shall carry
In spite of all their gabble.

3.

Speed us on our way,
Better not to tarry,
If we try we may
Drive 'em to old Harry.
Harry, Billy, Tom,
We shall win 'tis sartin,
Let the Demos come
We'll give 'em " Betty Martin."

4.

How shall we contrive
To let the matter out ?
They're snugly in their Hive,
'We'll try to ring 'em out !
Tommy, Harry, Bill,
We'll rob them of their honey,
Mind us when you will
We look out for the money.

5.

Let us talk no more
How can we endure it;
Push the Bowl from shore
Then we can ensure it.
Tommy, Harry, Bill,
Never mind the weather,
We've no sails to fill,
Let us stick together.

6.

Jimmy now said they
Let us see your master,
But he told them NAY—
What a sad disaster !
Billy, Harry, Tom,
What the Tophet ails you,
Better now go home
Before your courage fails you.

proceed to Washington and "make an earnest and respectable application" to the Federal Government, "requesting their consent to some arrangement whereby the State of Massachusetts may be enabled to assume the defense" of her territory, and to use "a reasonable portion" of federal taxes for that purpose.

On that very day the general court's object was partly fulfilled. President Madison signed an act of Congress authorizing him to receive into United States service and pay "any corps of troops, which may have been, or may be raised, organized, and officered under the authority of any of the States"; which corps shall be "employed in the State raising the same, or in an adjoining State, and not elsewhere, except with the assent of the Executive of the State so raising the same." A surrender, indeed, of Madison's administration to Federalist views. The "principal measure" of the Hartford Convention, Otis afterward claimed, was thus "virtually adopted, and the egg that was laid in the darkness of the *Hartford Conclave,* was hatched by daylight under the wing and incubation of the National Eagle!"

But, we may ask, if this act of 27 January hatched out the principal egg of the Hartford Convention, why did Governor Strong appoint commissioners and send them to Washington? Obviously because the act did not authorize the states to impound federal tax money to reimburse themselves for war claims. That is what the Federalists wanted. Otis said so explicitly in a letter of 21 January 1815 to Christopher Gore: "so that a portion of them [federal taxes] may *as collected* be paid into our State Treasury." Governor Strong must indeed have licked his chops at the prospect of a free dip into the heavy war taxes! It was to press this point that the state commissioners proceeded to Washington. As additional proof that the Governor intended no nonsense, and had given up his plan of a separate peace or armistice, he had already, on 2 January, returned to the federal arsenal at Watertown a large quantity of ordnance and ammunition borrowed during the alarm of the previous September. Obviously a state governor would not hand over arms and munitions to federal authorities if he contemplated secession or a violent confrontation with the national government.

Otis did not see any sense in sending a special mission to Washington; the Massachusetts delegation in Congress "could do all which can be done." Nevertheless, on the last day of January, Governor Strong appointed as the three commissioners Harrison Gray Otis and his friends Thomas Handasyd Perkins and William Sullivan. This was an impressive delegation. Tom Perkins, Otis's friend since boyhood, had become the leading China merchant of New England, with extensive European connections as well. In 1812 he had done the government a good turn by bringing some very ticklish dispatches from the American legation in London to Paris, and later he helped Samuel Gridley Howe to found Perkins Institution for the Blind. Lawyer William Sullivan, nine years younger than Otis but his close political ally and comparable to him for wit and charm, was a pioneer in public education, author of several history textbooks and of the once famous *Public Men of the Revolution*. Like Otis, he did not relish this appointment, but at an after-church meeting at 45 Beacon Street, Otis and Perkins persuaded him to accept. There could not have been a more congenial trio or one better calculated to impress the national administration. Otis's pretty sixteen-year-old daughter Sophia accompanied them as far as Philadelphia, where she stayed with the George Harrisons.

On 3 February the "three ambassadors," as Otis jocosely called them, departed for Washington, followed by the hopes and prayers of Federalists and the sneers and jeers of Democrats. Detained at New Haven over Sunday by the Blue Laws, and at New York by ice in the Hudson, they did not reach Philadelphia until the 9th, when Otis wrote to his wife:

> My dearest friend,
> We came here safe about sunset this evening, after breaking down without damage which detained us an hour or two. We lost one day at New York the ice running so violently down the

Thomas Handasyd Perkins, by Thomas Sully.

William Sullivan, by Gilbert Stuart Newton.

river as to render the passing dangerous and nearly impracticable, but yesterday morning, by watching for an opportunity we came over in a *row* boat with great ease and expedition. The steam boat is occasionally interrupted for a day or two but she is not hauled up *in winter* as Harry supposed. . . . We have been exceedingly amused by the circumstance of *three* black crows, constantly preceding us from N York to Philadelphia. Whenever a flock alighted which was every ten minutes, *Three* of them seperated from the rest and stalked over the ground, waddling and looking wise till they were frighten'd away. These are *ill omen'd* birds and in days when augury was in fashion would have been considered as sad precursors of the three Ambassadors. What the Blackbirds at Washington will say or do with us remains to be seen.

The three black crows were indeed prophetic. News of Jackson's victories at New Orleans, which knocked from under them the rotten prop of national calamity on which all hope of their success was based, reached Washington as early as 4 February, and confirmation reached the "three ambassadors" at the same time as the symbolic blackbirds. That Otis clearly realized this situation is indicated in his letter to Mrs. Otis dated "Baltimore Sunday Evg. 12 feby":

> The *miraculous* success of our arms at N Orleans and the pacific character of the floating rumours of the day, will probably put the Administration upon stilts, and augur no favorable issue to our mission. Still am I sincerely glad for the former occurence, and am quite willing to take peace when it comes, with all the inconveniences resulting from the benefit which bad men will derive from an event, for which they will deserve no credit.

Hard on the heels of the news of New Orleans came that of the Peace of Ghent, which turned not only Otis's mission, but the Hartford Convention itself, into a pitiful farce. Otis, in his first letter to his wife after his arrival at Washington, tells the story:

Georgetown feby 14 tuesday

I came here safe last night, my dearest love, and am safe and
well. The road from Baltimore bad but not yet intolerable. My
lodgings here are comfortable; I am in the same house with Mr
King and Mr Gore, and with other worthies. The ladies of those
two Senators are I think more disgusted with Washington and
more impatient to return than any homesick lady of my acquaintance who has ever been here. This is no matter of astonishment
with me, for though the City of Washington is considerably augmented and improved, and that of Georgetown very much so;
the state of Society is so different from our own, and all the associations of ideas which tend to afford comfort and pleasure so
utterly precluded by the circumstances and politicks of this atmosphere, that those alone are fitted to enjoy life here, who are
disqualified to enjoy it rationally anywhere. — There is at this
moment a rumour of peace which throws the natives into a great
bustle. But such is the nature of rumour that we believed here,
for some time that Madisons house was illuminated though only
one mile distant from us, and though there was no foundation
for the story. — God grant the intelligence may prove correct. . . .
[P.S.] I would not seal this letter untill I could have an opportunity of ascertaining the truth of the news of peace. Gods holy
name be praised. It is the most desireable event which could
have occurrd to me, and will enable me, I trust, still to maintain
the wife of my bosom and the children of my love in a situation
which I have struggled hard to support; with many an anxious
fear and with hard and laborious exertion. I say again, Gods
name be praised.

Otis was not alone in blessing God for the peace. Perkins wrote
to a friend on 16 February calling it a "joyful event . . . thanks to
the Giver of all good things." But the immediate effect of peace
on the "three ambassadors" was to render their mission bootless
and themselves figures of fun, subjects of numerous squibs, car-
toons and doggerel in the Democratic press. A friend wrote to
Senator Mahlon Dickerson on 15 February, "Harry Otis is here in
a most pitiful plight. He is pregnant with most weighty concerns

— the period of gestation is expired, and he is 'groaning to be delivered,' but finds no accoucheur." One of the best squibs appeared in the form of an advertisement in the New York *National Advocate:*

MISSING

Three well looking, responsible men, who appeared to be traveling towards Washington, disappeared suddenly from Gadsby's Hotel, in Baltimore, on Monday evening last, and have not since been heard of. They were observed to be very melancholy on hearing the news of peace, and one of them was heard to say, with a great sigh, "Poor Caleb Strong." . . .
P.S. One of the gentlemen was called *Titus Oates,* or some such name.

Besides the ridicule that he had to endure, Otis suffered at Washington a violent attack of the gout, which confined him to his lodgings. Both ills combined to put him in a peccant humor toward the world in general and President Madison in particular. This appears in his letters to Mrs. Otis:

23 feby 1815

. . . I presume I have already told you, that we have recd no invitation from Madison.[1] What a mean and contemptible little blackguard. Had we been sent with the declaration of a secession of our State from the Union, an open hearted and magnanimous President, under the exhilarating impressions & softening tendencies of the present moment would have extended to us the Olive branch & assumed a gracious demeanor. But it now suits his purpose to affect great distance & to permit it to be given out that we should not have succeeded in our mission under any circumstances. I believe however we should have succeeded, and yet the little Pigmy shook in his shoes at our approach. From Mr Munroe and Mr Dallas, we have recd every civility. . . .

---

[1] He means a social invitation, since in their official report to Governor Strong dated 16 February 1815 the commissioners state, "We have . . . called upon the Secretaries of the Treasury and of War, and have been introduced to the President; and by all of them have been received with great courtesy."

Georgetown friday 24 feby 1815

. . . The ball *here* on birth night was select and genteel. The party consisted of Gentlemen and ladies. The ball at Washington was of a different Complexion, it was made up chiefly of the Court Party, and strangers allurd by curiosity. After the Company was assembled, upon a flourish of drums and trumpets, the doors open'd seemingly upon sympathetic hinges, and enterd Mrs M—— who I am told Compensates by graciousness and good humour for the want of polished elegance and culture. And who led her in, do you think? No less a personage than *Joe Gales,* editor of the national intelligencer. This fellow has very much the face & manner of a Malay and stared about him I am told with ineffable self complacence and impudence. He acts I suppose as manager, but then she should have gone into the room as a private lady. If she intended to be announced with form and eclat, as the queen of peace, or the woman of first rank in America; some other gentleman usher or lord in waiting should have been selected for the purpose, rather than this dirty editor. What can be more characteristick of the style of the place, of the knowledge of propriety, and of the subservience of dignity and decorum to Party views and services. I am told, all was of a very consistent uniformity. Uncovered benches, naked walls, fiery muslins, and bloody flags, Clerks and Clerkesses, Members of Congress, Officers of the Army with fresh epaulettes that will never now be tarnished.

Why, then, did the "ambassadors" tarry in Washington? They, and the commissioners similarly appointed by Connecticut, hoped to obtain repayment for state militia called out for defense but not placed under federal command. At the time of their arrival a bill to this effect had been passed by the Senate, but news of peace made it no longer necessary to humor New England, and the House killed it. The mission, nevertheless, had one useful result, in removing a possible conflict between the federal and state governments. Otis persuaded Secretary of the Treasury Dallas to dismiss suits pending against certain publicans of Old Hampshire who had refused to pay their federal excise for 1815 in the hope that the state legislature would sequester United States taxes.

Madison's tactful consent to this act of clemency, for which Otis tendered his "respectful thanks" (21 February) laid a foundation for the Era of Good Feelings.

Otis began his homeward journey in high spirits, as this lively account of his gouty departure from Washington indicates:

Baltimore tuesday 28 feby 1815

Here am I my love, safe and sound with whole bones, having accomplished what I consider the worst part of my homeward journey, though I am yet but 43 miles distant from that enchanting city which is nicknamed the Metropolis. Nothing was farther from my mind than the intention of departing on sunday, when I went to bed on saturday evening, but the weather in the morning was fine; our comfortable coach with 4 good horses and a skilfull driver were waiting my nod; I felt free from pain, and quite strong in all my joints, except my two ancles, both feet, all my toes, my left wrist, and the fingers of of my left hand, and a slight affection in both shoulders: — All these were more or less weak & swollen though not painful, but these constituted but a minority, and as there were other joints without them, that were sufficiently strong and flexible, I was inclined to respect the rights of the majority. So said I to P[erkins] & S[ullivan] "Suppose I should tell you that I am ready to march in one hour." "Why," says P, "you must judge of your own feelings, and ought not to expose yourself but if you could bear it, it would certainly be a great affair to get on to Baltimore. The thaw is already rapid; The *runs* will be full, the roads frightful and every hour is worth saving." — "Order the carriage Sir I am ready in an hour." — "You are not serious" said Sullivan with a look of incredulity that would have doom'd a Jew to be roasted by the Santa Germanada. "Sir I say I go with you in an hour." Off he flew without waiting to put on a fresh blister. . . . The Bladensburg *run, before we came to the bridge,* was happily in no one place *above* the Horses bellies. — As we passed thro', the driver pointed out to us the spot, right under our wheels, where all the stage horses last year were drowned, but then he consoled us by shewing the tree, on which all the Passengers *but one,* were saved. Whether that one was gouty or not, I did not enquire.

The *Chuck* holes, were not *bad,* that is to say they were none of them much deeper than the Hubs of the hinder wheels. They were however exceedingly frequent, but we got thro them all and arriv'd safe at our first stage, Ross's, having gone at a rate rather exceeding two miles & an half per hour. The "man of Ross" gave me a fine warm room and an admirable bed and I awoke on Monday morning still better. . . . This route is Turnpike throughout, but 40 miles further. It would not answer for me to take the other route, for in case of a *break Down* or other accident, I could not walk far at present, & I should be sorry to stick and freeze in over night (as I have seen happen to twenty waggons) for without an extraordinary thaw I could not be dug out in any reasonable dinnertime the next day.

On 6 March Otis awaited the thaw at Philadelphia, and on the 14th he reached home. All along the way he found people celebrating the return of peace with fervor and unrestrained joy. The doves rejoiced that the war was over, and the hawks believed that they had won. And, in the main, the hawks were right. Although not a single object for which the war had been declared had been attained, although Canada still remained British and England retained the right of impressment, Americans had shown that they could fight and defeat veterans of Trafalgar and the Peninsula.

Had there ever been any chance of the proposed constitutional amendments obtaining a respectful hearing, that chance was now lost. In their exultation over victory and peace, a majority of the American people regarded the Hartford Convention as a despicable attempt to break up the Union and give aid and comfort to Britain. Democratic politicians, seeking a foil to their own mismanagement of the war and to discredit the still formidable Federalist party, caressed and fed this infant myth until it became so tough and lusty as to defy both solemn denials and documentary proof. The proposed amendments, adopted only by Massachusetts and Connecticut, were ignored or rudely rejected by all other states and every 15 December members of the Hartford Convention were posted as traitors in Democratic journals. Outside their own section, where they were honored as long as they lived, they were punished by "the torment of eternal contempt," as the aged Jefferson wished them to be.

THOUGHTS ON THE CONVENTION

Thus the Hartford Convention, principal event of Otis's political career, ended in futility and contumely, though not in dishonor. It can no longer be contended that there was any mystery about it. The motives of Otis and his colleagues were clear and open, but idiotic timing fouled the whole business. Blinded by their hatred of the war, they failed to see that its character had changed during 1814; that from a party and sectional war of conquest it had become a struggle for national integrity, and that the assembling of a convention of disaffected states at such a time, but for England's overwhelming desire for peace, could have paralyzed the national effort. Timing is one of the essentials of statesmanship, even of life itself; and the worst one can say of these "wise and good" men is that they were both foolish and wicked in their timing.

The question remains, what would have happened had the war gone on? Would George Cabot have reconvened the Hartford Convention, and would it then have summoned a new federal convention? This is hardly worth serious consideration, because both governments were so sick of the war that they greedily swallowed the Ghent treaty, which settled nothing, and ratified it with almost indecent haste.[1] But it will do no harm to play around with the subject.

Suppose the commissioners at Ghent had been unable to make peace, that war had continued, and England decided to press it;

[1] See chronology in notes to this chapter.

what then? Would the New England states, or some of them, have seceded? And if they had, would the Federal Government have attempted to suppress the rebellion?

In my opinion, nothing would have happened. It is literally true, as Otis asserted in his 1820 pamphlet, that "the publication of the report had the immediate effect of calming the public mind throughout New England." Governor Cotton Smith's address to the general court of Connecticut, commending the Report, said, "Those who have believed that our sufferings called for more prompt and efficient modes of redress will be satisfied that moderation no less than firmness is the dictate of an enlightened and just policy, . . . and enliven the hopes of all who cherish our national union." From 5 January to mid-February, when the Peace of Ghent was announced, there were no more feverish calls for "action," even in those Boston newspapers which had furthered extremist proposals.[1] It became the Federalist party line to applaud the moderate Hartford proposals, and that of the Republicans to jeer at it as "very weak," imagining the fury of "Crazy Jack" Lowell over anything so mild and inconclusive. Canny Caleb Strong, by handing over munitions to federal authorities in early January, had obviously abandoned his secret policy of a deal with the British in Halifax, and in his address to the general court on 18 January he said: "I hope that the people of this Commonwealth however they may . . . think themselves injured by the national agents, will not resort to unauthorized and intemperate measures, which may prove extremely hurtful to themselves and the public, and cannot be advantageous to either." Thus, the New England sectional movement had run its course by the new year, Otis's "safety valve" policy worked, and the Federalists fell back into their normal nationalism. There was not a single leader

---

[1] The one exception was red-hot Federalist Newburyport, whose town meeting on 20 January adopted a memoir to the general court urging that federal laws be "temporarily suspended" in Massachusetts, and "that hostilities shall cease towards Great Britain on the part of the free, sovereign and independent States of New-England."

capable or even desirous of carrying the state rights struggle further. "Monarchy and all" Blake, in his October speech, declared
that civil war was the worst of all calamities, and if his proposed
measures had "the remotest tendency" to lead to it, he would
abandon the Convention.

But it does not unduly strain the imagination to predict that if
Madison's administration had been stubborn about concluding
peace, a very serious situation would have arisen. As a result of
Governor Strong's secret diplomacy, the British authorities at
Halifax had authority from London to intervene. If Madison refused to ratify the treaty and war continued, they were authorized
to sign an armistice with the New England states; and in the event
that these states were invaded by federal forces, to provide full
logistic support. That "short of war" policy would of course
have led to full military cooperation. There would have been a
civil war, with New England militia supported by the Royal Navy,
Canadian militia, and a fresh British expeditionary force. The
British-Yankee coalition might have won had the British been
determined — but they distinctly were not. Insuperable obstacles
to a New-and-Old England victory would have been the loyal
Democrats of New England (even the governor's secret envoy to
Halifax warned that they were very strong), and the New England
regiments in their regular army. And yet — extremists almost
always get on top in times of panic and stress. Federalist hatred
of the national administration had boiled up into something
pathological, like the feelings of the white South against "Black
Republicans" in 1860. The Virginia convention of 1861, elected
with a Unionist majority, voted for secession when Lincoln called
for volunteers.

As a consequence of this hypothetical Anglo-Yankee alliance, a
New England Confederation might have been set up in 1815 to
run the war; and who would have been chosen President of New
England but Harrison Gray Otis? Would Madison then have
acted as Lincoln did in 1861? Leaders of his party certainly

threatened that he would; but if the British had kept American forces busy on the Canadian front, Madison would have had no troops to spare for putting down a Yankee rebellion. Would officers of New England regiments along the Canadian frontier have remained loyal to the flag, or, like Robert E. Lee in 1861, followed their states out of the Union? One can imagine President Madison trying to blockade New England with the United States Navy, which then might have enjoyed its long-desired fleet action with the Royal Navy. One can imagine General Jackson leading an army with the slogan "On to Hartford!" and also anticipate the result. The Yankees "with their dander up" might have fought valiantly but they would certainly have been overwhelmed, and the New England states reconstructed in an era of bad, not good feelings. And Harrison Gray Otis as leader of a lost cause would now have a position in Yankee hagiology similar to that of Jefferson Davis in the South.

On the other hand, suppose the Madison administration had allowed the "erring sisters" to go in peace, and recognized the independence of a New England Confederacy? New England would hardly have been a viable state, even in the relatively simple conditions of the early nineteenth century. One of two things would have happened: The Yankee Republicans would have recovered power, repealed the ordinances of secession, and rejoined the Union; or the Federalists, finding New England falling into worse poverty than she had supposedly been subjected to by Jefferson and Madison, would have opened negotiations to join British North America. The addition of so many rebellious Yankees to Canada might have brought confederation to that country forty or fifty years prior to 1867; or New England might have joined the maritime provinces in a separate confederation.

All this is pure fantasy. Remembering the avidity with which both governments ratified the Treaty of Ghent, and the fact that the British recalled General Pakenham's expeditionary force from Louisiana without even knowing whether it had won or lost, it is abundantly clear that the Peace of Christmas Eve 1814 was inevitable. And peace caused the entire sectional movement in New England, based as it was on false premises, to collapse.

After all is said on both sides, we should remember that Otis and his colleagues represented the majority in a section that from 1807 to 1814 had been governed with less regard for its feelings and interests than any other section of the United States at any other period. They followed the example of Jefferson and Madison in 1798, with greater provocation. They endured, with no attempt to resist the laws, wrongs which, though greatly magnified in their eyes, were still far more real than the supposed wrongs for which eleven states attempted to break up the Union a half century later. If love of the Union had been no stronger in the New England of the early nineteenth century than in the South of midcentury, New England would have seceded when Jefferson was elected President.

CHAPTER XIX

Good Feelings and the United States Senate

1815–1821, AET. 49–55

POST-WAR LIFE AT NUMBER 45

THE WORLD PEACE of 1815 brings us to the end of the colonial epoch in America, and begins a new era of nationalism. "In a single day, almost in a single instant," as Henry Adams wrote, "the public turned from interests and passions that had supplied its thought for a generation, and took up a class of ideas that had been unknown or but vaguely defined before." The nation turned its back on Europe and set its face westward. New problems of the frontier, of transportation, of free trade and protection, occupied its attention for the next fifteen or twenty years, and the black cloud of the slavery question presently showed itself above the horizon. The same year proved to be a watershed for Massachusetts and for her loyal son Harrison Gray Otis.

We are fortunate in having accounts of life at No. 45 Beacon Street immediately after the war, owing to the absence of Sally, Harry Jr. and Sophia, whom their husband and father kept constantly informed. It was a happy home atmosphere. Otis wrote to his wife on 29 May 1815, "I never had less cause for gloom or anxiety . . . . God has filled my cup of comfort to the brim." Sophia, seventeen years old in March, spent several months with the childless George Harrisons and, by all accounts, made a brilliant debut. The Harrisons loved their namesake, for she closely resembled her mother. "Mrs. Henry Sargent gives a ball next week," writes Otis to Sophia on 29 March. "Some college boys give another at Cambridge, W[illiam Howard] Gardiner one of the managers — *we* are invited. This is a bad practice . . . they had better mind their books." And to Sally, on 19 May: "I was last night at our neighbors — a very smart party — some singing, more talking, *considerable* crowding and a great deal of solid eating constituted the amusement of the evening."

William, aged 14, is so enthusiastic about the United States Navy that the family have nicknamed him "The Admiral." The front chamber which he shares with brother James (15) "is turned into a drydock," with a model of a full-rigged 74, overlooked by a "most tremendous and ugly likeness" of their naval hero Commodore Bainbridge. The purchase of this portrait bankrupted "William's Museum." Poor little William! A sensitive soul, and the only one of the family who loved the sea, he tried to stow away on a ship bound for the Orient but was apprehended and brought back, abashed, to continue his preparation for Harvard.

Mrs. Otis returned home in early June 1815 from a visit to Philadelphia, but suffered delicate health. Appalled at the prospect of another cold winter in Boston, she started for Charleston, in November, with her own horses and carriage, in company with her daughter and son-in-law the George Lymans, and the George Harrisons in their carriage. They took plenty of time, stopping in every city en route to visit friends and rest the horses, but had some rather rough nights at inns in what her husband called the "semi-savage country" of North Carolina.

Sophia writes to her mother at Fredericksburg, Virginia, on 3 December that the Thanksgiving dinner at No. 45 was "most merry." The whole family and the Apthorps, among others, were present, and "we played 'Stir the Mush' etc. as in old times." Sophia made her Boston debut in a cotillion on 9 December. "The dance is to be in the two front rooms," wrote her father, "supper in Harry's and Sophia's chambers," which also were on the *piano nobile* ell. Sophia and two Foster and Apthorp cousins "are as busy as Macbeth's witches" over the preparations. At the party, he reports, Sophia's behavior "was in every respect worthy

of such a mother. . . . Your married friends stood by her and I
thanked them all in your name." William precociously helped his
sister by livening things up when "there was a little hanging back
of partners," and "led off the second cotillion in good style." "The
Navy Department" — William's museum — "is evidently in a
state of languishment." William and James teased their father
into giving a cotillion for young people of their own age. Otis
consented grudgingly; he did not believe in age-segregated parties.
But he delighted in his little boys George (7) and Allyne (10), and
their two Lyman nephews of about the same age, George and
Arthur, the latter "a chubby little rascal." All four boys rode
hobbyhorses around the breakfast table while Otis shouted "Hur-
rah, boys!" and he amiably submitted to being drilled in the military company that they organized.

By March 1816, after passing a very enjoyable winter in Charleston, Mrs. Otis and Eliza Lyman are ready to start their long
carriage journey home, in company with the George Harrisons.
Otis charges his wife to carry plenty of codline "to keep one
carriage in repair," and a couple of sidesaddles to enable the ladies
to ride for help if the carriages bog down. It took Sally and Eliza
about three weeks to reach Boston, and the warmth of their reception may be judged by a letter they received from Otis en
route: "No princesses have been expected to arrive at any court,
with more importance than you and your child, in Beacon street;
& no Queen has attained a more absolute dominion than you have
over the little territory of my heart. It is not a domain worthy of
being boasted of, but all that grows in it is first for the Lady of the
manor and then for her Children. A Dieu dearest, yr H G O."

ERA OF GOOD FEELINGS

James Monroe, last of the Virginia Dynasty, easily captured the
presidency in 1816, and, following Washington's precedent, decided to make a tour of the country. Otis was the first to see that

his visit to Boston in July of 1817 could be turned to the profit of the groggy but far from defunct Federal party. Characteristically, he offered to place No. 45 Beacon Street at the President's disposal. Monroe naturally refused so to honor a private citizen, and put up at the Exchange Coffee-House.

Nevertheless, Otis won the second round. Town meeting appointed him chairman of the committee on arrangements, and his friend Colonel Perkins as grand marshal. The local Democracy, not caring to be eclipsed by their political enemies, appointed a rival committee in the hope of waylaying the President en route. But Otis and the Federalists were too smart for them. They captured the presidential cortege at Providence where, according to General Joseph Gardner Swift, the President's military aide, "Mr. Otis, in an eloquent address, alluded and compared the visit to its only precedent, that of Washington." The Democratic committee turned up next day at Pawtucket, giving Swift some trouble; and more awaited him at the Roxbury-Boston line on the Neck, where the retinue arrived on 3 July. The general, forced to decide which committee should take the presidential party in tow, gave the palm to the Federalists since they had been officially appointed. Otis, after delivering a short speech of welcome, rode beside Grand Marshal Thomas Handasyd Perkins, heading a mile-long procession. Militia companies, truckmen in white aprons, freemasons and plain citizens escorted the presidential party through streets crowded with enthusiastic citizenry and lined with children wearing red and white roses as symbols of political peace. The Salem *Gazette,* carried away by enthusiasm, described this display as "equal to that of an ancient Roman triumph." After the President had been installed in his lodgings, he drove to a reception at the State House, where, again quoting General Swift, "the influence of fruit and champagne seemed to quiet for a time the ground swell of party."

The following week there was no rest for the President or for Otis, who loved occasions of this sort. On the Glorious Fourth Monroe presided over several patriotic celebrations and dined

with former President Adams at Quincy. Forty gentlemen, including Otis, Josiah Quincy and President Kirkland, were there;
no Republican politicians and only one lady — Mrs. Adams.[1] On
Saturday 5 July, after a light *first* breakfast, the President visited
the Charlestown navy yard to inspect ships and buildings, followed
by a "sumptuous and elegant *dejeuene*" at the residence of the
commandant, Commodore Isaac Hull. At noon the President
"mounted his charger and proceeded through Charlestown toward
Breed's and Bunker's Hills," where he received survivors of the
battle, inspected the old earthworks, heard speeches, and "par-
took of a neat collation on the *Heights of Bunker*." There followed a cruise on the Middlesex Canal, dinner at four in the
afternoon at Governor Brooks's mansion in Medford, and a return to Boston in time to hear an oratorio by the Handel and
Haydn Society. "He then honored Mr. Otis with his company
at a brilliant party" at Number 45 Beacon Street, "enlivened by
a band of music placed in the garden, and a display of fireworks."

Here, for the first time in twenty years, Boston Federalists and
Republicans participated in the same private entertainment. It
was thus described in the diary of Eliza Susan Quincy, aged nineteen: "Evening with my father and mother to Mrs. Otis's party.
The windows of the house were all open and as we waited in
Beacon Street for the carriage to get up to the door we had a view
of the apartments — three drawing rooms opening into each other.
Mrs. Otis received us at the door of the third, a room with a bow in
the garden, toward Mr. Sears's house." From that oval room
French doors opened directly on the garden. Miss Quincy continues:

> The company were assembled when suddenly the door of the
> bow room was thrown open and Mr. Otis in a loud voice said,
> "Ladies and gentlemen, the President of the United States."

[1] An English eighteenth-century custom which Boston long followed: the lady
of the house presided at a gentlemen's dinner but retired when the cloth was removed and the men began their serious after-dinner drinking.

A band struck up on the balcony toward the garden from which a flight of rockets ascended. Mr. Monroe, a very plain unassuming gentleman entered, — but from his official station, "to him each ladies' look was lent, on him each politician's eye was bent." Mrs. Otis received him and he sat on the sofa beside her a few minutes, and then Mr. Otis came for Mrs. Quincy and introduced her. Mrs. Otis gave her the place next Mr. Monroe and then the other ladies were successively introduced and I also had the honor, of being named by Mr. Otis, whose manners are admirably adapted to such an occasion.

The crowd was great both within and without the mansion. I passed a most amusing evening, walking about the rooms, talking to the beaux and belles and listening to Mr. Monroe's conversation with my father and mother, and I stood next Mrs. Otis when the President took leave.

Another guest, William H. Gardiner, recorded that "there were at least 300 persons present, of whom about two thirds were introduced to the President. . . . Mr., Mrs., and Miss O. were all in their element — swimming in fashion and courtesy — saying and looking pretty things to all of their 300 *dear friends*. Mr. O. never left the presidents side, but acted as a kind of gentleman-usher, a grand chamberlain to his majesty from the time of his entrance, to that of his exit."

The *Columbian Centinel,* reviewing the presidential visit, published this editorial:

ERA OF GOOD FEELINGS

During the late Presidential Jubilee many persons have met at festive boards, in pleasant converse, whom party politics had long severed. We recur with pleasure to all the circumstances which attended the demonstration of good feelings.

This headline gave the name to an era; and without exaggeration one may say that the Otises inaugurated this Era of Good Feelings at Number 45 Beacon Street.

President Monroe rested on Sunday, but on Monday Harvard held a convocation to confer on him an honorary LL.D., and Tuesday he proceeded to Salem and points east. His geniality and political tact won him the entire New England electoral vote in 1820 — excepting one stubborn New Hampshire elector who voted for John Quincy Adams; and Adams himself was given a testimonial dinner when he returned from Europe in August 1817, Otis being one of the Federalists present. It was he who informed John Adams on 5 March that the Senate had confirmed his son's appointment as secretary of state, with but one dissenting voice. Old John, acknowledging Otis's courtesy, wished to know the name of that dissenter!

In society, the reconciliation of the Adams and Otis clans prepared for a general breaking down of party lines. George Ticknor was astonished, when he returned to Boston in 1819 after four years' absence in Europe, to find Judge Story and William Sullivan, George Blake and Daniel Webster, sitting down at the same dinner table.

HARVARD HAPPENINGS

Otis continued his close interest in the affairs of Harvard College, which he served either as overseer or fellow from 1810 to 1825. Son William, thwarted in his ambition to be a sailor, entered college in the fall of 1817 and next year distinguished himself as ringleader in a student uprising. The faculty attempted to enforce discipline after college crockery had been broken during a glorious battle between freshmen and sophomores in commons. George Washington Adams, Josiah Quincy, Jr., and young Otis rallied the sophomores at the traditional rebellion tree in front of Hollis Hall. President Kirkland summoned them into his presence and warned them against returning to the tree — which they promptly did. Finally (wrote Quincy), this "burlesque of patriots struggling with tyrants" played itself out and ended with several rustications and suspensions. Harrison Gray Otis, absent in Washington, could not intervene, but William was saved from serious punishment by the interposition of elder brother Harry. President Adams, grandfather of the ringleader, wanted severer measures, as appears in a letter from Otis to Sally of 22 November 1818:

> I presume order is restored at Harvard. Old Mr. Adams mistakes the genius of the age, to tell of whipping and to practice scolding. The principles of Government in States & Families are changed. The understanding and the heart must be addressed by persuasion and reason, & the bayonet and rod reserved for the last emergency. A boy of 18 for all the purposes of *Government,* is as much a man as he ever will be. He needs advice constantly, and sometimes must be punished by privations of the objects of his desire or pursuit.

Otis's conciliatory policy worked, and every former rebel graduated with honors.

We are fortunate to have an account of their commencement, in August 1821, from the diary of Josiah Quincy, Jr.'s sister, Eliza Susan. William Foster Otis, Ralph Waldo Emerson, and Robert W. Barnwell, future senator from South Carolina, shone at the morning exercises, which lasted at least three hours. After that, a bountiful "spread" (as college banquets used to be called) was laid out in Porter Hall for Quincy friends and kindred. Governor John Brooks, President Kirkland, Dr. Nathaniel Bowditch and other notables joined the company in time for the dessert and toasts. Then came a reception at Wadsworth House, the college president's lodge. Eliza, Josiah and their younger sister Abby drove into Boston to attend the Otises' party for their graduating son, first changing clothes at the Isaac Davises' house on Boylston Street. Eliza in her diary describes Number 45 that evening:

> The external appearance of the mansion was brilliant and foreboded a delightful party. . . . There were three large drawing

rooms open communicating with each other & the spacious hall,
— a splendid house for a party, — brilliantly lighted and filled
with gay and handsome ladies formed a beautiful scene. . . .
James Otis met me at the head of the staircase & led me into
the crowded drawing room and up to his mother. Polite conversation on the day from him and Mrs. Otis. I introduced Abby
who was cordially greeted. Mrs. Otis offered me her seat which I
of course declined & introduced me to her friend Mrs. Harrison
of Philadelphia. Wm. Otis then came to offer congratulations
& receive us as he considered the party as his Commencement
entertainment.

It must indeed have been a charming spectacle: the oval room,
"saloon," and dining room lighted by candles in Waterford glass
chandeliers and silver sconces, young girls in the becoming dress
of that era — bare arms and neck, low-cut bodice flattering to
young bosoms, billowing skirt — and slim young men in close-
fitting dress suits with brass buttons, ruffled shirts and choker
collars. Most of William Otis's Porcellian clubmates were there,
including Barnwell, the first scholar of the class, and Joseph Manigault, both of Charleston. Sixteen-year-old Abby Quincy "had
more partners on her hands than she could dispose of," and Eliza
did not do too badly, since William Havard Eliot, Allard Belin of
Charleston, and Francis Cabot Lowell were her partners for the
three cotillions, and Horace Gray, Manigault and George Washington Adams took her for the contra-dances. Number 45 was full
of fashionable Southerners; Eliza particularly admired Mrs. John
Wickham of Virginia, "a celebrated beauty & who with her diamonds was very conspicuous." Her son was then a junior at
Harvard.

At the conclusion there was a lot of giggling over Abby's getting
by mistake into the carriage of Robert Goodloe Harper, whose
son Charles had just been her partner; but things were straight-
ened out and the girls reached the Davises' in time for a little
sleep before the next party.

Some Otis Relics.
Portrait by Harding, 1830; decanters, ice cream jars and
candelabra on the mantelpiece; Lowestoft punch bowl and pepper
and salt, on the table. Arranged by Priscilla B. Morison.

That took place next day at the Lyman mansion, The Vale, in
Waltham. Most of the beauty and fashion which had attended
Commencement assembled there, to honor the majority of Mary,
younger sister of George W. Lyman who had married the Otises'
eldest daughter Eliza. Here were the same guests as at 45 Beacon
Street, together with three more young swells: "Mr. Clay of
Georgia, Mr. Arthur Middleton of Carolina, and Mr. Lee of Virginia,"[1] and again we are regaled by the diary of a gossipy Quincy
girl. "The guests included Mr. J. Q. Adams, Mr. Otis, Mr. Ritchie,
who had then just returned from Europe and just appeared in
fashionable society with a double eyeglass looking pretty awkward.
However, he had the reputation of being a great fortune and was
soon engaged to Miss Otis." This was Andrew Ritchie, Jr., who
married Sophia Otis the following December. Miss Quincy continues: "Waltzing was first introduced that evening in a dance
called the Spanish dance." When Otis first saw couples waltzing
at a Washington party in 1817–18 he considered it an "indecorous
exhibition." Evidently a few more years were required for this
delightful Viennese dance to reach Boston.

The balls of that period, and until after the Civil War, were
held in private houses. There were no formal comings-out for
young girls; when considered old enough they took their places
at their parents' parties, and were then asked out by their parents'
friends; no "dating" by young men was permitted. Dancing assemblies were held at Concert Hall on Hanover Street; but to
give a private ball there would have been considered ostentatious.
Ostentation of any sort was then taboo in Boston.

Harry Otis, Jr., in this same inaugural year of good feelings,
married Eliza Boardman of Boston. His father hoped that Harry
on his southern tour would lose his heart to some "pretty little

---

[1] The three young men were Thomas Savage Clay, Harvard 1819, son of a Judge
Clay of Georgia, later pastor of First Baptist Church of Boston; his classmate Charles
Carter Lee, elder brother of Robert E. Lee; and Arthur Middleton, Harvard 1814,
of the foreign service. All three were members, and Clay grand master, of the Porcellian Club.

Carolina rice bird," but he had been virtually engaged to Eliza since 1814. Old Otis found her pretty and vivacious but too forward for a young lady — she and her mother left cards on naval officers after meeting them at 45 Beacon Street, but before they called! Her father, William Boardman, a wealthy China merchant, Otis regarded as grasping and vulgar, especially after Boardman had demanded a dowry of $50,000 for William. Otis wrote to Boardman early in 1817 that in his opinion the couple "have remained too long in the relations of lovers,"[1] and, although he did not wish his son "to marry at so early an age" as 24, he would promote the union by giving the young man $10,000 and a house, if Papa Boardman would provide a dowry of $25,000. So it was arranged; the pair were married in May and old Otis turned over his office in Court Square and his law practice to his son, when he went to Washington as United States senator. Harry Jr. was regarded as a very lucky man; another Boston beau described Miss Boardman as "distinguished for her beauty and acquirements . . . enchanting in conversation and of pleasing manners."

SOCIAL LIFE AT THE CAPITAL

Envious persons then, and superficial historians later, have accused Otis of having entertained President Monroe in hope of political reward. There is no evidence that he ever wanted, much less expected, a federal job, and recent insinuations to that effect are not justified by the letters on which they are based. Otis, who would have made an admirable minister to Great Britain or a continental court, was passed over, whilst the Madrid legation, already the traditional consolation for political lame ducks, was offered to, but declined by, solemn Samuel Dexter. Even had Otis aspired to something like that, his membership in the Hartford

---

1 Meaning in love and affianced; "lover" as yet had no illicit connotation.

Convention disqualified him in the eyes of the Virginia Dynasty and their local satellites. For them, harping on "Hartford Convention treason" was the favorite election tune. "You are aware," Otis wrote to Theodore Dwight in 1821, "that a bountiful allotment of the odium attached to the Hartford Convention has been heaped upon me. . . . The very name is Tallyho, at the sound of which the 'hounds are all out.' "

In 1817 Federalists controlled the state governments of New England, Delaware and Maryland, and were still a formidable minority in New York, Pennsylvania and North Carolina. The situation bears a striking similarity to that of the Republicans in 1968. A party badly beaten for the presidency still hoped, with good state bases, to get "in orbit" and recover national power. In the meantime it had no intention of relinquishing state power without a battle. Otis himself received frequent and flattering testimony of popular esteem. In April 1815 he won an election to the state senate, and the following year he was offered the Federalist nomination for governor of Massachusetts. "I have authorized and requested particular persons to say in the most positive and unequivocal manner that I *will not* be a Candidate," he wrote to Sally on 19 January. "I wish not to espouse the Commonwealth while you live, nor to take charge of the immense family, untill my own boys are provided for." In spite of his protests, the formal nomination was tendered and promptly declined. A few days later he wrote to his wife: "There is great sensation produced by my declining what all the wise and sagacious heads believe to have been the object of my pursuit for years. . . . Nobody can imagine my motives for refusing what was never refused before, because nobody can conceive that the joys of domestic life and the command of ones own society and movements are to be placed in competition with the honor of the office."

This was another mistake in timing. Otis could have won the governorship in 1816 against Dexter. Benjamin Austin, who hated Dexter for defending his son's murderer, told Otis that if he accepted the Federalist nomination he would tip off the "bhoys" to vote for him. But Harry missed this flood tide, and the next time he tried he got stranded in the ebb.

Despite his unwillingness to "espouse the Commonwealth" while Sally lived, Harry on 9 June 1816, only two months after rejecting the nomination for governor, accepted an election to the United States Senate for the term beginning next 4 March. This change was the result of pressure that he could not honorably resist. Cold, aristocratic Senator Gore had done nothing, and Democratic Senator Varnum would do nothing, about the Massachusetts war claim on the Federal Government — upward of $800,000. Otis's friends begged him to take the seat soon to be vacated by the expiration of Varnum's term, as the only tactful Federalist with southern friends who had any chance of getting repayment through Congress. As Otis himself wrote, his leading part in wartime Massachusetts made him the obvious person "to explain occasionally those proceedings without sacrificing his dignity, and to soften the prejudices and dilute the venom of party feeling to which she was exposed." He regarded himself as an ambassador of peace and good will from Massachusetts Federalism to the national administration.

Senator-elect and Mrs. Otis journeyed to Washington in January–February 1817, making long stops with friends at New York, Philadelphia and Baltimore. At Baltimore he worked with Robert Goodloe Harper and others in the *Bothnea* prize case that we have already described. They arrived in Washington in good time for the President's inauguration and took a suite at the Union Tavern in Georgetown, the hostelry favored by Rufus King and other Federalist senators. From Lancaster, Pennsylvania, where she stopped with the George Harrisons on her way home, Sally wrote to her father her impressions of the inauguration:

Lancaster, March 12th 1817.

. . . The forth of March was ushered in by the handmaids of June, not an unruly breeze ruffled the plaits of the best handkerchief or disturbed the locks of the best powdered Beau, and had

Marshals been appointed and arrangements made, as they would have been with us, there never was a finer opportunity for a grand spectacle. but the differences between the two houses on the subject where the President should be received was derogatory to the Nation & effectually turned him out doors where under the Canopy of heaven the Oath was administered. — as there was no particular invitation or provision made for the diplomatic body — they of course could not appear — but the company assembled were in gay & handsome equipages well dressed and open; the multitude filling in back and front forming grotesque & fantastic groups, the contrariety of which are as light & shade in a well disposed picture — the number not equal I should think to those assembled on our last Artillery Election and by no means so well conditioned. A small scaffold received the *sages* of the nation, the two Presidents arrived, the one relinquished his credentials — the other received the Oath made his Speach which very few if any heard — made his bows & sat down. The Marshal now waved his white flag in mystic circle, that the People might rejoice — but whether grief at parting with one damped the pleasure expected on the acquisition of the other I know not — but certainly a very feeble acclamation was at length effected by a Comodore who came out with a *Huzza,* but it did not amount to a *boston cheer.* just at this moment as I stood on the box of our carriage an immense bird flew over the heads of the populace. Some imagined an eagle of glorious omen — but sorry am I to say that I could make nothing more nor less than an old Carolina acquaintance a Turkey buzzard. much laugh ensued & we turned our faces homeward; here the view was beautiful — the broad Pennsylvania Avenue three miles in length crowded as far as the eye could extend with carriages of every description, the sidewalks with foot passengers men women & children fiddles fifes & drums altogether presented a scene picturesque & animating. our next duty was to repair to the Palace to welcome the rising Sun, the concourse here appeared greater than on the ground — it was nearly an hour before we could get to the door & then pushing our way through all the Scavengers & wash women of the City who were laying violent hands on the waiters of cake & refreshments that were prepared & intended for the company above — in this solid column I moved upstairs, was introduced to his majesty, greeted graciously & passed on to Madame who could do little more than bow to hundreds who contented themselves in merely bowing to her.

As soon as decency would permit we hastened from this *jam* where one could with difficulty respire, to pass on to another no less *pressing* and *press'd*. Mrs. Madison behaved with her usual civility, she always finds time & occasion to speak to everybody, & what is a little remarkable never forgets the name of any one to whom she has been introduced — she was well dressed rather more pensive than common, but more interesting we all thought than ever. Mr. Madison was quite cheerful and conversible even complimentary — apparently glad to be rid of his Laborious State. I can easily imagine he is so. I therefore wished them all good and left them, glad to escape for an hours rest before joining a dinner party to which I was engaged at five & a grand inauguration Ball in the even'g — enough for one day.

Although Sally's letter is somewhat condescending toward the manners and customs of Washington — always at their worst during a presidential inauguration — the senator's letters are in complete contrast to those he wrote thence in 1801 and 1815. He entered with zest the social life of the capital and found it pleasant. His letters frequently speak of members of the dominant party as intimate friends and associates — Henry Clay, Martin Van Buren, Henry Middleton of South Carolina, and Senators Macon of North Carolina, Forsyth of Georgia, and Williams of Mississippi. He even discovered Joseph Gales of the *National Intelligencer,* whom he had called a "dirty editor" in 1815, to be a cultivated and delightful gentleman; "and yet," he remarked, "if I had been told ten years ago that I should be at a great party *chez ce Monsieur,* I should have certainly placed my prophet among the uninspired."

A letter to his father-in-law William Foster of 27 February 1817, five days before the inauguration, indicates that the Otises had already been adopted by social Washington:

Washington is undoubtedly on the increase. The public buildings are in progress to a state of reparation, though still bearing

marks of the savage scene which disgraced its authors. The indications of improvement since I was here two years ago are unequivocal. Many houses have been built, and more are ordered
to be put up this summer. Lots on the Pennsylvania Avenue
(the principal street) are selling from 75 to 100 Cents the square
foot. The state of society too is evidently improved — Indeed at
this season, the *materials* of good society are in the greatest
abundance, but there is a deficiency of cement to give it that
body and shape which constitutes its charm. This defect however is not attributable to want of pressure, for if mere squeezing
would form the Spirit as it consolidates the body of society,
that of Washington should be perfect — As it is however we get
on very well and are amused. We are not pursued with Solicita-
tions to dine and to evening parties *constantly*, but receive more
than the ladies can accept, and quite as many as our neighbours.
We have been twice to the Queen's drawingroom — To the
French ministers one night, British ditto, and this day dined
with the President. He and I are so gracious that I am almost
sorry it is too late for me to ask him for a place! I wish I could
obtain something for the Colonel, and if I see any opening I
shall ask for it, whatever may be the prospect of success.[1] The
weather has been intensely cold here but we have not suffered.
The ground is still covered with ice and snow. The Potowmac
is still fast and solid enough for carts opposite to this house, but
will I think be rotten in a day or two. As to public affairs, I can
tell you no news. There is no longer any demonstration of
party feeling in the debates or votes of Congress. No man
pretends to calculate the event of any question. The new administration will have more to apprehend from some of its friends
and the orators whose road to popularity lies open to every
splaw-footed brawler who cries out economy and votes against
taxes. They have already given them some trouble and alarm.

A jolly letter of 5 January 1819 from Otis to his father-in-law
relates the vicissitudes of returning from a visit only twelve miles
distant, in another cold winter:

[1] The "Queen" must mean Dolly Madison, as Monroe had not yet been inaugurated. By the President, Otis must mean President-elect Monroe, as Madison did
not make any midnight appointments. The "Colonel" was Thomas Handasyd
Perkins.

We have cold weather here, and the night before last a deep snow. This they call Boston weather, being used to consider Boston the great store house of political breezes and *high winds*, but they have not much to boast of over us. I was caught in the snow at a friend's house 12 miles from the city, and yesterday morning he insisted upon sending us home in a *sleigh*. So the negro carpenters were set to work to vamp it up, and in we tumbled, with a Maryland Senator for Coachman, and at the end of the first mile he bounced upon a covered stump, overset the apple cart, and choused all our dignities into the snow. The horses went off and the sleigh was broken up into *kindlings*. No harm to the bipeds. Our own carriages were near and we got home very tolerably. . . .

As you promised last year that I should be at your wedding, I take it for granted you will *forbear* untill my return this year, but remember Doctor Hunt. He tried all the widows in three counties and because he told them his object in a wife was principally to keep his back warm, they were all *hands off*, and he was obliged as he said to sleep with no live creature but a bedbug. Present my remembrances to Miss Charlotte and Miss Virginia and, as Rutledge says to me, I hope to see you soon without a grey hair in your head. Yours respectfully and with friendship

H. G. Otis

Two letters of November 1818 contain more social gossip. The first is to his youngest daughter, giving first impressions of the waltz:

My dear Sophia,

I wrote Mama yesterday about things in general and mentioned being at Madame De Neufville's Saturday evening at a sort of halfway party, pour commencer. There was present a Signior Christiani or some such name, an Italian musician said to have great talent. He played and sang. His execution I thought good but his voice coarse, and yet the effect was on the whole agreeable to my ear, and to those of the amateurs it was delectable. They relied upon it as a striking instance of what may be done by perseverance and art, towards vanquishing natural impediments. He is to teach Madame Herredia, and Miss Middleton, and I presume will be quite the rage in all the parties. An ugly sinner however I think him; and it strikes me greatly to see this sort of character assume airs of perfect equality and familiarity with the great folks, from whom we have been lead to believe, they at home observe a respectful distance — There was here the first waltzing I have witnessed in Washington — Madame Bagot, Mme Herredia & Miss Onis were the ladies, and Antrobus, Fenwick, Bourgonnais (Dixhuit) and Hughes[1] the gentlemen concerned. It was merely a little jeu de moment on the carpet. Well executed however. Little Herredia dances with astonishing elegance for so light and small a figure. It is however I think an indecorous exhibition, though now much in vogue in England as Mrs. Middleton says "to the dismay of all mothers."

The second, from Otis to his wife, describes a ball at the British legation, a simple little house, now No. 2017 I Street:

My dearest friend —
When the hour for dressing for the B. Ministers ball arrivd, I was reluctant to quit my comfortable little room and a new book on political economy, but as is sometimes the case with you enjoyed the scene with tolerable satisfaction . . . At ½ past eight I found the rooms well filled and the dancing begun. The ball was certainly brilliant and well conducted. The company I should judge not less than 250. All the foreign ministers were present, stiffened and sparkling in their laced costumes, and the heads of departments excepting Mr. A[dams]. The ladies extremely well dressed in my judgment, and a general spirit of ease and affability pervaded the rooms. The floor of one dancing room was handsomely decorated by a circle chalk'd with white crayons, in the centre whereof was the armorial shield of Great Britain with the motto of *Honi Soit,* and on different parts of the circumference were drawn the Prince Regent's crest & other

---

[1] La Baronne Hyde de Neuville, wife of the French minister; Mrs. Charles Bagot, wife of the British minister and niece of the Duke of Wellington; Miss Onís and Mme. Heredia were daughters of the Spanish minister. The others were attachés of the British and French legations.

ornaments, which were scuffled over before my entrance. The floor of the other dancing room was chalked with a corresponding circle, containing the arms of the US, and similar decorations. All your acquaintance was there — and some "that you never saw and never shall" the back buildings were occupied by cards. About $\frac{1}{2}$ past ten supper was announced. Mrs. B[agot] determined to command the rear guard, and allowd me to be her aid. She expressed a fear in going upstairs lest they should give way. On coming to the top of the stairs, the eye was met by a display of showy ornaments at the extremity of the entry placed on tables forming a sort of triple sideboard, the upper platform of which was decorated with plate and flowers and the lower one contained some very highly embellished dishes. The whole producing some thing like the effect of a handsome Roman Catholic altar. From this altar to the head of the stairs was laid one table protected from the wind and cold air by a curtain let down from the wall. Passing this table you discryed on each side into the two great chambers in which also tables were laid and covered with a most splendid variety of entremets, confectionary, porcelain and plate or plated ware. . . .

I find it difficult to remove the impression generally made here that your absence is owing to your reluctance to leave the comforts of your own house. Mrs. B's dress I fear would not appear to much advantage in my description for want of apt words and discriminating ideas. It was certainly silk covered with muslin — whether light blue or pink I could not swear. But the border was of very rich lama, besides other trimmings of the same material. White Prince Regent feathers to the amount of half a dozen, perhaps intended for a crest, nodded from her pretty head, and contested in vain for the palm of whiteness with a bosom and shoulders which were dressed in the *depth* of the fashion; a diamond necklace added to the effect of these charms. *Pour le reste* you know that eating, drinking and dancing are always done in the same way and afford no room for observation.

NATIONAL POLITICS

During Otis's sojourn in Washington, the distinction between Federalists and Republicans became obsolete in Congress as in Washington society. About half a dozen senators beside Otis, and a fair-sized minority in the House of Representatives were elected as Federalists, but never displayed this distinction in their voting. They uniformly supported the administration on questions of foreign policy, and followed their sections on questions like the Missouri Compromise, internal improvements and the tariff. In a letter to his constituents that appeared in the *Columbian Centinel* of 26 December 1818, Senator Otis argued as follows:

> As at present "all's well," — and the measures of government are favorable not less to the interests of your part of the Union than to the rest; as a due disposition has been manifested to provide for the great interests of navigation, the fisheries and manufactures, and you have no cause of complaint, I think the oftener your Governor, your Legislature, your able essayists, and your great and good men, shew a readiness to approach the national government, to give it just credit for what it deserves, and to support its measures, the more effectually will they baffle the wiles of those who wish that collisions may be eternal, wear off the edge of prejudices, and reconcile their opponents to the merit of their claim.

The only matter that threatened to revive the bitter feelings of former times happened to be the subject of a speech by Otis. A letter of 9 December 1818 to his wife explains the situation:

> You may remember the story of Matthew Lyon in the old Congress twenty years ago. The beast that spat in Griswold's face, and was tried and fined for sedition under the old obnoxious sedition act. This man lately applied to Congress to have this money reimbursed from the Treasury on the ground of the *unconstitutionality* of the law, which *expired 18 years ago*. It

was hardly supposed such a proposal would find advocates, but such is the case. A Member of Senate gave notice that he should *support* the petition, and *oppose* the report of a Committee of which I was one against it. This of course would bring into view the state of politicks and affairs in 1798 and upon looking round, I found myself the *only* remaining Federal member in *either house,* who voted for the bill, and one of *five,* the whole number, in both houses who composed the Congress of that day. This was no very pleasant predicament, but it was unavoidable and I determined at once, to shew them that I would not desert the cause of my old friends and shrink from my old principles when forced into discussion. Accordingly yesterday we had a debate of a more political and party character than has yet occurd. Crittenden and Barbour bore down upon the poor sedition act with full broadsides, & all eyes were turned towards me, as if meaning that I must give "my reasons on compulsion" — I never had a more difficult or delicate part to act. But I got through, and in consequence have receivd from King, Hunter, Hanson and many others compliments which I can't repeat, but from which I infer, and that is all I care to infer, that I have not committed my friends or myself, by a deficiency of firmness or redundancy of zeal. The skirmish will be renewd in the Senate today, but I shall probably say no more. I think they will make a party question and carry it. It is of no great consequence, but who could have supposed that this dead Lion as he was thot to be, should have stirred up the ashes of an old flame that was extinguished 18 years ago.

Otis's speech had a more pronounced effect than he anticipated, for the proposal to reimburse Matthew Lyon for his sedition fine was defeated by a vote of 20 to 17.

It must be confessed, however, that Otis was no great success in the Senate. He spoke infrequently, served on no important committees, and seemingly took little interest in the vital questions of foreign policy that culminated in the Monroe Doctrine. His position in the Senate was, to be sure, very difficult. Insinuations to the effect that he and his state had been guilty of treason during the late war were frequently heard in debate. Conscious as Otis was of having exerted a restraining influence in a time of great popular excitement, this attitude on the part of his colleagues goaded him, first, into making a factual statement of the several regiments of regulars recruited in Massachusetts who fought with credit in the northern campaigns; and, second, into making public the Journal of the Hartford Convention and publishing a formal defense of it in the *National Intelligencer,* under the transparent pseudonym "One of the Convention." John Bailey, a clerk in the state department, inspired doubtless by John Quincy Adams, followed these articles with a clever exposition of the conspiracy theory which neutralized any beneficial effect that Otis's articles might have had on public opinion. Unfortunately it became a habit with Otis to publish defenses of the Convention. He should have laughed it off, as George Cabot did. And the same may be said of Adams's implacable vindictiveness against the Convention; he would better have buried his anti-Federal hatchet.

Otis flattered himself that he had succeeded in the principal object of his senatorial career, the softening of national prejudice against Massachusetts. "It being apparent that I who was regarded as the arch fiend have neither horns nor a cloven foot nor a smell of brimstone, but on the other hand some features of a friend to his country," he wrote, "it begins to be concluded that my Associates may not deserve the doom of eternal penance and that my State is not disgraced." Yet he never felt at home in the Senate, being "sensible of the shyness with which any measure is regarded, that comes from *Massachusetts.*" The administration refused to meet him halfway in his offer of the olive branch. And he failed to accomplish the main object for which he had accepted his seat — payment of the Massachusetts war claim.

This claim, it will be remembered, was for the services of state militia and citizens called out by Governor Strong during the war to protect the coast, but not placed under United States command. The sum demanded amounted to $843,500, and could only be paid through an act of Congress. Otis found it to be generally believed at Washington that these militiamen were called out not to defend the state but to fight the Federal Government. He made every effort to correct this erroneous impression, and in some measure succeeded; but opponents to the claim replied that its payment would acknowledge the anti-national principle that a state has the right to judge whether or not a militia requisition from the President be lawful.[1] No criticism of this correct constitutional attitude would now be possible, had the principle been applied consistently. But Connecticut, which had taken the same position during the war, obtained reimbursement for a similar claim after she had turned the Federalists out of office. Otis and his state, too, were given to understand that there would be no obstacle to their satisfaction if Massachusetts elected a Republican state government.

One would think that state pride would have forced every Massachusetts man to support the claim in the face of such insinuations, but the Republican congressmen from Massachusetts and Maine proved the principal obstacles in Otis's path. The cry that the Federalists had lost the state a million dollars was too valuable a portion of their political capital to be abandoned. It was owing to their opposition that Otis never dared to bring the claim to a vote in Congress. In the face of such difficulties, his efforts were fruitless. In an open letter on the subject, written shortly after his resignation from the Senate, he concluded:

> Whatever may be the fate of the claim, I venture to predict that any allowances made towards it will never be the fruit of disavowals or retractions, but a result of a conviction . . . If the State has a claim in law or equity upon the national treasury, it ought to be paid — but if otherwise, it is a nullity: And there is no power in the Constitution enabling Congress to convert an unfounded demand into a just claim, on condition of dis-

---

[1] This objection applied only to a portion of the claim, the greater part of which was for services of militia called out by the governor in 1814 to resist invasion, without any requisition from or conflict with the Federal Government.

avowing political heresies, or of any sort of truckling or humiliation, — no power to give us on our knees, what we are not
entitled to receive in the erect posture of an independent State.

Nevertheless, after Massachusetts had "confessed her sins" by
electing a Republican governor, more than half the claim was
"admitted" by the treasury department's auditors, and in 1830
the Commonwealth received $430,748.26.

MISSOURI COMPROMISE

We have now reached a period when questions connected with
Negro slavery were becoming important and disrupting. As a
United States senator, Otis participated in the great debate over
Missouri, the "fire bell in the night" which J. Q. Adams recog-
nized as a knell of the Union.

Otis viewed Negro slavery from the standpoint of a conservative
northern gentleman. He shared the moral repugnance to it common to almost every American in the eighteenth century, but his
conscience was not greatly troubled by the existence of wrongs
for which he did not feel responsible. In the first decade of the
century, his southern friends at Newport occasionally asked him to
help catch slaves who had absconded from the fashionable summer
resort to Boston. He seems not to have taken this duty very
seriously. One such request from Rutledge he turned over to a
pettifogger, and to Rutledge he wrote flippantly about a coachman and cook who had absconded together and settled in Boston,
where they were "in a better situation" than if "the man had run
away with a French milliner, and she with a French count." In
1819, after a visit to the plantation of a Mr. Fitzhugh near Washington, he wrote to Sally:

He has *eleven thousand* acres in a body and nearly 200 slaves.
If he would sell the latter and give away the land, he would be

richer and happier ten years hence than by keeping the whole. I told him so plainly, and he assented. But he has a reluctance at selling the poor creatures. It is natural to a good mind like his. Thank God slavery does not exist with us. "I would not have a slave to till my ground," etcetera.

As early as 1798, Otis had been forced to take sides on a slavery question. Debates on the subject in the Fifth and Sixth Congress attracted little attention at the time, but showed every shade of pro- and anti-slavery opinion that became common forty and fifty years later. Slavery had been excluded from all territory north of the Ohio River by the Northwest Ordinance of 1787, but no decision had yet been made for that part of the national domain south of the Ohio until, in March 1798, a bill was introduced in Congress to organize Mississippi as a territory. In this bill, slavery was not prohibited. George Thacher, a Maine Federalist far in advance of his time, moved to strike out this exception and fulfill the original purpose of Jefferson to prohibit slavery in all United States territory. John Rutledge denounced this proposition as an invitation to the blacks to cut their masters' throats, and reminded Thacher that suggestions such as his "did much mischief" to the Federal party in "certain parts of the Union." Otis wished all northern gentlemen "to manifest that it is not their disposition to interfere with the Southern States as to the species of property referred to," and argued that an extension of slavery would not increase the number of slaves. And when Thacher's amendment came to a vote, only twelve members answered yea; and slavery marched into the remaining territory of the United States, where it so fattened and prospered the master race that they fought a bitter war to perpetuate and extend their "peculiar institution."

In 1819 the same question arose as in 1798, whether Congress could or should permit a further extension of slavery; but the task of preventing it was bound to be more difficult than it had been twenty years earlier. Emigrant slaveholders had now passed the Mississippi and occupied the fertile valleys of its western tributaries. The application of Missouri for admission with a pro-slavery constitution, as the second state to be formed west of the Mississippi, brought on a struggle between North and South to establish their respective systems of free and slave labor in the vast territory of the Louisiana Purchase.

The issue was raised in the House of Representatives on 13 February 1819, when James Tallmadge of New York proposed an amendment to the pending Missouri bill, providing that further introduction of slaves into the new state be prohibited, and that all slaves born in the state after admission be freed at the age of twenty-five. He followed this proposal with a brilliant plea for the restriction of slavery on moral grounds. The Tallmadge amendment passed the House, but the Senate rejected it by a vote of 22 to 16. Otis voted with the majority. Thus he evaded a second opportunity to check the advance of slavery.

Not long after he realized his mistake; on this issue depended the question whether "Virginian" rule should be perpetuated, or the balance of power be righted in favor of the free states. He was converted, apparently, by a remarkable speech delivered by Rufus King in the Senate debate. Senator King showed that, by virtue of the federal ratio of representation, the southern whites already had twenty Representatives and electoral votes based on slave population; that the further extension of slavery would be unjust to the free states and prejudicial to their interests. Congress had not only the right but the duty of imposing a slavery restriction on a new state as well as on a territory.

Rufus King's speech aroused the spirit of the North. His arguments were flung back at Congress from mass meetings and legislative bodies in almost every northern state. Unfortunately, King's arguments had the ring of New England Federalism; they recalled those employed in the Report of the Hartford Convention. The South suspected that Rufus King was trying to revive the Federalist party on an anti-slavery platform.

Otis's attitude is clearly shown in his letters to William Sullivan.

He disdained to use the Missouri question to revive his old party; even advised the Federalists to keep in the background, in order to avoid such a suspicion.

I think the Massachusetts resolutions on the Missouri question are about right, and if they are to be passed, it is no matter with how much unanimity. My opinion is still the same that no good purpose would have been promoted by your being more prominent or zealous, but *tout au contraire* — Let the other white peopled States commit themselves as much as possible, and let us support them. Had we foreseen all that has happened, before I left home, I think I could have made some useful suggestions. But I am persuaded that if you had tried to lead, you would not have been follow'd with the same alacrity by the other States. Some of my best friends however think otherwise. It is a fact, though to my shame be it spoken, that none of us anticipated the magnitude and political tendency of this question last year. Mr. King admits that he did not — Indeed I first told him of the debate in the house, and he treated the question as of little or no importance, but of this more hereafter. It was the terror discovered by the opposition that opened my eyes, while on my road hither — I awoke as from a trance. The thing has now taken such a turn that first or last probably Missouri will gain her point, though the restriction will be applied to the territories. But we ought to have stopp'd it, *in toto* — and the sceptre would then have passed from the ancient dominion forever. As it is, her hand shakes — Pennsylvania unanimous against her is what she has never seen that I remember. It is a fearful looking for of judgment to her. But she may yet come upon her legs — The fear of federalism and of *Massts* federalism may save her. . . .

A speech of mine in the *Intelligencer* of 1 feby, I wish you would read. It produced some effect and was well received here though I dare say there are not ten men in my own state who have read it. . . . I feel as if I had been working hard again for my old friends and old principles. . . . I have the satisfaction of feeling well upon the occasion, & that is about as much of a reward as any federalist in our Country is entitled to expect. . . . The Massachusetts federalists are the most disinterested men on earth — They stand by and extol all merit but that of their own friends and citizens. You will find this true one of these days, with all your growing popularity, so dont learn to love it too well. . . .

yrs Sincerely H. G. OTIS

Washington, 13 Feb'y 1820

Dear Sir,

I send you a Richmond enquirer, whence you will be able to discern the movements in Virginia. The Caucus it seems in *that State,* will not nominate Munroe untill they ascertain that he will reject a bill compromising the Missouri question, should such a bill pass — Thus you see they are reviving the system of intimidation by which they have always governed the Union. The object is to shake weak and wavering folks in the House of Representatives. The times require great firmness and prudence on your part — Let the Democracy *lead,* and urge them into the foreground, and take care to *support* them — Let them be irretrievably committed on the slave question before the fears on this subject become merged in their fears of federalism which are always likely to predominate. — Dont permit violent expressions, or reflections, or recrimination to appear in the *Federal* papers; but let them shew a firm solemn determination — and if you can manage so as to cause to be inserted in the Democratic papers, essays a little higher spiced, I know of no injury that would come from it. — On this you should have an understanding among you. If the House stands firm, and Virginia resists compromise, and the bill is lost — Amen — I shall not be frightened at the prospect of consequences, — If the house gives way and the bill passes without restriction, their feet will be upon our necks forever. But for Gods sake, let our course be dignified and erect, but not marked by intemperate expressions or local caustic satire. Express always the desire of Union, which we all feel, but say boldly, that if it can't be had, but by a farther subversion of the political ballance, you are sorry but will not consent to that. See a little to the Salem paper and other federal Papers out of town, and persuade our friends in those concerns to give the editors this cue. You may show this to Mr.

Mills, to Perkins, and to any discreet friend, but dont quote me, nor print me. You will have the extracts printed of course.

Is it not a queer world? Just as I have demonstrated that Massachusetts did not mean to break up the Union; (for which by the way I have not yet had "woman, child or man" to say thank ye) it is about to be shown by Virginia that the thing itself is no crime.

Yours in haste, very truly   H. G. Otis.
If Harry is at hand, you may let him read this, as I cannot write to him today.
Burn this after you have done with it

Before Otis reached these alarming conclusions, the town of Boston, under the leadership of William Tudor, had placed itself in the forefront of the new anti-slavery movement. At a great meeting in the State House on 3 December 1819, Daniel Webster presented the anti-slavery case with his usual skill, and a strong memorial was sent to Congress. But before long, complaints were made that by influence from Washington — Otis's letters, evidently — anti-slavery was being hushed up in the Federalist press. Curiously enough, Jack Lowell, the fire-eater of 1814, and Josiah Quincy, the leader of the movement against admission of Louisiana, added their influence to that of Otis; whilst William Tudor and John Quincy Adams, both critics of the Hartford Convention for its supposed disunion tendencies, were almost ready for a secession of the North if Missouri entered the Union as a slave state. Otis's counsels prevailed and Massachusetts kept well in the background. But that did not succeed in laying the ghost of Federalism. Thomas H. Benton, on arriving at Washington in 1820, found the fear of a Federalist renaissance prevalent among northern Democrats, and believed that to be their chief reason for supporting the Compromise.

The result of this agitation was to key up members of the Sixteenth Congress, which first met in December 1819. And Maine was now ready for admission as a state. A bill to carry out the will of the down-easters passed the House on 3 January 1820 and, on arriving in the Senate, went to the judiciary committee, of which Otis was a member. Much against his wishes, the committee tacked the Maine bill to one admitting Missouri *with* slavery. This was a clever maneuver on the part of the pro-slavery forces; for as Massachusetts had given her assent to the separation of Maine only if Congress should agree by 4 March 1820, the friends of Maine were forced to support slavery in Missouri or leave the new eastern state stranded.

When the Maine-Missouri Bill was reported in the Senate on 13 January 1820, there commenced one of the most prolonged, significant and ably conducted debates that has ever occupied that body. First, an attempt was made by Otis and several other northern leaders to recommit and separate the two sections of the bill. Their efforts were defeated by a vote of 25 to 18. Then came the vital debate on the bill itself, and on renewed motions to impose a slavery restriction on Missouri. Otis made the greatest effort of his senatorial career in answer to William Pinkney's oration of 24 January. After the Marylander, a master of the flamboyant school of rhetoric, had held a huge audience spellbound for five hours, Otis's reply, delivery of which occupied the whole of next day's session, must have seemed an anticlimax. Long and pedantic, it opened with a minute exposition of the powers of Congress, and concluded with an exposure of the fallacy of the southern argument (which Otis had supported in 1798) that a diffusion of slavery would mitigate the acknowledged evils of the system. The speech had at least the merit of straightforwardness; for Otis, like Rufus King, acknowledged that his motives for opposing slavery extension were not moral but political:

> I do not wish to be distinguished as a zealot in the cause of emancipation. . . . I acknowledge too that I am not influenced by maxims or indications from any religious or moral code, that might serve as a rule for my private conduct, or for my opinions as a man, neither do the claims of humanity, as affecting

the wretched beings who are doomed to bondage, decide me in my course on this occasion. I look to it entirely as a question of policy, affecting the equitable right of the various parts of the Union, and the security and welfare of the whole people, now and hereafter.

For three more weeks the debate continued, growing more intense toward the close, with frequent threats of secession from the southern members if their wishes were not carried out. On 16 February 1820 the Maine-Missouri Bill passed, providing that slavery forever be prohibited in the territories north of 36 degrees 30 minutes (the southern boundary of Missouri), but not in Missouri itself. This was the best part of the famous Missouri Compromise. After complicated maneuvers, the Compromise passed on 20 March, Otis and Rufus King still voting against it; and Maine entered the Union by a separate act.

Otis's course during the Missouri controversy, although neither bold nor brilliant, seemed so good to his friends that they proposed to give him a testimonial dinner upon his return to Boston before the spring session ended. He declined; primarily on account of the recent death of his daughter Sally (Mrs. Israel Thorndike), but also, he wrote, because the "kindness and courtesy" received from fellow citizens in the course of his Boston walks were far more gratifying to him than any "splendid or emphatical display."

The Missouri Compromise did not put the problem to bed. When in December 1820 the new state applied to Congress for formal admission to the Union, a clause of her constitution forbade the admission of free Negroes from other parts of the United States. This, as northern leaders pointed out, violated that provision in the Federal Constitution guaranteeing to the citizens of each state the "privileges and immunities of citizens in the several states." The southern senators maintained that this did not apply; that Negroes were not and could not be "citizens." Otis, in a terse and forcible reply to Senator William Smith of South Carolina, insisted that free blacks had always been considered citizens in Massachusetts — an argument that resembled the dissenting opinion of Judge Curtis in the Dred Scott case. He doubtless remembered their helping to vote him into Congress in 1796. He repelled the insinuation that he sought to undermine slavery where it already existed. He would never countenance emancipation by violence:

> But, with these convictions, I shall strenuously and forever oppose the extension of slavery, and all measures which will subject a freeman, of whatever color, to the degradations of a slave. Believing, therefore, that every free citizen of color in the Union is joint tenant with myself in the public lands of Missouri, . . . and that he is entitled to his protection equally with those born to a happier destiny, I cannot consent to an act which would divest him of his property and rights, and interdict him from even passing into a country of which he is a legitimate coproprietor with myself.

Since the South controlled the Senate and the North the House, a deadlock lasted until 21 February 1821 when, by virtue of a compromise arranged by Henry Clay, Missouri was admitted to the Union with the understanding that the objectionable clause should not be construed so as to violate the Federal Constitution. On this measure, which passed both House and Senate, Otis and Rufus King voted nay because, as King wrote, "the pretended Concession, for it is revocable at pleasure," being a legislative act and not a constitutional amendment, "is itself of no value." Both men foresaw what actually happened, that the South would obtain new slave territory to the south and west by purchase or conquest, and then break the Missouri Compromise as soon as the northwest, which Charles Pinckney called "a vast tract, inhabited only by savages and wild beasts," became eligible for statehood.

CHAPTER XX

State Politics and Manufacturing

1822–1837, AET. 56–72

INDIAN SUMMER OF FEDERALISM

THE IMPRESSION conveyed by sundry historians that former members of the Hartford Convention were consigned to the politician's hell of complete oblivion is incorrect. As James Schouler put it, "Twenty-six respectable men, politically dead, . . . swung in their chains like Rizpah's sons"; and more recently, says Samuel F. Bemis, "The delegates from the Hartford Convention, the Essex Junto defeatists of 1814, slunk home in obscurity, speedily to become forgotten men." On the contrary, their local prestige remained undiminished; Otis, far from slinking home in obscurity, was reëlected to the state senate in April. All his colleagues who wanted election or a political appointment obtained it. Five besides Otis served in state legislatures (Benjamin Hazard winning no fewer than 25 elections after 1814); six others were elected to constitutional conventions, Wilde became a justice of the supreme judicial court, Longfellow won an election to Congress, Otis and Goddard were chosen mayors of their respective cities; and Otis, as we have seen, went to the United States Senate. The governorship of Massachusetts remained in "safe" hands. Canny Caleb Strong won his eleventh election in 1815 against the "renegade" Samuel Dexter, but refused to run again. Otis having (as we have seen) declined the honor, the Federalists put up General John Brooks, a ruddy, genial veteran of the War of Independence. He defeated Dexter again. In 1817 the Republicans nominated a supposed hero of the late war, General Henry Dearborn; he lost

heavily to Brooks, after which President Monroe "took care" of
the General by appointing him minister to Portugal. Senator Otis
voted against confirmation on the ground that Dearborn was a
notorious nepotist — "His business has been . . . to 'cluck' in all
his family chickens to live in the barnyard."

For governor, the Republicans next tried Benjamin W. Crowninshield of Salem, who had been Madison's navy secretary; in two
tries he did even worse than Dearborn. Finally they put up Dr.
William Eustis, a surgeon in the Continental Army, secretary of
war in Madison's cabinet, and minister to the Netherlands. Under
his leadership the Republican vote for governor fell to an all-time
low, Brooks being reëlected handily. This era has aptly been
called Federalism's Indian summer.

Otis resigned his United States senatorial seat 30 May 1822,
almost a year before the end of his term. He had threatened to
do so two years earlier but forebore because the general court was
not in session, so no successor could be appointed. He found this
service "unprofitable exile" from Boston. Sally could not accompany her husband to Washington for every session of the Senate,
and he was miserable without her. Sick of beating his brains
against a stone wall of prejudice in furthering the Massachusetts
war claim, Harry longed to return to Sally and his beloved home,
which still housed a bevy of children. It sounds odd today for a
United States senator to resign, but in that era many did. When
the Senate numbered only forty-eight at full strength — a meager
audience for an orator — its debates were so ill reported that
senators who wished to circulate the text of a speech had to pay
for the printing. Few stuck it out term after term until they died
or were defeated, as has been the custom since 1870. Two senators
from New York, for instance, resigned their senatorial seats to
become respectively mayor of New York City and its postmaster.
Of Otis's sixteen Massachusetts predecessors in the Senate, only
three finished one term; and only Tim Pickering enjoyed more
than one. Not until the Senate attracted giants of debate such as

Clay, Calhoun, Benton and Webster, did it acquire greater prestige than the House.

So, Otis again transferred his talents from the national capital
to "the Hub of the Solar System" as Dr. Holmes would shortly
name Boston. Municipal problems had always interested Harry.
Since 1784 at least five attempts to obtain a municipal government
for Boston, promoted by him and other Federalist leaders, had
been thwarted by popular attachment to the traditional town
meeting. By 1821, however, it was clear that something must be
done. Faneuil Hall could not hold more than a fraction of the
voting population, hence the government and finances of a town
of 45,000 inhabitants were controlled by the men who came early
to secure places near the moderator, and choose the officers: selectmen, school committee, the town clerk and treasurer, and traditional but obsolete offices such as cullers of dry fish and surveyors
of hemp and wheat. So far these early birds had invariably been
leading Federalists with a sense of responsibility; but (horrible to
contemplate!) might not Democrats or other low fellows of the
baser sort get up a little earlier, seize control of the town, and
profit by the opportunities for corruption that so loose a system of
government offered?

At a town meeting of 22 October 1821, a committee of thirteen,
including Webster, Sullivan, Prescott, Quincy and Lemuel Shaw,
was appointed to report on the advisability of making Boston a
city. Another town meeting accepted a rough outline of city
government on the last day of December, a popular vote adopted
it a week later, and the general court issued a city charter which
provided for an annually elected mayor, a board of aldermen chosen
at large, and a common council of delegates from the wards. William Sullivan wrote to Otis (still at Washington) that this pattern
pleased the people because it reproduced the familiar form of
government. The senator, however, found much to criticize. He
observed that the office of mayor was superfluous, were he subject
to "advice and consent" of the board of aldermen; the office could

only be made "respectable" by giving the mayor power. He opposed abandoning the old method of holding state and federal elections in Faneuil Hall in favor of separate polling places, since this change might break the power of the Federal party. "It is easier to manage the town of Boston," he wrote, "by a Lancastrian system[1] of political discipline than to institute numerous schools." In Faneuil Hall every voter had to stand up and be counted; the leaders shuddered at the thought of ward polling places.

Earliest name mentioned for the mayoralty was that of Harrison Gray Otis. Sullivan promised to "mount the stump" for him, if he desired to "live in the mansion house," and Thomas H. Perkins formally inquired whether he would accept the nomination. Since Otis had decided not to finish his senatorial term, he found the offer attractive. He therefore promised to "yield to the wishes of his fellow citizens," if a "general unsolicited sentiment" prevailed among them that his "humble services might be useful in the organization of the new government." He did not wish to "run against any other Gentleman of the Federal party who might be thought of."

Unfortunately for Otis's municipal aspirations, a movement known as the Middling Interest sprang up at this time. Led by Roulstone, the riding academy proprietor, it represented the "little people" — small shopkeepers, mechanics and laborers. These, the bone and sinew of the Federalist party, resented the gentlemen who gave them few offices and disregarded their interests. In particular they objected to a law forbidding the erection of wooden buildings more than ten feet high within city limits, which Otis considered necessary to prevent cheap construction and devastating fires. This "revolutionary movement," as Otis called it, attached itself to Josiah Quincy, another aspirant for the mayoralty, and proposed his name at the Federalist nominating caucus on 4 April. Otis received 175 votes to Quincy's 170 and received

---

1 This referred to the English schoolman Joseph Lancaster, who taught hundreds of children their letters in one school by means of monitors and strict discipline.

the official nomination; but the Middling Interest refused to accept the result. Claiming that they had been "robbed," they held a caucus the same evening, nominated Quincy in opposition to Otis, and Quincy accepted.

The astonishment and indignation of Boston Federalism at Quincy's "bolt" may well be imagined, and Otis commented acidly, "As he gets nothing by being a great man among gentlemen, he will try his hand by shewing himself a good one among whores and rogues." Harry's friends were too indignant to withdraw his name as he wished, so there resulted the undignified spectacle of a United States senator and a distinguished ex-member of Congress competing for a mayoralty. Quincy actually spoiled Otis's chances without gaining anything for himself; he polled 1736 votes; Otis, 1384; scattering, 580. No candidate having received a majority, as required by the city charter, there was no choice. Both Otis and Quincy then withdrew, and at a second polling on 16 April, John Phillips, a Federalist acceptable to the Middling Interest, was elected first mayor of the City of Boston.

Otis showed such mortification at this, his first defeat since 1795, as to move that kindly Democratic politician Martin Van Buren to write: "I have frequently figured to myself the distress he must have undergone & from my heart felt sorry for him, for with all his excentricities & imperfections there is something about him which I like & especially his uncommon devotedness to his family."

RUNNING FOR GOVERNOR

In 1821 the District of Maine had become the State of Maine, and she elected as her first governor William King, who had helped Otis to pull off the Bingham land deal in the state senate. Josiah Quincy thought that the separation of Maine would make Massachusetts "a snug little Federal state for the rest of our lives." How

William Eustis, by Gilbert Stuart.

wrong he was, as usual! Unseasonable snow would soon bury the brilliant foliage of Federalism's Indian summer under a white funeral pall.

There were no signs of it in 1822. Massachusetts elected Federalist state administrations with monotonous regularity after the war. Governor Brooks, dignified and efficient, gave general satisfaction, and a Federalist majority in both houses afforded the honest, stable government that the people wanted. But the governor, having nearly completed a seventh term at the age of seventy, refused to run again in 1823. Otis now intimated a desire to succeed Brooks, his friends were willing, and he easily obtained the Federalist nomination. It looked like a pushover for popular, silver-tongued Harry, especially since the Republicans nominated seventy-seven-year-old Dr. William Eustis, President Madison's notoriously incompetent secretary of war, after having been defeated thrice by Brooks. And, to revive the patriotic associations of the name Otis, Harry's friend William Tudor brought out his *Life of James Otis* just as the campaign began.

The opposition now prepared for a mighty effort, since experience showed that when Massachusetts elected a governor she usually reëlected him for as long as he cared to serve. Eustis, as a veteran of the War of Independence, a favorite town meeting speaker, and withal an eminent physician and polished gentleman, made an unexpectedly strong candidate. Otis, on the contrary, proved to be vulnerable. He had voted for Burr in 1801. As a proprietor of the Charles River Bridge he had fought the building of a free bridge to Charlestown. He had been retained by the selectmen and school committee of Boston in 1818 to oppose a movement for establishing public primary schools. He had invited John Henry the British spy to dine. He had voted on both sides of the Missouri question, and his vote against the tariff bill of 1820 showed that he was no friend to domestic manufactures. And, most heinous of all, he was a leader of the treasonable Hartford Convention!

Who was at *Hartford?*
I, says SIR HARRY
At Hartford did tarry,
And I was at Hartford.

Whom met you at Hartford?
Three and twenty *wise men*
Separation devising,
These met I at Hartford.

And honest men frown whenever they mention
The names of Sir Harry and the Hartford Convention!

The people of Massachusetts knew the history of the Hartford Convention too well to believe the absurd charges brought up against it, but they were unwilling to vote for a candidate simply to vindicate the Convention, which is what the Federalists demanded in 1823. The *Centinel* opened the campaign with a series of questions and answers on the Hartford Convention; the Federalist central committee issued the *Short Account* by Theodore Lyman, Jr., of the Otis clan, and the Federalist press overflowed with apologetic literature. A backlash against Hartford smugness doubtless helped to defeat Otis; but the main factors, in the opinion of contemporaries, were the college and religious issues.

Clergy and leading citizens of "Old Hampshire" (Hampshire, Hampden and Franklin Counties) had long been trying to obtain a collegiate charter for their favorite school, Amherst Academy. Every previous attempt had been defeated in the legislature owing (they believed) to the influence of Harvard, Yale and Williams graduates who felt that New England already had enough colleges. After Dr. Eustis had pledged his support to an Amherst College charter, the friends of the institution decided to go all out for the Republican ticket. Under the lead of Samuel F. Dickinson (Emily's grandfather), they initiated a whispering campaign against Otis on the ground that he was "notorious for his profanity and disregard of the Sabbath," a radical in religion, and a Harvard snob who would deny college education to honest farmers' sons of the Connecticut Valley. Republican newspapers appealed to the orthodox Congregational clergy on the ground that Otis was a Unitarian, and, even worse, "one of the corporation of Harvard University, which is well known to be devoted to the propagation of a particular creed, to have exerted an undue and highly prejudicial influence to depress other literary institutions." This sort of talk appealed to simple voters, and meshed in with a new religious controversy inside the Congregational fold.

Deep resentment had been aroused among Trinitarians because Chief Justice Isaac Parker of the Commonwealth, in the case of Baker *v.* Fales (1820), had declared that any town parish which wished to elect a Unitarian minister could legally do so, even if the church (the communicants) opposed. Parker's decision caused a general secession by orthodox Trinitarians from parishes which had "gone to hell," and the seceders, who in general were the less affluent members of Yankee society, had to go to the expense of building a new meeting house on the village green, and supporting a second minister. This created a social rift almost as deep and bitter as the earlier political one. By a curious paradox, the most conservative Federalists of eastern Massachusetts were Unitarians; they controlled the government of Harvard College, and Otis served on both Harvard governing boards. Hence *odium theologicum* entered into this spring state election, making it more bitter and nasty than any since 1812. Otis polled 1684 more votes than Brooks had in 1822, but Eustis increased his vote some sixty percent and beat the Federalist champion by a plurality of more than four thousand. Old Hampshire went Republican for the first time in history, as did Essex County, where the Amherst alumni put on a strong campaign. A study of the figures indicates that thousands of citizens who had not troubled to go to the polls during the last few years went this time and voted for Eustis.

Otis, deeply mortified, asked the winner when they met on

'Change a few days later, "How are you pleased with your new party, Mr. Eustis? I understand you have joined the Orthodox?" For once our famous wit did not have the last word. The Doctor snapped back: "I am not fully initiated, but I believe in the doctrine of *election!*" Emerson relates another amusing anecdote in his Journal. Otis and an old Harvard classmate, Ambrose Spencer, who had been unceremoniously dumped from the chief justiceship of New York, met in the summer of 1823. Each reported the conversation to their common friend Judge Joseph Lyman of Northampton. "I said to him," said Judge Spencer, " 'Well, my old friend, we are both disappointed — I have fallen and you have failed to rise,' and I was very much mortified to have said this, as I found it touched Mr. Otis to the quick." But Otis, dining with Lyman shortly after, said "that it really made him ashamed to see how much Judge Spencer was offended by so trifling a thing as this political disappointment!" The truth is (Lyman told Emerson), "Both felt it very much."

Otis, years later, admitted his mortification to his minister Samuel K. Lothrop, but acknowledged that he had been "a happier and a better man" for his defeat. So the old Otis optimism triumphed; but in the meantime it was tough not to be governor or anything official, when Lafayette paid his last visit to Boston in 1824. Otis gloomily viewed the ceremonies on the Common from the windows of 45 Beacon Street and, if invited, refused to attend those at Bunker Hill and elsewhere.

FINIS FEDERALISM

The unseasonal (or, some will say, long overdue) frost of Otis's defeat terminated the golden Indian summer of Federalism. Governor Eustis, profiting by Gerry's mistake, avoided a general proscription of officeholders, but offended the Federalists by a scathing denunciation of their war policy in his inaugural address.

"These measures and this course had cast a reproach on the good name of the State," remarked the governor, "which is now disavowed and removed. Massachusetts is at length restored to the American family. Her character is redeemed in the estimation of the patriots of our own country, and of every statesman in Europe."

Otis wisely refused renomination in 1824, but with singular lack of wisdom published in the *Centinel* during the campaign, and also in a formidable pamphlet, another defense of the Hartford Convention. The first installment consisted mostly of sarcastic comments on Governor Eustis's address, such as these:

> His Excellency, by throwing into one dark group the deformities of the factious monster, has presented to the world the picture of a degenerate State, resembling the decayed and rotten republics of which we read, in the last periods of their decline. It is true, however, that with the pretentions of a skilful painter, he aims to relieve the *obscuro* by the *claro*, and exclaims (in substance) in a sort of gubernatorial ecstacy,
>
> > "What though your sins were many and were great,
> > What though they shook the basis of the State,"
>
> Yet now you have made me Governor, your sins which were of scarlet, are made as white as snow, and you are readmitted to the "American family." *Jam nova progenies cœlo demittitur alto!*

Apart from this *jeu d'esprit,* Otis's *Letters in Defence of the Hartford Convention* are turgid, rambling and inconsistent. They add nothing to the history of the Hartford Convention, and did their author no good.

Massachusetts Federalism gradually blended into the conservative wing of the old Jefferson party. In the four-cornered contest of 1824 for the presidency, among J. Q. Adams, Henry Clay, William H. Crawford and Andrew Jackson, New England without distinction of party supported her native son. A few old Essex leaders such as Pickering, who never forgave Adams for his sin of apostasy in 1807, united with radical Democrats to support an "unpledged electoral ticket" which would probably have voted for Crawford if chosen; but the Adams ticket carried Massachusetts by an overwhelming majority. In state elections no Federalist stood for governor after 1824. Chaos reigned in elections for state senators and representatives; over 800 persons received votes to represent Boston in 1826. During the following summer, the Federal party delivered its swan song.

Since Daniel Webster had been promoted to the United States Senate, it was necessary to hold a by-election to choose a new congressman. A Federalist caucus was accordingly summoned, to which the central committee presented the name of Benjamin Gorham, expecting this nomination would go through in the usual cut-and-dried fashion. Greatly to their surprise, an unknown young man mounted a bench and harangued the caucus in favor of Harrison Gray Otis. Although he broke down in the midst of his speech, and had to read the remainder from a manuscript hitherto concealed in his hat, this obscure champion developed so strong a sentiment for Otis that the caucus adjourned until the veteran politician could be consulted. The name of this bold youth was William Lloyd Garrison. Although but twenty-two years of age, and a humble journeyman printer, he had long been an ardent admirer of Otis, and had published a glowing panegyric of him when a candidate for governor. But young Garrison's efforts on this occasion were in vain, for Otis refused absolutely to reënter the political arena. Benjamin Gorham, finally nominated, defeated both the Adams and the Jackson candidates for Congress. This was the last occasion on which the Boston Federalists acted together under their old banner.

In the presidential election of 1828 the Federalists played the unhappy role of scapegoat, the ownership of which each side attempted to force upon the other. The Boston *Statesman,* representing the hungry office-seeking element in the Democratic party, attempted to prove that John Quincy Adams was a Hartford Convention Federalist in disguise, and that his candidacy was a Federalist plot to revive the "reign of terror" of the elder Adams. During the month before election day, its pages became fairly spotty with "Hartford Convention" in italics and capitals. At the same time the *Statesman*'s only ally in the Boston press was the *Jackson Republican,* founded and edited by Theodore Lyman, Jr., kinsman both of Otis and of Timothy Pickering. The clientele of this sheet came almost exclusively from that class of old Federalists for whom John Quincy Adams's defection overshadowed any live issue of the campaign. On 29 October President Adams published in the *National Intelligencer,* in reply to certain imputations against his motives for deserting Federalism, that in 1808 the object of the Massachusetts Federalist leaders "was, and had been for several years a dissolution of the Union, and the establishment of a separate confederation." Boston was still gasping for breath over this startling announcement when it learned that Daniel Webster, one of Adams's most eminent supporters, was about to bring a libel suit against Theodore Lyman, Jr., for casually mentioning him in the *Jackson Republican* as one of the old Federalists whom the President intended to impugn.

A more complicated and ridiculous political situation would be difficult to imagine. One Jackson paper accusing Adams of Federalism; Adams charging the Federalists with treason; and an Adams Federalist suing a Jackson Federalist for implying that he was among the traitors! Otis wrote to George Harrison that he considered Lyman's publication "indiscreet and indecorous," but that Webster was "ill-judged to make a fuss about it." As a protest a number of "Federal young men" who had been supporting Adams nominated a Federalist ticket of presidential electors, having at the head Otis and William Prescott and including three other members of the Hartford Convention. It received the pitiful total of 156 votes in Boston and none, apparently, in the rest of the state. Adams swept the city and state as cleanly as in 1824; but Andrew Jackson was elected President by a majority of 95 electoral votes.

The Federalist party, then, ceased to exist as a state organization in 1825, and as a local Boston organization within three years. In other states there were still Federalists (Roger B. Taney and James Buchanan started their political careers as such), but these were mostly engaged in trying to make patronage deals with Adams or Jackson. The eleventh-hour list of presidential electors in 1828, headed by Otis, was, so far as I know, the last ticket ever voted for that bore the name of the once powerful party of Washington and Hamilton.[1]

Even before Adams lost to Jackson, most Federalists had joined the National Republican, later renamed the Whig party; and the Whigs were regularly attacked by the Democrats for absorbing "Hartford Convention Federalists." But the old party survived as a social cult. Ancient Federalist leaders and their descendants long occupied a position in New England corresponding to that of prominent Confederate families in the South.

Adams's accusation of disunion against the leaders of Massachusetts Federalism left a heritage of bad feeling in Boston after the election of 1828. It started a controversy, in which Otis bore a prominent part, and brought forth charges and counter-charges which Henry Adams collected fifty years later and published in his *Documents Relating to New-England Federalism*. Otis and twelve other Federalists challenged the President to produce names and facts, mainly in the hope of refuting once and for all the secession charge, never before made upon such high authority. Adams replied evasively shortly after Christmas, 1828. Otis and four supporters then published an "Appeal to the People of Massachusetts" disavowing knowledge of or connection with any plan, plot or party to dissolve the Union. The President, smarting over his defeat for a second term, and ascribing this counter-blast to a desire to humiliate him, prepared a lengthy "Reply to the Appeal"

---

[1] Among the Otis papers for 1843 is a broadside signed by Robert Anderson of James City, Va., nominating himself for Congress and Otis and Louis McLean for the presidency and vice presidency, on a platform composed of the old Federalist principles of 1798! This was undoubtedly the work of an isolated crank, not a late survival of the party.

directed mainly against Otis and filled with unjust aspersions on his character and motives. But by the time this paper was completed, Adams, advised by his friends that his language was too personal and bitter to create a good impression, decided to suppress it. And (wrote Henry Adams), "It was not long before the patriotic course of Mr. Otis, at the time of the nullification excitement, led Mr. Adams to rejoice at the suppression and to look upon Mr. Otis with more kindly eyes."

Even though Adams suppressed his "Reply to the Appeal," he did more than anyone else to solidify the Hartford Convention myth. People naturally said, "Mr. Adams must know; this was his community, these traitors were his old friends." Actually, Adams had been absent in Europe — mostly in Russia — from 1809 to 1814, and knew very little of what went on in Massachusetts; his "Reply to the Appeal" is more rhetorical than factual. Although every reputable American historian for the last century and a half has discounted the myth, it is too popular, especially among Yankee-haters and New England-baiters, ever to die. When Colonel McCormick edited the Chicago *Tribune* he used to refer to New England as "the Hartford Convention states," and even raked up the "Henry plot" of 1812. President Lyndon B. Johnson in a press conference of 17 November 1967, contrasting his plight over Vietnam to that of President Madison, declared that the Bay State commission of February 1815 came from Boston "to secede," but "didn't quite make it" owing to Jackson's victory. The President contributed a new trimming, to the effect that Otis, Perkins and Sullivan dropped in at the White House next morning "to congratulate" Madison and to say "they thought he was right all along."

Otis, characteristically, again proffered the olive branch to Adams, eliciting angry protests from some of his old friends, to one of whom (George Harrison), he wrote on 20 May 1833:

I am told you are curious and puzzled for an explanation of
my call on J Q A last year. It was the result of reflection and
principle. In regard to the Bank and other great measures, he
had conducted himself with propriety and ability. I knew he
wanted to bury the hatchet, because *entre nous,* he sent me word
to that effect. The state of the nation, makes it desireable to
strengthen the hands and encourage the hearts of all who are
able and disposed to render services to the Country, on great
occasions, although reliance is not to be placed upon their consistency, and as I could have no personal or selfish motive, & he
must know it, I gave him a call which he return'd & there the
matter drop'd.

And in 1840 Adams was invited to Thanksgiving dinner at No.
45 Beacon Street!

Otis, unfortunately, would not leave the Hartford Convention to
the "verdict of history." He never could resist an opportunity to
sound off on the patriotism of that virtuous if despised conclave.
Even when called upon to address a rally of Boston's volunteer fire-
men, or some such association, he would conclude with a ringing
peroration, declaring that when admitted to the Assembly of the
Just made Perfect ("if such should be my lot") he would confidently expect to find the spirit of every deceased member of the
Hartford Convention occupying a seat near the Throne of Grace!

MANUFACTURING AND THE TARIFF

Commercial and free-trading interests having dominated New
England under the Federalist party, some time elapsed before the
rising manufacturers became sufficiently powerful to influence
state politics. Otis, when in the Senate, wrote to his wife about
the Baldwin tariff bill of 1820 that he considered it contrary to
"the interests of Boston and indeed of Commerce," and his nega-
tive vote in the Senate killed it. Massachusetts members of Congress joined those from the South in voting against the tariffs of

1824 and 1828. In the meantime, New England completed an economic revolution which had begun during, and as a direct result of, embargoes and war. While John Lowell was threatening the Union if Madison did not stop persecuting New England shipping, his brother Francis Cabot Lowell made economic history by establishing the first complete cotton manufactory, with power looms, at Waltham, Massachusetts. And a vast extension of the factory system began with the establishment of cotton mills in the newly founded city of Lowell in 1823.

Otis early fell in with this movement. Before 1823 he had purchased a majority interest, worth about $100,000, in the Taunton Manufacturing Company, a consolidation of several cotton, woolen and rolling mills; and he put his son James William in charge of it. Also, from time to time, Otis acquired large blocks of stock in the Chicopee, Neponset, Hampshire, Bristol Print, Perkins, and Amesbury manufacturing companies. He wrote to George Harrison on 21 March 1823:

There has been a curious *"revival"* in the spirits of men and a reaction in the affairs and business of this city which is quite remarkable. Two years ago our sun had sunk never to rise again, as many said and more feared. Manufacturing stock with its liabilities made a man to be considered so much minus, — All is now reversed and the stocks as well as spirits have risen *inordinately*. I have never known an impression so deep and general in favor of the prospects as well as actual prosperity of the business people. No doubt it is exceedingly overrated, but the change is certainly for the better. Those who held on to their stock in companies whose capital was paid have all come well upon their legs. I am offered 10 per cent above par for my stock in Chicopee & Amesbury of which I hold 38000 dollars. Last year I could not have sold it for more than 50 per cent. It was as good then in fact as it is now — It gives 10 per cent, and I mean to hold it. Taunton in fact is doing *better* than any of them — Yet the market value is yet less. It is amazing to see what is done by the puff on one hand and the panic on the other.

The following year Henry Clay promoted in Congress the policy of internal improvements and protection to home industries, which he christened the "American System," and in Boston the protection issue soon dominated congressional elections. Otis, then in his second term as mayor of Boston, took an active part in the congressional campaign of 1830 in favor of Nathan Appleton, the protection candidate, and presented in a speech many of the time-worn arguments for protection that the Republican party used to dish up every two years. He first replied to the assertion of sundry newspapers that His Honor the Mayor should not interfere in national politics. "I did not understand," he said, "that . . . while every man in the city showed his colors, it was my duty to sit in the Mayor's chair like a reverend Owl brooding over chaos amid the strife of the political elements" — a sentiment in which Mr. Otis's modern successors will heartily concur. He explained his change of attitude, as Webster had already done, on the ground that New England capital had been kicked into manufacturing by the policy of the Federal Government and now depended on a continuance of that policy. *"Tempora mutantur,"* Otis wrote to Henry Clay two years later, "and I am among those who have been coerced by the policy of government *mutari in illis."*

Jacksonian Democracy having adopted no definite attitude on the tariff question, Otis thought best to seek tariff favors from the powers that were, rather than commit himself irrevocably to Henry Clay. His bitter controversy with Adams also tended to attach him to "Old Hickory." Shortly after Jackson's first inauguration in 1829, Otis wrote to Secretary of State Martin Van Buren, expressing his confidence in the General and offering him the use of his mansion in the event of a presidential tour of New England. In 1831–32 he addressed ten-page letters to Jackson's secretary of the treasury, pointing out that many old Federalists could be attached permanently to Jackson's party by tariff favors and a conservative attitude toward the United States Bank. At the same time, he kept in close touch with the leading National

Republicans in Congress. Among his papers for 1832 are letters from Daniel Webster, Henry A. S. Dearborn, Nathan Appleton, and John Davis, informing him of the progress of the tariff bill of that year. He even made a short visit to Washington, in order to consult with the leaders.

South Carolina, at this stage, was preparing to nullify the protective system by a practical application of the principles supported by Otis between 1809 and 1815. If Otis saw the similarity, he did not acknowledge it; like all exponents of state rights, he denied the doctrine when applied by others contrary to the interests of his section. South Carolina, on her part, was loath to appeal for precedent to the "Patriotick Proceedings" or to the Hartford Convention, which her statesmen had been accustomed to denounce as treasonable. Otis's opinion of state rights as construed in the South is expressed in a letter to George Harrison of 20 November 1832, four days before the South Carolina convention passed its ordinance of nullification:

> Public affairs will give you and me who had resolvd to think no more of them, sufficient excitement for the rest of our lives, I fear. I never remember a gloom, foreboding & uncertainty respecting public affairs, so general since Lexington battle, when I was 9 years old. That we shall have treason and insurrection in fact, I can no longer doubt. If called by their right names, and treated with their appropriate remedies, they will be put down, and *the consequences of an unsuccessful revolt will be more beneficial than all other measures* to bring & for a time to keep everything right. But if tamper'd with, as I fear they will be — "My native land good-night."

President Jackson struck a vigorous blow for the Union in his proclamation of 11 December 1832 against the nullifiers. In order to show the President that Boston, although opposed to him in politics, would back him up on this occasion Otis "went to work *con amore,*" so he wrote to George Harrison, to organize a mass meeting in Faneuil Hall, acted as presiding officer and addressed an enthusiastic assembly with a speech second only to Webster's. The rest of his letter to George Harrison of 20 February 1833 is full of unconscious humor for readers who have followed his state rights career during the War of 1812:

> The proclamation of Jackson was one of those measures which a federal saint of the old school has a right to call providential, and which a federal sinner may regard as most wonderfully opportune and happy for the Country. The absurd heresies respecting State rights, consolidation, secession, &c, which were from the first the sources of our dangers were revived under circumstances favorable to their spread, and men were growing wild with these fantasies. A small bias in a wrong direction would have given a tremendously dangerous turn to affairs in the South — and at this juncture, to see such a *poser* to the State rights sticklers from such a source was certainly a source of great joy and comfort to me. . . . Thousands who would have regarded the doctrines as diabolical if broached by a federalist, will now read, ponder & inwardly digest and the true character of State sovereignty will come to be better understood. For my part I thank old Hick'y, tho' I never conceived that such wholesome waters would come from a bitter fountain.
>
> But with all this we have & shall have troubles eno'. "The South when they cease to govern will refuse to be governed." This is an old maxim of the "Boston Port." They are united by their black belt & are an overmatch for us as yet.

While the President and South Carolina shouted defiance at one another, the more cautious members of Congress, led by Henry Clay, began to revise the tariff in order to avoid a clash of arms. Otis regarded compromise with dismay, as this letter to Henry A. S. Dearborn of 29 December 1832 indicates:

> . . . Taking it for granted, that some reduction in the scale of protective duties must sooner or later, (and indeed very soon) be made in compliance with the plausible tho' unsound notion, that import duties should not exceed the amount required for

mere revenue, the question arises, whether it be expedient for the present Congress to act in effecting such reduction, rather than leave it to their successors. To bring my mind to a state which I consider proper to dispose of that question, I first ask myself whether any reduction made *at this time* in the Tariff system, will not be forever claimed & considered, & justly too, as a concession made to an Organized Conspiracy to oppose the laws, securing to the Conspirators an effective triumph, of most dangerous example, furnishing a fatal precedent, that will be often resorted to, for bullying, browbeating and threatening the non-slaveholding States in all future as it has been in all past time into an abandonment of their own and the adoption of the Virginia policy and doctrines. . . . Give alms to a beggar who wears a drawn sword in his hand and tell him if you please it is *pour l'amour de Dieu,* he will laugh in his sleeve and impute it to *au peur de l'Epée,* and he will never beg afterwards without a sword. So it will be with the Cavaliers and Wrongheads of the South, who are all united against us in fact. Rice birds like other birds will flock together and crow at the victory they have obtained. The men who with an effrontery without parallel, have given to treasonable conspiracy the sacriligeous mask of holy insurrection, will in all time hereafter be quoted and canonized as the Pyms & Hampdens & Sydneys of an oppress'd people by the advocates of State rights if their exactions are complied with, while they preserve this offensive & menacing attitude.

Events of the next thirty years proved Otis a good prophet. Nevertheless, his affairs prospered. On 9 January 1835 he wrote to Samuel Crocker, fellow director of the Taunton Manufacturing Company:

The rumour of your profits will make people *delirious.* I hope however you will make hay while the sun shines. . . . I should have voted with you for 15 per Cent, though I want the 20 enough — But it seems too good. You remember my fears and prophecies about the former 20 per cent. If I could afford it, I would nail up the post notes at the side of my drawer, as they nail up a horseshoe sometimes, to keep the Devil out.

When the panic of 1837 broke, Otis estimated the value of his property at $533,000, of which about $400,000 had been invested in Boston real estate and the rest in cotton mills. And he lived through the following depression without serious loss. In 1846, two years before he died, a pair of enterprising Bostonians brought out a gossipy pamphlet listing the "first men of Boston" and guessing at their wealth. Otis came thirteenth on the list with an estimated fortune of $800,000. In that happy era for the rich when there was neither income tax nor inheritance tax, we have no means of checking the accuracy of this gossip; but according to family tradition it is approximately correct, and the bulk of it was still invested in Boston real estate.

Otis was no philanthropist. His contributions to the good causes of his day were meager, in view of his income; and he left no foundation as did his contemporaries Lowell, Perkins, Dwight and Carney, to keep the name of Otis in grateful remembrance. An overwhelming desire to leave his descendants well off was responsible. His will, dated 29 January 1846, with a codicil of 8 April 1848, left several stores on Cornhill to the three sons of Harry Jr., those for Harrison Gray Otis III (who had settled in Switzerland) being placed in trust for his benefit. Since his daughters Elizabeth and Sally had married men of wealth, he left nothing substantial to their families; but as a remembrance bequeathed a few shares of cotton-mill stock and a small sum of money to each grandchild. The rest of his estate, real and personal, he divided equally among sons James, William and Allyne and daughter Sophia Ritchie; and Sophia's share he placed in trust for her benefit. He did not inaugurate one of the "great American fortunes" that the less fortunate like to gloat over. Some of the Otis descendants were prudent investors, and others became lavish spenders; but none were ever able to attain a scale of living in our so-called affluent society comparable to what Harrison Gray Otis enjoyed at 45 Beacon Street.

CHAPTER XXI

Mayoralty and Slavery

1829–1835, AET. 64–70

THIRD MAYOR OF BOSTON

OTIS FELT VINDICATED by public opinion, and consoled for his earlier defeat, by being elected the third mayor of the City of Boston. Josiah Quincy, having aroused opposition by his sweeping reforms and increased taxes, was opposed for reëlection in December 1828 by two other candidates; and, as in the first municipal election, nobody obtained a majority at the first trial. In the meantime a movement had begun to "draft" Otis. A letter purporting to be from a Jeffersonian Republican who wished Otis's talents to be used by the city appeared in the Boston *Courier* of 8 December. "I like the honesty of this man," announced the writer. "I admire his consistency and genius. . . . Otis in his latter, as well as in his earlier days, is destined to prove an honor and an ornament to the city of his birth." When a second balloting failed to break the deadlock, Otis accepted nomination by a non-partisan caucus, and won at the third trial by a fair majority.

This election marks the restoration of his former popularity and the beginning of another epoch of his life, when occasional public employment and frequent participation in public discussions relieved an affluent retirement.

The mayoralty of Boston, in the years 1829–1831, was the last public office held by Harrison Gray Otis. His administration is not to be compared with that of Quincy who is always referred to as the "Great Mayor." Otis, when being inaugurated, praised Quincy's new market and new prison, which still stand, and the

new schools, too many of which still exist. Family tradition relates
that "the only thing Grandfather Otis did for Boston was to exclude cows from the Common." He did that, as we shall see; but
he also promoted sundry enterprises and reforms that were carried
out by future administrations.

Mayor Otis presided over a very congenial little city government — he knew every member. Defense of the Hartford Convention comprised one quarter of his first inaugural address, delivered 5 January 1829 in the thick of his controversy with John
Quincy Adams; but he did touch on several current questions.
Railroads must be built, as "indispensable to save this State and
City from insignificance and decay. . . . This State and City must
be up and doing, or the streams of our prosperity will seek other
channels." Massachusetts as yet had granted no railroad charter,
although rails had already been laid in Maryland and other states,
and railways had been a "transcendant success" in England.
Country members of the legislature blocked every project for state
ownership, but frightened private capital by providing a free
bridge adjoining the Charles River toll bridge, of which Otis and
other wealthy Bostonians were stockholders. When charters were
finally granted to railroad corporations, Otis refused to subscribe
for a single share of stock; but he and a few other capitalists with
similar views made the Western Railroad (the future Boston and
Albany) a gift of several thousand dollars that tided it over a
critical period.

In 1830, owing to His Honor's "indisposition" (a flare-up of the
gout), "the members of both branches of the City Council proceeded to the mansion house of the Mayor" for their inauguration.
"The meeting was opened with prayer by the Reverend Francis
Parkman," and closed (we assume) with appropriate libations from
the Lowestoft punch bowl. In September, when the city government moved from the old town government's quarters in Faneuil
Hall to the Old State House, Mayor Otis gave them a lecture on the
history of that building; there "Uncle Jim" had argued against

writs of assistance and (according to John Adams) started the American Revolution.

Reëlected a second time for the year 1831, the Mayor congratulated his city on new streets being laid out on filled land along Boston Neck and in the old Mill Pond; on the success of an experimental Institution for the Reformation of Juvenile Offenders; on a threatened smallpox epidemic having been thwarted by free public vaccination; and on organizing a police court so as to do away with "the administration of injustice in some of the petty tyrannies called Justice Courts." These were courts of first instance held by individual justices of the peace in the old English and colonial tradition. They had become inadequate in a growing city, as Otis well knew from his earlier experience as judge of the court of common pleas.

Other progressive recommendations in Otis's mayoralty addresses were harbor improvements, soon to be carried out; filling the Back Bay, fast becoming "an immense morass . . . a receptacle of seeds of disease" (postponed for twenty-five years) and a "Copious Supply of Fresh Water," not obtained until after his death in 1848. Up to that time, even the Otis mansion contained no plumbing of any description.

The humanitarian movement began to make weight in politics while Otis was mayor, and he warmly supported it. The Reverend Joseph Tuckerman, a missionary pastor, addressed an open letter to the mayor in 1829, disclosing a shocking state of affairs in the local jail and house of correction. No attempt had been made to classify prisoners other than by sex; first offenders and the harmless insane were confined in the same cell with hardened criminals; within six years, fifty-eight lunatics had been committed to Boston jails for the sole purpose of saving their board in the state asylum. Otis recommended immediate segregation of the insane and hardened criminals, and that was done.

He had long been active in the movement to abolish imprisonment for debt, which then existed in every state of the Union except Kentucky. When a member of the Fifth Congress, Otis had secured a law abolishing imprisonment for debt to the Federal Government, and he renewed his efforts to procure a similar reform in Massachusetts when mayor. In September 1831 he presided at a meeting which drafted resolutions favoring the total abolition of this practice, and showed himself so zealous for reform that a "Committee of Gentlemen friendly to the Abolishment of Imprisonment for Debt" nominated him for state senator. Otis replied, "I am not aware of any possible inducement that would allure me again to be a candidate for a seat in any legislative body upon earth." But in 1834 the legislature passed the law that he advocated.

Although Boston had become a city, she retained many features and customs of a New England country town. Annually, members of the most respectable families, such as Loring, Thayer, Williams and Bradlee, were elected to offices with obsolete duties, redolent of a pastoral age: field drivers, hogreeves, haywards, fence viewers, surveyors of hemp, cullers of dry fish, hoops and staves. Most amusing to the present generation were the privileges of cow owners. Since time immemorial, Bostonians had enjoyed the right to pasture cattle on Boston Common, along Boston Neck, and in the graveyards. On a famous occasion during the War of Independence, when hundreds of French naval officers suddenly descended on Governor John Hancock, his servants had to milk everybody's cow on the Common in order to have enough for milk punch. Otis, when building up Beacon Hill, provided a cow lane under and between houses on Pinckney, Mount Vernon, Chestnut and Beacon streets so that cattle owned by working people on the north slope or West End could walk to the Common without mucking up the streets or lunching off front gardens. But their presence on the Common was becoming a nuisance, and after Mayor Otis's gallantry had been appealed to by sundry ladies, William Foster (his brother-in-law) petitioned city government in the spring of 1829 to exclude cows from the Common. Mayor and aldermen, after receiving numerous protests against this revolutionary step, ordered "that the Cows be permitted to go at large upon the Common" provided their owners pay five dollars a head for the privilege and "that each Cow wear a strap, with the name of the owner thereon."

So matters rested for a year. Then Amos Lawrence, a wealthy merchant who had built one of the two houses on Park Street which have become the Union Club, started new tactics in the War on the Cows. The barnyard aspect and odor of the Old Granary Burying Ground, on which his house backed, annoyed him and his neighbors. He tactfully offered the city government to plant trees in the graveyard at his own expense if cattle were excluded. Mayor and aldermen did that, and more; they issued instructions that no cow "be suffered to pasture in *any* of the burial grounds."[1]

This victory stimulated a flood of petitions, some anti-cow, others that cattle be permitted "to run at large on the Common, as usual." The city government turned over this acrimonious subject to a committee, Mayor Otis chairman. He reported that the number of cows annually grazing on the Common had declined from 152 in 1824 to 65 in 1829; that the Common was used more and more by timid women and young children; that plenty of good country milk was available; and, in short, "a public square in a city whose population exceeds 60,000, enclosed and preserved as a pasture for the accommodation of 65 cows, is an anomaly for which it will be difficult to find a parallel in any City in the World." So in May 1830, mayor, aldermen and common council solemnly voted No Cows on Boston Common. Outraged cattle-owning citizens then bombarded the city government to repeal the prohibition; and Otis as usual thought up a happy compromise. In July, mayor and aldermen restored to the cows the right of pasture "on that part of the Common West of Charles Street" —

[1] This action made the Old Granary Burying Ground a sort of private park for dwellers on Park Street. Children and dogs played there, and on warm evenings in spring and autumn, the gentlemen and ladies gave *al fresco* suppers, the flat-topped tombs serving as tables for strawberries and champagne!

the future Public Garden. But since this tract had no fence to prevent bossy penetrating the sacred Common or browsing along Charles Street, owners must provide a cowkeeper "to keep Cows within the allotted boundary." Moreover, each cow must wear on her neck a "tally" stating her owner's name; and she may not spend the night out — must be at home between sunset and sunrise.

Filled-in land along the Neck and the wide open spaces of South Boston were now the only places where Boston cows could be "home on the range," and the pioneers of "Southie" were already protesting. Soon there would be no cow country left in Boston.

The three years of Otis's mayoralty were the last in which "General Election" — the inauguration of governor and general court — came on the last Wednesday of May. On that occasion, dozens of booths were set up to sell gingerbread, candy, beer, cider and rum; and all boys and apprentices, white or black, were given a holiday. Amos Lawrence, representing the Massachusetts Society for the Suppression of Intemperance, munificently provided a band of music to play on afternoons and evenings of General Election and the Glorious Fourth, in 1829. Not to give pleasure to the citizenry, he explained, but for the worthy purpose of "promoting order, and to suppress an inclination to riots and intemperance." Mr. Lawrence hoped that the city government would not leave him holding the bag this year but would appropriate $80 for "the performance of music on the Common on holidays." They did; and they still do, at a vastly inflated cost.

Of course, the 200th anniversary of the founding of Boston — 17 September 1830 — had to be celebrated. It was an embarrassing situation, because the committee who arranged the ceremonies consisted of the three Federalist "ambassadors" to Washington — Otis, William Sullivan and Thomas Handasyd Perkins — whom John Quincy Adams had denounced as wicked conspirators. But they had to invite Adams, New England's most distinguished citizen; the ex-President graciously accepted and had a place of honor in the parade. In the evening he attended a reception, not at

45 Beacon Street, but at the home of Lieutenant Governor Thomas Lindall Winthrop who had defected from Federalism. The principal celebration took place in the Old South Meeting House; Josiah Quincy, now President of Harvard College, delivered an oration, and Charles Sprague the "banker-poet" recited an original ode, described in the city records as "elegant, interesting and instructive." The best part of it was his tribute to the Red Indians.

> Alas! for them — their day is o'er,
> Their fires out from hill and shore;
> No more for them the wild deer bounds,
> The plough is on their hunting grounds.

The mayor's personal contribution to the Bicentennial was to buy a Copley portrait of John Hancock from his widow's heirs, and present it to the city.

From the city records it appears that a mild boom had hit Boston. Many streets were widened and those not already macadamized were paved with Maine cobblestones. Gaslight began to replace whale-oil streetlamps. New sewers were laid, ahead of a sufficient city water supply to flush them properly. Abutters complained of the noise made by the stand of hackney coaches and "hourly stages" on Washington Street between Bromfield and the Old South; the aldermen instructed Mayor Otis to speak to the "hackeys" in the hope of better behavior. They also asked him, on his way to City Hall, to superintend the planting of trees on Tremont Street. Otis and Thomas C. Amory obtained an appropriation of $500 toward indemnifying city firemen for injuries sustained in line of duty. The one subject on which the mayor expressed petulance was street cleaning, which he declared to be "practised to a needless and pernicious extreme." Apparently it was done by horse-drawn rotary brushes in dry weather, raising clouds of dust which the southwest wind blew into No. 45 Beacon Street, to Sally's distress. But, said Harry with his usual geniality, he would not press the point, as the citizens seemed to like the system. He did manage partly to lay the dust by starting a private subscription for sprinkling carts, which got their water from the harbor. Apparently this offended some of his neighbors, for he had to write the following letter to John P. Bigelow of the Board of Aldermen, on 25 June 1832:

> Dear Sir,
>
> I beg leave to express the hope that we in Beacon Street shall not be deprived of the privilege of watering the street, without which existence would be hardly endurable. We have found it a most salubrious, & comfortable practice for many years, and pray that the crude suggestions of old Crones or young Quacks in the newspapers may not compell us to leave town or be Suffocated. The vapour from salt water sprinkled on the streets unwholesome —! too absurd.

Tremont Street, Boston, c. 1840, from

The routine work of the mayoralty, the weekly meetings of mayor and aldermen that went on all summer, dulled Otis's appetite for governing Boston; and in 1831, at the end of his third term, he refused to stand for reëlection. Harrison Gray Otis may not be enrolled among the few (and, alas, how few!) really great mayors of Boston, but no one ever equaled him in dignity or surpassed him in genuine love for the city's welfare. At his last session with the aldermen, they spread on the records their thanks to the mayor for "the pre-eminent ability and assiduity with which he has discharged the duties of Chief Magistrate of the City, for a series of years, and for the courtesy and punctuality with which he has presided over their deliberations, and for his cheerful co-operation in all the labors of this Board." They "tender their

nary Burying Ground to the Albion Hotel.

homage to his exalted talents, and to the dignity with which he has discharged the duties of his office; with a wish that he may long enjoy perfect health, and the blessings of this world, with the consciousness of having acted well his part, for the public good."

To which Otis made a long but graceful acknowledgment, declaring that in his long experience of federal, state and municipal offices, he had never found anything comparable to "the disinterested and arduous services of an Alderman who does his duty."

And he failed to mention the Hartford Convention!

Boston and the Abolitionists

All these issues of Otis's three years' mayoralty are insignificant, compared with one that had national importance — the beginning of Garrisonian abolition; and that was never even noticed in the city records.

In September 1829 a colored old-clothes dealer of Boston named Daniel Walker published an inflammatory pamphlet called *Walker's Appeal,* addressed to the members of his race, exhorting them to gain freedom by force. Walker believed that he had a divine commission to write; he seems to have been a black John the Baptist heralding Garrison. Somehow he managed to circulate his pamphlet in the South, where it aroused the liveliest resentment among the whites. In December 1829, the mayor of Savannah wrote to Otis calling his attention to the publication, and requesting its suppression. Otis replied that he regarded the pamphlet "with deep disapprobation and abhorrence," and that no disposition was lacking on the part of the city authorities "to avail themselves of any lawful means for preventing this attempt to throw firebrands" into the South; but Walker had violated no law of Massachusetts, and could not therefore be punished or silenced.

Another copy of the *Appeal*, which got into the hands of the Virginia authorities, was made the subject of a special message from Governor Giles to the legislature. Otis, in sending him a copy of his reply to the mayor of Savannah, wrote:

You may be assured that your good people cannot hold in more absolute detestation the sentiments of the writer than do the people of this city, and, as I verily believe, the mass of the New England population. The only difference is, that the insignificance of the writer, the extravagance of his sanguinary fanaticism tending to disgust all persons of common humanity with his object, and the very partial circulation of this book, prevent the affair from being a subject of excitement and hardly of serious attention.

Governor Gilmer of Georgia requested Otis by letter (23 March 1830) to make an inquisition of Walker's effects in order to obtain for the state authorities his correspondence with a certain Burrit who was accused of circulating the *Appeal* in that state. Otis refused peremptorily. And Walker died in 1830.

William Lloyd Garrison, the young journeyman printer who had twice supported Otis enthusiastically, now took Walker's place. On 1 January 1831 he printed the first number of his *Liberator* in Boston, on borrowed paper, with type set by his own hand, and with a preliminary subscription list that he could count on his fingers. On the first page he announced:

I shall strenuously contend for the immediate enfranchisement of our slave population. . . . On this subject, I do not wish to think, or speak, or write, with moderation. . . . I am in earnest — I will not equivocate — I will not excuse — I will not retreat a single inch — AND I WILL BE HEARD.

Had Garrison aimed to arouse the most violent indignation in the South, he could have chosen no better time than this year 1831. In August there broke out at Southampton, Virginia, the famous Nat Turner slave insurrection in which some sixty white people were murdered. As soon as Southerners heard of the *Liberator,* they attributed the insurrection to its influence. The influential *National Intelligencer* in late September inquired of "the worthy mayor of the City of Boston, whether no law can be found to prevent the publication, within the city over which he presides, of such diabolical papers as we have seen a sample of here in the hands of slaves, and of which there are many in circulation to the South of us?" At the same time Otis began to receive personal protests, of which none excited his sensibility so much as the following appeal from Mrs. Lawrence Lewis, formerly "Nelly" Custis, granddaughter of Martha Washington:

Alex[andri]a Oct 17th 1831

Dear Sir,

I hope you will pardon my appeal to you, in consideration of our long acquaintance, & of the momentous & vital interests of which I am about to treat. The dreadful events of Augst last in our State, the want of confidence & insecurity produced by those horrors, *compel* me to address you. To a wretch outraging the Laws of God & Man, to the Editor of the "Liberator" — one of your community, — protected by your Laws, we owe in *greatest measure* this calamity. His paper is widely circulated even in this Town. Think you not that the blood of the innoment, the helpless, will be required of those who suffer such inflammatory publications to issue from their community, without the slightest check of *fine* or imprisonment. I think he merits *Death* — you would pronounce sentence of Death, on an Incendiary who would fire your City, throw a match into your powder magazine. Is not the Editor of the Liberator an incendiary of the very worst description — He inculcates insurrection, murder, cruelty, & baseness, in every shape. The most *lenient* are as frequently the victims, as the most rigorous, & even *more* frequently; since *nine* times out of *ten,* a negro loves those best who are *least* indulgent — *fear* not *principle* governing the *far far* greater part. Our whites unhappily evince *too much fear* of these wretches — they can *never* succeed in subjugating the Whites, but our young & lovely females, infant innocence, &

helpless age will be their victims — it is like a smothered vol-
cano — we know not when, or where, the flame will burst forth,
but we know that death in the most horrid forms threatens us.
Some have died, others have become deranged from apprehension, since the South Hampton affair. Can you reflect on the
instrument employed for our destruction — that we may trace
the *train* as far as *Boston,* & not use your efforts to arrest its
course, to make an example of the Author of evil. Your
Southern Brethren incurred this curse by no act of their own,
they are endeavouring by degrees, & consistently with their
safety, & even existence, to remove it. Suffer them to do what
they know to be best, & let [not] their Eastern, & Northern
Brethren from a false principle of Philanthropy, make the blacks
miserable, discontented, & rebellious, & force the whites to
exterminate them. I have been assured by several Gentlemen
who have visited the devoted district, that should the blacks
attempt to rise there again, they will be exterminated; the excitement is so great. We cannot leave our State, our only means
of subsistence is here, we cannot dispose of our property to any
advantage. We must therefore risk the horrors that may be
impending. I have never *appeared* to *fear* them, & I *will not,*
but I cannot feel secure or happy now, I confess. My darling
children & grandchildren are dearer to me than life. Mr & Mrs
Butler, & their lovely son, will go to Louisiana the 1st Novr., I
expect & *fear.* My son & his family reside in Fredk. County
where I shall go with Angela the last of Novr, for two months,
after which we shall reside again at Woodlawn. My family
unite with me in respectful regards to yourself & family & to
our other tried Boston friends. . . .

Respectfully your friend

E P Lewis.

Mayor Otis received letters in the same vein from Benjamin
Faneuil Hunt, son of old Master Hunt of the Boston Latin School,
now an eminent lawyer of Charleston, and from Senator Hayne of
South Carolina, Webster's antagonist in the celebrated debate of
1830. Hunt complained not only against the *Liberator* but also
of certain printed calico handkerchiefs "exhibiting Negroes under
circumstances calculated to elicit sympathy," said to have been
manufactured in Massachusetts. He hinted that if Boston were the

source of this merchandise, her commercial intercourse with South Carolina would be cut off.

If Otis had really wanted to suppress the *Liberator* or harass Garrison, he could have found the authority somehow. Three years later the state authorities, no longer Federalist, "got" Abner Kneeland and his pantheistic *Boston Investigator* by applying a statute of 1782, reënacting a seventeenth-century law against blasphemy. Otis's old Democratic antagonist, Attorney General James T. Austin, kept after poor Abner with pertinacity and succeeded in jailing him and ruining his career. Why, then, did not Mayor Otis do the same? Abolitionists and Negroes were then as unpopular in Massachusetts as atheists.[1] Let us give him the benefit of the doubt that he really believed in free speech. So, all that he did was to have Garrison and the *Liberator* investigated. Not then, but seventeen years later, he reported that the city constable "had ferreted out the paper and its editor; that his office was an obscure hole, his only visible auxiliary a negro boy, and his supporters a few very insignificant persons of all colors."

This report inspired James Russell Lowell's poem to William Lloyd Garrison beginning:

> In a small chamber, friendless and unseen,
>   Toiled o'er his types one poor, unlearned young man;
> The place was dark, unfurnitured, and mean: —
>   Yet there the freedom of a race began.

Sardonic indeed is the contrast between Otis's offhand description of the young agitator's "obscure hole" and the revolutionary effects which flowed from it.

In his reply to Benjamin F. Hunt on 17 October 1831, Otis assured him that the *Liberator* enjoyed only "insignificant coun-

---

[1] Of the hundred-odd abolition societies in the United States in 1830, New England possessed not one. Garrison wrote in the first number of the *Liberator* that he found "contempt more bitter, opposition more active, detraction more relentless, prejudice more stubborn, and apathy more frozen" in New England "than among slave owners themselves."

tenance and support"; that although he, and Bostonians generally, entertained the same solicitude for eventual emancipation as frequently had been expressed by "the best citizens of your own and other plantation states, yet there has been displayed among us, less disposition to interfere with the actual relations of master and slave in our sister states, than has been manifested in other places." He concluded that he did not wish to tamper with slavery. "I am desirous of leaving the affair of emancipation of your slaves to yourselves, to time, to the Providence of God. . . . But I protest with deep horror against all measures of whatever description, tending to endanger their lives or make miserable the tenure of their existence."

Otis also made a wise answer to Hunt's request for penal laws against "incendiary writings." He promised to try any reasonable suggestion of southern statesmen for curbing abolition by public opinion; but, he remarked, Hunt "must perceive the intrinsic if not insuperable obstacles to legislative enactments made to prevent crimes from being consummated beyond the local jurisdiction." Such interference would drive every moderate person of anti-slavery leanings, and many previously indifferent, to make common cause with the fanatics "and justify themselves with the prejudices and arguments that abound against sedition acts."

He had learned the lesson, from the disastrous effects of the Sedition Act in 1798, that in the United States any attempt to suppress free discussion and criticism would boomerang. Unfortunately for the South, she had not learned this lesson. The subsequent struggle to stifle criticism of slavery in Congress, in the press and among the people generally, convinced the average northern citizen that this institution which could not bear the light of day must be inherently rotten, and must go.

Otis Attempts
to Solve the Slavery Question

Otis did not escape this problem when he ceased to be mayor of Boston. He spent time and thought on the slavery question. The idea of an irrepressible conflict may have occurred to him, as it did to Jefferson and Adams during the Missouri debates of 1820. The irreconcilable contradiction between the ideas of his southern correspondents and those of Garrison brought him to some such conclusion as Lincoln's, that the Union could not endure "half slave and half free." To Otis there seemed to be but one way out: a comprehensive policy of gradual emancipation and colonization of the slaves by the Federal Government, with the consent of the slaveholder. The time was ripe, if ever, for such a project. The Southampton insurrection made every thinking slaveholder, in Virginia at least, willing to listen to temperate appeals for emancipation; and Garrisonian abolition was not yet sufficiently powerful to be a serious obstacle.

Otis knew very well the American Colonization Society, founded at Washington in 1817 and dedicated to emancipating American Negro slaves and colonizing them in Africa. The founders and early officers (including Henry Clay and Francis Scott Key, Chief Justice Marshall, President Monroe and Justice Bushrod Washington) aimed to do for the American Negro exactly what the Republic of Israel has done for the Jews — to give him back a part of his old homeland, where he could live happily without white harassment. For the greatest obstacle to Negro emancipation was not the owners' greed but the problem of what to do with the freedmen, in view of their difficulty in adapting themselves to American society, and the bitter antagonism of the meaner sort of white people. The founders of the American Colonization Society, assuming that the African Negro would never fit into a predominantly white society except on an inferior basis, believed that he could only realize his potentialities through a government of his own in his ancestral continent.

Obviously the A.C.S. could not hope to repatriate all slaves in the United States, who then numbered about a million and a half; nor even all the free Negroes, who numbered over 230,000. But many planters were eager to emancipate their slaves, provided they could be removed to Africa instead of becoming victims of their own improvidence and of persecution by neighboring "poor white trash." The A.C.S. encouraged this movement in every way. It founded, supported and protected the Republic of Liberia, whither several thousand emancipated slaves had emigrated prior to 1830, setting up a Negro version of the later Republic of Israel.

This was the project that Otis wished to further in 1830. The difficulties were far greater than they had been fifteen years earlier, because the slaves in the United States now numbered three million, and the lower South, at least, had got its back up and insisted that slavery must be immutable and permanent. But the fact that the A.C.S. had its principal support in Maryland and other border slave states encouraged Otis to back the movement. Debates in the Virginia assembly of 1831–32 also encouraged him; a motion for the gradual abolition of slavery was defeated by only 15 votes out of 131, and a bill to promote colonization of free or to be freed Negroes passed the lower house and was lost by a single vote in the state senate. Otis thought (very erroneously) that these events proved that Virginia had "seen the light," and that this was the time to make a massive, concerted effort to get rid of Negro slavery and the Negro problem at the same time.

He described his project in a long letter of 5 February 1832 to Nathan Appleton, the Boston representative in Congress, and in an essay that appeared in the Boston *Courier* for 16 February under the pseudonym "Suggestor." The article begins with the statement that the abolition of slavery is the most important question before the people of the United States. It continues:

Yet such is the natural and feverish sensibility upon this subject among the proprietors of slaves, that hitherto they have protested with indignant remonstrance against all approach to it by others. They feel correctly that their property in their slaves is recognized by the Constitution. They notice with pardonable apprehension the ravings of the fanatics and the indiscretions of the zealots, as the call of crusaders stimulating their slaves to deeds of death. Unable to determine between projects of emancipation originating with those who feel with them and for them, and those infatuated persons who are ripe for abolition by any means and at all hazards, they have concluded that their security could be found only in repelling all interference with what they consider their peculiar rights.

[Should this attitude be maintained, all reform would be hopeless; but] a new era has commenced. The people of Virginia, at least, are no longer disposed to shut their eyes or bridle their tongues. . . . Their statesmen and orators do not affect to disguise or palliate the evils of slavery, or to deny the necessity of measures suitable to meet and remove them. Language, to which they would not have patiently listened from the lips of others, is now used by themselves, with a pathos which comes from their hearts and which must reach the hearts of all who regard them as fellow-citizens, and as a high-minded, patriotic race, who with us have shared the toils, and faced the danger, and borne the burdens, and supported the principles, which have made us a great and free nation.

[Not only is the time propitious for abolition, but] the means of effecting it are at the command of the national government. [The national revenue is so great as to] leave a competent amount to be annually appropriated to the raising of a fund which might be apportioned among the Plantation States, in the ratio of their slave population, and applied by each state, *in its own mode,* to the purchase of the slaves owned by their citizens, and to the colonization of *all* their colored people.

. . . If the abolition of slavery could by these means be effected, the public blessings that would result to this nation transcend the power of calculation. But they may all be comprehended in one. IT WOULD FIX THE STABILITY OF THE UNION. We should become one people, with the same habits, feelings, pursuits, and interests, and should all experience a common prosperity. We should hear no more of the fearful

array of conflicting interests on the different sides of Mason and
Dixon's Line, and our sectional jealousies would be obliterated
and forgotten. All calculation of dollars and cents, sink into
contempt in comparison with the value of this magnificent
object, especially when we have enough to spare for its attainment. [The member who might make this proposition would
immortalize himself, and] a measure inferior only to the declaration of independence would crown with unfading glory the
Congress in which it had originated.

Otis also corresponded with several members of Congress on
this subject, and attempted, though in vain, to secure a place for
his suggestions in the columns of the *National Intelligencer*. To
Daniel Webster he wrote, on 12 June 1832:

> After all my dear Sir, there will be no peace or security for
> us, untill you buy up the Virginia negroes & send them off —
> If Virginia could be whitewashed she would say with St. Paul,
> "now I am a man I put off childish things," and *pour ces
> autres*, they could do us no harm. I do believe, perhaps too
> fondly that a proposition to this end coming from the North,
> and managed with judgment and address and introduced with
> such a speech as I could make, (if I was somebody that I wont
> name); however unfavorably it might be received at first, by
> those whose interest it would chiefly promote would ultimately
> obtain, and prove to be the most feasible and felicitous of all
> schemes that have been or can be devised for saving this confed-
> eracy. So please to remember after I am dead, & you see this
> project realized after all, "Old Otis was not so raving about the
> matter as he appeared to be."

Not raving indeed! His comprehensive project, if carried out,
would have prevented the Civil War, if anything under Heaven
could have averted that calamity, and even solved the racial problems which are racking the Republic more than a century after
that war ended. There were great practical difficulties. Liberia
could not have absorbed more than a fraction of the slaves, but
there were plenty more territories in Africa which could have
been obtained for Negro colonization. The fact that Abraham

Lincoln, a practical idealist, proposed in 1862, when the slaves were twice as numerous as in 1832, an emancipation and colonization plan with an initial appropriation of $100 million, suggests that there was nothing visionary about Otis's plan. The insuperable obstacle was simply this: in the lower South, Negro slavery had come to be considered an economic and social necessity, and a positive blessing. On 2 April 1832 Charles Fenton Mercer of Virginia presented to Congress a petition for national aid to the American Colonization Society in furthering plans for emancipation and colonization identical with those of Otis. James Blair of South Carolina called Mercer a "recreant to the cause" of the slave states, and added, "I can tell gentlemen, that when they move this question seriously, we from the South will meet it elsewhere. It will not be disputed in this House, but in the open field, where powder and cannon will be our orators, and our arguments lead and steel."

Having retired from political life, Otis was in no position to forward his project effectively, and never succeeded in interesting any of the great men of the period. Finally he gave up colonization as hopeless and turned his remaining energy toward counteracting Garrisonian abolition. He had promised, in 1831, to apply the curb of public opinion on Garrison. That time arrived in 1835 when southern indignation broke out afresh, owing to the discovery in the Charleston post office of a mass of abolitionist literature. Southern mass meetings and the press called on northern public opinion to show itself. The Boston *Atlas* summoned a mass meeting in Faneuil Hall and urged leading citizens like Otis to attend and "vindicate the fair name" of the city. Faneuil Hall on 21 August was filled with the best elements of Boston society, among whom were scattered numerous Southerners who had come to observe Boston's attitude on a question vital to them. Mayor Theodore Lyman took the chair, and Peleg Sprague opened the discussion with a pungent attack on the abolitionists. Harrison Gray Otis, now seventy years of age, followed him with one of the most noteworthy speeches he ever delivered. His tone was calm and moderate; abstaining from invective or questioning of motives, he dwelt on the thesis that Garrisonian abolition must cease, or at least grow no stronger, if the Union were to endure. Closely acquainted as Otis was with the southern temper through friendship, travel, correspondence, and a long public career, he was able to prophesy with remarkable accuracy. The slaveholders, he told his audience, would regard any measure of militant abolition as

war in disguise, upon their lives, their property, their rights and institutions, an outrage upon their pride and honor, and the faith of contracts — menacing the purity of their women, the safety of their children, the comfort of their homes and their hearths, and in a word all that man holds dear. In these opinions they might be mistaken, but in support of them they would exhibit a spectacle of unanimity unparalleled among so numerous a population on any subject, at any time, in any part of the world. These opinions almost seem to be instinctive. They are in fact hereditary, and habitual from infancy to age. The citizens of those States have no occasion for meetings to compare sentiments, for speeches to stimulate to action, for plans to arrange and organize means of opposition. They would be ready in the case supposed for a *levée en masse* — a universal *Landsturm* — to seize and to use for life and for death, whatever arms their impassioned resentment could furnish, to resist every approach to interference with their domestic relations. Meetings indeed they have already begun to call — but they are like the meetings of clouds charged with the same fiery material, the occasional flashes of which serve only to show the stores of hidden thunder which are in reserve.

With this eloquent appeal Otis closed his speech:

The right of thought, and of speech, and of freedom of the press is one thing — that of combining to spread disaffection in other states, and poison the sweet fountains of domestic safety and comfort, is a different thing. This I hope my fellow citizens will see. In any event, I can have no motive to mislead them — my days are nearly numbered, and I have nothing to gain or to wish from public favor. I witnessed the adoption of the constitution, and through a long series of years have been accustomed to rely upon an adherence to it as the foundation of all my hopes for posterity. It is threatened, I think, with the most portentous danger that has yet arisen. I pray it may be dissipated — that the thirteen stripes may not be merged into two dismal stains of black and red, and that my grave may close over me before the Union descends into hers.

Commenting in a letter to his old friend George Harrison, Otis said he had been amused by a Virginia newspaper saying that he broke forth "like a lion from his lair," whilst he had been nothing better than "an old founder'd horse" on his last gallop. In sober tone he predicted that neither silence nor sympathy on the part of the North will "ultimately satisfy" the South. "The force of opinion in favor of emancipation throughout the world, must blow upon them like a perpetual trade-wind, and keep them in a constant state of agitation & discomfort. But the end of these things no man knoweth — we shall not see it."

William Lloyd Garrison retorted to the Faneuil Hall meeting with a stinging review of the leading speeches in the columns of the *Liberator*. Otis's speech he discussed with comparative decency, but in his finale pictured Otis as a hoary-headed old sinner who, on the brink of the grave, "under circumstances of peculiar criminality" had not scrupled "to pander to the lusts and desires of the robbers of God and his poor." He even composed an epitaph for the aged statesman, in part as follows:

Here lies the body of
H_____ G_____ O_____
Reader, weep at human inconsistency and frailty!
The last public act of his life,
A life conspicuous for many honorable traits,
Was an earnest defense of
THE RIGHTS OF TYRANTS AND SLAVE MONGERS
To hold in bondage, as their property,
The bodies and souls of millions of his own countrymen!

As the years went on, and the strength of Garrisonian abolition increased, Otis tended to become more conservative on the slavery question, and to urge that not only abolition, but all anti-slavery agitation should cease. In a published letter to John Whipple, in 1839, he attacked the Rhode Island legislature for protesting against the Atherton ("Gag") Resolutions of Congress, and for petitioning Congress to abolish slavery in the District of Columbia. He adopted the southern doctrine that any such proposition was unconstitutional, in spite of the exclusive federal jurisdiction over the District, because it would affect a domestic institution of adjoining states. Apparently he had become reconciled to the perpetual duration of slavery, since he wrote: "If slavery is a stain, it is one with which the Union was born, and which cannot be removed by our effort unless by cutting off the limb which wears it." He could "perceive no justification" for his "fellow citizens on this side of the line of Mason and Dixon, to throw firebrands, arrows of death, on the other side of that line." He foretells "that if this mania for tampering with the slave tenure of the plantation States . . . be permitted to go much further, the days of the Union will shortly be numbered."

We have recently celebrated the centenary of the Civil War, which abolished slavery through blood and iron. Probably a vast majority of those who think at all on this subject believe that emancipation could have been brought about in no other fashion. But in the future, men will realize that if more midcentury leaders, North and South, had possessed the moderation, foresight and wisdom shown by Harrison Gray Otis in 1832, there need have been no Civil War, no civil rights agitation, no "Black Power"; that "Old Otis," in very truth, "was not so raving about the matter as he appeared to be."

CHAPTER XXII

A Brisk Old Age

1834–1848, AET. 69–83

THE IRISH CATHOLICS

BOSTON AGAIN exhibited her genius for perpetual renewal. Gone with the east wind were the dismal forebodings of 1815. Her merchant marine staged a spectacular comeback; sail packet lines were established to Europe, a brisk trade sprang up with South America, and a new ice-export trade to southern ports and even India. As a financial center, Boston became second only to New York; profits from the cotton and woolen mills of Lowell, Lawrence, Chicopee, Fall River and New Bedford flowed into her banks and overflowed into railroad stock and western investments, usually so shrewdly that the city suffered less from the panic of 1837 than any other North American center. Learning and the arts, too, flourished; the Concord group were at their prime, and people who called Boston "the slough of despond" in 1815 now hailed her as "the Athens of America." She started to grow and kept on growing — the population jumped thirty-three percent in the last decade of Otis's life, and he shared in the prosperity and general euphoria. His Beacon Hill land became too valuable for gardens; the detached houses were now hemmed in by solid blocks. Even the garden to 45 Beacon Street, where President Monroe had been entertained, now supported two houses. And, for the first time since the Indians moved out, Boston had a racial problem — the Irish.

Otis had long since lived down his "wild Irish" speech and become a favorite of the Boston Irish, who prior to 1830 were a small minority in the city. The official historian of the Boston Archdiocese observes the curious fact that the people who welcomed the Irish and other Catholics who poured into Boston thereafter were Unitarians, poles apart from Rome in theology, and former Federalists who won no Irish votes; whilst those Yankees who persecuted the Paddies were the same Congregationalists and Baptists who helped defeat Otis for the governorship. Of course the Unitarians, cultivated and well-to-do, took no stock in popish plots and the like, whilst the orthodox, brought up on Foxe's *Book of Martyrs,* included the laboring classes with whom the Irish immigrants competed. Another reason for this Federalist-Hibernian entente was the Abbé Jean-Louis Cheverus who became Bishop of Boston in 1810 and eventually Cardinal Cheverus. The Abbé did not, as we have seen, embrace Otis at a town meeting in 1796 and declare that future generations would "call him blessed," simply because he was not there; but as a cultured priest of *l'ancien régime* he naturally belonged with the Boston patricians. Together with Otises, Lymans and Lowells, he founded the Anthology Club which is now considered to be the womb of literary Boston, and he was a frequent guest at 45 Beacon Street. Otis cheerfully contributed toward building the first Cathedral of the Holy Cross on Franklin Street.

There were no racial riots, fortunately for Otis, during the three years of his mayoralty, but in 1834 occurred the notorious burning of the Ursuline Convent in Charlestown. A Protestant mob, the core consisting of Protestant Irish bricklayers and truck drivers from New Hampshire, inflamed by false stories of a pretended nun, attacked and burned the convent until only a shell was left. The next day a public meeting was held in Faneuil Hall in which Otis, in "a speech of great power and eloquence, . . . denounced the perpetrators of this dastardly outrage on defenseless women and children." But nobody was ever punished for it, and even a petition to the general court for compensation to the Ursulines, signed by almost every respectable member of Boston society, failed to move the rural members.

The next major mix-up was the so-called Broad Street riot of

1837. This almost fatal riot occurred when a Yankee volunteer fire company, answering an alarm, cut through a Catholic funeral procession. It created such ill feeling between the races that the Boston Irish had to organize their own militia company, the Montgomery Guards. At the annual muster on Boston Common in September, when this outfit appeared, every other company of the regiment to which it belonged, excepting three, marched off in protest. Of these three, one was the New England Guards of which William Foster Otis was captain; and another, the Boston Light Infantry of which Harrison Gray Otis was still an honorary officer. The old gentleman, summoned to the Common, made such a tactful impromptu oration to the Irishmen that a sanguinary free-for-all was prevented.

By this time Otis had ceased to coquette with Jacksonian Democracy and had become a stalwart Whig. But his admiration for the President's courage in 1832 could not withstand the shock of Jackson's attacks on the bankers. "I have just read the Old Turk's firman against the Bank. Another appeal to the worst passions of the community — jealousy, envy & cupidity," he wrote. The removal of the deposits drove almost every old Federalist into the Whig party, which now became the protector of financial and commercial property. But the decade of the thirties proved a disheartening one for conservatives. Democracy installed at Washington; democracy tinkering with state constitutions and corrupting the civil service; substitution of stump-speaking, personal canvass and ballyhoo for New England's genteel electioneering customs of the Federalist era. Otis's letters for the last twenty years of his life are not lacking in *joie de vivre,* but are black-laced with dismal forebodings of the catastrophic nature of democracy.

Bishop John Cheverus, by Gilbert Stuart.

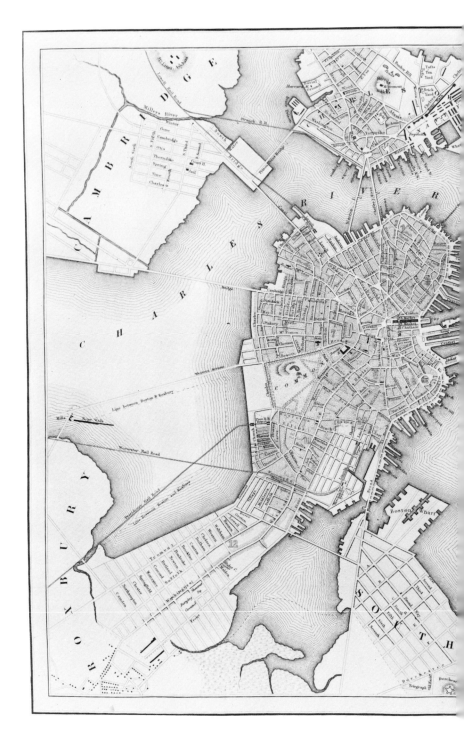

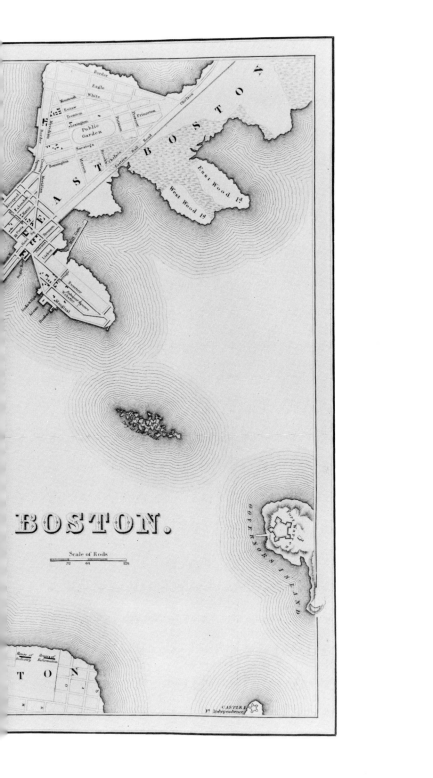

EAST BOSTON

Border
Eagle
Monmouth   White
Eutaw
Trenton   Princeton
Lexington
Public
Garden
Saratoga
Bennington

West Wood 1ˢ   East Wood 1ˢ

Sumner
Maverick Square

Marginal

BOSTON.

Scale of Rods
32   64   128

GOVERNORS ISLAND
CITY WAY

House of
Industry   House of
Reformation

T O N

CASTLE I.
Fᵗ Independence

SOCIAL LIFE AND FAMILY GOSSIP

Despite politics, crashes and panics, social life among the well-to-do
in Boston went on in the same pattern, and with much the same
diversions, as it had thirty years earlier. With the building up of
Beacon Hill, Number 45 Beacon Street had houses on three sides,
and all belonged to Otis's friends or family: David Sears, Jr., just
uphill, and next to him, on the corner of Walnut Street, the
Honorable John Phillips. Four doors downhill, on the corner of
Spruce Street, lived Otis's son-in-law Israel Thorndike, Jr., and on
the opposite corner, in the house that Otis had built for his
father, his stepmother Mrs. Samuel A. Otis and two half sisters
Harriet and Mary. Next them came the widow Mrs. Catherine
Powell of whom Harry wrote teasingly to Sally after sitting next
to her at a supper party: "I was next to the frisky old widow Powell,
all bedizened with flackets and diamonds . . . and her old fingers
stuck as full of rings as a set of curtain rods. I animated the old
skeleton in a style that should entitle me to a premium from the
Humane Society. . . . You had better come home for I am informed that it is not uncommon in Europe for men past my time
to be seduced and run away with."

Masons, Sullivans, Amorys, Joys, Eliots, Lowells and other
friends were now on the Hill, but other old Federalist families
such as Cabots, Perkinses and Cushings remained faithful to the
other side of the Common.

A few intimate glimpses of Otis and his circle are afforded by
the diary of Philip Hone, the New York political and social leader:

> June 6, 1834. The girls and I dined with Mr. Harrison G. Otis
> and Mrs. Ritchie, his daughter. They had an exceedingly agree-
> able party to meet us, and our dinner was pleasant as possible.
> We went from Mrs. Otis's to a party at Mr. William Sullivan's,
> where we found pleasant company and good music. Mr. Sullivan
> got a bottle of Eclipse wine for special benefit, of which I had to

Numbers 43, 44 and 45 Beacon Street in 1968.
Otis's garden once extended to the right of the picture.

drink two or three glasses, notwithstanding the copious libations to which I had been tempted where I dined. This Eclipse wine was imported into Boston in 1806, and arrived at the moment of the great solar eclipse, to which circumstance it owes its name, although it might claim it upon the ground of its eclipsing almost all other wines. I think it is perfection.

April 2, 1835 [in New York] I dined with Mr. Abraham Ogden. . . . Mr. Webster was there, and Mr. H. G. Otis, and Meredith. The great senator has been more uniformly cheerful during his present visit than I have ever seen him, and he is, when "in the vein," one of the best talkers in the world. Mr. Otis, when the tyrant of the limbs allows him to dine out, is always a most delightful companion; his voice is perfect music, his choice of words scrupulously nice, and talent gives a charm to his narrative, which makes his hearers regret that his longest stories should ever come to an end. He appears to me sometimes a little pedantic and too studious of effect, but no man of taste and feeling can listen to him during the social hours of a dinner-party without improvement and delight.

September 6. In the afternoon I visited and had a delightful talk of two or three hours with Mr. H. G. Otis, where I drank tea, and went in the evening to Mr. Peter Parker's, Mr. Samuel D. Parker's and Mr. Sullivan's, at each of which places I had been invited to those agreeable Sunday-evening parties for which the Bostonians are so celebrated, and which I enjoy so much.

September 9. I dined at Mr. H. G. Otis's, and had, as is always the case in the house of this agreeable and hospitable gentleman, a most capital dinner. Mrs. Ritchie (who came with her mother yesterday from Newport) presided at the dinner, and imparted to it the charm which always attends her presence.

Boston, Oct. 5, 1843. Mr. Otis called in his carriage to take us out to Brookline to see Colonel Perkins. I was highly gratified. The house and grounds are in the highest taste, the gardens beautiful, and the grapes and other fruits unequalled. It was a pleasant sight to witness the meeting of these two gouty old gentlemen, — fine old gentlemen of the old school; and a capital school it was. Mr. Otis will be seventy-eight years old on Sunday next. We drank his health yesterday in anticipation of his birthday. Colonel Perkins is a year older. We drove around the beautiful country of Brookline, and called to see a new house of General Lyman's. . . . In the evening my wife and I went to a party at Mrs. H. G. Otis's, — a travelled lady, a virtuoso, and a lion-hunter.

Boston, Nov. 12, 1845 . . . Mr. Blatchford and I made two pleasant visits this morning; the first to Mr. Otis, who is in good health and spirits, and has invited our little party to dine with him to-morrow; the second, to Mr. Prescott, the amiable and accomplished historian of *Ferdinand and Isabella* and *The Conquest of Mexico*. Mr. Prescott is engaged in fitting up a fine house in Beacon Street, which he bought lately from Augustus Thorndike. He showed us his new library and study, which will be in admirable taste, and a number of curious manuscripts, autographs, and pictures illustrative of his two great works, and collected with that object. I have been busily employed all the morning walking about the city. Boston is improved prodigiously, especially the southern part, where the great railroad depots are situated.

Boston, November 13, 1845. We dined with my venerable friend Mr. H. G. Otis, the most perfect gentlemen of my acquaintance. Besides our party, and the family of the host, there were Mrs. Harry Otis and her son, a handsome young fellow of about twenty years of age; Mr. Belknap, Mr. Nathan Appleton, and Mr. Truman. Mr. Webster was engaged in a cause in the United States District Court. The dinner and wines, as usual, were excellent, and Mrs. Ritchie charming.

Allyne and George Harrison Otis, the two youngest sons of Harry and Sally, graduated from Harvard in 1825. George, who died at the age of 23, is a rather shadowy figure; but Allyne left a few footsteps on the sands of time by being a class and club mate of Charles Francis Adams, future minister to Great Britain. In Adams's college diary Otis is referred to as "mean" and "stupid," but Charley admitted that Allyne had good manners and "knew the rules of society," and called on him almost every evening to drink wine or porter. He had it in for Allyne because his father (John Quincy Adams) refused to let him make the grand tour of Europe, on the ground that Harrison Gray Otis had done that for Allyne, who returned from it an "ass." But, objected young Charley, Allyne "always was an ass!" Both he and his brother George were typical members of the affluent dilettante, those faint and futile Americans abroad whom Henry James so well described.

Allyne, after spending a few months in his elder brother James's New York office, decided that work was not for him, and lived to a ripe old age without doing another day's labor. He had a separate apartment in the Otis mansion on Beacon Street, and there suffered the most mortifying experience of his life, in connection with the Boston engagement of Fanny Elssler, the celebrated Austrian ballerina. "In that city, noted for its austerity, she won unprecedented popularity," states her biographer. Emerson and Margaret Fuller, neither of whom had ever seen a ballet, attended one of Fanny's performances somewhat timidly, and for a long time were speechless. Then said the Sage of Concord, "Margaret, this is poetry!" To which she replied, "No, Waldo, it is not poetry, it is religion!"

Allyne Otis regarded Fanny neither as religion nor as poetry but as an exceedingly beautiful woman with whom he could easily have fallen in love — possibly he did. Anyway, taking advantage of his father's absence on a summer excursion, he gave a terrific party for her at 45 Beacon Street. Respectable Bostonians were not invited, but theatrical, artistic and Bohemian Boston, seldom if ever admitted to the Otis mansion, turned out in force and consumed quantities of madeira, sherry and champagne from the paternal wine cellar. In the midst of the party Allyne, feeling a call of nature, rushed to the privy next to the stable and fell in. When rescued, he was unable to reappear at his own party.

If Fanny became aware of this sad mishap she did not show it; and when she returned to Boston the following year, Allyne Otis

EL SAPATEO DE CADIZ.

THE CELEBRATED SPANISH DANCE

As danced with enthusiastic applause

BY

MAD.^{lle} FANNY ELSSLER.

At her last Benefit

and Kirk Boott squired her about the city. For this she thanked them in this charming note:

> Philadelphia 14 janvier 1842
>
> Mon cher Monsieur Otis
>
> Je ne puis partir sans vous remercier pour le zèle que vous avez mis à m'obliger. Quoique un tel dévouement de votre part ne m'étonne pas, je ne suis pourtant pas moins sensible à une telle bonne Amitié. Il m'est très doux, je vous assure, de savoir, que même loin de mes vrais amis, ils saisissent toute occasion de me prouver leur bonne amitié.
>
> Agréez donc, je vous prie Monsieur mes sincères remerciements pour vos bons services et permettez moi de vous dire un dernier adieu.
>
> fanny Elssler
>
> N'oubliez pas je vous prie Monsieur de nous rappeler un bon souvenir de Monsieur Boot. Ma cousine me prie de vous présenter ses compliments.

James William Otis, the second son to grow up, had no taste for books, so his father apprenticed him to Israel Thorndike to learn business, which he did to very good purpose. During his first job, to manage his father's manufacturing interests at Taunton, he wooed and won Martha Church, the belle of Providence. They were married in 1825; and after moving to New York, James prospered. From their two sons, James Allyne and William Church, are descended most of the Otises who have graced the social scene in New York and Boston during the last century.

Harrison Gray Otis, Jr., over whose health and well-being his father watched as tenderly as if he had been an only child, did fairly well in the law, but never shook off the malady which had been attacking him at intervals since childhood. He died in 1827 after fathering five children. Eliza, his widow, was not much consolation to her parents-in-law. On 21 November 1831 Otis wrote to George Harrison, "Mrs. H. Otis is going to Washington to flourish and talk loud, and will be some time in Phila. She never c[alls on] me or mine, knowing we would not but disapprove so long absence from her children. But we have *said* not a word to her against it. If she lives to come home I mean to take her in hand and give her a 'Spring dressing,' trimming down some other exuberances." Loud, vain and energetic, Eliza Otis unsuccessfully teased her father-in-law to recognize her son Harrison Gray Otis III as his sole heir. But she asserted leadership in Boston society with aplomb and traded on her connection by always signing herself "Mrs. Harrison Gray Otis." Thus she is often confused with her gentle mother-in-law.

In 1833 this bonny, bouncy young widow became the object of public satire. At a charity bazaar in Faneuil Hall for the benefit of the Perkins Institution for the Blind, Eliza Otis's trumpeting voice "was heard above all the rest, talking, laughing and selling," according to a chatty Quincy girl. All Boston attended; and not long after, social Boston was amused or outraged by the appearance of a pamphlet called *Scenes at the Fair*. In this saucy skit on Boston society, "Mrs. Harrowby Grey" presides "before a table covered with showy articles, and surrounded by a multitude of persons of all descriptions whom her marshals are vainly endeavoring to keep back." She declares that everybody is making love to her — "Hundreds of proposals before ten o'clock this morning!" The two la-di-da Otis bachelors stalk in; Allyne, "biting his stick," says "Absurd idea! attempting a thing of this kind in Boston! Siberian climate. In Paris par example this might have been worth seeing. There would have been some taste in the selection and display of the articles — but *really* here it is too *absurd!*" George echoes, "Too ridiculous! Beauty enough — but what tournures!" And it ends with Mrs. Harrowby Grey exclaiming, "Every thing sold — what a day! I am nearly stifled with the men coming up to look at me!"

This not too witty or malicious skit blew up the biggest social storm in Boston since "Sans Souci." Everyone knew who wrote it

— Fanny Inglis, who with her mother, brothers and sisters, *émigrés* from Edinburgh, conducted a fashionable private school on Mount Vernon Street. Hot words were exchanged, threats uttered to withdraw patronage from the school, even to bring suit for libel. Allyne and George Otis simply laughed it off, but Eliza Otis and her sisters Mrs. Rice and Mrs. Bates, who had been lampooned as "Mrs. Sago" and "Mrs. Whitebait," were not amused, and egged on their husbands and brothers-in-law to "do something" to get back at "that creature." George Parish, a young man in love with Fanny, and who perhaps had collaborated with her, gallantly assumed sole authorship and publicly apologized for giving offense. As even this did not satisfy the Boardman tribe, "Mr. Sago" and Parish, instead of fighting a duel as the Boardman ladies wanted, appealed to the patriarch as mediator. He issued a statement that in his opinion "No offense was intended," and that the aggrieved parties had better forget it. Whether or not Otis relished the skit on his relatives, he always stood by the Inglises; ten years later he, George Ticknor and a couple of bishops figure as patrons in the advertisement of "Mrs. Inglis's Establishment for Young Ladies" in Boston. Naughty Fanny in the meantime had jilted her Boston gallant and married Angel Calderón de la Barca, Spanish minister to the United States. A year later, Don Angel was promoted to the new Spanish Embassy in Mexico City; and Fanny's witty, descriptive letters to William H. Prescott, published by him as *Life in Mexico,* have become a classic.

Two years before this social tempest, in 1831, the Otises acquired a new daughter-in-law, Emily Marshall. In those days, when there were no cinema queens and few actresses, the American public worshipped society beauties; and the reigning belles who "stopped traffic" were Cora Livingston of New Orleans, Julia Dickinson of Troy, Elizabeth Bordley Hawkins of Baltimore, and Emily Marshall of Boston. When Emily visited Philadelphia, schoolgirls were let out to see her pass; in the New York hotel where she stayed, strangers eager to have a look at her thronged

Emily Marshall, by Chester Harding.

William Foster Otis.

the lobby; when she attended the Boston theater on the same night as Daniel Webster, Emily received the standing ovation. The poet James Gates Percival wrote an acrostic in her honor beginning, "Earth knows no fairer, lovelier form than thine"; dozens of Boston youths fell in love with her and used to tramp up and down Franklin Street hoping to see her at the window of her parents' house. And she was as popular with women as with men; one of her contemporaries declared to Josiah Quincy, "No envious thought could have been possible in her presence; . . . she was as kind and attentive to the stupid and tedious as if they were talented."

Emily first became affianced to Sidney Brooks, a member of the Adams clan, but William Foster Otis cut him out and the engagement was broken. William's parents opposed the match. Emily's father, a respectable China merchant, belonged to the middle class, and after experiencing one merchant's offspring as daughter-in-law, the Otises wanted no more. But they were reconciled in the spring of 1830. William, having been elected to the general court, made a good speech, after which his delighted father asked what he could do for him. William said, "Call on Miss Marshall and treat her as your future daughter!" He did so, and was captivated; but Papa Marshall refused to let Emily marry William until he was in a position to support her, and that took about a year. Papa Otis helped by giving his son No. 71 Beacon Street, one of the block of granite-faced houses that he had lately built below Charles Street, opposite the future Public Garden. In the meantime, according to the Otises' neighbor Mary Appleton, "Mrs. Otis, the Lady Mayoress, had quite a fashionable tea-party, last week. Miss Marshall was present at it, for she returned from Philadelphia the day before, where she has been staying with her sister, and she looked, as usual, *bellissima*."

William Foster Otis and Emily Marshall were married on 18 May 1831 when she was twenty-three years of age, and he not quite thirty. The bridegroom's sister, Mrs. Andrew Ritchie, thus describes the occasion:

There were fifty guests at the wedding, an enormous crowd at the visit, which kept us until half past ten from supper. The bride looked very lovely, and was unaffected and modest. Her dress was beautiful, a white crêpe lisse with a rich line of silver embroidery at the top of the deep hem. The neck and sleeves trimmed with three rows of elegant blonde lace very wide. Gloves embroidered with silver, stockings ditto. Her black hair dressed plain in front, high bows with a few orange blossoms, and a rich blond lace scarf beautifully arranged on her head, one end hanging front over her left shoulder, the other hanging behind over her right. No ornaments of any kind either on her neck or ears, not even a buckle. I never saw her look better. Mr. Lyman said she was extremely beautiful, and that every one was remarking on her beauty as they passed in and out of the room. . . . William looked quite as handsome as the bride, and seemed highly delighted. The groom & bride went to their house alone, about one o'clock. Finch & Boott went to bed about six in the morning, after serenading until the birds sang as loud as their instruments.

Mr. and Mrs. Otis were speedily reconciled upon better acquaintance with their daughter-in-law, as the following extract from a letter from Otis to George Harrison, dated 28 November 1831, indicates:

William's wife turns out to be one of the most amiable, domestic and artless creatures in the world. My wife grows *very* fond of her. And once, when William was calld to the country on professional business (she having a cold & complaining) the former would have her bro't home, and actually *divided her bed* with her several nights, fearing that she would be timid & nervous left alone in another chamber. How I said nothing but laughed in my sleeve, & remembered *your prophecy,* that this would be so! Do you likewise say nothing but laugh with your wife.

After only five years of an almost ideally perfect marriage, and shortly after the birth of her third child, Emily Marshall Otis died, a martyr to the primitive surgery of the period.

Within three weeks there came for Harrison Gray Otis the

greatest calamity of his life, the death of his beloved Sally. In the following note of 6 September 1836, he informed the chief marshal of the Harvard Bicentenary, Robert C. Winthrop, of his inability to preside at the alumni meeting the next day:

> My dear Sir
> Though I felt that the death of my daughter a few days since disqualified me in a great measure from assisting at the approaching festival, yet feeling it to be an occasion in its nature solemn as well as joyous, I perseverd as you know in my intention to preside at the meeting. It has pleased the Almighty this day to remove by a sudden dispensation the wife of my youth, & it will be less unexpected by you that I should now find myself totally incompetent to that duty, than, that I should have the recollection and the power of announcing it under my own hand.
> With great respect
H. G. OTIS.

Obituary notices of ladies were unusual at that era, but Sally was so well known in other cities as well as Boston that the following appeared in a Philadelphia paper:

> Mrs. Otis was closely associated in the affection and esteem of many friends in this city, and it is due to her memory to record the strong sense they entertain of her virtues, and of the endearing features of her character, which made her beloved by all, and the ornament of the circle of friends by which she was surrounded on her frequent visits to Philadelphia.

To John G. Palfrey, his former pastor, who had proposed to preach a funeral sermon on his wife, Otis wrote:

> It is hard parting after 46 years of love & harmony from a person too who liv'd for me and for others & less for herself than any person I have ever known. But the blows come on me so fast & heavy that I am too much amazed to indulge other feelings than those of terror on account of those who are left to me. The fear of surviving all I love predominates over other agonies.

Otis's fears were well founded. He had lost his eldest son Harry Jr. and his youngest son George, his two elder daughters Mrs. Lyman and Mrs. Thorndike, and the two little Lyman boys who used to play with his boys at 45 Beacon Street. Before Otis himself died, he had also lost two grandsons — little George, and "Gus," one of the little Thorndikes who used to run in and out of the Beacon Street mansion.

It was on the great occasion which Otis felt he could neither preside at nor attend, the Harvard Bicentenary, that William H. Gardiner, after a brief tribute to him, offered the following toast:

> Harrison Gray Otis; the *first* scholar of the *first* class of a *new* nation; the career of his life has been according to the promise of his youth; he has touched nothing which he has not adorned; he has been rewarded with no office, nor honor, nor emolument, to which he was not richly entitled; and in the dignified retirement of declining years, he must always possess . . . the kind remembrance and most respectful consideration of the Alumni of Harvard.

The speech which Otis could not deliver, a somewhat turgid lamentation on the state of the Union — especially over Texas and its "sparse population of speculators and adventurers" — may be found in Josiah Quincy's official account of the celebration.

Sally's place in that large and happy family could never really be filled, but her daughter Sophia Harrison Ritchie tried. With her two lively ten- and eleven-year-old boys "Harry" and "Monty," she moved into No. 45 Beacon Street and undertook to be a mother to her brother William's orphaned children — Emily aged four, Mary aged three, and baby George whose mishandled birth had caused their beautiful mother's death. William, inconsolable for his loss, could not bear to live long in Boston and vainly sought solace in travel. But as Uncle Allyne lived at No. 45, and Andrew Ritchie occasionally joined his wife, Harrison Gray Otis always had one or two sons, a daughter, and five grandchildren living with him. To the little girls he became a second father. When

Emily was nine years old, her grandfather took her to see Faneuil Hall decorated for a ball to be given to the Prince de Joinville that evening. She always remembered her astonishment at the respect and attention shown to Otis. "I had considered him hitherto in the light of a delightful companion and . . . failed to imagine that he had ever been a celebrity."

This ball, on 25 November 1842, was Boston's homage to the son of King Louis-Philippe. It was a fancy-dress party, of which the sailor prince recorded in his *Vieux Souvenirs:*

> Je fis mon entrée à ce bal précédé et entouré d'une armée de commissaires, portant gravement de gigantesque mirlitons[1] et accompagné d'une assez belle femme, inconnue de tout le monde, que se fait appeler Amérique Vespuce et qui se met a jurer en français comme un païenne, parce qu'on lui renverse un verre de limonade sur sa belle robe de velours.

Our curiosity as to the identity of this lady is not satisfied by newspaper accounts of the ball, which merely describe the costume of "Princess Vespucci" as a long claret velvet dress "low on the shoulders and lace chemisette," but respected her *incognita*. One strongly suspects that she was Mrs. Harrison Gray Otis, Jr., who played this role to perfection in 1860 when the Prince of Wales was given a ball in Boston.

THE LAST YEARS

Otis came into touch again with national politics in 1838, owing to Henry Clay having sent him a copy of one of his speeches. In acknowledging the favor, he expressed his wish that Clay might be the next Whig nominee for the presidency. Now, Clay's most formidable rival for this honor was Daniel Webster for whom

---

[1] A shako helmet worn by troops of the First Republic and imitated by some of the élite Boston military groups such as the New England Guards. Mistranslated "wigs" in the English edition of Joinville.

Massachusetts had voted in 1836; but Otis, although a friend and admirer of Webster, was enough of a politician to see that no New England candidate, especially one with a Federalist background, could possibly win; and Clay in his reply adroitly dropped a hint to the effect that Otis might persuade the "god-like Daniel" to abdicate. Thus began a lengthy correspondence lasting for two years between Clay and Otis on the subject of the Whig nomination. The old Federalists seem to have had little influence over Webster, who reluctantly withdrew his name but supported Clay's other and successful rival, William Henry Harrison. There followed the famous log-cabin, hard-cider, Tippecanoe-and-Tyler-too campaign of 1840, into which Otis entered with the ardor of a young politican, notwithstanding the fact that a prominent feature of the campaign was the accusation of Hartford Convention Federalism which each side brought against the other. Philip Hone, who attended the great Whig Festival at Boston in early September, recorded his pleasure and astonishment over "the noble hospitality with which the first people in the city have opened their doors, spread their tables, and vacated their bedchambers for the accommodation of the delegates. Mr. Otis is to have a table spread for all comers. The committee of arrangements are constantly receiving notices from the most respectable of the citizens; 'I have so many beds;' 'I shall have a luncheon;' 'Send me so many strangers to take care of!' It is so like Boston."

The following letter of Otis to George Harrison, of 31 October 1840, is typical of the old Otis spirit:

I am marvellously well for 75 — and think of this time last year with a thankful heart. Were it not for my feet I should be *frisky* but so many old fools play the part of Lord Ogleby, that it is perhaps best for me to be warn'd constantly not to attempt it. Yesterday was the D——l to pay with you [in Pennsylvania] no doubt. I have of course no sort of information as to your agitation. But prophesy that you are beat in your State. If I am wrong, I will addict myself to democracy, confess my sins, and die in a bonnet rouge. What a "glorious winter" of blood & carnage would accompany the present struggle of factions if we had such a place as Paris. . . .

What an important week is this coming, and who expected in our "palmy days" to see the federalists glad to make backs for others to play leap frog! Yet such is our position as a pis aller. If all will do, to stop the progress of the infernal machine, universal suffrage, before it comes to the place where it will blow up the "entire concern" we may congratulate ourselves.

Otis, delighted at the success of Tippecanoe and Tyler too, wrote to George Harrison after the election that the *bonnet rouge* was already purchased and ready for him to be laid out in. But this keen old politician, observing danger ahead for the Whig party, sent a warning letter to Henry Clay on 16 December, opening with a sapient analysis:

The whig party is a coalition of persons, brought together from the four ends of our earth, led by instinctive impulse, not merely by compact of leaders, & united, (so far as the evidence goes,) as yet in only one defined object — a change of men. The other object, a change of measures, is far enough from being *defined*. It would be a fair & wise step in Genl. Harrison to throw upon the shoulders of yourself and a few leaders and representatives of the great subdivisions of party, the responsibility of forming his cabinet of persons who should be consulted & agreed beforehand, upon the principal features of the system to be pursued. The project of the Campaign should be arranged in such a Cabinet. Such measures only should be attempted as all are agreed in, & this should be pushed with vigor and carried. Thus a broad foundation could be laid for the formation of a great "Country party," on primary principles and mutual concession, extending in every direction & embracing all the great interests of the Country. Such a party has not yet existed among us; Events seem to indicate the practicability of forming it. Unless it be done, the cossacks will be upon you in one or two years. *Mais peut-etre cela ne sera pas mon affaire.*

Henry Clay's reply, expressing a belief that the Democratic party was "annihilated," showed very little perspicacity. Undiscouraged, Otis wrote in the same vein — the Whigs' golden opportunity to form a nationwide party — on 13 January 1841. The untimely death of President Harrison, and the breach between President Tyler and his party, rendered barren the Whig victory of 1840 and made Otis again a pessimist in politics. He wrote to George Harrison on 25 October 1842:

> Harrisons election shook my confidence in my opinion as to the certain ultimate result of universal suffrage, & the irresistible tendency of the masses to acquire & abuse power. But this only *pour le moment.* Mob principles, hatred to elevated character, jealousy of property, & a disposition to make all interests subservient to the views of the Canaille. In a word, agitation, incessant & unmitigated will keep this people in perpetual turmoil & render the Country an uncomfortable domicil for honest men & quiet gentlemen. But these troubles cannot come to you or me — at least not stay with us long. Happily you have no children, on whose uncertain fate to ruminate with anxiety.

Since Cicero was one of Otis's favorite authors, he doubtless read and reread *De senectute.* Consciously or unconsciously, he patterned his life on what the great Roman wrote about Appius Claudius Caecus:

> Four lusty sons, five daughters and a great household Appius ruled over when blind and aged. He did not lazily succumb to old age, but kept his mind taut as a bow. He maintained absolute command over his household, . . . his children venerated him and everyone loved him. In that house the manners and discipline of old time flourished. For old age is honored only so far as it defends itself, retains its rights, appeases no one, and rules over its domain to the last breath. As I approve an adolescent in whom there is something aged, so approve I the old man in whom there is something youthful. For he may be old in body, but never will be in spirit.

Harrison Gray Otis in 1844.

That Otis well succeeded in emulating old Appius, and in a more genial manner, may be judged from what a younger contemporary, Augustus C. Perkins, wrote about the amenities of No. 45 Beacon Street:

> The family of Mr. Otis was remarkable for great intelligence and personal beauty. I well remember numerous parties at the fine old mansion-house in Beacon Street, with its spacious hall and three beautiful rooms *en suite*, decorated with pictures by Copley, Blackburn, and Smybert, which threw over the place the air of good old colony times. There Mr. Otis, surrounded by his children and grandchildren and their friends, moved, the ruler of the revels. He always remembered all our names, and had a kind word and often a pat on the head for each of us.
>
> After an experience of more than forty years in such matters, I have never seen Mr. Otis surpassed in the perfection of his dress, his equipage, his entertainments, or his manners. He always reminded me of a fine old French nobleman, one of those we read of as uniting wit with learning, and great elegance with profound acquirements.

The gallery of family portraits had already been, as we have seen, augmented by purchases abroad through Washington Allston.

Gaiety at the Otis house was confirmed in her old age by one of those tots who received a kindly pat on the head; she remembered a party at Number 45 in which the patriarch, the most lively person present, entertained the company by singing an old English hunting song.

Although frequently suffering from recurrent attacks of the gout, Otis managed to keep up horseback exercise until the age of eighty, to make every year a journey by stage and rail to Newport, Philadelphia, Ballstown or Sharon Springs, and to preserve his good nature unimpaired. "We shall not quit Beacon Street," he writes in July 1843, "as our name is legion, and two or three generations like to come here to eat drink & smoke it." But, in September, off he goes on a "jaunt," as he calls it, to Albany by the newly opened Western Railroad, followed by a river trip to West Point and New York.

Most of his time was spent in his library, acquiring new friendships with books to make up for the friends he had lost. He taught himself Italian at the age of 69, and the wealth of literary allusions in the writings of his later years testifies to the breadth and depth of his reading in English, French, Italian, and classic literature.

A few of Otis's pleasant letters to George Harrison will best indicate his thoughts and pursuits during these last years of his life:

Boston Sepr 2 1841

Well my dear friend, the summer has gone again like a butterfly, & you and I with railroad speed are getting to the end of our journey. Dont you wish you knew what sort of accommodations await us there. We have no right to expect them to be *comparatively* as good as we have had here. It would be more than our share. Perhaps you would be satisfied to know that they will be not worse than at Longbranch. I hope dear Mrs H has enjoyed herself among the mermaids, & am glad that none of the Gods have descended in any shape to swim away with her. I have been doing little more than vegetate — making some repairs in my earthly tabernacle & driving out to visit Sophy who is 5 miles in the Country at a farmhouse which she seems to like for the occasion of moving around ad libitum with her girl. But I generally sleep at home, though I have a room there — but I want a servant & appliances, having conquered all lusts of the flesh except that of a fleshbrush. . . . I wish you could see my new wineroom. Old children want baby houses as well as "beads & prayer books" for the toys of old age. I have much comfort in my drosky. If you ever see Doctor Jackson enquire if his forewheels turn *quite round* to the crane neck — mine do not but I think they should. God bless you.

Afty

H. G. Otis

The "drosky" here mentioned was the vehicle to which Josiah Quincy alludes, in his *Figures of the Past,* as the first low-hung carriage ever seen in Boston. It saved Otis the pain of climbing the formidable flight of steps by which one entered an old-fashioned coach. The gouty old gentleman's first appearance downtown in his new vehicle created a sensation. "What will you take for your carriage, Mr. Otis?" inquired an impudent bystander. "The worst pair of legs in State Street!" he replied.

To proceed with the letters from Otis to George Harrison:

5 March 1842:

> I wonder if you & I shall ever meet again. The chances are against it, for though I am amazingly well in the *organics;* & have been to two soirées this winter, with a blue coat, yellow buttons plum tree velvet vest, & made a prodigious sensation; yet I cannot walk a mile without pain & have more or less *light* chronic gout flying about me, so that I am cowardly about being haul'd up from home, without a man to rub my back.

7 December 1844, after Clay's defeat by Polk:

> What fine encouraging times since we met . . . though I have had strong hopes, I have indulged as in the late struggle but feeble expectations. The general complexion of parties has been the same since the days of Jefferson — the predominance of ignorance and *mulishness* in Pennsylvania has also been conspicuous — ever since and before Israel Israel[1] was a candidate for public honors & Peters said "right, Gentlemen — let us have stable men and stable measures." I have lately seen a letter from the *elder* Adams to a lady — in which he stated that among other causes of his then late defeat in his canvas for President of the United States was a story propagated and believed thro all the German population, that he had imported three mistresses from England, but finding them un peu de trop, had sent them back at the public expense. And still equally absurd stories were current. . . .
> The difference however — & it is very great — consists in this. The problem to be solved under the Federal Govt, was whether by means of its peculiar modification, the conservative principles

---

[1] Israel Israel was the actual name of a livery stable keeper and publican who owned the "Cross Keys" at Chestnut and Third Streets in the last decade of the eighteenth century, and helped to organize the Pennsylvania Democratic Society. His apparent election to the state senate in 1797 was declared invalid.

indispensable to the salvation of every government, could be maintained against the steam power of universal suffrage, and the ignorance and passions of the masses. The trials have been for the most part discouraging but not so as to extinguish all hope. But this is a consummation which leaves nothing to be expected. The intelligent, educated, substantial and patriotic portion of the community are under the everlasting ban and power of a nominating caucus — in fact an elective body — representing all the anticonservative passions & prejudices & bad feelings of increasing millions. Are you sorry that they will have no chance to torment or push you long? — God bless you

yr H G OTIS

7 February 1845:

The only amusing occurrence of any note is the new subscription for Webster. The project is to raise a fund of 100,000 dollars here & in N York, the income to be settled on him & his wife for life, reversion to ye subscribers. It is confidently said that it will be filled — indeed is nearly so at this moment. I think his good fortune is almost equal to his political preëminence and quite equal to his claims. This is at least the third time that the wind has been raised for him and the most curious fact is that thousands are subscribed by many, who hold his old notes for other thousands, and who have not been backward in their censures of his profusion. I am not a subscriber — not able to be one — though I think it a great point to have him replaced in the Senate — of which the Whig minority will combine great talents, and afford the possibility of preventing or mitigating mischief. This affair of W's reminds me of George Selwyns wit. When a subscription was raised for Charles Fox, somebody adverting to the delicacy of the subject, expressed his wonder how Fox would *take it*. "Take it" said Selwyn "quarterly to be sure!"

In this same year (1845) the death of George Harrison brought an end to the sixty years' friendship between him and Harrison Gray Otis, who had now reached his eightieth year. Most of his friends and contemporaries having passed on, he clung tenaciously to those who survived — such men as Colonel Perkins, and the Maryland diplomat, Christopher Hughes — witty, delight-

ful "Kit" Hughes, everybody's friend. There are several of his
quaintly punctuated letters among Otis's papers of the forties.
The two old gentlemen loved to match good stories, to compare
notes on the gout, and to send each other presents of champagne
and of "Eastern Sho' " hams, of which the Otis family managed
to consume several barrels yearly. Otis's mind dwelt more and
more on the past; he delighted younger men, like Josiah Quincy,
Jr., with racy anecdotes of the great men of the Federalist era;
and he frequently furnished biographers and others with letters
of reminiscence.

During the winter of 1847–48, in his eighty-third year, Otis was
attacked by an unusually severe fit of the gout, followed by gan-
grene of the big toe. Yet his marvelous constitution pulled him
through; and so irrepressible was his spirit and energy that once
more he was able to take an active part in politics. The temperance
movement, which won its earliest victories in Massachusetts, drew
him from retirement. It seemed to this ancient conservative the
height of democratic tyranny for a legislature to prescribe what
he should or should not drink. He therefore wrote, in April 1848,
a long argument against coercive temperance measures, in the
form of a letter to a member of the Massachusetts legislature. It
was shortly published, as from "An Aged and Retired Citizen of
Boston," and was thought good enough to be republished in 1867.

Nor was this activity sufficient to exhaust the energy of Harrison
Gray Otis at the age of eighty-three. Eighteen-forty-eight was a
presidential year; the Whigs, defeated in 1844 on the Texas question, now prepared to draw advantage from the Mexican War by
nominating a military hero, General Zachary Taylor, for the
presidency. Otis addressed a Whig caucus in the beginning of the
campaign. Daniel Webster's statement, in the heat of disappointed
ambition, that the nomination of Taylor was "not fit to be made,"
and the Free Soil defection, caused Otis to fear for the success of
his party. He put all his remaining energy into an article in defense of the Whigs and their nomination. The result was no
ordinary production, but a letter of over five thousand words ad-

dressed "To the People of Massachusetts," and written in all the freshness and vigor of his early style. It appeared in the Boston *Atlas* of 2 October 1848, six days before his eighty-third birthday. He exposed the corruption and executive usurpation of past Democratic administrations, the danger to the Union of the Abolitionist and Free Soil parties, and the necessity of letting the South manage its internal affairs in its own way. The most eloquent passage is that in which he disposes of the objection that General Taylor was a soldier, not a statesman:

> The truth, however, is that a truly great man will always show himself great. The talents called forth by the strategy of a succession of military campaigns, in a country new and unexplored, and inaccessible by ordinary means, where resources must be created, and embarrassments not to be foreseen are constantly met and surmounted, would easily accommodate themselves to the varying, though less difficult exigencies of civil affairs. For myself, I rest satisfied that General Taylor would be found fully competent to the office of president, for the same reasons that I think Daniel Webster would make a great general. Each would require some little training and experience, in a new harness, and, perhaps, a good deal of consultation with others. History is replete with heroes transformed into statesmen. Who is unacquainted with the agency and influence of the great Marlborough, in the councils as well as in the wars of Queen Anne? Where did the greater Duke of Wellington qualify himself to settle the peace of Europe, which he had won by his sword, associated in congress with emperors and kings, and the most accomplished diplomatists from the principal cabinets of the old world? And whence did he derive the faculty which since that period has been displayed, in the intuitive sagacity with which he has controlled the measures of the British cabinet and peerage, and enabled his country to persevere in her career of power and glory, despite the most novel and serious embarrassments? In what school did the great Napoleon acquire the knowledge of affairs which enabled him to hold the strings of his administration in his own hands, to reform the interior management of the whole empire, and to preside in a council of the most distinguished jurists and civilians in the formation of the civil code,

himself initiating some of the most essential improvements? Finally, our great Washington was a Samson in combat before he became a Solomon in council. On very mature reflection, I am satisfied that General Taylor, in a short time after he shall have taken the chair, will acquit himself of his high duties to the entire public satisfaction.

This "Letter to the People of Massachusetts" was Otis's supreme effort. For months he had been troubled by a severe pain in the back. Exhaustion and weakness now confined him to his bed, his stomach refused food, little by little his strength ebbed away, and, surrounded by devoted children and grandchildren, he quietly awaited the end.

Knowledge of a family tragedy that occurred only two days before his own death was mercifully kept from him. This was the sudden death of his twelve-year-old grandson George Harrison Otis, a boyhood friend to Henry Adams, who vividly remembered him sixty-five years later. Every evening George used to play a game with his sister Mary. They sat at either end of a short sofa, bracing their little backs against the arms, placed the soles of their feet together and tried to push each other away. One evening George said, "I can't play tonight, my legs won't move." It was poliomyelitis, which no doctor then had the faintest idea how to treat, much less to cure; and next day the little boy died.

Every function of Otis's vigorous mind remained unimpaired almost until the last. He followed with keen interest the details of the presidential campaign, and read with dismay the comments on his "Letter" by the Democratic press which reiterated, as usual, the charge of Hartford Convention that he had so long and fruitlessly endeavored to explode. As he lay dying, the aged statesman could hear the Whig processions marching up Beacon Hill; hear the lusty shouts as company after company halted and gave with a will "Three cheers for Harrison Gray Otis!" — for the people of Boston had not forgotten their old favorite of Federalist days. On 26 October he lost the power of speech, and fell into a sweet

and tranquil slumber from which he never awoke; and at two
o'clock in the morning of Saturday, 28 October 1848, his gentle
breathing grew more and more faint, and finally ceased.

In his funeral sermon his pastor, the Reverend Samuel K.
Lothrop of Brattle Square Church, quoted some appropriate verses
by Dryden, one of Otis's favorite poets:

> Of no distemper, of no blast he died,
> But fell like autumn-fruit that mellowed long;
> Even wondered at, because he dropt no sooner.
> Fate seemed to wind him up for fourscore years;
> Yet freshly ran he on ten winters more:
> Till, like a clock worn out with eating time,
> The wheels of weary life at last stood still.

He was buried beside Sally in Mount Auburn Cemetery. Philip
Hone's *Diary* contains the best obituary:

> Mr. Otis was one of a class almost extinct, — a gentleman, in
> the full extent of the term; of shining talents and the most pol-
> ished manners. He has held many important public stations;
> as a senator from Massachusetts in the Senate of the United
> States, his eloquence shone with a lustre the rays of which have
> been transmitted to his illustrious successors. As the Mayor of
> Boston, his legal knowledge, sound judgment, and dignified de-
> portment imparted strength and grace to the magistracy. De-
> scended from a family and inheriting a name sacred in the annals
> of the Revolution, he was a Federalist in the best days of that
> glorious and abused party; a Whig then, and a Whig ever since.
> His intellect was unimpaired to the last hour of his life, and it
> is remarkable that a few weeks since, whilst suffering under the
> pains of a hopeless disease, and sinking beneath the weight of
> fourscore and three years, he wrote and published a long letter
> . . . marked by all the strength of argument and brilliancy of style
> which characterized the productions of his middle age. I have
> again to lament in the decease of Mr. Otis, the loss of another
> dearly-valued friend, whose uniform kindness and hospitality
> always constituted one of the greatest enjoyments of my visits to
> Boston.

Harrison Gray Otis had acquitted himself more than creditably in the career marked out for him by heredity, education, and unusual attainments of mind and heart. He had not shown, it is true, much evidence of great or original statesmanship. The sectional movement that culminated in the short-sighted Hartford Convention was the policy on which he had exerted the most pronounced influence. But his worthiest efforts in the national portion of his career, his spirited nationalism of 1798, his wise policy of sectional reconciliation in 1816, and his proffered solution of the slavery question deserve high praise. Otis, moreover, represented all that was best in a class — the ruling aristocracy of New England — and of a party — the Federal party, which he followed through all its aberrations, from lofty nationalism to narrow and selfish sectionalism; and led the way back to nationalism. His guiding principle, throughout his life, was a belief that the government of the United States and of the several states should be conducted by the wealthy and educated classes. He was firmly convinced that democracy would lead to a leveling downward of society, and a social revolution. The self-sacrifice, endurance, and devotion to the Union that the American democracy showed fifteen years after his death, he would never have imagined possible.

Otis, in truth, belonged more to the eighteenth than to the nineteenth century. He had no ambition for territorial expansion or world power for his country; Oregon, Texas, California, meant nothing to him. He would have kept the United States a "right little, tight little" nation backing the Mississippi and facing the Atlantic, ruled by merchant princes and country squires. Since America has followed the setting, not the rising sun, we may feel that Otis and his friends deserved to be excluded from a national power and destiny that they could neither share nor serve, only carp at and obstruct. But Massachusetts has little reason to complain of her long Federalist rule. While other states, taken over by the Democracy, were swimming in political corruption and extravagance, the Federalist administrations in Massachusetts set a standard in honesty, efficiency and moderate reform that no government of and by the people has surpassed; and only since the Bay State became Democratic has she become famous for political corruption.

The personality of Harrison Gray Otis was singularly well rounded and attractive. In him were blended all the qualities that make up a man beloved by men; and he was indeed beloved, during and after his lifetime, as few men have been. Sociable without dissipation, clever without affectation, brilliant without hypocrisy, he retained through years of political disappointment and domestic misfortune a genial, sunny nature that shed happiness. Few men have extracted so much pleasure from mere living as did he. With a wife whom he dearly loved, a little clan of relatives and descendants who adored him, a city proudly displaying the results of his taste and enterprise, devoted friends in all parts of the country, an enviable reputation as a lawyer and orator, and a public career crowned by the approbation of his fellow citizens, he could have asked for little more than he possessed. Had Otis been inclined to seek from Providence one more boon, it would have been that his countrymen should take him at his word, when he told them that the Hartford Convention was intended to preserve, not to destroy, the Union of the States.

APPENDIX

Children of Harrison Gray Otis
and Sally Foster Otis
and Some of Their Descendants[1]

H.G.O., B. 8 OCTOBER 1765, D. 28 OCTOBER 1848

S.F.O., B. 10 JANUARY 1770, D. 4 SEPTEMBER 1836[2]

THEY WERE MARRIED 31 MAY 1790

1. ELIZABETH GRAY OTIS, b. 1 June 1791, m. 31 May 1810 George Williams Lyman, Harvard 1806, s. of Theodore Lyman 1753–1839 of The Vale, Waltham, and Lydia Williams, niece of Timothy Pickering. Elizabeth Lyman d. at St. Croix, W.I., 20 Dec. 1824; her husband lived until 1880. Children:

George Theodore Lyman, b. 25 Apr. 1811, d. 11 Oct. 1816 (Otis Mss.)

Arthur Wellesley Lyman, b. 28 Mar. 1813, d. 24 Feb. 1826.

Elizabeth Otis Lyman, b. 29 July 1817, m. 1844 Francis Boott, d. 12 Jan. 1847. Their one child Elizabeth Otis L. Boott, m. 1885 Frank Duveneck the artist (see *Dictionary of American Biography,* hereafter *D.A.B.*) and d. the following year after giving birth to Francis Boott Duveneck, Harvard 1909.

Mary Ellen Lyman, b. 8 Sept. 1819, m. (1) 1840 James Amory Appleton (1818–43); (2) 1856 Charles S. Arnold of Savannah, Ga., who

---

[1] Based on a manuscript Otis genealogy compiled for Mrs. Samuel Eliot prior to 1906, and continued to date by her daughter and grandson; on Harvard class records (H.U. Archives) and on printed genealogies of the Lyman, Thorndike, Foster and other allied families. I have not attempted a complete list of all the Otises' descendants, but have tried to include all men with the surname Otis.

[2] Sally's parents were William Foster (1746–1821), Boston merchant, and Grace Spear, m. 29 Sept. 1768. Of their several children, twin girls Grace and Mary successively m. John Trecothick Apthorp; Joseph, a merchant mentioned by Abigail Adams as "a gentleman of soft and delicate manners" when he crossed the ocean with her; William Foster, Jr. (1772–1863), who after many years abroad returned to Boston with a French wife in 1809; Charles, Leonard, and Charlotte, who m. Jeremiah Van Rensselaer.

d. 17 days later. George L. Appleton, b. 1841, was her one child. She
d. 29 May 1875.

George Theodore Lyman, b. 23 Dec. 1821, Harvard 1842, d. 1908;
m. 17 Apr. 1845 his cousin Sally, dau. of James William Otis; she d.
1894. Their son George Gray Lyman m. Milly Parker and was
father of James Otis Lyman, Harvard 1906; daughter Alice m. William Platt Pepper, an Englishman; a second daughter Elizabeth
Gray Lyman m. Albert A. H. Meredith of Milton, Mass.

2. HARRISON GRAY OTIS, JR., b. 7 Aug. 1792, Harvard 1811; read
law with his father and in office of C. W. Hare, Philadelphia; admitted to Suffolk Bar 1814, m. 6 May 1817 Eliza, b. 1796, dau. of
William and Elizabeth (Henderson) Boardman of Boston. Otis
d. 3 Jan. 1827. His widow, who signed herself "Mrs. Harrison Gray
Otis," became a social leader and organizer of charities, prominent
on the Civil War Sanitary Commission, preserving Mount Vernon,
etc., and published a novel *The Barclays of Boston* (1854); d. 1873.
Mary C. Crawford *Romantic Days in Old Boston* (1910), pp. 306–12;
Famous Families of Mass. (1930), II pp. 250–52, and Colonial Soc.
Mass. *Publications* XVII, p. 157. Children:

Harrison Gray Otis III, b. 1822, Harvard LL.B. 1842. After fight-
ing a duel in Washington in 1844 with one Schott, he settled in
Thun, Switzerland, m. Blanche Müller, and d. 1 Apr. 1884. His son
Harrison Gray Otis IV d. 1901 in Switzerland, leaving a son Harrison
Gray Otis V, who died without issue around 1940.

Arthur Henderson Otis, b. 1824, entered U.S. Navy as midshipman
1841, served in U.S.S. *Columbia* and *John Adams* during Mexican
War. Entered Naval Academy 1848 but resigned next year and d.
19 June 1852 unmarried.

Edmund Dwight Otis, b. March 1827, d. unmarried subsequent to
1848.

3. SALLY OTIS, b. 22 Dec. 1793, m. 17 July 1811 Israel Thorndike, Jr.
(1785–1867), son of Israel Thorndike, merchant-shipowner of Beverly
and Boston, primarily trading with Germany, and benefactor of Harvard College. She d. 2 Dec. 1819. Their children:

Sally Ann Thorndike, 1812–79, m. 1837 Erich F. Oelrichs of
Bremen. No issue.

Elizabeth Frances Thorndike, 1813–85, m. (1) James J. Mason of

Portsmouth, N.H.; (2) Stephanus Theodore Oelrichs of Bremen, her brother-in-law. Numerous German descendants.

Israel Augustus Thorndike. b. 1814, Harvard 1839, m. Frances M. Macomb, dau. of James Macomb, Cuban sugar planter; he entered that business and d. at Sagua la Grande 1845. Children: James Macomb Thorndike 1841–68 who inherited the Sagua la Grande estates, m. Augusta Talmadge; Henry Huth Thorndike, 1843–1908, m. Elizabeth C. Gorton; Augustus Otis Thorndike, 1845–91.

Sophia Harrison Thorndike, 1815–85, m. her cousin George Herbert Thorndike, who was lost in the wreck of S.S. *President* in 1841. No issue.

4. MARY FOSTER OTIS, b. 15 Jan. 1795, d. in infancy.

5. ALLYNE OTIS (the first), b. 16 July 1796. Drowned bathing, July 1806.

6. GEORGE OTIS, b. 1797, d. in infancy.

7. SOPHIA HARRISON OTIS, b. 29 March 1798, m. Dec. 1823 Andrew Ritchie, Harvard 1802, who spent most of his time in St. Croix where he had inherited a sugar plantation from his first wife, a Danish lady. He d. 1862. H. G. Otis built No. 44 Beacon Street for the Ritchies. After the death of her mother in 1836, Sophia moved in with her father at No. 45, ran the old gentleman's household and brought up his motherless granddaughters and grandson. Lived in Newport from 1852; d. 1874. She had three children:

Harrison Ritchie, b. 23 Feb. 1825. Sent with his brother on grand tour of Europe under tutelage of Thomas G. Bradford, 1839–41. Harvard 1845 with honors, and one year in Law School. Admitted to bar 1848. M. 1849 Mary dau. of Frederick R. Sheldon of New York. Twice member of general court from Boston, trustee Mass. General Hospital, captain of the New England Guards and colonel on staff of Governor Andrew 1861–65. Moved to Paris 1868, d. there 24 Nov. 1894, as did his widow in 1913. Only surviving child, Sophia Harrison Ritchie (1857–1948) of Paris.

Montgomery Ritchie, b. 20 March 1826. Abroad with his brother, Harvard 1846, rowed on first college boat, the *Oneida*. In East India trade and toured Far East 1849–51. M. 1857 Cornelia, dau. of Gen.

James S. Wadsworth of Geneseo, N.Y. (see *D.A.B.*). As captain U.S. Army, helped cover retreat at Bull Run, later captain 1st Mass. Cavalry. After Wilderness Campaign discharged on account of chronic dysentery, of which he d. 7 Nov. 1864. Left son James W. Ritchie, from whom there are many descendants. *Harvard Memorial Biogs.* I (1866), pp. 116–23.

Elizabeth Gray Ritchie, 1830–96, m. 1858 Dr. Edouard Duplessis Beylard of Paris and Château de Rabodanges, Normandy. They had two daughters, Sophy and Marie ("Mimi") who died, unmarried, in France. Their son Edouard ("Zed") Duplessis Beylard (1859–1925), a noted sportsman, m. Julia P. Howard of California and lived at San Mateo. One dau. Sophia m. twice but d. without issue.

8. JAMES WILLIAM OTIS, b. 18 May 1800, m. 4 Jan. 1825 Martha, only dau. of Capt. William Church (1776–1849) and Martha (Crapon) Church of Providence. Studied for mercantile career under Israel Thorndike, took charge of his father's manufacturing interests in Taunton, settled in New York, agent for New England manufacturing concerns, president North America Fire Insurance Co., d. 1869. Children who left issue :

Sally Otis, b. 4 Oct. 1825, m. 1845 her cousin George T. Lyman; d. 1894 (see above, No. 1).

William Church Otis, 1831–89, m. 1855 Margaret, dau. of Henry and Margaret Sigourney; she d. 1885. Described at his death as "leading clubman of Boston." Their children were (a) Harrison Gray Otis 1856–1915, Harvard 1878, m. 1893 Louise McNamara whose descendants are William Allyne Otis, b. 1895, Harvard 1917, m. Alice Merriam who d. 1966, leaving son Michael P. Otis b. 1948, and Harrison Gray Otis (1902–67); (b) William Sigourney Otis (1857–93), Harvard 1878 (and 2 years in Law School), m. Pauline Root; (c) Herbert Foster Otis (1861–1921), m. Ethel Whiting; their descendants are James Otis b. 1898, Harvard 1920, m. 1937 Martha M. Brown, their son Samuel Allyne Otis, Harvard 1962, m. Elizabeth L. Stockton; (d) Margaret Sigourney Otis, b. 1866, m. Rev. Roland Cotton Smith; (e) Violet Otis, 1871–1965, m. 1891 Rev. William Greenough Thayer, Rector of St. Mark's School; they left five sons, two daughters and numerous grandchildren.

James Allyne Otis, 1836–98, m. Adelia (or Delia) Ludlam; lived at 111 Fifth Avenue, New York and Bellport, L.I., which he represented in the state senate 1884–85; major 22nd New York Infantry in Civil War; famous cotillion leader at New York and Newport. In

William Church Otis
and
Mary Ellen (Lyman)
Appleton.

Martha Church Otis

Elizabeth Otis
(Boott) Duveneck

business as commission broker but "on his marriage to the wealthy Miss Ludlam he retired . . . and devoted himself to the care and cultivation of his country place at Bellport, L.I." Three daughters: Mary L. Otis, b. 1865, m. Robert R. Livingston Clarkson; Martha C. Otis, b. 1867, m. George P. Munroe of Paris, Sara Birdsall ("Birdey") Otis, b. 1872, m. Frederick Edey. Numerous descendants.

Frank Allyne Otis, 1842–1903, Columbia 1861, of Bellport, L.I., a prominent Roman Catholic layman, m. (1) Almira Smith, one son Francis J. Otis, 1873–1939; (2) Marie Wiedenfeld.

9. WILLIAM FOSTER OTIS, b. 1 Dec. 1801, Harvard 1821. Practised law, elected to general court 1830–32; m. 18 May 1831 Emily, dau. of Josiah and Priscilla Marshall. Emily d. 1836, aged 29. William, senior warden of the Church of the Advent and trustee of St. Paul's School, d. at Versailles 29 May 1858; funeral sermon by Rt. Rev. Horatio Southgate, 20 June, printed in Boston. Children of William and Emily:

Emily Marshall Otis, b. 13 March 1832, m. 7 June 1853 Samuel Eliot, Harvard 1839. She d. 6 March 1906; he, 14 Sept. 1898. Their daughter Emily Marshall Eliot (1857–1925) m. 1886 John H. Morison (1856–1911), Harvard 1878. The writer of this book is their son.

Mary Allyne Otis, b. 9 Oct. 1833, d. 26 May 1918, m. 4 Dec. 1860 Alexander H. Stevens, Yale 1854, grandson of Albert Gallatin, a New York banker. Lived at Lawrence, L.I., and "Ardsheal," Paget, Bermuda. Their children who grew up were (a) Mary Otis Stevens, 1861–1950; (b) Frances Stevens, 1863–1910, m. Major Harington Swann of the British army; (c) Emily Stevens, 1864–1937, m. Adolf Ladenburg, New York banker (their only child Eugénie Mary, b. 1895, m. 1930 Preston Davie 1881–1967, Harvard 1904); (d) Eben Foster Stevens, 1871–1926, Yale 1892, New York stockbroker, m. Evalena B. Dixon (parents of Byam K. Stevens 1897–1967, Yale 1919, and William Dixon Stevens, 1901–60, Yale 1923, this writer's friend and shipmate); (e) Francis Kerby Stevens, 1877–1945, Yale 1897, New York City realtor, m. Elizabeth Shaw Oliver and has three married daughters.

George Harrison Otis, b. 11 July 1836, Henry Adams's boyhood playmate. D. of polio 24 Oct. 1848.

10. ALLYNE OTIS (the second), b. 27 Aug. 1807, Harvard 1825. Built a house in Newport 1852 and there d. 1873.

11. GEORGE HARRISON OTIS, b. 4 Sept. 1810, Harvard 1825; d. 1833, unmarried.

There are several Otises sufficiently distinguished to have sketches in the *D.A.B.* who are descendants of the original John Otis of Hingham, and remote cousins of H. G. Otis. These are Bass Otis (1784–1861), painter and lithographer; Charles Eugene Otis (1846–1917), jurist of St. Paul, Minn., Elisha Graves Otis (1811–61), inventor and manufacturer of the Otis elevator; General Elwell S. Otis (1838–1937) commanding U.S. Army in the Philippine Insurrection; Dr. Fessenden Nott Otis (1825–1900), specialist in genito-urinary diseases; George Alexander Otis (1781–1863), translator of the *Storia della Guerra dell' Independenza d'America* by Carlo Botta (1820), and his like-named grandson (1803–81), surgeon in the Union Army and author of *The Medical and Surgical History of the War of the Rebellion;* and Harrison Gray Otis (1837–1917), officer in the Union Army, who moved to California in 1876 and became owner-editor of the Los Angeles *Times.*

A number of other and less distinguished Otises named after our H. G. O. will be found in William A. Otis *Genealogical and Historical Memoir of the Otis Family in America* (Chicago, 1924).

BIBLIOGRAPHY & NOTES

Bibliography and Notes

My *Life and Letters of Harrison Gray Otis* (1913) is thoroughly anno-
tated and has a bibliography of manuscript sources and of Otis's published works (II, pp. 313–17). Here I am attempting only to indicate
important changes, and new material used.

Manuscript Sources

The Harrison Gray Otis Mss. given by me, and by Sophia Harrison
Ritchie, to the Massachusetts Historical Society in 1926 and following
years, have been broken down into a single chronological series, with
these exceptions: Otis's Letter Book of 1788–1803, the copies of his
mother's letters to Harrison Gray, and documents relating to the development of Beacon Hill. These last I gave to the Society for the
Preservation of New England Antiquities which occupies Otis's first
house on Cambridge Street. There are also Otis letters in an autograph
collection which my mother gave to the Boston Athenaeum.

Other manuscript collections which have come into the Massachusetts Historical Society since I first wrote on Otis are the Theodore
Sedgwick, David Cobb, Elbridge Gerry, Mercy Warren, and Josiah
Quincy Mss. The Otis letters collected by Herbert Foster Otis are now
owned by his son James Otis Esq. of Needham, Mass. A very important
collection is the John Rutledge Mss. in the Southern History Collec-
tion of the University of North Carolina Library, Chapel Hill. This is
available in microfilm. Other Otis letters are in the Palfrey Mss. in the
Houghton Library, Harvard; in the Boston Public Library; the Robert
G. Harper, Martin Van Buren and William H. Harrison Mss. in the
Library of Congress; and (especially his correspondence with William
Sullivan) in Miscellaneous Mss., New York Public Library.

CHAPTER I. CHILDHOOD

OTIS'S BIRTHPLACE. His parents' home was torn down to build the Revere House, and that was replaced by a fire station which in turn has fallen to the bulldozer and has been replaced by a little open space in front of the State Office Building.

Mrs. Samuel Eliot, Otis's granddaughter, left me some ms. notes of his childhood.

CHAPTER II. A YOUTH OF PROMISE

"THE GRAY MAGGOT." This is *A Few Remarks upon some of the Votes and Resolutions of the Continental Congress, . . . and the Provincial Congress.* By a FRIEND to Peace and good Order (1775).

Harvard Univ. Archives have been combed for Harry's student life. His letter to Van Rensselaer, the only one known to me to which he signs his full name, belongs to James Otis Esq.

CHAPTER III. LAW, FUN, AND REBELLION

SANS SOUCI. Charles Warren in Mass. Hist. Soc. *Proceedings* LX (1927), pp. 318–44, with key to the characters. Authorship of the pamphlet was a well-kept secret. I suspect Mercy Warren herself. Mrs. Perez Morton, *née* Sarah Apthorp, became a locally famous poet under the pseudonym "Philenia," but did not (as many supposed) write that "scandalous" novel *The Power of Sympathy* (1789). Concert Hall, on the corner of Scollay Square and Hanover Street, was Boston's principal hall for concerts, dances and social meetings from 1755 for almost a century. "This was the most elegant Hall in the Town, and was much admired for its symmetry and elegant architectural finish. . . . Superb mirrors adorned its walls," says Samuel G. Drake in his *History and Antiquities of Boston.*

FAIRBANKS-FALES CASE. *Report of the Trial of Jason Fairbanks* (Boston, 1801) contains a speech by "one of the prisoner's counsel." Ferris Greenslet (*The Lowells and Their Seven Worlds*, 1946, p. 104) agrees with me that this was by Otis. Charles Warren *Jacobin and Junto* (1931) devotes a chapter to this case, as does Thomas C. Amory in his *Life of James Sullivan* (1859), II, pp. 17–26.

CHAPTER IV. MARRIAGE, BUSINESS, AND FAMILY LETTERS

MOUNT VERNON PROPRIETORS. The original partners were Otis and Jonathan Mason, each with a three-tenths interest, and Joseph Woodward and Charles Ward Apthorp, each with two-tenths. Woodward sold out to Mrs. James Swan, whose son-in-law William Sullivan inherited that share; and he or Apthorp sold to Benjamin Joy. A few others figured briefly, but Otis, Mason, Sullivan and Joy had a majority interest for most of the Proprietors' history. Allen Chamberlain *Beacon Hill. Its Ancient Pastures and Early Mansions* (1925) is supplemented by his article based on the Otis Mss., in the Boston *Evening Transcript* 12 March 1927. Mary C. Crawford *Old Boston Ways and Days* (1909), Harold and James Kirker *Bulfinch's Boston* (1964), and Walter M. Whitehill *Boston: A Topographical History* (1963) have additional details.

OTIS'S PROPERTY IN 1798. In the Boston assessment for the direct tax of 1798 (Boston Record Commissioners' *22nd Report*, iv, p. 19) Otis's Cambridge Street house is assessed at $16,000, four wooden buildings near by at $11,000, land on Cambridge Street which he owned in partnership with Samuel Parkman, $26,200, a brick dwelling on Common (now Tremont) Street, $9,000, and two stores on Long Wharf, $5,000. Otis sold the Cambridge Street house in 1801 for $20,000 to a Boston merchant, John Osborne, who lived in it for 18 years. In 1834 it became headquarters of a noted midwife named Mott, and an engraving of it, offering "Shampoo Baths" and other ministrations, is the frontispiece of *The Ladies Medical Oracle; or, Mrs. Mott's Advice to Young Females, Wives and Mothers,* printed and published for the authoress at her residence at the corner of Lynde and Cambridge streets (Boston, 1834). In 1916, the house was purchased by the Society for the Preservation of New England Antiquities and beautifully restored to serve as their headquarters and museum. It is now numbered 141 Cambridge Street. The best pictorial description is in *Great Georgian Houses of America* (1933).

CHAPTER V. HAMILTONIAN FEDERALIST

OTIS'S QUOTATIONS on the conservatism of the American Revolution: Boston *Courier* 14 June 1831, and a letter to George Harrison of 4 April 1837. He elaborated the thought in the address he prepared for the Harvard Bicentenary of 1836: "Those persons [Radicals and Democrats] do not admit, that the Revolution was completed by the establishment of independence. They would identify revolution with perpetual motion. They would put all ancient institutions, laws, customs, courts, colleges and schools upon wheels and keep them whirling for ever with the steam of their own eloquence." Josiah Quincy *Hist. of Harvard Univ.* II, p. 666.

THE BAY STATE REPUBLICANS. The contempt with which the Massachusetts Democrats were treated in Congress was notorious; e.g., Edmund Quincy *Josiah Quincy*, p. 95 and Wm. C. Bruce *John Randolph* II, p. 724. Of eight Massachusetts Republicans who signed an open letter to Otis and Timothy Bigelow, 13 Dec. 1808, supporting Jefferson's embargo, four are not even mentioned in Paul Goodman *The Democratic-Republicans of Mass.* (1964) . Two of them, Ezekiel Bacon and Richard Cutts, when defeated by Federalists in 1812, were "taken care of" by appointments as comptrollers of the Treasury. Good sketch of Varnum in *D.A.B.*

ESSEX JUNTO. Gerry's remark is in his *Life* by James T. Austin (1829) II, p. 86; Parsons's ideas are in the *Memoir* by Theophilus Parsons, Jr. (1859), pp. 116–18. Important sketch of Parsons's services to American law by Zechariah Chafee in *D.A.B.* For Fisher Ames, see my essay "Squire Ames and Dr. Ames" in *New Eng. Quart.* I (1928) and *By Land and By Sea* (1953), pp. 200–18. Otis's description of the Essex Junto, dated 1811 or 1812, is in Edmund Quincy *Josiah Quincy* (1868), p. 242. David H. Fischer "The Myth of the Essex Junto," *William and Mary Quart.* XXI (1954), pp. 191–235, argues that there was no such thing (which would certainly have astonished Otis!) and that the "Essexmen," as he calls its members, were merely "dreamers, hopeless idealists." Junto was a pejorative word meaning a political clique or faction, and to call the *émigrés* from Essex County, who were the right-wing Federalists, the "Essex Junto," came naturally to New Englanders who had read about the Junto of Charles I, especially as Essex had been the most powerful county, politically, since the seventeenth century (see John G. Palfrey *History of New England* II, p. 157n). Parsons *et al.* had been instrumental in having the 1778 state constitution defeated, by a powerful pamphlet known as the *Essex Result,* and in getting the 1780 constitution adopted. Besides the references to them in this book, see Nathaniel Ames's diary in Charles Warren *Jacobin and Junto* (1931), pp. 94–5, 149, 234, referring to the same group. According to a letter of Pickering in 1808,

Henry Adams *Documents Relating to New Eng. Federalism,* p. 369, he first heard the phrase from John Adams in 1797. Otis to James Swan, 23 Nov. 1797, is in N.Y.P.L. Misc. Mss., H. G. Otis. The consul referred to was probably Fulwar Skipwith, a cousin of Jefferson's whom he had appointed consul general in Paris. Cf. Dumas Malone *Jefferson* III (1962), p. 379.

CHAPTER VI. FIRST TERM IN CONGRESS

FEDERALIST EXTREMISM. Vernon Stauffer *New England and the Bavarian Illuminati* (1919). Jedidiah Morse, best known for his *American Geography,* got his ideas largely from the sensational books of John Robison and the Abbé Barruel, published in England the year before and reprinted in the United States. This Illuminati myth never dies. It reappeared in the propaganda of the Anti-Masonic party in 1828; Nesta Webster *World Revolution* (1921) ascribed the origin of the Bolsheviks to the Illuminati; the story was used to discredit the New Deal; and Robert Welch of the John Birch Society uses it in his pamphlets, e.g., *The Truth in Time* and *The New Americanism* (1966), to prove that the welfare state, communism and the two world wars are part of a conspiracy started by the obscure Weishaupt in 1776. Robison and Webster have recently been reprinted in Texas for the edification of the faithful.

CHAPTER VII. THE REPUBLICAN COURT

Rufus W. Griswold *The Republican Court* (1855). Manuscript memoir by Joshua Fisher, Jr., son of Joshua Fisher (1755–1806) who married Elizabeth Powel Francis, sister of Mrs. George Harrison. His son George Harrison Fisher (1849–1925, Harvard 1870) placed the manuscript at my disposition in 1910 with this statement about the author (whom he did not then allow me to name): "Born after the events described, he wrote his account of society during the Washington and Adams administrations for the amusement and information of his children, from first-hand testimony of members of that society, and from family tradition." Although Mr. Fisher informed me that he was giving the ms. to the Historical Society of Pennsylvania, apparently he never did so, and it cannot now (1968) be located.

CHAPTER VIII. FRANCE BACKS DOWN

FRENCH POLICY. E. Wilson Lyon "The Directory and the U.S.," *Amer. Hist. Rev.* XLII (1938), pp. 514–32, has accurate data on French policy. The key document, Victor Du Pont's *Mémoire* to Talleyrand, 21 July 1798, is in Mass. Hist. Soc. *Proceedings* XLIX (1916), pp. 63–79. Létombe's account of Otis's consternation when Adams's nomination of Vans Murray came out is in the Foreign Office Archives, Paris. Otis's quotation from Charles Churchill in his letter to Rutledge (Chapel Hill, date missing) is from "The Ghost," in Churchill's *Poems* (1766) I, p. 23. Page Smith *John Adams* (1962) II is a fresh account of this administration.

BANKRUPTCY. In my possession are a broadside *Mr. Otis's Speech on the Bankrupt Act, in the Senate of the United States, February 7, 1821;* a pamphlet *Letter to the Senate and House of Representatives of the United States upon the Expediency of an Uniform System of Bankruptcy* (31 pp., Boston, 1821), and a broadside *Remonstrance* against the bill addressed to Senate and House by certain "Merchants, Traders and Mechanics of the Town of Boston." Otis's bill did not pass, nor did another introduced by Daniel Webster in 1824. Except for a temporary act of 1841, the first real national bankruptcy act was that of 1867. *Collier on Bankruptcy,* the standard work (14th ed.), gives the history of this class of legislation.

CHAPTER IX. THE ELECTION OF 1800–1801

"MIDST CHAINS AND BOLTS" (Otis's letter of 4 Feb. 1801 — it should have been "bolts and bars") is quoted from Lord William Russell's *Epistle* from Newgate in 1683 to Lord Cavendish (London, 1773).

The confusing final count is explained in Edward Stanwood's *History of the Presidency 1788–1897* (1898), p. 72. "The 36th ballot, on the 17th of February, resulted in the choice of Mr. Jefferson. The Federalists, excepting those from New Hampshire, Mass., R.I. and Conn. declined to vote. This action gave the votes of Vermont and Maryland to Jefferson, raising his number to 10; it rendered blank the votes of Delaware and So. Carolina; and left to Burr the 4 New England States above named."

CHAPTER X. HARRY OTIS, FRIEND AND HOST

WILLIAM WIRT. The quotations are from his *Memoirs* by John P. Kennedy (1851) II, pp. 232–33, 237.

NO. 85 MT. VERNON ST. S. Parsons & W. D. Garrett "The Second Harrison Gray Otis House," *Antiques* XCII (1967), pp. 536–41.

NO. 45 BEACON ST. The houses on Beacon Hill were not numbered until 1823, when Otis's mansion became 20; this was changed to 42 in 1830, and to 45, which it has since remained, in 1846. The site of the present numbers 43 and 44 was Otis's garden. Uphill from the garden, on Otis's plan here reproduced, is "Vinal's land." John Vinal, a schoolmaster, bought Copley's old wooden house before the Otis deal. He and his son were living there in 1816 according to the Boston Directory of that year. Shortly after, Vinal sold to David Sears, who pulled the old house down and in 1817 began to build the granite mansion which became the nucleus of the Somerset Club, No. 42. In 1831 Sears bought a 25-foot-wide strip of Otis's garden and there built an addition to his mansion, now No. 43, the ladies' entrance to the club. In 1967 a bottle-shaped well or cistern about 60 feet deep, once the water supply for the Otis house, was found under No. 43. At about the same time that Otis sold half his garden to Sears, he built No. 44 Beacon St. for his daughter Mrs. Ritchie on the remainder. Apparently she never lived there but let it. For later history of No. 45, see notes to Chap. XXII, below. The best description is in *Great Georgian Houses of America,* published for the benefit of the Architects' Emergency Committee (New York, 1933).

SERVANTS AND ALLEGED EXTRAVAGANCE. Among the grossly inaccurate statements about Otis circulated by gossip columnists turned social historian are that Otis lived in "extravagance on a truly horrid scale," wore gold-laced hats, and spent $10,000 a year on servants. Considering that maidservants in his day got $5 to $7 a week, and menservants $7 to $12, a slight calculation will show that Otis could only have spent $10,000 a year on servants by filling every room in the house with them.

From 1815 on, Otis was so afflicted by gout that he needed a manservant to massage and dress him. "Gentlemen's gentlemen" were not to be had from the Yankee population, and Otis had to make do with a series of French-speaking Germans who did not stay long after discovering that flunkies were despised in Boston.

HARVARD REBELLION OF 1805. My *Three Centuries of Harvard* (6th ed., 1963), pp. 211-12. In this book, p. 198, I said it was "not certain that young Lee entered Harvard." But a letter from his father to Otis, dated 2 March 1807, repaying money that Otis had advanced to John at Harvard, proves that he did; he belonged to the Class of 1808 but did not graduate.

SANTAYANA. The quotation is in his *Character and Opinion in the United States* (1920), p. 52.

SCANDALS. Rutledge Mss., Chapel Hill. The nameless Boston scandal is related in "Sigma" (Lucius M. Sargent) *Reminiscences of Samuel Dexter* (1857), pp. 65-70.

CHAPTER XI. BUSINESS, ORATORY, AND FAMILY AFFAIRS

BOSTON FAMILIES. Mary Caroline Crawford *Famous Families of Mass.* (2 vols., 1930) is the best for unraveling family relationships.

BOSTON REAL ESTATE. Allen Chamberlain *Beacon Hill, Its Ancient Pastures and Early Mansions* (1925); Walter M. Whitehill *Boston: A Topographical History* (1963), Harold & James Kirker *Bulfinch's Boston 1787-1817* (1964). An article by Chamberlain in the Boston *Evening Transcript,* 12 March 1927, adds piquant details on the nuisance suits to which the Proprietors were subjected; and Abbot Lowell Cummings "Charles Bulfinch and Boston's Vanishing West End" in *Old-Time New England* LII (1961), pp. 31-41, adds details on the houses. H. W. Winkley "Annals of Louisbourg Square," Bostonian Society *Proceedings* (Jan. 1926), pp. 22-37; Carl J. Weinhardt, Jr. "Domestic Architecture of Beacon Hill 1800-1850" in same (Jan. 1958). Bainbridge Bunting *Houses of Boston's Back Bay* (1967), pp. 49-52, 402, 467, has data on Otis's granite block, now 70-76 Beacon Street — but these numbers were not always the same.

MOUNT WHOREDOM. The change of name did not change the character of the north slope village. In 1814 we hear of disorderly conduct there by sailors of U.S.S. *Constitution;* and an early vice crusader, the Rev. James Davis, reported that "Satan's Seat" lay on Southack (now Phillips) Street, where dwell "three hundred females wholly devoid of shame and modesty." Although certain streets have become respectable, this area even at the present day is the Boston headquarters for beatniks, hippies and other unsavory characters who have appropriately made Charles Street, built on the fill from Mt. Whoredom, their Broadway. The so-called "nigger hill" of the early 1800's lay on the north slope of Sentry Hill directly behind the State House, and is not to be confused with Mt. Whoredom, and was far more respectable.

MAINE LANDS. The Bingham deal is fully documented by Frederick S. Allis, Jr., in Col. Soc. Mass. *Publications* Vols. 36 and 37 (1954), and in Paul Goodman *The Democratic Republicans of Mass.* (1964), pp. 155–61. William S. Spurr *History of Otisfield* (n.p., n.d.); Alphonso Moulton *et al. Centennial History of Harrison* (Portland, 1909); G. L. Varney *Gazeteer of State of Maine* (1881). In the 1960 census Harrison had a population of 1,014, a drop of 12 in ten years; Otisfield had 549, a drop of 50 from 1950. Otis in Hancock County attained its highest population (304) in 1880, and today has barely half that.

OTIS'S PAINTINGS. The artists can be identified as Domenico Marchi, called Tempesta (1652–1737); Jan Dirksz Both (1618–52) and Adam Pynacker (1622–73), imitators of Claude Lorrain, and Anthonie Waterlo (1610–90) and Jan Siberechts (1627–1700). In a fragmentary list of his paintings in Otis's hand are two not shown in the Athenaeum exhibits: "Tankard, lemon &c, Teniers," probably a copy of a still life by that artist, and "Venus & Cupid with the Arms of Aeneas. Bourdon." This must be Sebastien Bourdon (1616–71) whose "Vénus et Enée" at the Hermitage is reproduced in *Chefs-d'Oeuvre de la peinture française dans les musées de Leningrad et de Moscou* (Paris, 1965), p. 6. Apart from this last, Otis's — or Allston's — taste seems to have run to the Dutch and Flemish schools of the nineteenth century. Lillian B. Miller *Patrons and Patriotism* (1966) chap. x.

LITERATURE AND ORATORY. Emerson on Otis's 1822 speech is in his *Journals* (1909 ed.) I, p. 142. Thirty years later Emerson recorded (*Journals* VIII, p. 339), "From 1790 to 1820, there was not a book, a speech, a conversation, or a thought in the State." Hardly fair to the Federalist period, but the Federalists were deaf and blind to the new voices and scenes that were rising around them. Otis's contemporary Alden Bradford, in his *Biographical Notices of Distinguished Men in New England* (1842), pp. 450–1, wrote of Fisher Ames: "He was contemporary and intimate with Judge Tudor, Rev. John Clarke, Rev. John Eliot, Rev. James Freeman, Hon. Samuel Dexter, Hon. H. G. Otis — who, forty-five and fifty years ago, formed a literary constellation, not since surpassed; probably not equalled."

This, after Emerson had published his first addresses and essays, Longfellow had published "Voices of the Night" and the "Psalm of Life," Whittier's, Holmes's and J. R. Lowell's first books of poems had appeared, and Hawthorne had published *Fanshawe* and *Twice-Told Tales!*

HENRY LEE'S REMARKS ON ESSEX COUNTY CLANNISHNESS are in the *Memoir* of him by John T. Morse, Jr. (1905), pp. 8–9. Mrs. Peabody's memoirs are *To Be Young Was Very Heaven* (1967).

CHAPTER XII. FEDERALIST REORGANIZATION

David H. Fischer *The Revolution of American Conservatism, The Federalist Party in the Era of Jeffersonian Democracy* (1965) has broadened this subject to all the states. He uses material from my first edition but attacks my conclusions as "erroneous," arguing that the Federalist party, as reorganized, was democratic. Which, I maintain, is contrary to fact.

WASHINGTON'S MEMORY. Greatly though the Federalists admired Washington, they notably did not respond to an appeal by Benjamin Russell, editor of the *Centinel,* in 1811, to raise money for an equestrian statue of the general. Cabot, Pickering, Otis and other prominent men of means begged off. John Lowell renewed the project in 1818, and negotiations were begun with Sir Thomas Chantrey, the British sculptor, to execute it; but in 1831 the Bostonians were still talking and failing to raise the money. (Letters in Boston Public Library, Ms. Collection). Next, the City of Boston took it up, designating Thomas Crawford as the sculptor, but Crawford died in 1857 before even starting work. Finally, Thomas Ball of Boston made a half-size model which aroused so much enthusiasm that the money was raised; Ball worked on it during the Civil War, and in 1869 his magnificent equestrian statue of Washington was unveiled on the Boston Public Garden.

CHAPTER XIII. CONSPIRACY AND THE *Chesapeake* AFFAIR

AUSTIN-SELFRIDGE AFFRAY. Thomas C. Amory *James Sullivan* II, pp. 165–67; Boston *Gazette* 4 Aug. 1806; Boston *Democrat* 6 & 9 Aug. 1806; *Trial of Thomas O. Selfridge . . . for Killing Charles Austin* (1807); T. O. Selfridge *A Correct Statement of the Whole Prelimi-*

nary Controversy (1807); Charles Warren *Jacobin and Junto* (1931), chap. vii. For Mellimelni, innocent instigator of this fray, see Ray W. Irwin *Diplomatic Relations of the U. S. with the Barbary Powers* (1931), pp. 164–66. Warren gives references to discussions of the case after 40 years had elapsed, and I can add one even later. When Rear Admiral Thomas O. Selfridge, grandson of the acquitted slayer of Charles Austin, visited Newport in the present century, he caused careful inquiries to be made as to whether Miss Catharine Austin, grand-niece of Benjamin Austin and a social leader of Newport, would "receive" him! I am glad to say that Miss Austin assured him that she considered bygones should be bygones.

Chapter XV. Embargo to War

OTIS'S CONVENTION LETTER of 15 Dec. 1808 is in Quincy Mss., Mass. Hist. Society.

SOUTHERN SECESSION. *Columbian Centinel* 22 Aug. 1812, quoting *United States Gazette;* it adds that this suggestion caused such an uproar in Washington that Colvin had to apologize. Otis copied the *Centinel* article, probably intending to use it in one of his rebuttals of Hartfort Convention treason. This *Monitor* article may have suggested to the Rev. William Jenks of Bath, Me., a fantastic pamphlet that he wrote, late in 1808, and published over a false imprint, "Quebeck, A.D. 1901." It is called *Memoir of the Northern Kingdom, written A.D. 1872 by the Late Rev. Williamson Jahnsenykes LL.D. . . . in Six Letters to His Son.* Here he tells how Virginia, pressured by Napoleon, seceded in 1808 and was consoled by Jefferson's being chosen viceroy for the "Southern Kingdom" (which all the slave states joined) until Betsy Patterson's son by Jerome Bonaparte should come of age. New England, ruined by the embargo, joined Canada, which became the "Northern Kingdom," under a member of the House of Hanover, leaving out on a limb the "Illinois Republic." This in 1872 was being pressured to join the Northern Kingdom. Whether Jenks intended this as a warning, or a mere fantasy, does not appear.

MASSACHUSETTS GENERAL HOSPITAL. Incorporation was conditioned on $100,000 being raised for the hospital by 1816; but when the hat was handed, all the big contributions (Phillips $20,000; Thomas H. Perkins, James Perkins and David Sears $5000 each; the Humane Society of Mass., officered by Federalists, $5,140.56; Theodore Lyman, Samuel Parkman, Joseph Peabody and Joseph Coolidge $2000 each; Otis, $500) were Federalists, and the only Democrats on the list of incorporators who gave anything were Benjamin W. Crowninshield ($200) and Billy Gray, wealthiest shipowner in Massachusetts ($500). Nathaniel I. Bowditch *History of the M.G.H.* (1851), pp. 399–417; Mark A. DeWolfe Howe *The Humane Society of Mass.* (1918), pp. 201–10.

THE GERRYMANDER. Prior to 1812 state senatorial districts were identical with county boundaries; this meant that Essex County chose a solid Federalist delegation of five. The Democrats accordingly created a new district starting at Salisbury and running around the back of the county, where the poorer farmers were of their persuasion, terminating at Chelsea in Suffolk County and including only one strongly Federalist town, Salem. This secured them three state senators. Benjamin Russell, editor of the *Centinel,* posted up a map of this amorphous district in his office. Gilbert Stuart the painter dropped in, added a beak, wings and claws, and said, "That will do for a Salamander." "Gerrymander!" said Russell, and the name stuck. Note that the "monster's" back shows Gerry's profile.

OTIS-GRAY CORRESPONDENCE. In the Public Record Office, London, F.O.5.73, is a letter of Harrison Gray to Lord Wellesley the foreign minister, of 8 March 1810, enclosing extracts from two earlier letters from Otis to him along the same lines.

HENRY PLOT. My detailed account is in Mass. Hist. Soc. *Proceedings* LXIX (1956), 207–31, and *By Land and By Sea* (1953), chap. xii. The origin of the odd friendship between John Henry and Henry Cary (the "H.C." of Harriet Otis's diary entry) has since been explained. John Henry gave Henry Cary, who had put him up on an earlier visit to Boston, a letter of introduction to a rich uncle in New York, Michael Hogan, who made him his secretary; and this led to Cary's fortune. Perry Miller *The Raven and the Whale* (1956), pp. 37–9 *et passim.* The Carys owned a lavish country estate in Chelsea and were intimate friends of Harriet Otis — see C. G. C. *The Cary Letters* (privately printed 1891), pp. 183–93.

BALTIMORE RIOT and "FEDERALIST OUTRAGES." The Boston *Independent Chronicle,* Aug. 1812, condoned the Baltimore riot on the ground that the Federalists irritated the mob by defending themselves and deserved what they got for disapproving the war. It also tried to balance the Baltimore affair with stories of "Federalist Outrages." These took the form of breaking windows in Benjamin Austin's house, hooting at two pro-war congressmen (Seaver and Widgery) on State Street, and hustling a third in Plymouth. Here the descendants of the Pilgrim Fathers, remembering perhaps how their ancestors had treated "Mad Jack" Oldham, gave congressman Charles Turner, Jr., the equivalent of a modern "bum's rush," shouting, "Here goes the fellow who voted for war, here goes the War Hawk!" Turner claimed that he had been kicked on the backside, but the Plymouth selectmen issued a statement that the kickers merely *aimed* at him but failed to register! Turner, an unsuccessful preacher, had squeaked into Congress in 1810 through falsification of election returns, but was heavily defeated in 1812. Cape Cod was as violent against the war as Boston. On 21 July 1812 a popular convention on the Cape resolved, "We consider the War in which we are now engaged, as having originated in hatred to England, and to Commerce; in subservience to the interest, or obedience to the mandates of the Tyrant of *France*."

MILITIA QUESTION. Winfield Scott *Memoirs* I (1864), p. 35. See also S. G. Goodrich *Recollections* (1856) for the unsavory characters commissioned to command federal troops stationed at Hartford. Herman V. Ames *State Docs. on Federal Relations, No. 2, State Rights and the War of 1812* (Phila., 1900) has a full account of the militia controversy, which the Supreme Court finally decided against the states in Martin *v.* Mott (1827).

MERINO SHEEP AFFAIR. Documents in Otis Mss. 14–17 Dec. 1814. On 23 Oct. Otis's cousin Henry Warren wrote him that he was sending a servant to Boston to bring to Plymouth certain merino rams, including one named "Grand Turk" — probably a prize of the privateer of that name.

BOTHNEA CASE. Charles Warren *The Supreme Court in U. S. History* (1926) II, pp. 427–28 notes. The R. G. Harper Mss. he cites are in the Library of Congress, and copies I made in 1911 are in the Otis Mss. The case is in 2 Wheaton Reports, pp. 176–77 (4 U. S. Reports, pp. 81–2) and 1 Wheaton, pp. 408–14 (3 U. S. Reports, pp. 608–10).

FEDERAL LOANS. Otis to Cabot 2 July, and Cabot to Otis 3 July, Otis Mss.; J. D. Forbes *Israel Thorndike Federalist Financier* (1953), pp. 112–14.

CHAPTER XVII. THE HARTFORD CONVENTION

The only serious attempts since my 1913 *Life and Letters of H. G. Otis* freshly to study the Hartford Convention are Edward Channing *History of the United States* IV (1917), Charles A. and Mary Beard, *Rise of American Civilization* (1927), and J. Truslow Adams *New England in the Republic* (1926). All three are very fair.

TOWN MEETING RESOLVES. One of the most vehement was Deerfield's of 10 Jan. 1814. The war was "impolitic, unnecessary and unjust," against the nation which has been the only barrier against the universal domination of "that modern 'scourge of God,' the Emperor of France." The war has been "infamously and profligately conducted" in such manner as "to pave the way for an iron despotism." Protests in Congress against measures destructive to New England interests have been "contemptuously voted down . . . by mad tyros and slave representatives of the South and their sycophants." If the Madison administration insists on continuing the war, and creating new States in the mud of Louisiana" whose inhabitants are "as ignorant of Republicanism as the alligators of their swamps," disunion will be better than continued submission to this nefarious system. The nomination of Albert Gallatin, "a renegade from his native Country, . . . a ringleader of insurrection," to the peace commission proves the insincerity of peace negotiations. Mass. Archives.

RUFUS G. AMORY'S STATEMENT. In Otis Mss., undated, probably 1819 or 1829.

DEBATE ON OTIS'S REPORT. Boston *Weekly Messenger* (Fed.) 4 Nov.– 9 Dec. and *The Yankee* (Rep.) 14–28 Oct. 1814.

STRONG'S SECRET PEACE MISSION. The documents, from the British Archives, were printed by J. S. Martell in *Amer. Hist. Rev.* XLIII 1938), pp. 553–66. The editor did not know the name of Strong's emissary. Sherbrooke described him as a "respectable inhabitant" of eastern Maine, a member of the state house of representatives, well known to him and to Rear Adm. Griffith of the occupation force. Eight Federalists were elected to the general court from Hancock and Washington Counties in 1814, but Thomas Adams was the most prominent; and one of the Republican papers of Boston in mid-November has a squib about his being passed through the lines to Castine in a double-bottomed wagon. His secret was well kept for a century and a quarter. There is no record of the date when Bathurst's dispatches of 13 Dec. 1814 were received at Halifax, but it could hardly have been before 10 Jan. 1815, and, if Adams was there, waiting for the reply, it would have taken him at least another week to reach Boston. By that time Gov. Strong could not have been interested.

OLD THIRTEEN STATES UNION PROPOSAL. *Thoughts in a Series of Letters, in Answer to the Question, respecting the Division of the States by a Massachusetts Farmer* (Boston 1813; the letters are dated 25 April–13 May). Undoubtedly by Lowell; in same style as his other pamphlets in which he liked to pose as a farmer, and same substance as his letter of 3 Dec. 1814 to Pickering in Henry Adams *Documents*, pp. 410–14. This concept was promoted by the Boston *Centinel, Spectator, Gazette, Weekly Messenger, Repertory* and *Daily Advertiser*, in which Lowell had a series of articles under the pseudonym "Refederator" in Nov. 1814. The Salem *Gazette* was neutral on this question; the Northampton *Hampshire Gazette* and Worcester *Massachusetts Spy* reprinted some of the violent articles in the Boston papers. Matthew Carey *The Olive Branch* (10th ed., Phila., 1818), filled chapter lxxv with quotations from extremist articles in the Federalist papers, without indicating what they were driving at. An article in the Georgetown (D.C.) *Federal Republican* (the paper broken up by the Baltimore mob in 1812), supporting the Lowell-Pickering plan, was widely quoted in the Boston press.

OTIS'S LETTERS TO GORE of 3 Dec. 1814 and 21 Jan. 1815, first printed in Mass. Hist. Soc. *Proceedings* XLVIII (1926), pp. 24–9. Rufus King's correspondence, in Charles R. King *Life and Correspondence of Rufus King, V* (1898) is illuminating.

SPENCER ROANE'S THREATS. Edwin J. Smith "Spencer Roane," *John P. Branch Hist. Papers of Randolph-Macon College* (1905) I, p. 18; cf. Richmond *Enquirer* of 19 Nov. 1814.

OLD STATE HOUSE, HARTFORD. In 1879 it became the Hartford City Hall. When I saw it in 1910 the interior was in a pitiful state, smothered by brown paint and liberally garnished with spittoons. Since 1915 it has been restored to the original condition and preserved as an historic building. The council chamber where the Convention sat is now called the senate chamber.

CHAPTER XVIII. THE MISSION TO WASHINGTON

The following chronology may clarify events mentioned in this chapter and the desperate eagerness of each side to conclude the war.

24 Dec. 1814	Peace Treaty signed at Ghent.
27 Dec.	Peace Treaty ratified by Prince Regent.
2 Jan. 1815	H.M.S. *Favorite* sails with both copies of Treaty, and with orders to British armed forces to stop fighting on every front as soon as Treaty is ratified by United States.
5 Jan.	Hartford Convention adjourns *sine die*.
8 Jan.	Battle of New Orleans.
15 Jan.	U.S.S. *President* captured.
27 Jan.	Gov. Strong authorized to send three commissioners to Washington.
28 Jan.	President authorized to pay state armies for service within state.
3 Feb.	Otis, Perkins and Sullivan leave Boston.
4 Feb.	First news of New Orleans battle published in Washington; reaches London 9 Feb.
11 Feb.	H.M.S. *Favorite* arrives New York; Mobile surrenders to Gen. Jackson.
12 Feb.	Otis, Perkins and Sullivan reach Baltimore.
13 Feb.	They arrive Washington; American copy of Treaty of Ghent delivered to Madison.
14–15 Feb.	President discusses Treaty with Cabinet and submits Treaty to Senate.
16 Feb.	Senate votes unanimously to advise ratification.
17 Feb.	President ratifies Treaty and exchanges ratifications with the British envoy.
18 Feb.	President proclaims Treaty in effect. Peace is definite.

CHAPTER XIX. GOOD FEELINGS AND THE UNITED STATES SENATE

MONROE IN BOSTON and Other Parties. The Quincy girls' accounts are in M. A. DeWolfe Howe *The Articulate Sisters* (1946). For the party at The Vale, Ella L. Cabot *Arthur Theodore Lyman and Ella Lyman* (privately printed, 1932).

SOPHIA'S LOVE AFFAIRS. Sophia Otis, the one unmarried daughter, petite, pretty and vivacious, had numerous aspirants in Boston, Philadelphia and Washington. In 1819, she was formally engaged

to Charles Thorndike, younger brother of her brother-in-law Israel
Thorndike, Jr. She broke the engagement on the ground that the
young man was dissipated, and this caused more social flap in Boston
than a divorce would nowadays. Should Mrs. Otis call on Mrs.
Thorndike? Should Sophia appear in society? etc., etc. While the
engagement was still on, two Williamses, of the Roxbury family
who had moved to Baltimore after the war, dined with Senator
Otis in Washington and inquired whether his daughter was engaged
to Charles Thorndike. Otis allowed that she was, upon which one
of the Williamses remarked rudely, "The Baltimore ladies are not
so easily won!" Yet a Miss Purnell of Baltimore married Charles and,
prior to his death in 1833, bore him six children: two of the girls,
after the fashion of Baltimore belles, married foreign noblemen.
(Morgan H. Stafford *Descendants of John Thorndike,* 1960, pp.
105–7).

OTIS'S ALLEGED OFFICE-SEEKING. Shaw Livermore, Jr. *The Twilight of
Federalism* (1962), pp. 25–6, 44–5, charges that Otis's letter of
22 March 1816 to Secretary Dallas (Dallas Mss., Hist. Soc. Pa.), offering to help him open a branch of the new United States Bank in
Boston, was a come-on for a federal job. Otis, as director of the old
U. S. Bank's Boston branch, of the Boston Bank, and of several other
banks, should be allowed to render valuable courtesies to Dallas,
who had done the same for him in 1815, without being accused of
office-seeking. Livermore repeats an insinuation of Gore's in a
letter of 25 Dec. 1816 to Rufus King (King Mss., N. Y. Hist. Soc.)
that a forthcoming "pleasure trip" by Otis and Perkins to Washington was to look for a federal appointment for Otis. Yet Gore must
have known that Otis had been elected to the Senate in June 1816,
making him ineligible for appointive office. Nor did Perkins accompany the Otises to Washington.

WASHINGTON SOCIETY. Bagot "Notes on Housekeeping and Entertaining
at Washington, 1819," Colonial Soc. of Mass. *Publications* XXVI,
pp. 439–46. S. E. Morison "Life in Washington a Century and a Half
Ago," (Washington, Cosmos Club 1968).

U. S. SENATE. Mr. Richard W. Hale, Mass. State Archivist, has kindly
verified dates of Otis's election and resignation. In Otis's time, if
a senator wished to have a speech printed in full he had to do it
at his own expense. Thus Otis's speeches on a bankruptcy bill that
he introduced, on the services of Massachusetts troops in the War of

1812, and on the Missouri Compromise, were printed as broadsides and distributed by Boston newspapers. His Sedition Act speech with a rebuttal was printed as *Mr. Otis's Speech in Congress, on the Sedition Law, with Remarks by the 'Examiner'* [Benjamin Austin] *on this important subject* [Boston 1819]. General Eleazar Ripley's detailed tabulation of the Mass. regiments is in the Otis Mss. Walter K. Watkins "Defence of Boston in the War of 1812," Bostonian Soc. *Proceedings* 10 Jan. 1899, pp. 35–74, includes a detailed history of the war claim.

MISSOURI COMPROMISE. Otis's letters to Sullivan and letter to Perkins refusing testimonial dinner are in N.Y.P.L. Misc. Mss., Otis. The insinuation of Dangerfield *Awakening of American Nationalism,* p. 122n, that Otis's course on Missouri was dictated by his desire to win votes for the Massachusetts war claim, is punctured by these letters. His principal speech, on 25 Jan. 1820, was printed as a 22-page pamphlet *Speech of Mr. Otis, on the Restriction of Slavery in Missouri* (n.p., n.d., copy in A.A.S.). His second speech is reported in *Annals of Congress* 16 Cong. 2 Sess., pp. 88–99.

CHAPTER XX. STATE POLITICS AND MANUFACTURING

"POLITICAL OBLIVION." James Schouler *History of the U. S.* II (1895), p. 476; S. F. Bemis *J. Q. Adams and Foundations of Am. Foreign Policy,* p. 226. It may be said that Otis's election as governor was prevented by the Convention stigma; but, as I have pointed out, there were other factors as well.

LETTER ON DEARBORN. Otis to Rufus King 1 May 1822, in King Mss., N. Y. Hist. Soc.

CITY CHARTER AND FIRST MAYORALTY CONTEST. Correspondence with Sullivan in N.Y.P.L. Misc. Mss., Otis.

RUNNING FOR GOVERNOR. The doggerel is in Boston *Patriot* 25 March 1823. For the college issue, William S. Tyler *History of Amherst College* (1873), pp. 158–59. Claude M. Fuess *Amherst* (1935), p. 64. The Northampton *Hampshire Gazette* 2 April 1823 defends Otis from these charges — he "is too much of a gentleman to be profane . . . he is not bigoted," etc. R. W. Emerson *Journals* (1909 ed.) II, p. 238.

ADAMS-OTIS CONTROVERSY. S. F. Bemis has a fair account in *John Q. Adams and the Union* (1956). The documents were printed by Henry Adams in *Documents Relating to New Eng. Federalism* (1877).

TARIFF. Otis's letter to Henry A. S. Dearborn belongs to James Otis Esq. His letter to Samuel Crocker is in the Crocker Mss., which in 1911 belonged to Miss Sarah L. Guild.

OTIS PROPERTY. [A. Forbes & J. W. Greene] *Our First Men, a Calendar of Wealth, Fashion and Gentility, containing a list of those persons in the City of Boston credibly reputed to be worth $100,000* (Boston, 1846.) Peter C. Brooks tops the list with $4 million. Next come Abbot Lawrence, $2 million; Thomas H. Perkins and David Sears, each $1.5 million, and the following $1 million each: Samuel, Nathan and William Appleton, John Bryant, Amos and William Lawrence, Robert Gould Shaw and John D. Williams. In the 2nd ed. of this pamphlet, *A Statement of the Reported Wealth of about Fifteen Hundred Persons*, (1851), Otis's estate is estimated at $750,000, and six more Bostonians have been added to the millionaire group.

Copy of Otis's will furnished by James Otis Esq. Other details: Family portraits were left to son James to distribute. Copies of my list telling where they may be found in 1969 will be placed in the Frick Art Reference Library, New York, and the Massachusetts Historical Society. Other minor legacies were a pair of silver wine coolers each to his daughters-in-law Mrs. Harrison Gray Otis, Jr., and Mrs. James W. Otis, and to his half sister Mary; and to Deborah Hastings his "faithful nurse," $200 and "a suit of mourning, . . . handsome, suitable for her condition & not extravagant." Although a member of the Brattle Square Church, whose minister the Rev. Samuel K. Lothrop preached his funeral sermon, Otis also owned a pew in Trinity Church which he left in joint occupancy to his children Sophia Ritchie and William F. Otis. Not one charitable bequest.

CHAPTER XXI. MAYORALTY AND SLAVERY

OTIS'S INAUGURAL ADDRESSES, and *Address on the Removal of the Municipal Government to the Old State House* (1830) are printed in *The Inaugural Addresses of the Mayors of Boston* (1894) I, pp. 119–71. Most of my data are from the City of Boston Archives, "Records of

Mayor and Aldermen," VII–IX (1829–31). Roger Lane's account
of the mayoralty of "General Harrison Grey Otis," as he calls him,
in *Policing the City of Boston 1822–1885* (1967), is grotesquely inaccurate. Otis's letter on watering carts, Houghton Library, Harvard.

BOSTON BICENTENNIAL. S. F. Bemis *John Quincy Adams and the Union*
(1956), pp. 215–16. Sprague's Ode in his *Writings First Collected*
(1841). Bemis (p. 219) notes that at a memorial meeting to President
Monroe on 25 Aug. 1831, which Adams attended, "Otis and company
kept studiously out of sight." This is hardly believable of Otis!

ABOLITION AND EMANCIPATION. Otis's report on his investigation of Garrison, Boston *Atlas* 2 Oct. 1848. H. S. Commager "The Blasphemy of
Abner Kneeland," *New Eng. Quart.* VIII (1935), pp. 29–41. The
same statute was brought up in the present century to "get" a local
anarchist, but that attempt did not succeed. A similar case was the
Tresca one of 1923. Tresca published a violent anti-fascist paper,
Il Martello in New York, which got into Mussolini's hair. The
Italian Ambassador in Washington demanded its suppression as
"communist propaganda." The complacent Harding administration
prodded the federal district attorney in New York, who arrested and
tried Tresca for publishing an advertisement advocating birth control, and he was sentenced to a year in prison. American liberals
smoked out the Italian initiative, made a row, and President Coolidge let Tresca out of jail after four months. John P. Diggins in
Journal of American History LIV (1964), p. 583.

CHAPTER XXII. A BRISK OLD AGE

ANTI-IRISH RIOTS. Very Rev. Wm. Byrne in Justin Winsor *Memorial
Hist. of Boston* III, p. 524; John T. Morse, Jr. *Memoir of Henry Lee*
(1905), p. 288; Rev. Robert H. Lord *Hist. of Archdiocese of Boston*
(1944). On the Broad Street riot, President Charles W. Eliot told me
that he could remember being in King's Chapel on Sunday, 11 June
1837. A messenger summoned his father, then Mayor of Boston, from
the family pew, and Samuel A. Eliot marched into the thick of the
riot and managed to quell it.

SOCIAL LIFE. Bayard Tuckerman, ed. of Philip Hone's *Diary* (1889) I,
pp. 107, 136, 159–60; II, pp. 195–6, 265; III, pp. 264–5. T. H. Perkins's Brookline estate is (1969) owned by his descendants Dr. George
C. Shattuck and Henry Lee Shattuck Esq. "General" Lyman means

Theodore Lyman, Jr.; the house, designed by Upjohn and latterly the home of Prof. Theodore Lyman the physicist, has only lately been torn down to make way for a "development." The Mrs. Otis mentioned was Eliza, widow of H. G. Otis, Jr. She then lived at 41 Mt. Vernon St., corner of Joy. Prescott's house, No. 55 Beacon St., now belongs to the Colonial Dames of America. His study, where he wrote *The Conquest of Peru*, has been preserved almost unchanged. Fanny Elssler's letter to Allyne Otis is in Boston Athenaeum "Morison Autograph Collection." The story about Ralph and Margaret is in Barrett Wendell *Literary History of America*, p. 301.

H. G. OTIS, JR. When, at the age of 23, Harry Jr. was living at home and had not entered the house by 2 A.M., his father roused son James and both went in search of him at his law office and houses of his friends. They were unable to find him, but Harry nonchalantly came home about 3:30. He had been whooping it up with Franklin Dexter and another friend at Mrs. Delano's fashionable boarding-house; and, being still sober, was forgiven.

I have Allyne Otis's copy, with key to the characters of *Scenes at the Fair* (N. Y., printed for the publisher, 1833, 14 pp.). It ends with "To be continued," but no sequel was printed. Howard T. and Marion Hall Fisher, in their edition of Mme. Calderón de la Barca's *Life in Mexico* (1966), state that Fanny Inglis and "a young man known to admire her" were the authors.

HARVARD BICENTENARY. Josiah Quincy *Hist. of Harvard Univ.* (1840) II, pp. 651, 662–70, 699–701. Quotation from Otis's undelivered speech in Chap. V above. Mrs. Otis's obituary, Phila. *American Daily Advertiser* 14 Sept. 1836. Otis's letter to Palfrey, Harvard College Library.

PERKINS QUOTATION. From A. T. Perkins's sketch of Otis in *Memorial Biogs. of New Eng. Hist. Gen. Soc.* I (1880), p. 160. Otis was elected an honorary member of this society shortly before his death. The hunting song anecdote was told to me in 1910.

NUMBER 45 BEACON STREET. The executors sold the mansion after Otis's death to Samuel Austin, who had been living as a tenant in No. 44, which was then sold to Robert Gould Shaw, Jr. (Allen Chamberlain *Beacon Hill* p. 178). Austin, a bachelor, was so afraid that he or his friends might stumble at the top of the Bulfinch spiral staircase and roll down to the bottom that he replaced it by an ugly squarish one with broad landings. He did, however, introduce gaslight and a modicum of plumbing. From him the mansion went to his kinsfolk the Austin Wadsworths of Geneseo, N.Y., who used it as their town house until the 1920's. They sold it to the Lathrop Browns, owners when the mansion was described in *Great Georgian Houses of America* (1933) and they partially restored the Bulfinch staircase. In 1941 the Browns were about to sell it to a wrecker for $38,000 when a public-spirited young architect, Mr. James Lawrence, Jr., stepped in and together with Mr. Paul Courtney, President of the Boy Scouts of America, raised the money to turn it over to that organization as headquarters. When the Scouts found it beyond their means to keep up the mansion properly, Mr. Temple Pond persuaded Miss Eleonora Sears to buy it, and she held it until 1951 when she, or her trustees, sold it to the Meteorological Society of America, to become their national headquarters. The friends of this Society raised $140,-000 for a complete restoration, and it has since been well maintained.

INDEX

Index

HGO: Harrison Gray Otis

Abolition, 272, 464–77; bibliography, 546

Adams, Abigail, 28, 39n, 70n, 102, 128, 136, 404; letter to JQA, 191–2

Adams, C. F., 190, 193, 487–8

Adams, G. W., 406–8

Adams, Henry, 93, 446, 510, 545; quoted, 310, 400, 447

Adams, John, 17, 40, 85, 89, 207, 276, 367, 406–7, 457; asserts himself, 158–65; campaign of 1800–01, 170–5; defends Gerry, 154–5; entertains Monroe, 404; letter to HGO, 160–1; president, 96–8, 106, 112–8, 123, 131, 150, 168–9, 171, 266, 445; quoted, 2, 18, 122–3, 158, 188, 192, 359–61; "snubbed," 128–30

Adams, John Quincy, 49, 268, 305–7, 368, 406, 410, 470, 488, 546; defeated, 444–5; defects, 86, 251, 280, 301; Missouri question, 424, 429; president, 443, 446–7; quoted, 50, 250–1, 353, 382; relations with HGO, 190–3, 271–4, 354, 456; view of Hartford Conv., 372, 380, 422

Adams, Samuel, 31, 42, 43–4, 60

Adams, Thomas, 363, 540

Alexandria, Va., 349–51, 356

Aliens, Alien Act, 116–8, 121

Allston, Washington, 234–6, 504, 535

American Colonization Society, 470–1, 474

American Revolution, 18, 31, 40–2, 63, 83, 86, 108, 315, 439, 457; HGO on, 87, 529

Ames, Fisher, 85–95, 100, 114, 163, 259, 272, 530, 535; quoted 101, 268, 271

Amherst College, 440–1

Amory, Rufus G., 356, 540

Amory, T. C., 284–6, 461, 528

Appleton, Nathan, 450–1, 471, 487, 545

Army, U. S., 165–6, 176, 349

Austin, Benjamin, 44, 92, 277–8, 412, 537, 544

Austin, J. T., 314, 468

Austin-Selfridge affray, 277–9, 536–7

Bagot, Sir Charles and Lady, 418–9, 543

Bailey, John, 422

Bainbridge, Commo. William, 336, 351

Baltimore, Md., riots of 1812, 149n, 327, 330–1, 343, 538, 541; HGO there, 1815, 389, 393–4

Bankruptcy, 138–9, 168, 532

Banks, 95, 123, 268, 341, 383, 450, 480, 543

Barnstable, Mass., 2–4, 22–30

Barnwell, R. W., 407–8
Bassett, Francis, on HGO, 333
Bayard, J. A., 98, 146, 160–1, 184
Benjamin, Asher, 79, 220–1
Benton, T. H., 429, 435
Bernard, Gov. Francis, 8–10, 21, 30
Bidwell, Barnabas, 85
Bigelow, J. P., 213, 462
Bigelow, Timothy, 57, 258, 330, 359–61, 375, 530
Bingham, Maria, 134–7, 319
Bingham trust, 137–8, 205, 230–2, 257n, 346, 535
Bingham, Sen. William and Mrs., 82, 123, 131–8, 230
Blair, James, 474
Blake, Francis, 347, 355–7, 397
Blake, George, 308, 406
Boott, Kirk, 490
Boston: abolition, 429, 464–9, 474–6; arts and letters, 232–6, 478; Athenaeum, 233–6; Beacon Hill, 10, 76–9, 196, 219–21, 458, 484, 534–6; celebrations 7–10, 50, 277, 335–41, 403–4, 460; city charter, 251, 435; clubs, 205–6, 233, 479; Common, 7–10, 456–60; Concert Hall, 42, 47, 204, 250, 410, 528; development, 75–9, 218–26, 461–2, 478; Exchange Coffee House, 209, 223, 250, 313, 335, 339, 403; Faneuil Hall, 61, 92–4, 238–40, 250–1, 313, 332, 435–6, 451, 456, 479, 491, 499; India Wharf, 221, 224; Latin School, 1, 14–6, 33, 237; Mass. Gen. Hospital, 318, 537–8; Monroe's visit, 402–6; population, 64, 218; resolutions, 303; society, 188, 204–7, 213–5, 242–3, 404n, 410, 484–7, 500; theater, 59–61; in War of 1812, 331–2, 335, 340–2, 349–51
"Boston Seat," 93, 250
Bothnea & *Jahnstoff* cases, 338, 413, 539

Bowditch, Nathaniel, 407, 538
Bowdoin, Gov. James, 49, 85
Bowdoin, James, Jr., 85–6, 155
Bowdoin, James T., 284, 297
Bradford, Alden, 535
Breck, Samuel, 141, 144, 149
Brooks, Gov. John, 50, 404, 407, 433–4, 439–41
Bulfinch, Charles, 76, 79, 193, 200, 219–21, 224, 299, 372
Burke, Edmund, 85, 91, 300
Burr, Aaron, 149, 172–4, 178–84, 272, 439
Burrows, W. W., 150–2
Bussey, B. I., 40, 206

Cabot, George, 87, 94, 158, 163, 256, 259–60, 272, 316, 342, 536; Hartford Conv., 359, 375, 380, 395, 422; quoted, 154–5
Calhoun, John C., 320, 345, 435
Canada, 320, 327; HGO visits, 284–97
Canning, George, 311–3
Carroll, Charles, 364
Casa Yrujo, Marqués and Marquesa, 123
Caucuses, 260, 428, 445; Federalist, 181, 184, 246–50, 301, 313–5, 444
Champlin, Christopher, 132–4, 142–4
Channing, F. D. and W. E., 248, 339–41
Chesapeake affair, 156, 280–1, 301
Cheverus, Cardinal, 94, 351, 479
Chittenden, Gov. Martin, 334, 361
Clay, Henry, 89, 320, 415, 432, 435, 443, 450–2, 470, 506; correspondence with HGO, 499–502
Clinton, DeWitt, 260–3, 343
Clinton, George, 259–60, 263
Cobb, Gen. David, 205, 230
Congress, First, 91; Fifth, 98, 102–3, 110–1, 124, 153, 320, 425, 458; Sixth, 145, 167, 174–82, 425; Twelfth, 319–20; Sixteenth, 429

Constitution, U.S.S., 107, 335–6, 351, 534
Copley, J. S., 76, 220
Crawford, William H., 443–4
Crocker, Samuel, 249, 453
Crowninshield, B. W., 316, 434, 538

Dallas, A. J., 391–2, 543
Dane, Nathan, 359, 373–5, 379
Davie, Gov. W. R., 162–5, 175
Davis, I. P., 234, 407, 410
Dawson, John, 34–7, 112, 150
Dayton, Jonathan, 98, 106
Dearborn, H. A. S., 451–2, 545
Dearborn, Gen. Henry, 433–4
Debtors, 110, 457–8
Democratic party: beginnings, 83–6; bogus martyrs, 167; campaign of 1800–01, 170–4; controls N.Y., 172, 355; fears Federalism, 428–9; foreign policy, 91, 105, 280, 300, 304; in Mass., 91–2, 95, 171, 251, 274–9, 315–6, 330, 530; Jacksonian, 480; view of Hartford Conv., 353, 358, 362, 367, 373, 394; War of 1812, 325, 332, 347–8; *see also* Jacobins
Dexter, Samuel, 202, 239, 308, 335, 535; lawyer, 74, 214–5, 278; letter to HGO, 261; politician, 87–9, 173, 232, 250–2, 343, 347–8, 355, 411–2, 433; threatens HGO, 240, 351
Dickerson, Sen. Mahlon, 390
Dickinson, S. F., 440
Dupont, Victor, 97, 532
Dwight, Theodore, 372, 412

Earthquake, 363
Eaton, Gen. William, 284–5
Election Day, 7–10, 251–2, 460
Elections, congressional, 362, 444; national: 1800–01, 170–85, 246, 532; 1804, 274; 1808, 257–60; 1824 and

Elections, 1848 *(cont'd)*
1828, 443–6; 1840, 499–502; 1848, 508–9; state, 266, 301, 303, 315–6, 344, 347–8, 355, 444
Electors, 170–4, 260–3, 326, 445–6
Eliot, Samuel, 11, 235, 342
Ellsworth, Oliver, 162–5, 169–70, 175
Elssler, Fanny, 488–90
Ely's amendment, 270, 379
Embargoes, 310–1, 447; French, 157; Jefferson's, 191, 220, 232, 254, 283, 298–300, 303–11, 315, 327–8, 530; Madison's, 346–9, 355–6
Emerson, Ralph Waldo, 238, 407, 442, 488, 535–6
Era of Good Feelings, 393, 402–5
Essex Junto, 174, 190, 242, 248, 258, 280, 316, 359; attitude toward HGO, 88–9, 101, 154, 162–3, 169, 266, 301; French policy, 154, 157, 162–3, 169; secession plot, 271–4; bibliography, 530–1
Eustis, William, 86, 308, 316–20, 434; governor, 439–43
Everett, Edward, 188, 214, 236

Fairbanks-Fales case, 53–5, 528
Feast of Shells, 275–6, 284
Federal party: character and distribution, 83–9, 174, 185, 263; decline and fall, 403, 412, 442–6; factions, 153, 159–61, 172–5, 190; financial policy, 341–2; foreign policy, 90–3, 153–62, 165–6, 269, 279–80, 298–300, 312–3, 321–3, 326; in Mass., 91–5, 170–2, 257–8, 266–8, 274, 301, 311, 344, 362, 512; "Indian summer," 433–42; opposes Louisiana Purchase, 268–70, 311, 313; organization, 246–59; "outrages," 538–9; and secession, 306–7; slavery issue, 426, 429; society, 122–30; war policy, 320–1, 327, 333, 336, 342–51;

Federal Party (cont'd)
  see also Essex Junto; Hartford Convention
Force Act, 305, 308–9
Foster, Sally, see Otis, Sally
Foster, William, 57, 85, 145, 191, 207,
  358, 415–6
Foster, William, Jr., 208, 458
France: American attitude toward,
  97–8, 102–6, 164, 307, 378; backs
  down, 153–69; influence, 313–4;
  memos on HGO, 156, 159, 532;
  quasi-war, 112–6; Revolution, 90–1,
  101–2, 107, 331; bibliography, 532
Freeman, Rev. James, 339, 535
Frobisher, Joseph, 288–9
Fuller, Margaret, 488, 547

Gales, Joseph, 392, 415
Gallatin, Albert, 37, 94–5, 100, 107,
  119, 540
Gardiner, William H., 400, 405, 498
Garrison, William L., 444, 464–70,
  474–7
Georgetown, D. C., 145, 149, 175, 413,
  418
Gerry, Elbridge, 88, 106, 153–7, 173,
  344, 530; governor, 86, 312, 315–6,
  442
Gerrymander, 86, 316, 344, 538
Ghent, Treaty of, 91, 354, 368, 389,
  395–8; chronology, 541–2
Giles, William B., 100, 111, 465
Goddard, Calvin, 360, 374, 433
Goodrich, Chauncey, 360, 372–3, 380
Goodrich, S. G., on HGO, 372–3
Gore, Christopher, 74, 92, 216, 276–8,
  321, 367, 380–1, 543; politics, 250,
  258–60, 301, 413
Gorham, Shubael. 226–7
Gray, Harrison, 6, 17–32, 50–2; letter
  to HGO, 60; property, 61–4

Gray, Harrison, Jr., 18, 28, 297, 321–4,
  538; letter to HGO, 243–4
Gray, "Jack," 27–8, 243–4
Gray, William, 86, 206, 538
Great Britain, 97, 164, 303, 378;
  American policy, 92–3, 280–2; Fed-
  eralist policy toward, 91, 94, 156,
  269, 299–300, 312–3; orders in
  council, 282, 299, 311, 319, 322–4;
  War of 1812, 320, 324, 349–50, 362
Griswold, Roger, 98, 110–1, 271–2
Guy Fawkes Day, 7–8

Hamilton, Alexander, 83–4, 91–2, 106,
  114, 131, 141–4, 216; backed by
  HGO, 156; campaign of 1800–01,
  169–75, 180–1; death, 238, 272; eulo-
  gized by HGO, 90; French policy,
  158–9, 162–5, 269
Hancock, John, 63, 76, 89, 458, 461
Harding, Chester, 236
Hare, C. W., 257, 341–2, 364; letter
  to HGO, 258
Harper, R. G., 107, 113–4, 119, 234,
  276, 338, 410, 413; Federalist, 98,
  165, 173, 258, 320; Observations,
  103; quoted, 185, 279
Harrison, George, 68, 87, 123, 134,
  139, 210–1, 445–52, 476, 490, 496,
  500–2, 505–7
Harrison, Me., 226–30, 535
Harrison, Sophia (Mrs. George), 68n,
  123, 132, 408
Harrison, President William Henry,
  500–2
Hartford, Old State House, 372, 541
Hartford Convention, 118, 321, 336,
  348, 351n, 352, 451, 464, 510–13;
  beginnings and objects, 305–7, 353–
  8; Democratic view of, 353, 358,
  367, 412; effects, 426, 433, 440;
  HGO defends, 353, 422, 443, 448,
  456; members, 358–61; mission to

Hartford Convention (*cont'd*)
Washington, 383–92, 447; Report, 270, 375–82, 396; secrecy, 373; sessions, 374–5; thoughts on, 395–9; bibliography, 540–2

Harvard College, 33–6, 63, 208, 440–1, 461; Bicentenary, 497–8, 547; commencements, 7, 10, 38, 48, 94, 201, 348, 407–8; student rebellions, 201–2, 406–7, 534

Hazard, Benjamin, 360, 373–4, 433

Heath, Gen. William, 103, 114, 155–6, 326

Henderson, Capt. Archibald, 336

Henry, John, "plot," 327–30, 439, 447; bibliography, 538

Higginson, Stephen, 87, 154, 158, 272; on HGO, 101, 162–3

Hillhouse, James, 271, 360

Holmes, John, 350, 358, 362

Hone, Philip, diary quoted, 484–7, 500, 511, 546

Howard, Gen. J. Eager, 146, 161*n*

Hughes, Christopher, 507–8

Hull, Commo. Isaac, 335–6, 404

Hull, Gen. William, 76, 239, 325

Hunt, Ben. F., 467–9

Hyde de Neuville, 417–8*n*

Illuminati, 118, 531

Inglis, Fanny, 491–2, 547

Irish, 10, 107–9, 116, 156, 478–80, 546

Israel, Israel, 506

Jackson, Andrew, 86, 190, 389, 443, 447, 542; president, 445–6, 450–2, 480

Jackson, Francis J., 311–3

Jacobins, 155, 206–7; American, 85, 105, 110–2, 118–9, 140, 158, 268, 316; defined, 98*n*; French, 91, 102–3, 164

Jarvis, James, 86, 92, 94

Jay, John, and Treaty, 86, 93–4, 97, 105, 238, 262

Jefferson, Thomas, 83–7, 98*n*, 105, 112, 123, 130, 149, 155–6, 163*n*, 190, 236, 257, 361, 395, 470; *Chesapeake* affair, 282; election of 1800–01, 106, 167, 171–5, 178–84; president, 100, 152, 264–5, 269–70, 283, 298–9, 303–5, 310, 335, 352, 379, 399, 530; quoted, 158, 310, 320

Jenks, William, *Memoir of Northern Kingdom,* 537

Johnson, William, 338

Joinville, Prince de, 499

Joy, Benjamin, 205–6, 220–1, 529

Judiciary Act, 176–7

Kendall, Amos, 330

Key, Francis Scott, 470

King, Cyrus, 346–7

King, Rufus, 258, 260–2, 413, 421, 426–7, 430–2, 543

King, William, 231, 437

Kingfield, Me., 231

Kirkland, J. T., 202, 205–6, 316, 339, 404–7

Kneeland, Abner, 468, 546

Knox, Gen. Henry, 230–2

Langdon, Sen. John, 40

La Rochefoucauld-Liancourt, Duc de, 128, 131

Lawrence, Amos, 459–60, 545

Lee, Henry, 140–1, 168, 242, 331, 536

Lee, John, 202, 534

Lemon, Capt. Clement, 51–2

Leopard, H.M.S., 280–2

Létombe, consul, memo on HGO, 159, 532

Lewis, Mrs. Ellen Custis, 148; letter to HGO, 466–7

Lexington and Concord, Me., 231

Liberia, Republic of, 471–3

Lincoln, Benjamin, 49–50

Lingan, Gen. James, 149, 331

Livingston, Edward, 94, 100, 115

Lloyd, James, Jr., 258, 301, 347, 355

Logan Act, 157

Longfellow, Stephen, 359, 373–4, 433

Lothrop, S. K., 188, 442, 511, 545

Louisiana, 105, 175; Purchase, 158, 268–74, 313, 426; state, 344–5, 364, 429

Lovell, John and James, 1, 14–6

Lowell, Francis C., 408, 449

Lowell, J. Russell, 468, 536

Lowell, Judge John, 40–2, 87, 177, 242

Lowell, John, Jr., 53–4, 74–5, 201, 209, 276, 348, 356, 429, 536; "Boston Rebel," 87, 315; Federalist, 89, 313, 316, 375, 396; pamphlets, 327, 368; quoted, 361, 370; plan to reorganize Union, 364–7, 382, 447, 541; bibliography, 541

Lyman, Daniel, 360, 374, 380

Lyman, Mrs. George W., see Otis, Elizabeth G.

Lyman, Joseph, 359, 442

Lyman, Theodore, 209, 218, 316, 342, 474, 538

Lyman, Theodore, Jr., 440, 445, 547

Lyon, Matthew, 110–11, 120, 420–1

Macaulay, Catharine (Mrs. Graham), 48

Macon, Nathaniel, 100, 415

Madeira wine, 11, 34, 205, 210–12, 215

Madison, James, 92, 262, 415; election, 263, 303, 343; embargo, 346–8, 355; Henry plot, 327–30; HGO on, 391; president, 86, 319–21, 335, 393, 415–6n, 447; quoted, 300; War of 1812, 257, 332, 341, 363–8, 385, 397–9

Maine, Bingham lands, 226–32, 535; state, 429–31, 437; in War of 1812, 346–9, 356, 383

Mansion of Truth, 316

Manufactures, 448–50, 453–4, 478

Marshall, Emily, see Otis, E. M.

Marshall, Chief Justice John, 106, 114, 153–4, 165, 190, 262, 326, 470

Mason, Jeremiah, quoted, 368

Mason, Jonathan, 74, 163, 192, 196; Federalist, 87–9, 95, 112–4, 146; letter to HGO, 160; partnership with HGO, 76, 529

Massachusetts, 189, 400, 512–3; defense, 383–5; embargo, 298; judiciary reform, 266–7; legislature, 2, 21, 40, 171, 218, 250, 257, 266, 270–6, 301, 305–8, 314, 316, 330, 346–8, 383–5, 434, 456, 508; militia, 49–50, 350, 403, 422; religious issue, 440–1; War of 1812, 326–7, 344–5, 348–50; claims from, 413, 412–4, 544

Massachusetts General Hospital, 316, 537–8

Mayhew, Rev. Jonathan, 17–8

McGillivray, William, 286–8

McKean, Thomas, 123

Mellimelni, Sidi Soliman, 277, 537

Mercer, C. F., 473

Merino sheep affair, 336, 539

Middling Interest, 436–7

Militia, Shays's Rebellion, 49–50; War of 1812, 333–4, 349–50, 361, 366, 377, 422–3, 539

Missouri Compromise, 381–2, 420, 424–32, 439, 470, 544

Monroe, James, 98, 281; president, 413, 416n, 434, 470, 546; secretary of state, 328, 391; visits Boston, 402–6, 411, 542

Morris, Gouverneur, 271, 355, 364, 381

Morris, Robert, 44, 123, 138–9

Morse, Jedidiah, 118, 531

Morton, Sarah (Mrs. Perez), 42, 47, 528

Mount Vernon Proprietors, 76–9, 196, 219–21, 529, 534

Murray, William V., 159–64, 175, 532

Muzzey, A. B.: on HGO, 239–40

Napoleon I, 103, 158, 269, 279–80, 299, 303, 313–4, 319, 352; conquests, 327; downfall, 338–41; Madison likened to, 346

Nash, Thomas, 167

Nashville Convention, 354

Navy, U. S., 114–6, 176, 335–6

Negroes, 9–10, 155, 424–5, 430–1, 467, 470–4

New England, 362, 377, 512; Convention, 305–8, 348–9, 364; see also Embargo and War of 1812

New York, controlled by Democrats, 172, 355; convention, 257–63; Mansion of Truth, 316; secession plot, 271–2

Newburyport peace protest, 396n

Newspapers, British, 322–4; Democratic, 94–6, 105, 174–6, 247, 258, 269, 274, 278–80, 330, 362, 390–1, 441, 510; Federalist, 172, 246, 250, 254, 258–60, 366–7, 429; on Hartford Convention, 367, 375, 381, 394–6, 440; Richmond Enquirer, 370, 428

Nicholas, John, 100–2, 119, 166–70, 176

Non-Intercourse Act, 311–5

Nullification, 313–5, 347, 376–8, 451

Otis, Allyne (1), 59, 82, 188, 196, 278, 287, 297; (2), 188, 212, 297, 402, 454, 487–92, 498

Otis, Elizabeth G. (Mrs. S. A.), 6, 23–9, 33

Otis, Elizabeth G. (Mrs. G. W. Lyman), 59, 70, 82, 196, 287, 316, 401–2, 410, 454, 498

Otis, Emily M. (Mrs. Samuel Eliot), 16, 497–9

Otis, Emily M. (Mrs. William F.), 221, 492–6

Otis, George H., 188, 402, 487–8, 491–2, 498

Otis, George H. (grandson), 510

Otis, Harriet, 39n, 329, 484, 538

Otis, Harrison Gray: Adams relations, 153–4, 160–4, 190–3, 272–4, 406, 446–8; appearance, 6, 7, 189, 240–1, 372–3; art collection, 235–6, 504, 535; birthplace, 528; Boston houses, 82, 195–9, 221, 495, 529, 533–4, 547–8; childhood, 1–24; college, 33–8, 48; congressman, 82, 94–169, 218, 320; death, 510–11; defeated for governor, 411–2, 439–42, 544; denounces Chesapeake outrage, 280; domestic and social life, 186–217, 243, 316–9, 400–2, 504–5; entertains Monroe, 404–5, 411; French memos on, 156, 159; Henry plot, 328–30; health, 213, 391–3, 456, 508, 533; lawyer, 39–42, 51–4, 61, 74–5, 214–5, 336–8; letters to: Appleton, 471–3; Bigelow, 213, 462; Clay, 501; constituents, 420; Dearborn, 452–3, 545; Dwight, 412; Foster, 145–6, 415–7; Giles, 465; Gore, 367–8, 381, 385; the Grays, 52, 93, 297, 321–4, 327; Hamilton, 180–1; Harper, 234, 276–7; Harrison, 87, 445, 448–51, 476, 490–1, 496, 500–2, 505–7; Heath, 103, 114, 155, 298; Hunt, 468–9; Sophia Otis, 319, 400–1, 417–8; Palfrey, 497; People of Massachusetts, 508–10; Quincy, 89, 305–7; Rutledge, 164, 173, 207, 259, 261, 264–6, 275, 278–81, 299, 307–8, 311,

Otis, Harrison Gray (cont'd)
345–6; Sullivan, 251, 427–9; Van Rensselaer, 36, 528; Warren, 218, 308–9; Webster, 473; Whipple, 477; wife, 65–74, 104–5, 111, 124–36, 139–44, 149–52, 165–9, 177–8, 181–3, 186–7, 233, 284–6, 289–91, 295–7, 374–5, 386–94, 400–2, 407, 412, 418–21, 425, 484; Winthrop, 497; marriage, 57–9; mayor, 433, 450, 455–70, 479, 545–6; Oakley, 200–1, 209; oratory, 50, 59, 94–5, 102, 238–42, 332–3, 339, 535; personality, 372–3, 511–3; political relations, 83, 88–9, 101, 154, 162–3, 169, 190–1, 246–8, 256–66, 301, 480; property, 75–9, 218–31, 449, 453–4, 478, 529, 545; quoted on: Adamses, 190–1; Aliens, 117; American Revolution, 87; Harvard, 36, 407; South and slavery, 425, 430–2, 452, 471–3, 475–6; "wild Irish," 107–9, 478; Wolcott, 176; religion, 11, 79, 188, 441; will, 454, 545; wit, 215–7

Otis, Harrison Gray, Jr., 59, 71n, 82, 196, 203–4, 255, 286, 292, 319, 400, 407, 410–1, 429, 454, 490, 498, 547

Otis, Harrison Gray, III, 454, 487, 491

Otis, Mrs. Harrison Gray, Jr. (Eliza Boardman), 410–1, 487, 490–2, 499, 545–7

Otis, Col. James, 2–4, 17, 21, 27, 39, 227

Otis, James, "the Patriot," 2–4, 17, 22, 39–40, 456

Otis, James W., 198, 209, 401, 408, 449, 454, 488–90, 545

Otis, Joseph, 4, 27, 32, 39–40, 61, 79

Otis, Mary (Mrs. S. A. O.), 39n, 58, 128, 191, 484

Otis, Sally Foster (Mrs. H. G.), 57–9, 132–4, 167, 177–8, 192–3, 201, 218, 233, 284, 358, 374, 391, 400–2, 412,

Otis, Sally Foster (cont'd)
484; character, 186–7; death, 497; describes inauguration, 413–5; in Philadelphia, 123–4; in Washington, 174; visits Mt. Vernon, 146–9

Otis, Sally Jr. (Mrs. Israel Thorndike, Jr.), 59, 82, 188, 196, 287, 316, 431, 454, 498

Otis, Samuel A., 1, 6, 22, 27–30, 39, 61, 178, 301, 309; business, 4, 31–3, 226; letter to Sally Foster, 58–9; secretary U. S. Senate, 40, 53, 163

Otis, Samuel A., Jr., 27, 70–2, 286

Otis, Sophia H. (Mrs. Andrew Ritchie), 140, 188, 196, 287, 316–9, 386, 400–1, 410, 454, 484–7, 495–8, 505, 533, 545; breaks engagement, 542–3; HGO's letter to, 417–8

Otis, William Foster, 196, 209, 221, 401–2, 406–8, 454, 480, 498, 545; marriage, 495–6

Otisfield, Me., 226–30, 535

Parish, George, 492

Parker, Isaac, 278, 348, 441

Parsons, Chief Justice Theophilus, 74–5, 88, 189, 206–7, 252, 267, 530; Federalist, 87, 180, 260, 272, 313

"Patriotick Proceedings," 308–9, 330, 451

Peabody, Marian L., 242–3, 536

Peace Convention, 354

Peale, Rembrandt, 236

Perkins, Augustus C.: on HGO, 504, 547

Perkins, T. Handasyd, 6–7, 24, 30, 89, 205–6, 209, 218, 235, 248, 260, 342, 403, 416n, 436, 447, 460, 486–7, 507, 537, 543–5; Montreal trip, 284, 291; Washington mission, 386, 390, 393, 542; wealth, 545

Perry, Commo. Oliver H., 335

Philadelphia, society in, 98, 122–4, 127–31, 138–40, 145

Phillips, John, 217, 248–9, 342, 437, 484

Pickering, Timothy, 31, 87–8, 101, 254, 301, 312, 347, 359–63, 370, 434, 536; character, 169, 190; endorses Lowell's plan, 364–6; plots secession, 271–2; quoted, 299–300, 313, 364; secretary of state, 154, 159, 163–5, 171–2

Pickman, Benjamin, 34, 193

Pinckney, C. C., 98–100, 262, 432; campaign of 1800, 169–74; candidate, 260, 303; mission to France, 106, 114, 153–4

Pinkney, William, 281, 430

Powel, Mrs. Samuel, 142

Powell, Mrs. Catherine, 484

Prescott, William, 74–5, 212, 359, 375, 435, 445

Prescott, William H., 236, 487, 492

Privateers, 32, 97, 115–6, 326, 338, 341

Quebec, 105, 289–95, 320, 368

Quincy, Abby and Eliza, 204, 404–5, 407–9

Quincy, Josiah, 74, 89, 174, 239–40, 305–7, 320, 334, 404, 435, 495, 498, 505; exposes Henry plot, 329–30; Federalist, 250, 313, 320–1, 347; mayoralty, 436–7, 455; president of Harvard, 461; quoted, 214–5

Quincy, Josiah, Jr., 186, 204, 215, 406–7, 508

Railroads, 456, 478, 505

Ramsden, Thomas, 51–2

Randolph, John, 85, 150, 166, 300, 320, 325; quoted, 334–5

Religious controversies, 440–1, 478–80

Republican Court, 122–44, 230, 531

Republican party, see Democratic party

Ritchie, Andrew, 410, 498

Ritchie, Mrs. Andrew, see Otis, Sophia H.

Roane, Spencer, 370, 541

Roulstone, Mr., 316, 436

Russell, Benjamin, 44, 536–8

Russia, 327, 338–40

Rutledge, John, 130–1, 164, 201, 207, 278–80, 299, 307, 311, 424–5; divorced, 214; Federalist, 98, 107, 173, 259–61, 264–5, 274–5, 320, 344–6; letters to HGO, 200, 203, 281; quoted, 175–6, 269

Rutledge, Robert, Hugh and John, Jr., 319

Saltonstall, Leverett, 357–8

Sans Souci Club, 42–8, 59, 491, 528

Sargent, Daniel, 248, 361

Sargent, Lucius M., 252, 341, 534

Scenes at the Fair, 491, 547

Scott, Gen. Winfield, 334

Sears, David, 235, 533, 537, 545

Secession, 85, 374–5, 429; plot, 271–4, 307, 354, 362; Southern, 430, 537; threatened, 310, 314, 346, 379–81

Sedgwick, Theodore, 87, 160, 168–9; letters to HGO, 259–60, 267

Sedition Act, 118–21, 149, 155, 268, 305, 419–20, 469, 544

Servants, 197, 533

Sewall, Samuel, 180–1

Shaw, Lemuel, 75, 435

Shays's Rebellion, 49–50, 87, 177, 343

Sheaffe, Col. R. H., 291–4

Sherbrook, Gen. J. C., 349, 363–4, 540

Sherman, Roger M., 360

Slavery and slaves, 115, 345; extension of, 308, 425–30; insurrections, 103,

Slavery and slaves (*cont'd*)
465–6, 470; power based on, 270,
344–5, 379, 426; *see also* Abolition
Smith, Gov. J. Cotton, 359, 396
Smith, Nathaniel, 360, 374–5
Smith, Robert, 325–6
Smith, Sen. Samuel, 115, 132, 184
Smith, William, 98, 431
Spencer, Ambrose, 34, 442
Sprague, Charles, 461
Stewart, Capt. Charles, 336, 351
Story, Joseph, 190, 238, 338, 406; let-
ter to HGO, 120–1
Strong, Caleb, 90, 542; character, 247;
governor, 171, 177, 231, 250, 266,
276, 316, 344, 348–51, 355–8, 433;
War of 1812, 326, 333, 363, 383–6,
396, 422, 540–1
Stuart, Gilbert, 236, 538
Sullivan, James, 53–5, 74, 85, 278;
governor, 279, 301, 305
Sullivan, William, 74, 85, 89, 186, 214,
393, 406, 427, 435–6, 447, 460, 484–
6, 529, 542; character, 386; Feder-
alist, 248, 251, 254, 260, 361; letters
to HGO, 205–6; property, 220–1;
quoted, 262
Swan, Mrs. James, 42, 47, 529
Swift, Gen. J. G., 403
Swift, Zephaniah, 360, 373, 375n

Talleyrand, 113, 131, 153, 157–9, 164,
175
Tammany societies, 246, 255
Taney, Roger B., 446
Tariff, 448–52
Taylor, Zachary, 508–10
Thacher, George, 425
Theater, 59–61, 73
Thorndike, Israel, 206, 248
Thorndike, Israel, Jr., 316, 361, 484,
542

Ticknor, George, 208, 236, 332, 359,
406, 492
Tilghman, William, 169, 348
Toasts, 253, 284, 312–3, 335, 339–40;
to HGO, 340, 498
Towne, Salem, 217
Tracy, Uriah, 271–2
Tudor, William, 233–4, 429, 439
Turner, Charles, Jr., 539
Turner, Nat, 466

Van Buren, Martin, 415, 437, 450
Van Rensselaer, Stephen, 34–7, 42,
528
Van Vechten, Abraham, 259
Varnum, Joseph B., 86, 316, 362, 413,
530
Vaughan, Sir Charles, 138
Vermont, 334, 343–4, 350, 361
Virginia, 189, 269–70, 272, 308, 342,
364–6; "dynasty," 185, 264, 380, 412;
politics, 85, 170, 428–9; slavery is-
sue, 428, 471–2

Walker, Daniel, 464–5
Waltz, the, 410, 417–8
War loans, 341–2, 383
War of 1812, 220–2, 233, 239–40, 257,
325–52, 355, 395, 452; approach,
316–23; declared, 253, 324, 330;
Federalists oppose, 239, 255, 325–6,
342–8; peace chronology, 541–2;
trade with enemy, 336–8, 367n;
Treaty of Ghent, 91, 354, 364, 389,
395–8; bibliography, 537–9
Warren, Henry, 309, 539
Warren, James, 2, 21, 31
Warren, Drs. John and John C., 85
Warren, Mercy Otis (Mrs. J. W.), 2,
4, 21–2, 31, 43, 48, 218, 308–9; *His-
tory,* 207

Washington, D.C., capital, 145; society, 415–20; War of 1812, 349–50, 356, 359; bibliography, 543–4

Washington, George, 32, 116, 256; president, 50, 53, 92–3, 98, 103, 128, 402; death and funeral, 140–1

Washington, Martha, 128, 146–8, 256

Washington Benevolent Societies, 246, 254–7, 336

Webster, Daniel, 186, 240, 406, 429, 435, 444, 450–1, 467, 473, 486–7, 499–500; expects government breakdown, 368–70

Webster, Noah, 75, 355

Welles, John, 248–9

West, Benjamin, 361, 373–4

Whig party, 480, 499–502, 510

Whoredom, Mt., 219, 504–5

Willard, Joseph, 36

Willing, Thomas, 123, 127, 131

Winslow, Isaac, Jr., 42, 47

Winthrop, James, 37, 84

Winthrop, T. L., 84, 461

Wirt, William, 188, 533

Wolcott, Oliver, 102, 159, 163, 172, 176

Woodward, Joseph, 157, 529

XYZ affair, 113–4, 118, 140, 153, 156, 280